The Ideas of Leon Trotsky

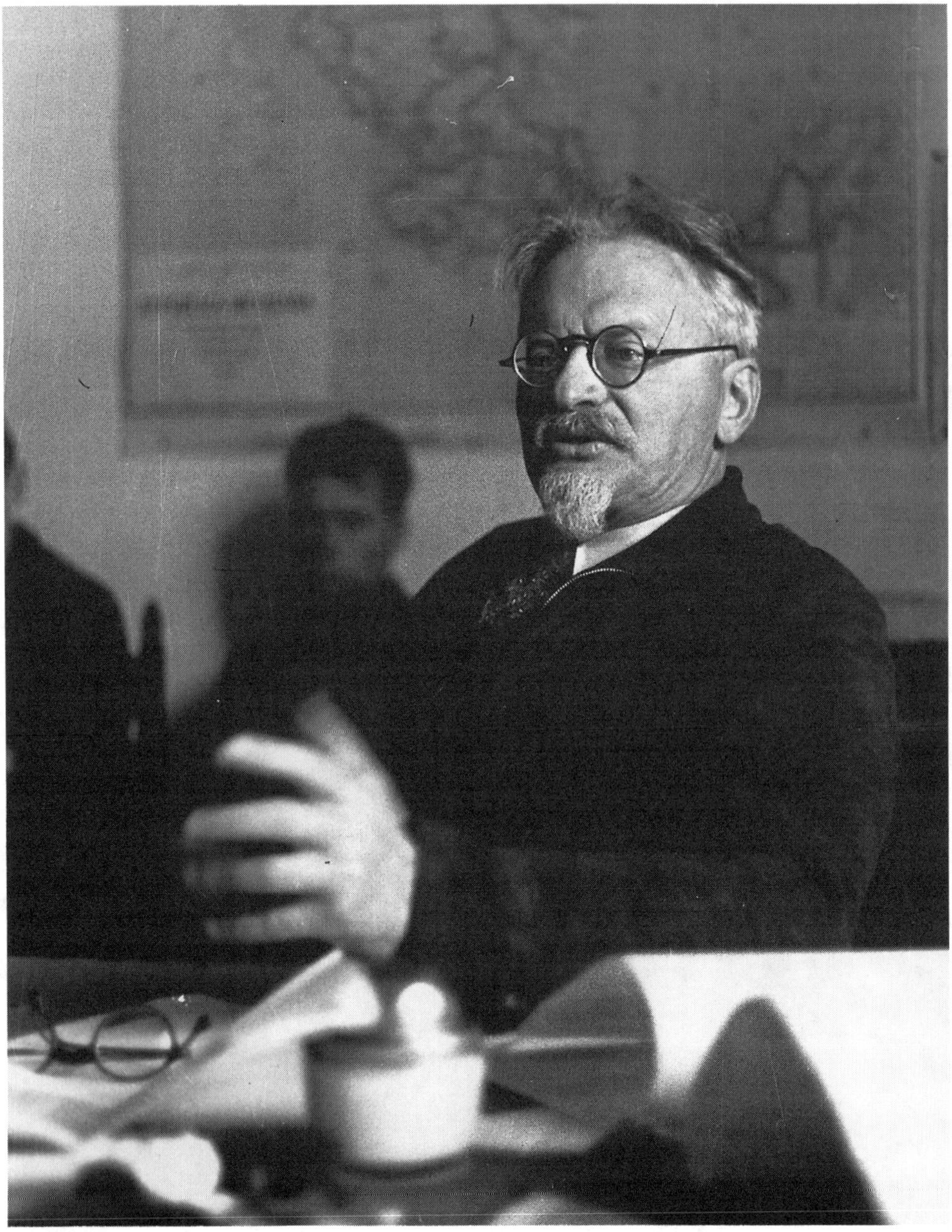

Hillel Ticktin and Michael Cox

The Ideas of Leon Trotsky

Porcupine Press

Published by Porcupine Press, 10 Woburn Walk, London WC1H 0JL

© 1995 Porcupine Press

Text processing and interior layout by Paul Flewers
Cover by Catlin Harrison
Photograph processing by Lesley Thompson

Printed in Britain by Biddles Ltd, Guildford

ISBN 1 89 943804 1

Contents

Hillel Ticktin and Michael Cox, The Ideas of Leon Trotsky 1

Political Economy

Hillel Ticktin, Leon Trotsky and the 'Russian Mode of Production': The Political Economy of Taking Power in the Russian Empire 23

Hillel Ticktin, Leon Trotsky and the Social Forces Leading to Bureaucracy, 1923-29 45

Hillel Ticktin, Leon Trotsky's Political Economic Analysis of the USSR, 1929-40 65

Hillel Ticktin, Leon Trotsky's Political Economy of Capitalism 87

Politics, Philosophy and Culture

Lynne Poole, Lenin and Trotsky: A Question of Organisational Form? 111

Antonio Carlo, Trotsky and the Party: From *Our Political Tasks* to the October Revolution 147

Stephen Dabydeen, Trotsky, the United States of Europe and National Self-Determination 163

Michael Löwy, From the *Logic* of Hegel to the Finland Station in Petrograd 187

David Gorman, The Political Economy of Defeat: Leon Trotsky and the Problems of the Transitional Epoch 201

Alan Wald, Literature and Revolution: Leon Trotsky's Contributions to Marxist Cultural Theory and Literary Criticism 219

History

David Law, The Left Opposition in 1923 235

Richard Day, The Myth of the 'Super-Industrialiser': Trotsky's
   Economic Policies in the 1920s 253

Susan Weissman, The Left Opposition Divided: The Trotsky-Serge
   Disputes 269

Debating Trotsky

Michael Cox, The Revolutionary Betrayed: The *New Left Review* and
   Leon Trotsky 289

Michael Cox, Trotsky's Misinterpreters and the Collapse of Stalinism ...305

David Law, How Not to Interpret Trotsky...317

John Molyneux, How Not to Interpret Trotsky — Again 329

Loren Goldner, Trotskyism and Trotsky: Pierre Broué as Biographer ...333

Trotsky and the World Economy

Leon Trotsky, Two Speeches on Developments in the World Economy 341

Leon Trotsky, On Party Education 371

Index..377

Notes on Contributors

The Editors

Hillel Ticktin was educated at Cape Town and Moscow Universities. He is Reader at the Institute of Russian and East European Studies and Chairman of the Centre for the Study of Socialist Theory and Movements at Glasgow University, where he has taught for 30 years. He is the author of numerous articles on the Soviet Union, in which he argued well before 1991 that it was doomed to collapse. His book *The Origins of the Crisis in the USSR: Essays on the Political Economy of a Disintegrating System*, appeared in 1992. He has also written a book on South Africa, and various articles on the nature of modern capitalism. He is the editor of the journal *Critique*, which was founded in 1973.

Michael Cox was educated at Reading and Glasgow Universities. He was Reader in Politics at Queen's University in Belfast until he transferred to the Department of International Politics at Aberystwyth in September 1995. He is Chairman of the Irish Slavists Association, and is on the editorial boards of a number of journals. He has written extensively on the nature of the Cold War and on US foreign policy in relation to the Soviet Union and Russia. He is one of the founding editors of *Critique*. His analysis of the Cold War as a system is one of the most important pieces to have been published on the subject.

The Authors

Antonio Carlo is a Professor at the University of Cagliari, Italy, and author of many works on the former Soviet Union.

Stephen Dabydeen is writing his thesis on Trotsky's views on nationalism.

Richard Day is a Professor in the Department of Political Science at Toronto University, and author of many works on Trotsky, Soviet economic thought and Soviet economic history, including *Leon Trotsky and the Politics of Eco-*

nomic Isolation and *The 'Crisis' and the 'Crash': Soviet Studies of the West, 1917-1939*.

Loren Goldner lives in Cambridge, Massachusetts, and has written extensively on political, historical and economic issues.

David Gorman is a member of the editorial board of *Radical Chains*.

David Law is an historian at the University of Keele. He wrote his PhD on Trotsky and the Soviet Union.

John Molyneux has written a number of books and articles on Marxist themes, including *Leon Trotsky's Theory of Revolution*.

Lynne Poole taught at the Department of Social Administration and Social Work at the University of Glasgow, and now teaches at the Department of Social Work at Edinburgh University.

Alan Wald teaches at the University of Michigan at Ann Arbor. He is a member of the editorial board of *Against the Current*, and has written a number of substantial works on literary and intellectual themes, including *The Revolutionary Imagination: The Poetry and Politics of John Wheelwright and Sherry Mangan*; *James T Farrell: The Revolutionary Socialist Years*; *The New York Intellectuals: The Rise and Decline of the Anti-Stalinist Left* and *The Responsibility of the Intellectuals: Selected Essays on Marxist Traditions in Cultural Commitment*.

Susan Weissman is Associate Professor at St Mary's College, California, and author of many works on the former Soviet Union, Victor Serge and socialism. She is a long time member of the editorial board of *Critique*, and is also an editor of *Against the Current*.

The Illustrations

The photographs reproduced in this book were taken by Alexander Buchman, an aeronautical engineer and amateur photographer, during a five month stay at the Trotsky household in Coyoacan, Mexico, in 1939-40. During this period, he was enlisted to improve the security system of the premises, and he served as a guard to fill a temporary vacancy. His motion pictures and still photographs of Trotsky are amongst the last taken prior to his assassination.

Hillel Ticktin and Michael Cox

The Ideas of Leon Trotsky

Lev Davidovich Bronstein, or Trotsky (1879-1940), was arguably the greatest orator of the twentieth century, certainly one of its finest writers, and undoubtedly one of its most influential revolutionary theoreticians. His talents were by any measure considerable; certainly quite extraordinary in comparison with those who have stood in judgement of him over the years. He was a brilliant organiser, and was in fact, according to Lenin, 'too much drawn to the administrative side of things'. He had an enormous intellectual range, making important contributions to the study of Tsarist Russia, literary theory, revolutionary history and our understanding of fascism in a world turned upside down by war and depression. Trotsky was also a principled and brave human being who refused to compromise with Stalin, something that cost both him and his family dear. He was no political saint, of course. As one of the two men bearing the greatest responsibility for the defence of the early Soviet state, that would have been nigh impossible. Nor was he always correct. In fact, some of his arguments now seem plainly bizarre, especially his mature characterisation of the USSR as a workers' state, and his strangely upbeat discussion about what was being achieved economically in the Soviet Union in the 1930s. Some have even argued, with some justification (though with little understanding of revolutionary psychology) that Trotsky was too much of an optimist as well. Yet even at his most optimistic, he never lost his objectivity. And when he was wrong or ambiguous, he was generally more interesting than those who are always right, but never actually say anything. Indeed, frequently locked away within some of his less assured assessments (notably those written in exile about the Soviet Union), there was more often than not a rational kernel of truth straining to get out. Even his mistakes live on in the works of those who might not even be aware of Trotsky's contribution to thought. That is why his work will last. An intelligent, well read, and, it has to be emphasised, a singularly honest man who refused to suffer fools or charlatans gladly, he was a rare phenomenon in a Machiavellian age. It is hardly surprising that he and his ideas have had a profound impact on our epoch.

Trotsky's influence can best be measured perhaps in the enormous literature on him. Certainly, for one of history's better known losers, he seems to have generated an extraordinary amount of interest, and not just by Marxist scholars or revolutionary activists alone. To a large degree, in fact, both his explanation and description of Stalinism have influenced nearly everyone who has written about the phenomenon. There are, moreover, hundreds of articles and literally thousands of shorter pieces on or about Trotsky himself. These range from the vicious to the plainly hagiographic, the utterly tendentious to the intellectually serious. Naturally, being an entirely political being dedicated to the proposition that neither capitalism nor Stalinism offered an answer to humanity's problems, Trotsky has attracted his fair share of political hate mail over the years. For the same reason, his life and work has inspired great loyalty — though it has to be admitted that many of his more dedicated and often courageous followers seemed to have spent more of their time attacking each other than critically assessing his thought. Fortunately (though somewhat ironically, given his own ambiguous attitude towards Trotskyism), Trotsky has been immensely well served by his first and really his only serious biographer, Isaac Deutscher. Deutscher was always something of a renegade in the wider revolutionary movement. A wonderful stylist with immense empathy for both his subject and the times through which he lived, Deutscher was, and still is, regarded by many on the left as having conceded far too much to Stalin. One of his severest critics, Max Shachtman, complained (and correctly so) that great writer though he may have been, in the end Deutscher provided a form of 'objectivist apologetics' for Stalinism by praising Stalin's historical role too highly. But one simply cannot underestimate the impact which Deutscher's truly remarkable trilogy had upon intellectual life in the 1950s and 1960s in particular. With its beautiful prose, its sense of history and feeling for the unfolding tragedy of the interwar years, his biography probably did more to bring people to a sympathetic view of Trotsky than any other work on the revolutionary prophet, who was — as Deutscher so poignantly noted — first armed by the revolution, then outcast by those who usurped it, and finally destroyed by its gravediggers.

Though we owe Deutscher a great deal, his work, like that of so many others, suffers from a real failure to engage theoretically with Trotsky's ideas. Reconstructing the life and times of the great revolutionary is useful; fascinating even. But it is no longer enough, if indeed it ever was. Nor is a solution provided by throwing together eclectic collections of conference papers — even less by bringing out journals about Trotsky edited and directed by those opposed to what he stood for. Critical distance is one thing, but one gets a distinct feeling that something's up when the first piece in the *Journal of Trotsky Studies* goes to inordinate lengths to prove that one of Trotsky's most profound works, his *History of the Russian Revolution*, is nothing more than a mere polemic; one which not only misunderstands the underlying causes of 1917, but deliberately (it would seem) overstates his own role during those heady months. To add academic insult to historical injury, Trotsky, we are told, did not even consult the archives. No doubt if he had done so, he would have been forced to tell a very different story than the one he does in his three volumes of invective and distortion. With friends like this, Trotsky obviously has no need of enemies![1]

Whilst bear-baiting Trotsky might still be fashionable, it hardly takes the discussion forward. Hopefully this volume will do so, not by damning Trotsky with faint praise, or by seeking to prove that he led the Russian Revolution single-handed, but rather by engaging with his intellectual and political legacy in an honest and open fashion. Moreover, though each author here treats Trotsky in a very different way, they all do so from a perspective informed by Marxism. We make no apologies for this. Marxism may have a bad name in parts of the academic world, and an even worse reputation in the land of the Russian Revolution itself. But in our view there is really no alternative framework from which to judge Trotsky properly. In this very special sense we thus challenge the thesis put forward by a leading American writer — one not entirely unsympathetic to Trotsky — who has argued that in spite of, rather than because of, his Marxism, Trotsky still had some interesting things to say about the world.[2] We proceed from the opposite assumption, adding that only through a critical and creative use of Marxist categories can we fully assess Trotsky's never less than engaged, and always engaging, analysis of our turbulent times.

A positive icon for his followers (and a negative one for his enemies), Trotsky often argued that great men were only made great by their times. This particular historical theorem certainly applies to Trotsky himself. Thus when there was hope and an expectation of change, he was at his most brilliant and incisive. But when the revolution ebbed, he almost lost his raison d'être. And while his analysis always remained powerful, it was no longer as profound as it had been in the years of revolutionary possibility. Things were made worse, inevitably, by his living outside of the USSR. He could never have known, for instance, of the extent of the famine, or guessed at the depth of the purges. He did not even have the neces-

---

1. See James D White, 'Trotsky's *History of the Russian Revolution*', *Journal of Trotsky Studies*, no 1, 1993.
2. See Robert V Daniels, *Trotsky, Stalin and Socialism*, Boulder, 1991.

sary Marxist texts to consult. And we can only guess as to the impact which the death of his daughters and the murder of his sons had upon him — before he too was murdered by Stalinist agents in Mexico in 1940.

Trotsky's Analysis

Possibly more than any other Marxist of his day, Trotsky's thought was the most historically sensitive, not in the empiricist sense of piling one fact on top of another, but in terms of uncovering the deeper tendencies at work, and seeking to understand where these might eventually lead. History itself may do nothing, as Marx once noted. In Trotsky's analysis, however, there is always a powerful historical dimension in which the present and the past seem to merge as he strives to anticipate the future. This almost panoramic quality, quite absent in the work of, say, Plekhanov or even Lenin, was first graphically revealed in his early and what turned out to be his crucially important writings on pre-revolutionary Russia.

On the basis of his own research of Tsarist society, Trotsky, as we know, came to the then heretical — to both orthodox Marxists and liberals alike — conclusion that the obstacles to 'normal' bourgeois development were so profound that there was no possibility of an authentic Western-style capitalism taking root in Russia. From this analysis, first advanced in his studies *Results and Prospects* of 1906, and *Our Revolution* of 1907, he drew an even more heretical set of political conclusions. These were somewhat more complex in nature than his followers later assumed, but at the time went under the simple (and, unfortunately, easily misunderstood) heading of *permanent revolution*. Neither the term itself, of course, nor the reasoning that lay behind it, were original to Trotsky. Marx had used the same concept in the mid-nineteenth century in his discussion of the revolutions of 1848. According to Marx, whilst other classes might seize power for a time, only the proletariat could make the revolution permanent. Alexander Helphand, or Parvus, had worked with Trotsky on the concept. Even more interestingly, two years after Trotsky had popularised the phrase, it was also endorsed by the leading Marxist of the day, Karl Kautsky. But it was Trotsky who really developed and extended the theory. Moreover, in his hands, it underwent a radical transformation, to the extent that it effectively became synonymous for him with the very idea of socialism itself.

For Trotsky, permanent revolution consisted of three related parts. The first was the notion (originally put forward by Marx in 1843) of the working class as the universal class. Its historic role, no less, was to emancipate itself, and in the process emancipate mankind as a whole. Trotsky then added and incorporated a second idea: that of a decadent Russian capitalism which could no longer fulfil its own tasks of introducing bourgeois democratic forms into Russia itself. That job, he insisted, would have to fall to the working class. Once in power, however, the proletariat could not stop half way, and would, out of necessity, be impelled to establish its own revolutionary dictatorship. The obvious question then was: what was to be done? If the Russian working class stopped at this point it would be crushed, if not by the force of arms, then by the social weight of the Russian peasantry in combination with the economic power of world capital. Thus there was no alternative. The revolution had to burst out of its national integument — or die. The workers in Russia, therefore, had to keep moving forward, and the only way forward was to assist workers in other countries — not, it should be emphasised, by direct military means (it was Trotsky, after all, who opposed Lenin in using the Red Army in 1920 to advance the cause of European revolution), but in other ways. These might include, amongst other things, theoretical support, diplomatic backing, and, if absolutely necessary, money and arms as well. But the main thrust of activity would be political, which after 1919 found its organisational expression with the formation of the Third International. It was no coincidence that Trotsky both wrote the Comintern's first *Manifesto* in 1919, and played the leading role in the organisation until its demise as a serious revolutionary body in 1923.

Once the proletariat of the advanced countries had taken power — a task which Trotsky certainly did not underestimate — the construction of socialism in Russia could begin in earnest. But until that point was reached, the most the besieged regime could do was to conduct a holding operation. This might (and indeed did) take several forms, such as the exploitation of contradictions within and between the main capitalist countries, the creation of the political and military instruments through which to defend the workers' state, and the pursuit of policies at home whose purpose was to strengthen the position of the working class. But these were temporary measures. They were not the answer itself. That could only be provided when help arrived from the outside. Then, and only then, could the really serious work begin.

But what did this work consist of? Several things naturally, including the expansion of democracy and the overcoming of material scarcity. But in addition, according to Trotsky (and here both he and Lenin were as one), there had to be a genuine cultural revolution as well. On this particular subject, Trotsky wrote at great length. Of course his argument had absolutely nothing to do with the waving of little red books or the sycophantic cult of the great leader that occurred in China in the 1960s. Rather, it looked forward to the education of the whole working population to the point at which it had the information and hence the self-confidence and the capacity to govern. And as Trotsky warned, without this 'accumulation of culture', new and politically significant divisions would inevitably arise between those who had knowledge and those who did not. A cultural revolution was not merely educationally desirable therefore, but politically essential. Indeed, only when everybody had achieved the highest level of education could there be genuine popular control. At that point the revolution would have become irreversible; in the very real sense of the word, 'permanent'.

Related to, though (according to some writers) analytically separable from the political notion of permanent revolution, was a second idea, one which has also become closely associated with Trotsky's name: that is the law, or more precisely *the twin laws of uneven and combined development*. Though implicit in his earlier writings on Russia, it was only later that Trotsky seemed to invest the two notions with the status of a more general law. In fact, according to Trotsky, the idea of unevenness was the most universal law of history, for it referred basically to the obvious fact that different societies developed at a different economic pace. The central problem for Trotsky, then, was to explain why Russia had failed to develop in the first place, and when it finally did emerge from its long torpor in the second half of the nineteenth century, why it did so in what he termed a most 'peculiar' way. This logically led Trotsky to the second part of his argument. Russia, in his view, or more precisely the Russian state, was forced to move towards capitalism, not out of internal necessity, but because of external pressure. Existing alone, Russia may have remained a backward society, located somewhere between classical European absolutism and Asiatic despotism. Situated in a sea of international capitalism, it had no alternative but to change. But it did so in a most extraordinary fashion, because onto its original primitive foundations was grafted or 'combined' the most advanced capitalist economic forms. Not surprisingly, the drawing together of these 'different stages' in the historic 'journey' created what Trotsky termed an amalgam-like formation in which the 'archaic' and the 'contemporary' coexisted and interpenetrated in such a way as to create a profoundly unstable society. Moreover, within this society, the Russian working class was likely to play a crucial role. Concentrated as it was into huge industrial concerns in a country where the indigenous bourgeoisie was weak (the bulk of Russian capital either being in the hands of the state or the West), its impact on politics was almost certainly bound to outweigh its sociological strength in the population as a whole. In fact, instead of being condemned to political irrelevance, in Russia there was every chance it could come to power before its peers in the West. Thus far from being fated to wait for an almost inconceivable length of time until the market fully matured, the Russian proletariat could leap over centuries, and, in a manner of speaking, move from the back of the revolutionary queue to the front. Such, according to Trotsky, was its privileged historic status.

The most obvious thing that might be said about Trotsky's argument was that it provided him (well over a decade before the event itself) with a great insight into what later happened in Russia in 1917. One might even suggest that it is virtually impossible to make much sense of the deeper causes of the Russian Revolution without reference to his two laws. But the theory of combined and uneven development was pregnant with all sorts of other intellectual possibilities as well. Firstly, it implied that Marxists would have to abandon their attachment to the more general thesis that all societies would of necessity have to pass through the same set of historical stages. It also suggested that the discussion of any one particular country had to be set in the context of a much broader analysis of its location within the wider world market. If the two laws could be applied to Russia, moreover, there was no reason to believe they could not be applied to other undeveloped societies as well. And finally, and perhaps most significantly of all, if a revolution was more likely to occur in Russia because it was backward in a 'special' way, then was not the same likely to happen in other backward countries that had also been compelled to develop under pressure from the West? In this way, Trotsky not only advanced a genuinely original theory about Russia, but provided a key to understanding the world revolutionary process in the twentieth century.

This brings us to a third concept linked to Trotsky's name, the idea of the modern era as being one of *capitalist decline*. The view that the accumulation process had entered a critical phase in the first decade of the twentieth century was not of course just held by Trotsky alone. It had been the position held by nearly all serious Marxists, from Rosa Luxemburg to Lenin. Moreover, whilst these two writers had a different view of the underlying cause of the crisis, both agreed that the main reason it had not fully expressed itself was because capitalism had been given a temporary lease of life by external expansion or imperialism. However, with the coming of the First World War, this temporary 'solution' had clearly reached its limit. Indeed, according to Lenin, the war could only exacerbate the system's underlying contradictions, and accelerate its disintegration. Capitalism had entered its final phase. As the first programme of the Bolshevik party put it in 1919, because of the war and the war's most important result — the Russian Revolution — the world had passed from a period of relative class peace to one of intensified class struggle in which the only conceivable outcome was the dictatorship of the proletariat.

Trotsky concurred with this general line of analysis, but he made a number of original contributions to the general discussion. The first was to root the debate about decline into a much wider historical perspective. Indeed, his discussion took him back to the French Revolution, through the critical events of 1848 to 1913 — the starting point in his view of the new epoch of decline. Secondly, Trotsky also made a clear distinction between waves — these being general and determinant — and cyclical downturns. The latter he characterised as 'periodic oscillations' situated within the former. Thus, for example, although the bourgeoisie had gained a temporary breathing space by 1921, the overall trend for capital, he insisted, was down. The period thus remained revolutionary. Finally, the new epoch would not necessarily last for ever. The bourgeoisie would take all measures necessary to prevent the working class coming to power; and if it could in fact defeat the proletariat then what Trotsky called 'some new sort of equilibrium' could be established, albeit at enormous cost to humanity.

This leads logically to a fourth contribution he made to Marxism: his analysis of *the role of democratic organisation in the revolutionary process*. Trotsky developed his own very distinct (non-Leninist) views on this question long before 1917. Trotsky, of course, was not against organisation as such, as his earlier writings show. What he was against, however, was Lenin's particular views on the party as outlined in *What Is To Be Done?*. Trotsky later claimed that he had been wrong, and that after 1917 there was no better Bolshevik than he. But in this one suspects he was being more tactical than historically honest. After all, by 1917 Lenin's original views had undergone something of a metamorphosis. Thus what Trotsky was accepting by then was something utterly different to that laid out by Lenin 15 years earlier. It was also clear that Trotsky had made no such adaptation, as his later disagreements with Lenin over the seizure of power clearly indicated. Lenin, it will be recalled, wished to take power through the party. Trotsky wanted to do so through the medium of the soviets. The difference was not a minor one, and it reflected still important differences between Trotsky and the Bolsheviks. And though he later espoused the cause of a Leninism he had rejected openly until the October Revolution, there was a very real sense in which he never was, and never became, a real Bolshevik.

A fifth idea associated with Trotsky's name is the belief that it would be *impossible to build socialism in one country*. The notion itself was not unique to Trotsky. Indeed, before Stalin and Bukharin suggested otherwise, it was taken as read within the broader Marxist movement that without successful revolutions in most if not all of the main capitalist countries, socialism could neither be built in one backward country like Russia, nor in fact in any single country situated in a sea of world capitalism. This was certainly the position adopted by Marx. Marx, it is true, hoped that Russia would be able to escape the brutalities of capitalism. But as he added in his famous introduction to the Russian edition of the *Communist Manifesto*, Russia would still require technical aid and support from what he hoped would soon be new workers' states in Western Europe. Otherwise the whole project was doomed.

Trotsky's specific contribution to the debate was not so much in advancing the idea that socialism in one country was a utopian project, but in his systematic defence of the argument and his careful analysis of what would follow — both at home and abroad — if the USSR proceeded along this path. Trotsky's thesis was as clear as it was obvious. No single country, not even the most advanced, could escape from the international division of labour. If it tried to do so, the results were bound to be disastrous, and in time the country in question would be impelled to rejoin the world market. For at least 50 years this most simple and eloquent of arguments was derided as pure fantasy by those who sought to defend the Soviet achievement. Not surprisingly, the collapse of the Soviet Union and its pathetic attempts to become reintegrated into the international capitalist system have done a great deal to rehabilitate Trotsky's original argument.

This brings us to Trotsky's sixth intellectual contribution: his explanation for the rise and his mature analysis of *Stalinism* as a system. Here, there is no point going into great detail. Nor should we seek to defend everything that Trotsky wrote on these connected problems. Suffice to make the observation that his discussion of the Soviet system remains both highly suggestive, but obviously unfinished. Moreover, his analysis of Stalinism was a very contradictory amalgam; in part a reflection of Soviet reality itself, partly a function of his attempt to find something progressive in the USSR, and partly a reflection of the fact that after 1929 he no longer had direct contact with what was going on in the country. Yet in spite of this, his writings were sufficiently rich to stimulate a potentially useful discussion between those like Ernest Mandel who followed Trotsky in regarding the USSR as a variety of degenerate workers' state, and others like Max Shachtman, who saw it as a new mode of production with a new ruling class, or Tony Cliff, who saw it as state capitalist. Unfortunately, what might have been the beginning of an open debate soon turned into a highly sectarian exchange of positions between dogmatists, who were more interested in defending their own political trenches against the real and sometimes mythical forays of their other political enemies on the Marxist left, than in advancing genuine understanding of the USSR. Onto this highly charged battlefield arrived the journal *Critique*. First issued in 1973, it attempted to move the debate beyond the banal and the tedious. And if it achieved little else it did at least anticipate the demise of the Soviet system. How it managed to do so will be explained in the next section.

The *Critique* Analysis

Because the editors of this volume have been closely involved with *Critique* since its foundation, it might be useful here to outline the theory that has underpinned what others now refer to as the *Critique* school of thought.

It starts from Trotsky's analysis of the defeat of the revolution by a new social group led by Stalin. It then employs the concept of the surplus product, a concept which Trotsky sometimes but not frequently deployed in his discussion of the Soviet Union. The crucial question here is one of control. According to *Critique* the

Soviet ruling group ruled by virtue of its control over the surplus product. However, it was unable to establish full control over the surplus. Moreover, under Soviet conditions, it was obliged to hide its appropriation of the surplus. The workers for their part were atomised by a very powerful state apparatus which acted in the interests of the ruling group. This atomisation was in turn buttressed by the political-economic individualisation of the worker at the point of production. The worker in this position, however, was able to establish a degree of control over his or her own work process. A conflict was thus set in being between the organisational function of the ruling group and the self-interest of the exploited and atomised worker. This system could function only as long as there was an absolute expansion of labour time. Moreover, because it was not a mode of production, it had a limited life span. It had to disintegrate. Naturally, the ruling group constantly tried to eliminate the workers' control over the labour process, but always failed. Thus ultimately it took the step, when the system was in terminal decline, of trying to go over to capitalism — the only method available to it of controlling the workers, and of maintaining the position of the ruling group.

The *Critique* school thus sought to develop a mature political economy of what it saw (correctly) as an historically unviable system. It also sought to develop Trotsky's theory of permanent revolution, which in its opinion had become absorbed, as it were, into the nature of our epoch. Beyond doubt, the concept of a transitional epoch was one of Trotsky's enduring conceptual innovations. Trotsky compared the transition from capitalism to socialism with the previous transition from feudalism to capitalism. He pointed out the way in which such epochs reflected the insecurity of the times, and gave rise to a politics which was well described by Nicolo Machiavelli. Indeed, our times are perhaps the most Machiavellian of all, reflected on the one hand in the lack of trust between people, and on the other in the high level of dishonesty and deception which are part and parcel of modern politics.

The change from one mode of production to another, according to Trotsky, could take many years. But the key question (one which led Trotsky to some of his most inspired insights of our age) was what happened if the proletariat overthrew the old order, but failed to install itself in power? Moreover, what would happen if the proletariat was unable to overthrow the old order, but continued to be capable of (though was not yet ready for) revolution? Then, of course, there would be a stalemate: the permanent revolution would become frozen. In fact, if we look at permanent revolution as a dynamic rather than a static category, then we have to conclude that the process can be — and indeed has been — held up. However, because capitalism was overthrown in Russia, the bourgeoisie was then impelled to implement reforms in the shape of full employment, the welfare state and the full franchise for all. These were all gains made after — and more critically because of — the Russian Revolution. The overthrow of capitalism in one country put the whole system into permanent jeopardy, with the consequence that the ruling class preferred to make concessions in order to stay in power. The working class in turn acquired a consciousness of the alternative, which made their demands impossible to refuse outright.

It is, of course, possible to argue that the granting of the franchise in the United Kingdom after the First World War (first to all men and then later to women) would have happened in any case. Yet governments only extended the franchise because they had to do so in order to survive. Today, it is impossible to extract the exact importance of any specific event which led to the granting of the franchise. It is not a question of anyone's individual consciousness, but a question of the logic of the events themselves. If revolution breaks out over Europe, as it did, the logical method of containing it is to provide a constitutional parliamentary structure, whereby the government can be removed in such a manner as to favour the ruling class. It has been a highly successful form of delaying the process of change to a socialist society, even though it has meant a series of economic concessions that might not have been made otherwise.

In short, it can be argued that the entire political economy of the post-1917 period was shaped by 1917 itself. But the question remains as to how far, and to what degree, the long pause or delay between the first revolution and its total consummation calls into question the theory of permanent revolution itself. Nationalist revolutions, for instance, seem to prove that the proletariat is not needed to consummate the bourgeois revolution. At this point, it is usual to point out that the ex-colonial world remains dependent on the metropolitan countries. Whilst the Third World is no longer part of a colonial system, it is still controlled through financial and economic institutions. Furthermore, the role of Stalinism cannot be ignored. Stalinism itself is an illegitimate product of the October Revolution, but is nonetheless a product of it. It has been crucial in engendering the modern forms of post-colonial states, many of which have collapsed following the collapse of the USSR.

Trotsky in the Post-Stalinist Epoch

In the Stalinist epoch, from which we are emerging, mistakes were seen as evidence of failure, backwardness and weakness. Great mistakes, however, can now be understood to result from great acts and great men. Today, we can discuss the thought of Trotsky in the context of the failure of the Russian Revolution, and we can ask the question that he dared not pose. Is the world better off for the Russian Revolution? Was it a mistake? The terrible disasters which followed represent the costs of the revolution. It may also be argued that the revolution led to Stalinism, which prevented a socialist revolution for most of the century. Was the attempt worthwhile? Of course, history cannot be undone, but the question is not academic because the answer is crucial to understanding the present day. Nor should anyone shirk the question, as most socialists have done for the last 70 years.

For those who are fatalists, the answer must be no. For those who see history as an interweaving of accident and necessity, the answer must be a qualified yes. The result was not a foregone conclusion. The revolution might have triumphed in Germany or elsewhere. The proletariat was bound to try to take power at some point, and there was no guarantee of victory. Any defeat brought the possibility of an unheard of retribution. The same problem remains today.

Furthermore, the Russian Revolution showed the world that capitalism was not eternal, and that an alternative was possible. In order to contain it, the bourgeoisie made concessions which altered the nature of capitalism itself. Nothing could justify the millions killed by Stalinism in the name of socialism. But that is not the point. In the period before Stalin, the Russian Revolution had already changed history. It gave the masses the world over the hope that they could some day determine their own destiny. It was the Russian Revolution which marked the beginning of the transition period through which we are still living. The ruling class did not then, and will not now, willingly give up, and unfortunately there may be many defeats before a truly human society arrives. It was Trotsky who understood the concept of the epoch of transition, even if he could not have known or predicted its depth or the extent of human misery.

Trotsky's role in history is already set. He was crucial to the success of the Russian Revolution of 1917, both as an organiser of the Red Army and as a theoretician. His *History of the Russian Revolution* is possibly his most important work, not just because it gives an unsurpassed non-Stalinist Marxist view of the Russian Revolution, but rather because it is a textbook on the nature of a revolution itself in the twentieth century. Luxemburg discussed the question of working class consciousness, Gramsci wrote much on how to alter working class consciousness, but it was only Trotsky who became part of the process itself. He understood the nature of the changing moods of the masses, and the relationship of those changing moods with the political actions and programmes of the political parties. Lenin was supreme in political manoeuvring, but Trotsky eschewed that process in favour of interaction with the masses. That was his strength as well as his weakness.

When the workers were worn out, maimed, injured or demoralised by the process of war, civil war and famine, Trotsky no longer had an audience. When Lenin proposed a bloc against Stalin, Trotsky did not follow it through. He later argued that he could not seize power without popular support because he would then have been forced to rely on the social forces which supported Stalin. The question remains open. If Lenin had been in his place, Stalin would have been removed without ceremony, but it is not clear that the situation would have been salvaged. With the benefit of hindsight, we can say that there would have been no forced collectivisation, no famine, no purges, and possibly even no Hitler. In that case Trotsky owed it to humanity to have taken power and saved the tens of millions who were killed in those barbaric episodes. But then, how could he have known?

Politics and the Political Party

Trotsky has been attacked on the grounds that he was no politician. As we have argued above, there is an element of truth in the charge. Not being a Machiavellian, he had no personal interest in taking power. Only latter-day Stalinoids try to foist the fantastic charge of self-promotion on him. Trotsky's problem (if there was one) was not ambition but self-denial. He wrote several times to Lenin that he could not become his successor as he was Jewish and the Russian people had not yet jettisoned anti-Semitism. This statement does not ring true. No Marxist could refuse to lead because of his ethnic background. We have to suspect that Trotsky at first was not prepared to lead. Later, of course, he refused to take power. He was the leader of the Red Army, and in 1924 Antonov-Ovseenko, the chief political commissar of the Red Army, actually proposed that Trotsky take over. Stalin suggested the same thing — though in the expectation that the offer would be declined. Lenin would not have had to be asked a second time! Trotsky was clearly the most able, intelligent, far-sighted and gifted member of the Bolsheviks' Central Committee, but he preferred to hold back

There is, however, an aspect of this charge which is worth exploring. It concerns Trotsky's view of the political party. In 1904 he expressed himself clearly against Lenin's concept of the party. He was against the centralisation of power in one man, the discipline of the factory, and the substitution of the party for the working class. His concept of the party was closer to that of the Social Democratic Party of Germany, shorn of its bureaucratic and conservative tendencies. Trotsky had served as president of the St Petersburg Soviet in 1905 and again in 1917. More than any of the Bolsheviks, he had a conception of what the soviets represented. Indeed, he refused to sanction the taking of power in October 1917 until it was endorsed by the soviets. As we have seen, this led him to refuse power in 1923-24.

On the other hand, Trotsky had expressed himself from 1917 onwards in favour of the Bolshevik party. Moreover, the Fourth International, which he founded in 1938, was based on the conception of the Bolshevik party. It is true that the Bolshevik party of November 1917 was very different from the earlier Leninist conception of the party, but it retained important aspects. It was vanguardist and highly centralised, and it showed Lenin's disregard for internal democracy. It was not that there was no internal democracy, but it was limited, and was ignored when required by the important leaders. This ambiguity has never been resolved. It is not clear whether Trotsky had rejected his 1904 critique of Lenin. It is possible that Trotsky accepted the party as a necessary evil, but then could find no way out when placed in an environment where loyalty to Lenin and the party was everything. Trotsky appears to have been trapped between his own need for democratic forms and his acceptance of the Bolshevik party. Whereas Lenin had no time for formal democratic niceties, and was consequently quite prepared to remove Stalin as soon as possible in 1923, Trotsky preferred a more constitutional course. Trotsky's Fourth International was similarly suspended between vanguardism and democracy.

All Marxists, as opposed to Stalinists, take the view that in the end, the working class must govern itself. The workers' councils or soviets are the obvious form for that self-government. Lenin, however, preferred to short-cut this elementary workers' democracy. There were two grounds on which he could do so. The first was that Russia was an overwhelmingly peasant country, and the peasantry was necessarily in favour of small private property. Hence the workers were both a small minority and themselves of peasant background. As a result, it became necessary to take power, but only as a means of assisting the revolution in other countries. As for the charge of the Bolsheviks' 'undemocratic' seizure of power, it has to be remembered that the full franchise for all male and female adults had not yet been fully granted in most countries of the world in 1917. In the second place, it was a period of generalised warfare and barbaric killings. It was also a period of massive discontent, with general strikes and a demand for a change of the old order. How, then, could the change take place? One way was to simply take power in the name of the proletariat, and short-circuit the whole process. Indeed, all other attempts, in Germany, Hungary, etc, failed. The very drastic action of the authorities of the old order, both internal and external, in Russia, Germany and Hungary showed that a simple seizure of power by workers' councils could not succeed without an organised and armed force on the side of the workers.

Trotsky went along with Lenin's party after July 1917, seeing the taking of power in Russia as the first step in the move to socialism in the world. He had never seen the peasantry as anything other than allies of the working class, but the destruction of the working class in the Civil War and the harsh measures required by that war meant that the Bolshevik party was left without a popular base. What could socialists do under those circumstances? They could not build socialism in one country. Until 1923, there was some hope that the workers could seize power in Germany, but after then it looked very unlikely. Indeed, the mutation of the Bolshevik party into a proto-Stalinist party was already under way after 1921, and its conversion now looked inevitable. The solution to Trotsky's dilemma is not obvious. He could have left the country in the early 1920s. Indeed, he did propose early in 1923 to go to Germany to assist the German revolution.

What would have happened if the Bolsheviks had not taken power in 1917? It is not difficult to see that Russia would have been no different from its neighbours. There would have been an early form of fascism, or at least White terror, with all the anti-Semitism and ethnic brutality that was shown in the Civil War by the Whites. The left would have been physically exterminated, just as they were at the time of the Paris Commune. At the same time, the economy would have remained as backward as it had been. Tsarist Russia was no Japan, and even if it had recovered somewhat by 1929, the world depression would have thrown it back.

In a sense, then, the Bolsheviks had no choice. They were chosen by history, and they won the battle of the Civil War only to lose the immediate socialist war. This at least is the sense that one gets from Trotsky. At the same time, there is another way in which they won in the end. Stalin's defeat of the October Revolution could not erase the October Revolution itself from its impact on world history. Capitalism had been shown to be vulnerable. An alternative became possible, which even the triumphalism over the fall of Stalinism cannot transcend. Ever since the October Revolution, the institutions of a declining capitalism have reflected that initial abortive triumph. Trotsky always looked to history, and in that sense he has been victorious.

Nonetheless, the question remains as to whether the short cut did not delay the world revolution and the move to socialism. It is almost 80 years since the October Revolution, and there are no substantial socialist parties today in any country. Socialism is here defined in the sense used by Trotsky — that of a new socio-economic system in which wage labour is abolished and the proletariat is in power. There is no mass party today which espouses such principles. On the contrary, the Stalinist parties have become at best social democratic, whilst social democracy itself now supports the concept of the eternal nature of the market and wage labour.

Trotsky's Fourth International never took off except as a flight of tiny sects. What is obvious is that the degeneration of many of these Trotskyist groups into semi-Stalinist sects has been helped by their absurd pretensions to be mini-Leninist parties. Trotsky had no successor, and he was unable to train one. He was a man of action who wrote the theory for that action. He was neither an abstract educationist, nor a mere political fighter. Nor, it has to be added, was he Karl Marx.

The Question of the Nature of Stalinism

The second charge against Trotsky is that he misunderstood the nature of the new regime under Stalin. This and the charge that he was no politician are linked in that it would have been his duty to have taken power from Stalin, if he had understood the nature of the counter-revolution that was to occur. His analysis of Stalinism became increasingly critical as time went on. But, and this is vital, he failed to understand the true nature of the beast in the crucial years when he could have prevented its rise. Others, such as those in the Democratic Centralists, took a very much stronger line much earlier. Trotsky, however, argued firstly for opposition within the party and then for loyal opposition outside it. It was only in 1933 that he finally declared the party dead and the Communist International dead with it. But even then he continued to support the USSR, seeing nationalisation and 'planning' as crucial anti-capitalist gains which had to be defended. Amazingly, he still characterised Stalinism — even in its most barbaric years — to be a centrist phenomenon. He viewed Bukharin as a rightist and therefore pro-bourgeois. And until his death he persisted in arguing that the Soviet Union was a degenerate workers' state which defended workers, however badly.

Thus Trotsky did not act against Stalin decisively enough precisely because he failed to understand the nature of the regime that was coming into existence. As a result, he not only failed to take power, but also stood opposed to direct popular action against the regime. Great men make great mistakes. Ordinary people may not make any mistakes because they do not have the opportunity or the ability to do so. Trotsky could not conceive of the magnitude of the retreat and the real defeat that had occurred. The Democratic Centralists, some Mensheviks, the anarchists and other Marxists opposed Stalin earlier and more strongly, but they never had any hope of success. Their failure largely arose from their inability to understand the process any better. In fact, a cursory look at all these left oppositions shows an analysis which is hardly worth reading. It is most usually no more than a series of empirical and worthy humanist and democratic statements.

Even the later opposition of Bruno Rizzi, James Burnham and Max Shachtman had almost no political economy. It was further marred by a quite obvious lack of empirical knowledge of their subject matter of the USSR. Their doctrine of bureaucratic collectivism was and remained little more than a slogan. The state capitalist viewpoint was put forward very early on by the Mensheviks, but again it lacked any reality. Its later reincarnation in the works of Tony Cliff and his followers, as well as in the sayings of Mao and his followers, could have little real meaning other than that of a slogan expressing contempt for Stalinism, or, in the latter case, Stalin's successors.

As a result, it is not surprising that Trotsky emerged unscathed from any and all theoretical battles. Indeed, the later Trotskyists, who dogmatically repeated all his sayings, still appeared often to be superior to their more critical opponents for the same reasons.

The theoretical result, however, has been disastrous. Whereas Trotsky himself was a complex, many-sided and sometimes contradictory thinker, his followers often became semi-Stalinist iconographers. The fault here lies in part in Trotsky's legacy insofar as he failed fully to comprehend the nature of Stalinism itself. One can, of course, argue that he did say that its nature was undetermined, and he therefore cannot be blamed for the wrong attitude of his so-called followers. The problem, however, is that he always regarded Stalin as a centrist even if he was politically worse than Hitler. It is almost impossible to square this circle. On the one hand, Stalin was counter-revolutionary, a monster responsible for the deaths of millions, whilst on the other he defended nationalised property. Trotsky insisted that there was planning in the USSR, but also said that there was no planning in the USSR. Stalin defended nationalised property, but on the other hand Trotsky said that he was the organ of the bourgeoisie. A scholastic follower might produce a formally logical reply, but no one else could do so.

Under conditions where opposition to Stalinism often meant death both in East and West, it is not surprising that with this legacy the Trotskyists often became scholastic sectarians — the monks of our time. The Soviet Union was not a workers' state, and there was no workers' movement left in that country. The defeat of our time was far more complete than Trotsky could have imagined. It may be that his revolutionary optimism prevented him from seeing the very depths of misery to which the one-time revolutionary country had sunk. It may well be that it was his optimism which kept the socialist candle burning at a time when Stalinism had plunged the world into a dark age with which no other is comparable.

Trotsky and the End of Stalinism

The death of Stalinism permits us to make a creative reassessment of Trotsky's ideas. His critical attitude to the former USSR and his savage critique of Stalin are vindicated. A number of critics, including Deutscher, argued that Trotsky had gone too far in his book on Stalin, his last unfinished work. In fact, the knowledge of the depth of Stalin's crimes gets deeper with the years. The concept of the impossibility and inherent falsity of the doctrine of socialism in one country is now widely accepted far beyond the ranks of Trotskyists. Permanent revolution as the modern version of the task of the proletariat in emancipating mankind is less well known, and is less generally accepted. Some consider that the countries like India show that national and bourgeois democratic revolutions are possible, whereas others hold that India is not independent economically, and thus is not politically independent. Others assert that we are in an epoch of contending forces, of which the outcome is not yet determined. In a sense the epoch itself is one of permanent revolution.

It is now clear that no 'national liberation movement' has succeeded beyond the immediate aim of removing the direct political control of the colonial power. In most cases, the country has succumbed to neo-colonial domination. In the case of countries in which Stalinism assumed power, we can now see a complex result. On the one hand, in those countries which have overthrown Stalinism, there is an overwhelming dependence on the West, whilst in the remaining Stalinist countries there is neither bourgeois democracy nor a real independence from the Western powers.

Whatever the conclusion, it is clear that the concept of permanent revolution may be used as a creative tool, but not as a dogmatic restatement of Trotsky's correctness. In part, the problem goes back to Trotsky's inability to cope with the theoretical nature of Stalinism. The reason may have to do with the accidental nature of Stalinism itself, or the fact that Trotsky was killed before he could comprehend its full horror, but it makes little difference. As long as Stalinism is regarded as centrist then its doctrines have a limited degree of validity, and its actions can deserve a limited defence. Then, in contrast to the doctrine of permanent revolution, it can be argued that local elites can achieve independence from imperialism. Put differently, the doctrine of permanent revolution stands resolutely against any two stage revolution in the movement to socialism, that is, a primary capitalist stage, and then a subsequent socialist stage, a strategy which Stalinism has consistently insisted on imposing. The effect has been to assist new elites in seizing power, who have then turned on the left and destroyed it. This happened from the time of Chiang Kai-Shek in 1927-28 onwards. Indeed, at that time Trotsky engaged in a written polemic with Yevgeny Preobrazhensky, who, against Trotsky's arguments, insisted on the necessity of a two stage revolution in China.

The failure of Stalinism in its homeland and in the Third World has led to considerable gloom within the left. Some speak of a crisis of Marxism. Trotsky's analysis leads to a different conclusion. Marx himself argued that for the revolution to be permanent, the workers had to seize power. Up to that point there can only be failure. The history of the twentieth century is replete with the failure of revolutionaries to introduce the socialism that they had promised the masses. It is not surprising that the masses do not trust any revolutionaries. For Trotsky, as for Marx, there is no such thing as a socialism without the working class in power. Undemocratic socialism is not socialism. Planning without democracy is not planning. The doctrine of permanent revolution is untarnished. As such it is a doctrine of hope and optimism in a world of despair and hopelessness.

❋ ❋ ❋

This volume consists of two main parts. In the first section, there are several essays analysing the ideas of Trotsky. In the second part, we have translated and here published for the first time in the English language two of Trotsky's key speeches of the 1920s. We also reproduce a letter by Trotsky written in 1909 on party education. Together the articles and the speeches make this the most significant volume ever to be published on Trotsky.

The book opens with four essays by Hillel Ticktin on political economy. The first deals with Trotsky's analysis of pre-revolutionary Russia, showing inter alia the important differences between Lenin and Trotsky, and why the debate on Russia has such relevance for understanding the more general phenomenon of underdevelopment in the twentieth century. The next two essays critically examine Trotsky's analysis of the USSR with special attention being paid here to both the strengths and weaknesses of his emerging theory of the transitional epoch. The last essay in this section looks at Trotsky's political economy of capitalism. The author begins with a discussion of method and the notion of equilibrium, then provides a detailed assessment of Trotsky's views on capitalism, and goes on to look at his theories of crisis, imperialism, Taylorism and fascism.

The discussion on political economy is followed logically enough by six essays dealing with politics, philosophy and culture. The first two — by Lynne Poole and Antonio Carlo — tackle the question of organisation and the degree to which Trotsky abandoned his earlier views on the subject in favour of Leninism. Both Poole and Carlo seek to challenge this thesis, and in the process provide us with a very different reading of the pre-revolutionary period to that normally advanced by both conventional and left wing historians. So too does Stephen Dabydeen. Concentrating on the debate between Trotsky and Lenin around the slogan of a United States of Europe, Dabydeen reveals how this discussion masked an even greater divide between the two men about the relationship they saw existing between Russia and the European revolution. The essay by Michel Löwy also deals with Lenin as much as it does with Trotsky, and seeks to show a connection between Lenin's espousal of *The April Theses* and his earlier reading of Hegel. David Gorman provides a critical assessment of Trotsky's legacy. While accepting that Trotsky was probably the most sophisticated Marxist of this century, Gorman insists that Trotsky's writings cannot provide a genuine foundation for understanding the present epoch. Finally, Alan Wald takes a look at Trotsky's views on literature and revolution.

The third section on history contains three essays. David Law provides useful empirical background on the origins of the Left Opposition in 1923. Richard Day goes on to examine the political economy of the Left Opposition, refuting in the process the absurd (but influential and popular) charge that Trotsky's economic ideas of the 1920s provided Stalin with a programme which he then implemented in the 1930s. And in the last essay, Suzi Weissman looks very critically at Victor Serge's stormy relationship with Trotsky in exile. Though sensitive to Trotsky's position, the author raises critical questions about Trotsky's often harsh judgements about one of his more talented and justly famous followers.

The last section of this part contains five review essays dealing with Trotsky and his various interpreters. The first two by Michael Cox deal with the way Trotsky has been interpreted, or more precisely misinterpreted, by both his friends and enemies. Firstly, in an extensive critique of Perry Anderson, he mounts a sustained polemic against the New Left. Then, in a bibliographical study, he goes on to show how Trotsky can be utilised to understand the collapse of the Soviet system. David Law follows up with an extensive analysis of how Trotsky should not be analysed. And this section concludes with critical reviews of two books on Trotsky: one by the historian Baruch Knei-Paz, and the other by the French Trotskyist, Pierre Broué.

While the contributors here might agree about basics, each has his or her own interpretation of Trotsky's work. Hence we have not attempted to make the book more consistent, but left it to the reader to note the differences in emphasis and interpretation. On the other hand, the essays are united in at least three very obvious respects. Firstly, though each of the authors have approached the subject with a degree of intellectual respect, none here merely seeks to repeat Trotsky's formulae. The authors are also united in a second equally important way: in their rejection of the simplistic and politically dubious argument that Lenin and Trotsky were as one. Indeed, nearly all the contributors demonstrate a clear distinction between Lenin's and Trotsky's Marxism. Once seen as a mark of Trotsky's obvious political and intellectual inferiority, these differences are taken here as an indication of Trotsky's innovative contribution to Marxism. Finally, part of the strength of this volume is that its various contributors attempt to examine Trotsky, rather than merely repeating him. In this sense they approach his ideas very much as Trotsky himself approached those of Marx and Engels: as tools to be used, and not catechisms to be repeated. We can only hope this book stimulates its readers in the same way.

Louis Sinclair (1909-1990)

This volume is dedicated to Louis Sinclair. Louis was a lifelong Trotskyist who dedicated the last 30 or so years of his life to producing a comprehensive bibliography of Trotsky's writings. He never asked for any recognition, and he even gave his collection of Trotskyana to Glasgow University free of charge, without any indication on the books from whence they came. Louis was a very modest man, who saw himself as making his contribution to the struggle for socialism through his bibliographic work. He provided a chronological list of Trotsky's works as they were published and republished. The book therefore served both as a list of the works of Trotsky in the various languages, as well as a list of republications of Trotsky's works over the world. The first task was probably more interesting to scholars, while the second served the purpose of the revolutionary movement in pinpointing the gradual rehabilitation of Trotsky himself. Louis was very excited that Trotsky was finally republished in the USSR. In a sense, Louis' task was never over.

Political Economy

Hillel Ticktin

Leon Trotsky and the 'Russian Mode of Production'

The Political Economy of Taking Power in the Russian Empire

Introduction

There has been very little theoretical discussion about the mode of production existing within Russia before the Russian Revolution. Such a discussion would of necessity require the use of the concepts of political economy, and not just provide a description of socio-economic conditions in Russia. Of all the Russian Marxists, however, it was only Trotsky who developed a genuine political economic and therefore theoretical analysis of Russian history. The only other Marxist who is sometimes recalled in this connection is Pokrovsky, but his analysis is so primitive that it is doubtful if it can be called either Marxist or even an analysis.

This chapter argues that Trotsky evolved a unique viewpoint on the nature of the Russian mode of production. His understanding of the forces driving Russian history was profound. His analysis led him to argue that a developed Russian capitalism was ruled out. This then led to three conclusions. The first, associated with the theory of permanent revolution, was that only the proletarian revolution could perform the tasks associated with bourgeois democracy.[1] The second was that a reversion to a form of underdeveloped capitalism, derived from the old mode of production, was entirely possible. There is also a further and third consequence of his analysis. Because Trotsky was able to site the development of Russia, as a semi-Asiatic mode of production, within the context of a world capitalism, he stood squarely on the need for a world revolution as an integrated whole. Lenin also stood for world revolution and never believed in the absurdity of socialism in one country, but he was more inclined to see the world through the prism of Russian revolutionary activity, a fault criticised by Trotsky. As I discuss below, Lenin's analogy of the chain breaking at its weakest link is misleading. The capitalist chain remained intact — less one link — in spite of the victory of the Russian Revolution.

In addition to Trotsky's specific views on Russian history and by implication his differences with Lenin, the article also addresses the question of the proposed alternatives to revolution at the time, in particular that advanced by the Mensheviks. I argue that mature industrialisation was not a realistic option in Russia in the early twentieth century, and has not been a possibility in most underdeveloped countries. In the process I develop a political economy of Russia which extends Trotsky's analysis.

The Nature of the Victory and Defeat of the Russian Revolution

The orthodox pre-Stalinist and anti-Stalinist viewpoint has been — and continues to be — that the movement to socialism must be on a world scale. It cannot be accomplished by one country or even a group of countries. What this would involve, however, is not at all clear. The Russian Empire could never become socialist in isolation. What is not so clear, however, is how the overthrow of a weak and underdeveloped capitalism in Russia could be translated into more than just a local victory, into a threat to the world capitalist system as a whole. The Russian Revolution was both systemic and local. It was systemic, in the sense that it was anti-capitalist on a world scale, but it was local insofar as it solved specific local bourgeois democratic issues such as the national question, the land question, etc.[2] It

---

1. LD Trotsky, *1905*, New York, 1971, p329. He argued against Pokrovsky there, and pointed out that the first chapter of *1905*, 'Russia's Social Development and Tsarism', was written for a Russian public, and he then says that: 'The direct motive for writing it was a desire to provide historical and theoretical justification for the slogan of the seizure of power by the proletariat as opposed both to the slogan of a bourgeois-democratic republic and to that of democratic government by the proletariat and peasantry.'
2. There is an underlying theoretical question here. I would argue that the local issues had to be

also taught the bourgeoisie, on a world scale, that it could be overthrown. The bourgeoisie lost a proportion of its capital in the USSR, but the world capitalist class itself was not overthrown. The capitalist system was damaged, but it remained operational. It was able to amputate the wounded limb, and launch a strategic social democratic retreat.

A defeat in Western Europe and particularly in Germany would have been very different. The capitalist system could not have survived. Of course, if the Russian Empire had developed to the point where it was tightly integrated into the world division of labour, as a major industrial capitalist power, then the taking of power in the Russian Empire would have had a much greater impact upon the capitalist system as a whole. Trotsky's analysis succeeded in showing both the relative independence from and special dependence of the Russian empire upon the West. Hence the Mensheviks were not entirely incorrect in arguing that the development of a Russian capitalism was crucial. They were nonetheless wrong, because they argued in terms of the internal development of the Russian Empire, and not of the international development of the international division of labour. They were parochial and mechanistic in their interpretation of Marxism.

But then no one in the Second International was clear as to the exact form of taking power, or the conditions necessary for such taking of power. Did it require a general strike? Was a war essential? Would crises induce capitalist collapse, or would capitalism gradually decline? While there was some discussion of these issues, notably by Luxemburg and Kautsky, it never went very far.[3] Lenin's enunciation of the three conditions under which the ruling class could be overthrown was only an analysis at the level of politics. Trotsky did discuss the attitude of workers at various times in relation to depressions and booms.[4] He did not clearly state the nature of the objective conditions that would be required for the overthrow of capitalism. It was this ambiguity and uncertainty that led to the dichotomy of a relative voluntarism on the part of Lenin, and a mechanistic attitude among the Mensheviks.

The problem, then, was that no one was clear on two crucial points concern-

---

    subsumed under the more general question of the overthrow of capitalism before the revolution became fully international. This, however, was not possible before the USSR had become a highly industrialised country and fully integrated into the world division of labour. The revolution had to be systemic and in no sense local to challenge successfully the world capitalist order.

3. R Luxemburg, *The Mass Strike*, London, 1986; K Kautsky, *Selected Political Writings*, London, 1983, pp53-73.
4. LD Trotsky, 'Report on the World Economic Crisis and the New Tasks of the Communist International', *The First Five Years of the Communist International*, Volume 1, London, 1973, pp199-213.

ing the overthrow of capitalism. In the first instance, the interrelationship between taking power in one or several countries and the overthrow of world capitalism was ambiguous. In the second place, no one was clear as to the social conditions which would lead to such a victory. As a result, revolutionaries could differ quite widely on the strategy and tactics of taking power and sustaining that power, without differing at all on the general principle of the impossibility of constructing socialism in one country.

Trotsky's Perspective

Trotsky's concept of the permanent revolution argued that only the proletariat could defeat the autocracy, but once it had done so, it would have to move forward to the socialist revolution. From this angle, the Russian Revolution appeared to be inevitable. Trotsky then argued that the new workers' state would have to proceed to assist the world revolution in order to survive.

Trotsky's theory was completely logical and was a natural extension of Marxism to the conditions of the Russian Empire. There was, however, a real problem. The workers of the Russian Empire could not do more than assist the world revolution. The German or French workers, on the other hand, could automatically upset the world division of labour. Hence, the success of the revolution in the Russian Empire required an extra component. It was this that was missing.

There never was any reason to assume that capitalism would simply break down by itself. Marx at various points in his life saw various opportunities for the workers to overthrow the system. He believed that there had to be subjective class development as well as the presence of objective conditions. In principle, this could have occurred at some point from 1848 onwards, but the capitalist class learned how to defend itself, and it could be expected that the workers would be constantly defeated until they finally won. Yet no one could predict when they would win, or how they would win.

It is this background which explains the possibility of various interpretations of the overthrow of capitalism. In a sense, the different socialist interpretations were correct, as all were applicable to a capitalism which was in decline. At some point, capitalist decline must compel an involuntary movement to socialism, which would assist the subjective movement to socialism. Time, however, is of the essence. While it could be argued that socialism could inevitably be victorious within 300 years of Marx's death, those who suffer the depredations of capitalism do not want to wait. As capitalism fails to be superseded, there could be many instances of chaos in which the capitalist class could no longer maintain order, particularly in peripheral areas of the capitalist system. The capitalist class has, as a result, come to fear any indications of instability and chaos. The instability of the capitalist system thus shows itself in limited ways.

It is, however, these limited forms which provide the opportunities for a restricted rejection of the capitalist system. Are the workers and peasants of such countries, or parts of countries, to ignore the opportunities presented to them? Are they to permit a dictatorial right wing regime to come to power instead of a workers' government?

Lenin used the analogy of 'a weak link' in a metaphorical 'chain' to describe the nature of the Russian Revolution. The problem with the metaphor is that it assumes that the breaking of the weak link in the chain will destroy the chain itself. Yet that is not what happened, precisely because the analogy itself was defective. The revolution in the Russian Empire was closer to the destruction of one pillar of a multipillar hall or building. It caused permanent structural damage, but the hall remained standing. Of course, if not for Stalinism, the USSR might have done much to bring down capitalism, but Stalinism itself represented a victory of the world bourgeoisie, or the shoring up of the defective pillar.

In other words, the taking of power in the Russian Empire was a short cut, which might have worked. One can then argue that what was wrong with Lenin was his conservatism in not gambling on losing the Russian Empire but gaining the world. It is at this point that one can bring out Trotsky's objection to Lenin as being too Russocentric.[5] Lenin, as is well known, was so desperate that in 1920 he ordered the advance of the Red Army through Poland to Germany, against the advice of Trotsky. It might have succeeded if not for Stalin.[6] Lenin was an internationalist in spite of Stalin's attempts to depict him in a different light. Yet, he was a Russian internationalist, who concentrated on the specific conditions of the Russian Empire. This was the main reason why Trotsky was reluctant to join up

---

5. Lenin's notes indicate that at the unity meeting with the Mezhraiontsi in May 1917 Trotsky had this to say: 'I completely agree with the resolution, but at the same time I agree to the degree to which Russian Bolshevism internationalises itself.' (*Leninskii Sbornik*, Volume 4, Moscow-Leningrad, 1925, p303)
6. See *Devyataya Konferentsiya RKP(B), Protokoly*, Moscow, 1972. This stenographic report of the congress, which discusses the advance on Poland, was distinguished by the suppression of Lenin's speech, recently printed for the first time in the Porcupine collection *In Defence of the Russian Revolution*, London, 1995, and the first speech, by Trotsky. Trotsky berates Stalin for providing Tukhachevsky, the Soviet general in charge of the advance, with the wrong information and advice. Tukhachevsky had expected that the population of Warsaw would rise against the authorities and welcome the Red Army. As a result, he marched his men to exhaustion in order to reach Warsaw in time. In fact, he was met by the Polish army, which easily defeated his army in its weakened state. Such is Trotsky's report. It appears that Stalin's incompetence prevented the advance of the Red Army to the German border, and thus denied the Soviet regime the possibility of rendering direct help to a socialist revolution in Germany. This accident of history may have played a pivotal role in the history of the world.

with him in 1917. From this point of view, the Bolshevik party, which Trotsky had opposed as being too centralised around one man,[7] appears to have been too sharp an instrument for its task. It succeeded in taking power by being so well adapted to Russian conditions, and for the same reason it could remain in power. That was both its strength and its weakness. By being so Russian, it was not able to relate in an organic way to the world revolution. The problem with the Bolshevik party was that it did not consider the effects of its actions on the world revolution.

Lenin was eager to take power and then use the Russian Empire as a base for world revolution. Trotsky preferred to link the taking of power to the Soviets, so making it a working class and not merely a party act.[8] Trotsky's attitude was not just more democratic, it was also more linked to the proletariat as an international entity.

By 1918, however, Trotsky had compromised with Lenin on withdrawing from the First World War. The Left Communists in 1918 preferred to continue the war, while Trotsky wanted to temporise in order to maximise the possibility of fraternisation of the armies that were under pressure from developing revolutions. The point was that Trotsky (until he sided with Lenin) and the Left Communists like Bukharin, Preobrazhensky, Uritsky, Pokrovsky, etc, recognised the deleterious effect of peace on the development of the world revolution itself. They were much less interested in preserving the Russian base in and of itself. It is not possible to argue that Lenin or Trotsky were less internationalist than the Left Communists. The difference actually lay in strategy. One group believed that it was better to keep a base than to hope that the destabilisation of the Allied armies and the movement of world revolution would lead to a socialist revolution in Europe. The other argued that the base itself would be corrupted once the organic link with international revolution was disrupted.

Luxemburg had refused to take part in the formation of the Third International as she considered it was too dominated by Russia, and she had opposed the undemocratic features of the October Revolution. Whether she was correct or not on the specific issues, she was undoubtedly right in seeing the international implications of the particular form of the October Revolution. It was not a question of whether the Bolsheviks had won a formal majority. There were few governments in 1917 which were truly elected by the whole electorate. In the United Kingdom

---

7. LD Trotsky, *Our Political Tasks*, London, nd.
8. 'I understood that it was only then that he finally made peace with the fact that we were not proceeding by way of a conspiracy and a plot.' (LD Trotsky, *On Lenin, Notes Towards a Biography*, London, 1971, p89) With that sentence Trotsky made clear that Lenin differed sharply from himself in proceeding conspiratorially as opposed to democratically.

not only did women not have the vote, but some 40 per cent of men did not have it either. Hence, the Bolsheviks' actions in basing themselves on the working class alone and effectively ignoring the peasantry were not entirely counterproductive in propaganda terms. The problem was that the course of the revolution itself became more undemocratic as the counter-revolution made itself felt, and the Bolsheviks did not realise the enormous impact on the world of a revolutionary party holding onto power when its social base had been destroyed.

While one can still argue that the Bolsheviks were justified in remaining in power, the problem of their impact on the revolution on the West becomes more problematical. We can never know whether a different policy in the USSR might not have led to a successful German revolution. At the same time, the isolation of the Soviet Union posed an impossible dilemma for the Bolsheviks. Were they to preserve the Soviet Union even though they had lost their social base? If so, did they not have to compromise with the regimes on their borders rather than directly support the revolutionary parties in those countries? The argument that the state would have the duty of preserving itself, while the Bolshevik party would have the duty of helping revolutionaries to overthrow capitalism wherever it existed, was never meaningful. Since the same people led both state and party, no one could be deceived, and any compromise was necessarily with both state and party.

Thus the Soviet Union compromised on peace with Germany, compromised with its border regimes like that of Ataturk, and compromised with the peasantry and petit-bourgeoisie in introducing the New Economic Policy. It compromised itself by maintaining a dictatorship over the workers and peasants because the peasants did not trust them, and the workers became progressively confused, disillusioned or simply politically exhausted. As a result, some socialists and workers, all over the world, were less attracted towards revolution. In other words, the methods required to maintain the socialist base repelled part of the socialist constituency. When the Bolsheviks did form an international agency — the Communist International — it was so dominated by the Russians that it was built in their image rather than that of Western Europe. If German socialism had been stronger this would have been very difficult, and in any case the Comintern would have played a lesser role in Germany itself. Unfortunately, one of the effects of this imbalance in the Comintern was its rapid Stalinisation.

Bolshevism, in other words, showed its strength in adapting to the specific conditions of the Russian Empire. In that respect Lenin was a master. But its weakness lay in its inability to integrate more closely into the world revolution as a whole. This was the fault of the world socialist movement as well as of the Bolsheviks. But the essential point was that the bourgeoisie was able to learn from its own overthrow in the Russian Empire, and successfully to contain and ultimately destroy the revolution. What neither Lenin nor Trotsky could have known before the event was the way in which the failure of the external revolution could lead to an internal overthrow of the system. In this respect the bourgeoisie proved resilient beyond expectation. Bolshevism in this respect was deficient because it failed to develop an international theory of revolution, as opposed to one which argued for the copying of the Bolshevik example.

What are the Requirements of a Marxist Theory of History?

History in this context is both a description of events and a theory explaining the reason for them. It is the interweaving of the accidental and the necessary components of movement. A Marxist history, however, also has a purpose, which is to understand the present in terms of the past, in order to change the present.

It must start from the extraction of the surplus product, and show the form of that surplus product, the nature of the group which is exploiting the subordinate group, the nature of that subordinate group, and the way in which the interrelations between them change over time. Because Stalinism could not admit that a surplus product was extracted in the USSR by a concomitant ruling group, it abolished the category of surplus product as a general category across social formations. It thereby prevented the possibility of the examination of the ruling group in the USSR and with it the category of bureaucracy or elite itself.

The theory must describe the contradictions of the mode of production or social system over time. In this respect there is a movement both of the categories over time, and also of the classes or social groups. It is the special task of history to interrelate that movement of categories and classes. In the context of the Russian Empire that would mean a movement of both the surplus product in its transformation over time eventually to surplus value, and the struggles of the peasants with the landlords. It is not an easy task, and that is why there have been very few Marxist historians, although there have been many Stalinist historians and many empiricists who have demonstrated a liberal regard for the working class.

Trotsky's Theory of Russian History

World Stalinism has so distorted the Marxist interpretation of Russian history that there is in fact very little Marxist theory of Russian history. In fact there are the views of Marx, Plekhanov, Pokrovsky and Trotsky. Of these, the second and third are quite simplistic, not to say even vulgar. It is not accidental that the novelist Anatoli Rybakov is able to poke fun at Pokrovsky.[9] It was really only Trotsky who put forward a consistent theory of Russian history.

9. A Rybakov, *Children of the Arbat*, London, 1988, p566.

Trotsky did indeed start from the surplus product. He argued that Russia had needed to defend itself on all frontiers, and had been permanently engaged in warfare in order to sustain its existence. A large part of the surplus product was thus spent on military needs. This surplus had to come ultimately from the peasantry. As a result, Russia had a developed bureaucratic apparatus to sustain the collection of that surplus product as well as its organisation of and expenditure on the military, which further absorbed that surplus product. In turn, the creaming off of such a large part of the surplus product meant that the forces of production could not be developed, and hence Russian agriculture remained backward and industry itself could not take off.[10] The backwardness of Russia meant that the surplus product was itself reduced, and hence taxation on the peasantry became an ever heavier burden. At the same time, the towns remained administrative centres, and the villages were largely self-sufficient in that they made their own tools and consumer goods, such as clothing. This description is very similar to that of the Asiatic mode of production where the Oriental despot owns all the land, but permits the peasantry to possess the land in return for taxes paid to the state. The taxes are collected by the bureaucratic apparatus. The latter in turn performs a crucial function in the economy, most usually that of irrigation. Towns are administrative centres, and the individual villages are more or less self-sufficient.

Marx and Trotsky saw Russia as being semi-Asiatic because the analogy with the Asiatic mode of production was only partial. The military function played a largely wasteful role, and hence did not raise productivity in the same way as irrigation. On the contrary, the semi-Asiatic nature of Russia meant that its productivity was lower than it might otherwise have been. In the second place, its low productivity but absolute need for a rising surplus product led to a late or second enserfment of the peasantry of a particularly onerous kind. The classical form of the Asiatic mode of production, on the other hand, had essentially free peasants cultivating the land, together with other forms of unfree labour.

The Nature of the Russian Empire

If we turn now to discuss the Russian Empire, its peculiarity did not lie only in its backwardness, because after all most of the world was backward, but in its unique mode of production, with a developing landlord-serf social relation encompassed within an autocratic state, within a world moving to capitalism. How was this to be explained? Marx and following him Plekhanov and Trotsky saw the Russian Empire as semi-Asiatic. Lenin did not follow up this discussion. Stalin could not admit this characterisation, and wiped out the discussion itself.

10. LD Trotsky, *1905*, op cit, p5.

For Trotsky, the semi-Asiatic nature of the Russian Empire meant that the USSR could very easily return to capitalism in the 1920s. One of the aspects of the Asiatic mode of production was that the villages were isolated and largely but not entirely self-sufficient entities. Trotsky noted how a single merchant under those circumstances could easily come to dominate an entire region.[11] The merchant or the traveller was the intermediary between the scattered producer and the scattered consumer. In this way, the sparseness and poverty of the population and the resulting smallness of the towns determined the immense role of commercial capital in the organisation of the national economy of old Muscovite Russia. He also used this argument against Bukharin in the 1920s, when the latter was arguing for concessions to the peasantry.[12] For Trotsky it was entirely possible to proceed along Bukharin's road, but it was the road to capitalism. Hence for Trotsky, his characterisation of the Russian Empire was crucial not just in providing an overarching conception of the Russian Empire, but also in order to understand the immediate nature of change in the Russian Empire and the USSR.

At this point, it is necessary to point out that when Trotsky spoke of the dominant role of the merchant in certain parts of Russia, it did not mean that he saw Russia as being capitalist. Such a view was associated with Pokrovsky, whom Trotsky attacked particularly strongly in his historical works. Marx had argued that the more developed was merchant capitalism, the less developed was capitalism. Merchant capital long precedes capitalism, existing in the ancient mode of production, feudalism and in the Asiatic mode of production. Its peculiar feature is that it can only acquire value and thus money by buying cheap and selling dear, and hence it not only does not develop production, but is its very antithesis. It absorbs the very surplus product that the producer needs to invest in his enterprise in order to expand it. That is why Trotsky was so scathing about Pokrovsky's absurd idea that Russia had a capitalist system.[13] Hence the presence of the merchant did not give rise to capitalism, but helped to maintain the old autocratic regime. On the other hand, once the autocratic regime had been overthrown, Trotsky saw the merchant as providing a link to world capitalism, not because the merchant had changed his nature, but because the merchant would necessarily provide a conduit for world capitalism into the USSR.

11. 'The merchant or traveller was the intermediary between the scattered producer and the scattered consumer.' (Ibid, p12) He repeats this point in a number of places, basing the argument in part on his personal experience. See, for instance, ibid, p336.
12. Dvenadtsatyi S'ezd RKP(B), *Stenograficheskii Otchet*, Moskva, 1968, pp399-401. Trotsky argued that the Asiatic nature of Russia was crucial in establishing the importance of merchant capital, and that under the NEP there was the ever-present danger that merchant capital would provide the basis of a return to capitalism.
13. LD Trotsky, *1905*, op cit, pp341-5.

Socialism in One Country and Capitalism in One Country

The fundamental conception of the overthrow of capitalism in the context of the Russian Empire lay in interrelating it with the world system. Capitalism was a world system.[14] Hence the problem was to overthrow it as a world system, and not just in one country, which was in any case theoretically impossible in the long run.

The Mensheviks rather oddly ended up arguing for socialism in one country in that they wanted an overthrow in the Russian Empire only when it was ready. It was true that in 1903 the Mensheviks stood to the left of Lenin in arguing for a socialist revolution in the Russian Empire.[15] It was only the failure of the 1905 Revolution that led them to conclude that an alliance with capitalism was necessary in order to overthrow the autocracy. Thereafter, they developed a unique theory of the necessary development of a country to the level of world industrial capitalism before a socialist revolution became possible. This was extremely odd, as Marx had argued in terms of the world development of capitalism right from its outset. He did not see capitalism as developing from some small village or town or country and expanding outwards, but as forming through interrelations with the whole world, whether on the basis of trade with China, or the plunder of South America and Asia. It was always a world system. It never was anything else. A world system could not be overthrown in one country, and Marx was quite clear on that. Engels put it even more clearly.[16]

Put differently, Marx had seen capitalism as a single entity, not as a series of different countries with different modes of production interrelated by a market.

---

14. 'The proper task of bourgeois society is the creation of the world market, at least in outline, and of the production based on that market.' (K Marx to F Engels, 8 October 1858, K Marx and F Engels, *Collected Works*, Volume 40, p347)
15. Theodore Dan put the point like this: 'Bolshevism took shape as the bearer of predominantly *general-democratic* and *political* tendencies of the movement, and Menshevism as the bearer predominantly of its class and *socialist* tendencies.' (T Dan, *The Origins of Bolshevism*, London, 1964, p259) He went on to point to the irony that the two factions ended up taking the opposite positions from that with which they had begun (p260). That Lenin was almost violently opposed to a direct call for a socialist revolution is described by Isaac Deutscher in *The Prophet Armed*, Oxford, 1954, p113. These statements refer only to the programmatic differences, and not to the differences over alliances and the nature of the party.
16. Engels, when discussing the possibility of Russia going directly to socialism, said both he and Marx argued in terms of 'the first condition to bring this about, [which] was the impulse from without, the change of economic system in the countries in which it originated' (F Engels to N Danielson, 24 February 1893, K Marx and F Engels, *Selected Correspondence*, pp508-9). He refers in particular to Marx's preface of 21 January 1882 to the Russian edition of the *Communist Manifesto* (ibid, p355).

Money was world money, or it was not money at all.[17] Hence socialism had to triumph as a world system, or not at all. Nor did Lenin differ at all in this conception, in spite of the later attempts by Stalin to assimilate him to that viewpoint. Indeed, no Marxist, as opposed to a Stalinist, could hold any other standpoint. But the views of socialism were really based on the conception of capitalism itself as a world system. It was here that the differences between Mensheviks and Bolsheviks came in a very convoluted way to be very profound. The Bolsheviks argued that the system was of a whole, and that breaking it at one point would weaken the whole system. It is clear that neither side understood the complexities of the argument as it has now come to show itself.

Towards a Political Economy of the Russian Empire

Trotsky started from a conception of world capitalism, and saw the Russian Empire as an entity which was faced with constant warfare and external pressure: 'The history of Russia's state economy is an unbroken chain of efforts — heroic efforts, in a certain sense — aimed at providing the military organisation with the means necessary for its continuing existence. The entire government apparatus was built, and constantly rebuilt, in the interests of the treasury. Its function consisted in snatching every particle of the accumulated labour of the people and utilising it for its own ends.'[18] The question was why it had to fight in order to exist. Trotsky did not provide a complete answer. I will attempt to reconstruct one here.

As Trotsky pointed out, in certain respects, Russia developed a similar absolutism to that of France or Britain, but there was no concomitant rise of the guilds, artisans, gentry and a capitalist class. Instead, the merchants were foreign, and goods were imported, while the landlords re-enserfed the peasantry. The second or late serfdom was in fact a feature of Eastern Europe in general, and in this respect was very similar to slavery — but under conditions where the forces of production were underdeveloped in comparison with other areas.

The development of Russia can only be explained through the prior development of capitalism in Britain and Holland, etc, which in turn reacted directly and indirectly on Eastern Europe and Russia. In other words, the Russian Empire and the regions that were to be incorporated into the Russian Empire were compelled

---

17 . K Marx, *Grundrisse*, London, 1973, p873. 'It is only in the markets of the world that money acquires to the full extent the character of the commodity whose bodily form is also the immediate social incarnation of human labour in the abstract. Its real mode of existence in this sphere adequately corresponds to its ideal concept.' (K Marx, *Capital*, Volume 1, Moscow, 1961, p142)

18 . LD Trotsky, *1905*, op cit, p5.

either to supply goods to the West for the Western market, or to fight states on their borders which were becoming incorporated into the world market. The development of Russia, Trotsky argued, was governed by conflict with other states, in particular Lithuania, Poland and Sweden, but that in itself is not enough to explain its development. It was the relative primitiveness and backwardness of Russia in relation to those countries that was crucial:

'As a consequence of this pressure on the part of Western Europe, the state swallowed up an inordinately large part of the surplus produce; that is to say, it lived at the expense of the privileged classes which were being formed, and so hampered their already slow development...The state pounced upon the "necessary product" of the farmer, deprived him of his livelihood... and thus hampered the growth of the population and the development of the productive forces.'[19]

The states of this time in Eastern Europe were constantly throwing off foreign yokes and expanding. What caused this process? It was not explained by appeal to a non-existent and mythical nationalism, or by a psychohistory of monarchs. The answer lay much more in terms of the internal dynamic of these regimes.

Expansion can be the result of internal instability, which implies a problem of control over labour and thus over the extraction of the surplus product itself. Landlords needed to establish greater control over adjacent territory to prevent the loss of labour or threats to the system itself. Territory also provided greater resources with which to expand production. The use of shifting agriculture necessarily led to an expansion of the regime. But the regime was not based on shifting agriculture, but on the three-field system, which permitted the soil to recuperate. An increase in the population would of course have led to an increased demand for land. Yet a non-class approach does not explain much. These regimes were not popular, but were rather ruled by a minority of landlords who would expand in order to serve a particular purpose. Before capitalism, there was no accumulation, and hence the economic need to expand would only arise from the need of landlords to increase their own income in order to reach a particular standard of living.

In the context of Russian Tsarism the question was why did the empire therefore expand? There are two answers to this. Firstly, the bureaucracy and landlords needed an increasing income to buy goods from the West for their own pleasure. Secondly, the expansion led to permanent wars, which absorbed the surplus product, which in turn led to a backward technique. The landlords required an increased surplus product in order to satisfy their increasing needs that arose from

---

19. LD Trotsky, 'Results and Prospects', in *Permanent Revolution and Results and Prospects*, London, 1962, p171.

the expansion of the market in the West. The wars themselves became increasingly costly with the improvement in military technique, which again had to be imported from the West, and the need to absorb more labour in these more intensive wars. The wars and the need to control the Russian Empire required a considerable bureaucratic apparatus, which also had to be paid for out of the surplus product. Hence the Russian Empire was caught in a vicious circle arising from the development of capitalism in the West without a parallel development in the Russian Empire. This inevitably resulted in underdevelopment. Without the growth of the surplus product, the peasants could only be ground down further and further. Yet the increasing demand for the surplus product by both the state and the landlords logically led to a declining standard of living for the peasantry. In turn they had no alternative but to revolt, which led to their suppression by the state or local landlords. Brutally controlled, such a peasantry could have no interest in producing a larger product for the landlord. Hence the state was driven both to expand and control its peasants more and more harshly.

The contradiction of the Tsarist system was its absolute need to expand the surplus product on the one hand, and the form of the extraction of that surplus product on the other. The form, that of autocratic serfdom, prevented the expansion of the surplus product itself. Yet the form itself had arisen out of the need to expand that surplus. Hence the whole drive to expand the surplus led to greater control over the direct producer, and to a lack of improvement of the technique of production. Thus the form of the expansion of the surplus product negated that very expansion. The mediation lay in the expansion of territory, and hence in the increase of the number of serfs.

As long as the number of serfs expanded and the territory of the Russian Empire itself expanded, the problems for the state could be limited. The intensification of serfdom and the expansion of the Russian Empire occurred precisely because of the rise of capitalism outside its boundaries. Once it ran out of populated territory, and the West had begun its industrial revolution, the Russian Empire became increasingly dependent upon the West. It moved from being a backward junior partner to becoming a neo-colony of France and other Western countries. Loans and the import of capital also served the purpose of expanding the surplus product, but they put the Russian Empire into pawn.

Under these circumstances, the question became one of the possibility of reforming this peculiar mode of production. In principle, concessions to the peasantry might have provided for the growth of agriculture. The 1861 Emancipation Act and the Stolypin reforms, whose failure some in Russia now regret, are seen in this context. Yet there was no good reason to assume that Stolypin would have succeeded.

The elimination of large numbers of peasants from the villages, leaving the land to be farmed by capitalist farmers, could have worked, provided that the necessary industrial outputs were forthcoming. There were, however, five conditions which had to be fulfilled. Firstly, industry would have had to expand rapidly in order to absorb the unemployed flooding into the towns from the countryside. Secondly, there would have had to have been large loans from the West to allow for the purchase of the necessary machinery, pesticides, pipes for irrigation and drainage, and fertilisers. Thirdly, the state would have had to invest colossal sums in the development of the infrastructure. Fourthly, the state itself would have had to establish a form of cooperative farming in order to maintain prices. Fifthly, the absence of a welfare state in the towns would have led to an enormous growth in both crime and working class militancy. Hence the payment of social security would have been required.

All this required very large sums of money from the West. In its absence, the simple institution of private property in farming would have merely led to the rise of a pauperised urban workforce, the growth of a small number of rich farmers, and a majority of poor farmers who would only scratch a living from a farm with declining fertility. Trotsky concluded that only through the elimination of capitalism would there be a 'final solution to the agrarian problem: no solution can be found under capitalism. But in any case, the revolutionary liquidation of the autocracy and feudalism must precede the solution which is to come.'[20]

It has to be remembered that one of the effects of the increasing growth of industry in that period was the decline of rural crafts. In a similar manner, a simple growth of capitalist agriculture would drive peasants to the towns in such a way that those peasants would lose the elementary life support systems that they previously maintained in the village. These range from the village crafts to common baby-sitting. In the absence of a welfare state, the plight of the ordinary peasant could only grow worse. In other words, Stolypin could never have succeeded even had he overcome all forms of bureaucratic resistance. Reformism never could have worked in the context of the Russian Empire.

Trotsky expressed the importance of understanding Russian history at the end of his chapter defending his view of Russian history against Pokrovsky: 'All these circumstances... directly determined the October Revolution, the triumph of the proletariat, and its subsequent difficulties...'[21]

Trotsky argued that it was the poverty of natural resources and the consequent small surplus product which made Russia backward in the first instance. That backwardness, however, was reinforced by the growth of the autocracy and its constant demand on resources in order to defend the Russian state. As a result, the

20. LD Trotsky, *1905*, op cit, p34.
21. Ibid, p344.

ruling class itself was stunted, while the peasantry was permanently discontented. In an era of capitalist decline, the bourgeoisie could not hope to sweep the old class structure away. On the other hand, the emerging working class appeared as the historical heir to the past opponents of the autocracy.

The Menshevik Solution

There remains the issue as to whether a social democratic Russia was feasible. This really involves two questions. Firstly, could capitalism have developed in the Russian Empire at all? Secondly, could social democracy have come to power in any stable way, and have introduced the reforms which would have ensured the necessary stability for the development of industry?

In the case of the Russian Empire, sufficient surplus had to be extracted internally to ensure industrial development, unless there was a massive inflow from foreign countries. Russia's enormous debt made such a further inflow rather doubtful, unless international conditions had been more propitious. Had there not been a revolution, the Russian Empire would have prefigured the South American debt default 70 years earlier. The repudiation of the debt by the Bolsheviks was a conscious anti-imperialist act, but was also the only alternative left to any semi-independent government. The enormous destruction wrought by the First World War was followed in 1929 by a world depression. The international situation never looked very propitious for a Russian government or bourgeoisie intent on investing in its own industry.

It might be argued that the peasants and workers could have been further repressed and squeezed to extort the necessary surplus product for industrialisation. As the standard of living was already very low, it is not easy to argue this case. What, however, made the whole viewpoint untenable was the socio-political situation as a whole.

There has been no lack of economists to support the intellectual position that Russia had reached a take-off stage at which the country could have been launched into a mature industrialisation phase. They are right, of course, that the preconditions for such a take-off were present. Translated into Marxist terms, Russia possessed the proletariat, potential proletariat, and the capital to invest in industry. The skills, the capitalists or entrepreneurs, etc, were all present. The problem with this simplistic argument is that it ignores the real class relations of the time. If there had not been a revolution, there would certainly have been a wave of protest movements and strikes. Land reform would have been demanded, but conceded only gradually, leaving a discontented peasantry. The government was weak, and could not repress the workers and peasants to the extent required for a high level of surplus extraction.

In other words, whatever the technical economic situation, the socio-economic and political conditions internally and externally would have made a rapid indigenous growth pattern unlikely.

Trotsky and Parvus, following Marx, formulated the above arguments in their conception of permanent revolution. Marx had earlier argued that the bourgeoisie had ceased to be revolutionary by 1848, and that the petit-bourgeoisie had become pusillanimous. Thus only the proletariat could carry out the tasks of sweeping away the remnants of pre-bourgeois society. From that followed the necessity for the proletariat to overthrow the autocracy, as the liberals could not do it.

After 1905 the Mensheviks began to argue the opposite, that the liberals and therefore the bourgeoisie were needed to overthrow the autocracy. They learned the lesson of the second general strike of that year, in November, which the employers had opposed. Unlike the first one, in October, which was supported by the employers, this one was lost. The differences between Bolsheviks and Mensheviks were obscure to start with, but from 1905 there could be no doubt that the Bolsheviks stood on the more militant wing of the Russian Social Democratic Labour Party. The Bolsheviks accused the Mensheviks of wanting a legal revolution, while Dan accused Lenin of not understanding that the masses were still under monarchist rather than constitutionalist illusions. This latter statement really encompassed the real differences. For Lenin the problem was not that some workers or peasants might still support the Tsar, but that some of them might support the Cadets.[22]

In a global sense, the Mensheviks were wrong not just in arguing that socialism was not on the agenda, but they were also wrong in believing that genuine reforms were possible in Russia. It was only the realisation that the bourgeoisie could lose power that forced the capitalist class to implement a welfare state and a global industrial growth strategy. But this new policy was only implemented after the Second World War. Before then, such a policy could not be implemented in any country. The Menshevik solution of bourgeois democracy was thus doomed. The bourgeoisie adopted the social democratic solution precisely because of the October Revolution and the threat that it could be regenerated, or be repeated in other countries.

The theoretical failure of Menshevism lay in its implicit acceptance of the doctrine of socialism in one country. If one started from the premise that the revolution could begin anywhere as long as it spread to Western Europe, then they were wrong to oppose the acceptance of power in 1917. One could, on the other hand, take the view that socialism was premature everywhere. Such a view has been propounded by such writers as Fernando Claudín and David Rousset. They argue that

---

22. Chertvertyi (Ob'edinetel'nyi) S'ezd RSDRP, *Protokoly*, Aprel'-Mai 1906, Moskva, 1960, pp205-9.

the forces of production had not yet sufficiently developed on a global level by 1917 for socialism to be possible. Claudín argues that it was not enough for the productive forces to be capable of sustaining socialism: 'It must also be the case that capitalism is incapable of developing new productive forces.'[23] Yet he is really producing an international Menshevik viewpoint, as it were. He says that Marx foresaw a revolution only at the point of terminal crisis, and such a crisis would occur when capitalism could no longer develop. There is no evidence that Marx ever thought along these lines. It would indeed have been extremely odd if he did, for the previous history of transitions is one in which the old system goes on developing, while the new one overtakes it, rather than a situation of absolute collapse as implied in Claudín's analysis.

When Marx said that no system would disappear before it had produced all it was capable of, it is unlikely that he was providing an absolute statement of collapse. It follows from his overall argument that all systems will decline and decay, but decline here has a different meaning from collapse or terminal crisis. Its first, theoretical, meaning refers to the growing ineffectiveness of its fundamental law or method of pumping out the surplus product. In the case of capitalism, that would be the law of value, which is in patent decline in the West in spite of reactionary attempts to reverse it. Those very attempts, like the reforms of Thatcher and Reagan, succeed only in increasing the power of the state rather than weakening it, and then destroy much of the industrial base of the country. The second, empirical, meaning refers to the growing gap between the potential of developing the productive forces and the reality. In our present time, it would refer to enormous possibilities in the total computerisation of production, popular transport systems, and in general a concentration upon raising the standard of living, instead of upon armaments and luxury goods for the rich. Claudín's viewpoint is both dubious and mechanical.

Claudín's attempt to justify himself by invoking the very high development in the postwar period has become a classic argument. However, the postwar period is entirely exceptional in the history of capitalism. In no other period has there been such a rise in the standard of living and such high growth rates in the metropolitan countries. If capitalism is capable of reforming, why did it not do so earlier? How was it that capitalism was able to introduce reforms without workers demanding the whole hog, as it were? To ask these questions is to realise the answers. Apart from the previous history of the war, fascism and the depression, what was crucial both in permitting these reforms and preventing any real change was Stalinism itself. At a certain point in history, the capitalist class will not invest if it expects

23. F Claudín, *The Communist Movement: From Comintern to Cominform*, Harmondsworth, 1975, p99.

the workers to be its gravediggers. When, however, the workers are controlled, then reforms become possible, and indeed are the only alternative for the system. In other words, Claudín, a former member of the Spanish Communist Party, would not admit the enormously reactionary role of Stalinism in holding back world history.

David Rousset, who rejects the concept of building socialism in one country, does not take the same line as Claudín. He argues that the absolute backwardness of the technology of 1917 made socialism impossible on a world scale.[24] This is Menshevism on a world scale, as opposed to Menshevism in one country. Was this the case? The obvious reply is that the productive forces would have developed very fast under the transition period to socialism, and in the initial period of socialism itself. At the same time, Rousset has taken a Marxist truth to its limit. Capitalism will develop over time, and, as it does so, production will become more and more socialised, so providing to an ever higher degree the base on which to build socialism. He concludes that it is best to wait until there is the maximum development of forces of production under capitalism.

The concept of decline and thus the concept of a declining capitalism does incorporate the idea that the decline will become decay, and ultimately terminal decay in an absolute sense. But there is no reason to assume that this absolute terminus, as opposed to a relative one, will be reached for hundreds of years. If capitalism is not overthrown for 200 years or so, it might be expected that the system will show advanced features of decay beyond that of the present day. The new socialist society would then be faced with the task of dealing with those forms of decay and reconstructing a new society.

The 'Russian Mode of Production'

Whatever the international situation, the peculiarity of the Russian Empire was its relative backwardness combined with its close integration into the world market. Finance capital, agricultural trade, raw material exports and imports of machinery were all closely integrated with Western Europe. Yet the level of education and skill of its workforce were close to illiteracy, while the infrastructure was far from what was necessary for industry.

Its nature was determined by its mode of production, one which was semi-Asiatic in that the centre extracted the surplus product for defence, the landlords extracted the surplus product in order to obtain Western goods, and the peasantry had no incentive to work. The result was declining productivity, and a declining

---

24. D Rousset, *The Legacy of the Bolshevik Revolution: A Critical History of the USSR*, London, 1982, pp1-16.

standard of living for the majority. The capitalist solution was therefore presenting itself at the time when the workers were conscious of alternatives, and when only Western capital could provide the real solution. Trotsky's law of combined and uneven development had a particular application to the Russian Empire.

Trotsky argued that a capitalist solution to the agrarian crisis in the Russian empire did not exist. What could have succeeded, however, was the growth of a merchant-finance capital predicated on the semi-Asiatic nature of the Russian Empire. This was Trotsky's point. The relative self-sufficiency of the village and the development of village crafts meant that trade was essential between the villages. Hence merchants played an historic role in the Russian Empire, but ever more so with the growth of mass-produced consumer goods. The villages then fell into a position of dependency upon merchants, and through them upon the world market. The long-term development of rich capitalist farmers and a mass of poor peasants scraping a living from an ever smaller proportion of land was inevitable. But that would not have altered the position of the mass of ordinary peasants who would be doomed to the grinding poverty that they had always experienced as peasants, or to becoming a member of the urban proletariat. This was then no solution to the agrarian crisis because the capitalist farmers would continue to use a relatively backward technique in association with a sullen, discontented peasantry, whose productivity would remain low.

Russia and its Development in an International Context

With regard to the development of capitalism in the Russian Empire, the problem is whether a backward country could have had its own industrial revolution, and established an independent capitalism. Although capitalism had, of course, already begun to develop in the Russian Empire itself, the question need only be posed to realise its impossibility. Prior to the Second World War, no backward country reached the first rank. Those that might be discussed, such as Japan, had a relatively backward industry, which needed a particularly rapacious imperialism in order to survive. Even in the post-Second World War period, only a small number of countries like Japan, South Korea and Taiwan managed to break through, and then only under very special conditions. Of course, there are a number of countries with a wealthy bourgeoisie, an industry of a limited kind, a starving peasantry, and massive surplus population such as Brazil, Chile and India, but they cannot be considered examples of successful mature capitalist development, if this is defined in terms of a self-sustaining growth of relative surplus value.

Special conditions appear to be necessary to ensure the development of real and self-sustaining relative surplus value extraction. These include the existence of a strong pro-capitalist state, the successful suppression of potential revolution, and the encouragement by a dominant capitalist country. In the period since the Second World War, the Cold War has also played a crucial role. The stability of Japan, Taiwan, Singapore, Hong Kong and South Korea was vital for the United States to contain the perceived Soviet/communist threat. A capitalist will not invest in an unstable country, while a powerful working class movement will see to it that there is a low rate of profit. Even an internal capitalist will not invest in his own country unless the rate of profit warrants it. It has, therefore, paid the United States to accept the growth of a relatively independent capitalist class in those countries, which have used economic forms of protection against the United States, and opened its own internal market to enterprises from those countries. The United States and its allies have invested in those countries in order to ensure their viability.

Theodore Von Laue has argued a similar case based on the conditions of pre-revolutionary Russia. He says that the socio-economic conditions did not permit of a democratic government.[25] Put differently, labour had to be well disciplined and politically controlled. It also had to be skilled and well-educated. Capital had necessarily to come from the outside, and be suitably rewarded with a rate of profit considerably greater than that obtainable in its host country. Historically, capital has flowed towards the developed areas of the world economy, and only exceptionally towards the underdeveloped countries in order to exploit their raw materials. In the post-Second World War period, however, there has been a significant development of industry in much of the Third World, but it has only been possible on the basis of a protective state mechanism, under conditions where the international bourgeoisie has accepted the need for such development, in order to secure its own future.

In this context, the future of a non-revolutionary Russia can be seen in India. In fact, this is precisely what Trotsky said.[26] His argument that the bourgeoisie was too craven in a period of historical decline to fulfil its own tasks has been vindicated by the course of world history.

Conclusion

Trotsky and Lenin took power in a backward Russia, intending that the snapping of the world capitalist chain would assist the world revolution. However, because the new Soviet republic was on the periphery of capitalism, it lacked any organic

---

25 . T Von Laue, *Why Lenin? Why Stalin?*, London, 1964, pp125-6.
26 . 'Only the foundations that have been laid by the October Revolution can guard the country from the fate of India or China...' (LD Trotsky, 'Alarm Signal!', *Writings of Leon Trotsky 1932-33*, New York, 1972)

link to the mass of the Western proletariat. The concept of establishing a base for world revolution proved to be flawed. It might have worked, but it was as much a gamble as the alternative — which was, on the one hand, to wage a revolutionary war, and, on the other, to take steps to ensure that the Soviet regime would be a socialist democracy of a hitherto unknown kind. The specific nature of the Russian Empire, however, forced the Bolsheviks to take power in a particular way. The only other realistic path for Russia was to have become a backward undemocratic finance-capitalist semi-dependency of the West. There were no other roads it could take. Trotsky's analysis of Russian history provides a basis for understanding the nature of the problem involved in taking and maintaining power in Russia.

Hillel Ticktin

Leon Trotsky and the Social Forces Leading to Bureaucracy, 1923-29

Introduction

The nature of the emerging social forces in the newly-formed USSR was and remains the primary political economic question of the first decade of that country. The economic basis of the 'bureaucracy' remains a question of considerable debate. How did Trotsky see the development of class relations in the USSR in relation to the process of accumulation in that country? The only specific formulation of the nature of accumulation in the USSR was developed by Preobrazhensky in terms of the contradiction of the law of planning and the law of value, but he did not relate this contradiction to the development of the real class relations existing in the USSR. On the other hand, Trotsky and Rakovsky had evolved a theory of bureaucratisation, but without discussing the laws of accumulation existing in the USSR.

It is still possible on the basis of Trotsky's writings to derive a picture of his political economy of the emergence of the new social group. I have done so in relation to the period from 1929 onwards in another essay in this book. The picture which emerges is different from that of either Richard Day or Isaac Deutscher. Trotsky and the Left Opposition saw the main danger to be on the right, which they took to be Bukharin, Rykov and Tomsky. Stalin was perceived to be a centrist. As the right was easily defeated by Stalin, and Stalinism proved to be far worse and more enduring than the Bukharinist forces, the left was compelled to revise its understanding of the class nature of the regime. As a result, the left's political-economic analysis had to take account of this shift on the question of who was the main enemy. Preobrazhensky never managed to do so. He avoided the question. Trotsky, on the other hand, gradually and grudgingly came to terms with his initial mistake, but he never formulated it in theoretical terms. To the end, he saw Stalin as a centrist, a point which is made again in the following essay. In political-economic terms, however, his thesis of necessary bureaucratisation was almost fully evolved by 1929. His argument about Stalin and Thermidor was a part of that discussion. The point here is to draw out how Trotsky's characterisation of the classes in the USSR and of the transitional epoch differed sufficiently from some of his fellow oppositionists, but most particularly from that of Preobrazhensky.

Preobrazhensky

Preobrazhensky's viewpoint did not enable him to produce a theory of political-economic degeneration. Preobrazhensky was the main economist of the Left Opposition, and it is clear from Trotsky's references to him before his capitulation and indeed in the 1930s, though not at the time of his defection, that he was held in high regard by the left and Trotsky.[1] In the second volume of his trilogy, Deutscher tries to provide a critique of Preobrazhensky from the point of view of Trotsky,[2] while Stephen Cohen points to the contradiction between the opposition to socialism in one country and the law of primitive socialist accumulation.[3] None of these conceptions makes much sense if one examines the actual speeches and references of the time.

The main concept was that of primary, original or primitive socialist accumulation.

1. In February 1929 Trotsky referred to Preobrazhensky as an economist with a 'profound education' (LD Trotsky, 'C'est la Marche des Événements!', *Writings of Leon Trotsky 1929*, New York, 1975, p23).
2. I Deutscher, *The Prophet Unarmed*, Oxford, 1979, pp237-9. Deutscher provides no evidence for the differences he sees between Preobrazhensky and Trotsky. Since Preobrazhensky specifically attacked the conception of socialism in one country, and indeed by 1927 argued its economic impossibility, it is difficult to see where Deutscher gets the idea that the two differed on the possibility of successfully concluding primitive socialist accumulation. Preobrazhensky's views are clearly articulated in EA Preobrazhensky, 'Economic Equilibrium in the USSR', *The Crisis of Soviet Industrialisation*, White Plains, 1980.
3. S Cohen, *Bukharin and the Bolshevik Revolution*, New York, 1973, p161. It is difficult to see where Cohen gets his views from as Trotsky and Smirnov obviously had no problem using the term before Preobrazhensky. The meaning they attached to the term was in essence no different.

It is paradoxical that the term also came to be employed for the transition from Stalinism to the market in the post-1991 period in Russia. As an idea it was invented by Vladimir Smirnov in 1920, and used by Trotsky in his famous speech at the Twelfth Party Congress in April 1923.[4] It was then theorised by Preobrazhensky as a law.[5] Smirnov was working in Gosplan, but he was also a member of the Democratic Centralist opposition, which later merged with the Left Opposition. By 1926-27 he took the view, unlike Trotsky, that the USSR was no longer a workers' state, but had become a bureaucratic dictatorship of the Secretariat.[6] Smirnov and the tendency he represented — which took the view that the bureaucratisation of the society was destroying its revolutionary character — were rejected by Trotsky.

Nonetheless, the two concepts remain as crucial tendencies in Trotsky's thought from 1926-27 onwards. There was no contradiction between holding that the immediate task was that of primitive socialist accumulation and arguing that in this process bureaucratisation could strangle the workers' state. There was a subtle difference between the formulation by Trotsky of primitive socialist accumulation as a stage, and the formulation by Preobrazhensky of the law of primitive socialist accumulation. It was not one of principle, but of method. Trotsky did take the view that there were specific laws of the transition period different from the laws of capitalism or socialism. But for whatever reason he never produced an exact formulation of these laws. The consequence is that it was quite possible, on the basis of Trotsky's views at this point, to argue that society was proceeding through a process of deformed socialist accumulation led by a bureaucratic caste. Furthermore, the danger from the right was such that it could have aborted this process. Even in 1932 Trotsky saw the role of the middle peasant as crucial in putting pressure to bear on the bureaucracy.[7]

4. Cf Trotsky's leading speech on the economy, XII S'ezd RKP, *Stenograficheskey Otchet*, Moskva, 1968, p351. Trotsky used the same term at the Fourth World Congress of the Communist International in November 1922, almost en passant, see LD Trotsky, *First Five Years of the Communist International*, Volume 2, London, 1953, p238. It is quite clear that the term in itself meant little politically until the struggle with the Stalin-Bukharin wing allowed the latter to use the emotional content of the words for agitational purposes. No one was anti-peasant. Indeed, Preobrazhensky had specifically been charged with drawing up theses on the peasantry for the Eleventh Party Congress. Lenin rejected them, but Preobrazhensky was retained on the subsequent committees. Lenin did not like Preobrazhensky's over-academicism and lack of practical measures. The fundamental thesis on the need for the proletarianisation and industrialisation of the countryside was general policy, but was certainly highly abstract (VI Lenin, *Sochineniya*, Volume 27, Moskva, 1936, p191).
5. References to Preobrazhensky are to his *New Economics*, Oxford, 1965, unless specified otherwise.
6. This was recounted by Victor Serge. See V Serge and N Trotsky, *The Life and Death of Leon Trotsky*, London, 1975, p140.
7. Trotsky spoke of the middle peasant still exerting an influence, and saw the peasantry as still

Market and Planning

Preobrazhensky did not allow for such a process in his description of the transition period. It is a curiously unrecognised fact that Preobrazhensky provided the laws of an ideal transition period, and not of the specific transition of the USSR. He argued in terms of the necessary conflict between the law of value and the law of planning. On the other hand, he argued that the specific nature of the USSR was such that planning was very restricted, and indeed was undermined by the market. He was not unaware of this undoubted situation since time and again he pointed out the small size of the nationalised sector.[8] He also, but quite separately, in his speeches pointed to the development of the bureaucracy. Indeed, having been a member of many oppositions, he constantly referred to this aspect of Soviet reality. It is even in *The ABC of Communism*, which he wrote with Bukharin in 1919.[9] Nor could it be said that he only saw bureaucratism and not the existence of a social group, for he was most vociferous on the question, and pointed to the corruption of the Communist Party managers.[10] Nonetheless, he did not integrate this social group into his theory of Soviet society. Logically, therefore, what he produced was a more or less pure theory of the transition period modified to take account of primitive socialist accumulation. This latter was simply adapted into the theory by placing the category into the specific period in which the law of planning was operating.

    trying to find a market solution to their problems. See LD Trotsky, 'The Soviet Economy in Danger', *Writings of Leon Trotsky 1932*, New York, 1973, p273; and 'Alarm Signal', *Writings of Leon Trotsky 1932-33*, New York, 1973, p99. The translation is not always accurate, so I have used the original in *Biulletin' Oppositizii*, 1932, no 31, p8, for the article 'The Soviet Economy in Danger'.

8. Preobrazhensky, speaking in a debate on the Soviet economy, produced a triangle showing the state sector at the apex, with the base of petty production (*Vestnik Kommunisticheskoi Akademii*, no 2, 1923, p181).

9. He spoke very early on in debates and his works of organisations succumbing to bureaucracy, see especially *The ABC of Communism*, Ann Arbor, 1966, p212. In his letter to Valentinov, Rakovsky spoke of Preobrazhensky devoting a special chapter to it in his new book, *The Conquests of the Dictatorship of the Proletariat in Year Ten of the Revolution*. His speeches at the party congresses did not overlook this theme, for example, the speech he made at the Ninth Party Congress where he spoke of the bureaucratisation of the Central Committee itself. The letter to Valentinov first appeared in *Biulletin' Oppositizii*, 1929, no 6, p18, and a translation appeared in *The New International*, November 1934, p108.

10. This he did in his speech at the Twelfth Party Congress where he argued that the communist directors of enterprises were affected by the law of value — to the detriment of the revolution. It is indeed odd that in spite of his intended chapter he never came to produce a theory of bureaucracy. Perhaps his exile proved too much for him, and the necessity of producing a theory of bureaucracy to compare with his theory of the two regulators was either consigned to a limbo or remained in a hidden place in his mind.

There is from a Marxist point of view an important problem which Preobrazhensky overlooked. He and Bukharin both continued to maintain, as indeed had all Marxists until then, that the law of value ceases to exist under socialism. In the debate on this question in the Communist Academy both right and left agreed totally on this question. They most vigorously opposed the truly confused viewpoints of Stepanov-Skvortsov, Pokrovsky, Bogdanov and others.[11] In fact, there can be no dispute that Bukharin and Preobrazhensky held the correct Marxist interpretation on the nature of socialism. The overthrow of the market is of the essence of socialism, but if this is so, however, it must mean that the laws of value and planning are mutually incompatible, and must involve the total destruction of the one or the other. In other words, there is no dialectical interaction — there is no superseding, overcoming or synthesis possible. Yet in fact the interrelation of these two laws was occurring, and was leading to the formation of new entities. Preobrazhensky in *The New Economics* did not see this, though he did in his political speeches quoted above.

This point needs to be elaborated. Development, in the Marxist sense, is seen as proceeding through a process of interpenetration of opposites, which in time are so changed that they are superseded by a new entity. Thus the two poles of the commodity — use value and exchange value — interpenetrate to the point where the commodity itself is superseded under socialism by planning. Capital and labour interpenetrate similarly to the point where capitalism is superseded. On the other hand, workers and capitalists fight with one another to the point where the one wipes out the other. Planning and the market are not two poles of an entity so much as forms of different socio-economic formations. Planning is the form of a socialist society. It can be defined as the conscious regulation of the society by the associated producers. In other words, it involves the direct and indirect participation of everyone in the society in order to decide on the shape of the economy and society. The anarchic forms of the market are rejected. Competition, regular slumps, unemployment, profit, abstract labour and the fetishism of the commodity are all eliminated as standing in direct antagonism with a truly planned society.

There are two problems here. The first concerns the reality of the antagonism. There can be no doubt that Trotsky and Preobrazhensky both saw the market and plan as antagonistic opposites.[12] Social democrats and many of those who see themselves on the left in the last decade of the twentieth century do not have the same view. They see plan and market as working in harmony. I have argued the contrary case in other articles.[13] This is not the place to expound on the point.

11. 'Debate on the Subject of Political Economy', *Vestnik Kommunisticheskoi Akademii*, no 11, 1925.
12. See the discussion in my next article in this book.
13. See my 'Socialism, the Market and the State', *Critique*, no 3; 'Is Market Socialism Possible or

Suffice it to say that Marxists at that time and indeed all traditional Marxists down to the present take the same view because they look forward to a society which has all the characteristics of a socialist society as described by Marx.[14] A fully developed socialist society would abolish money, and have an economy of abundance. It would be ruled through elections to all important posts, and would involve the elimination of the old division of labour.

At this point, it must be clear that for Marxists like Trotsky and Preobrazhensky or, for that matter, for Bukharin, there could be no compromise between the market and socialism.[15] Preobrazhensky and Trotsky therefore concluded that Soviet society had to move gradually in the direction of socialism. Planning would gradually oust the market over time. This was the nature of the transition period. The whole concept of the transition period was bound up with the elimination of the market. The other aspect of the transition period which had to be removed was the state itself, but it could not go until the element of force involved in compelling people to work in a market ceased to exist.

In the case of a move to socialism on a world scale, the matter is not unproblematic, but it is not difficult to see the way forward. In the case of the Soviet Union, the economy had not even reached the stage of a developed capitalism, and hence would have to maintain the market for some time before it could be eliminated. This was the stage of primitive socialist accumulation. This was the second problem. It was the period in which sufficient capital had to be accumulated in order to reach the same level as Western capitalism. At that stage the market could begin to be eliminated. Here the differences between Bukharin and Stalin on one side, and Trotsky, Preobrazhensky and the Left Opposition on the other, became important. Bukharin and at first Stalin argued that the market could coexist with planning until the market was eliminated, and that the market would not conflict with planning. The differ-

---

Necessary?', *Critique*, no 14; and forthcoming: 'The Problem is Market Socialism'.

14 .   See, for instance, my article 'What Will a Socialist Society be Like?', *Critique*, no 25.

15 .   A firm in which the workers elect the managers on a recallable basis and in which the manager does not necessarily receive any more than a highly skilled worker may function in a market environment, but it will not be able to compete with traditional capitalist firms very well. Workers will demand the best working conditions, the highest possible pay, and will regard profit as a secondary consideration, in contrast to the capitalist firm. The result is that the traditional firm will have higher profits, workers who are compelled to work harder, and as a result will introduce innovations more rapidly. The capitalist firm will fire workers as rapidly as possible on a decline of the market, or on the introduction of labour-saving machinery. The labour-oriented firm could not do so. However sophisticated the market socialists may make their model, they cannot get away from the basic antagonism between making profits and acting in the immediate interests of the direct producers.

ence between the two sides was, therefore, not in the final goal, but in the process of getting there.

The Social Groups Behind the Market and Behind the Plan

Both sides in the debate failed to take account of the socio-political consequences of retaining a market. Trotsky was clear that a market uncontrolled by the state and planning would lead to capitalism. No one, however, looked at the effect of the market on the society: the corruption of the managers, specialists, intelligentsia and smallholders of various kinds. These groups were acting within the market or law of value, and wanted to retain it or at least its consequences in terms of salary and position in society. On the other hand, the state planning bodies were unable to operate democratically, and as a consequence ultimately became instruments of control of the representatives of that very layer that benefited from the market.

The logical consequence of this failure to understand the laws, or his own laws, led Preobrazhensky later, in 1928, to see Stalin as a deformed upholder of planning, who was therefore required to be supported.[16] No doubt Preobrazhensky's capitulation may be understood in psychological terms as well, but there was a failure in his thought which made the defection easier. In his analysis of the process from the NEP to socialism,[17] he never once mentioned the degeneration which would tend to occur in the isolated socialist state, except in terms of socialism in one country being an absolute impossibility.

It is important to realise that behind the laws of which Preobrazhensky spoke stood social groups or classes, namely the bourgeoisie and petit-bourgeoisie on the one hand, and the proletariat on the other. The rise of a new social group, the bureaucracy, was never incorporated. Theoretically it could have appeared as the degenerate offspring of the interpenetration of the two laws, which had themselves been consequently transformed. This solution could then provide the basis for the analysis of the USSR as it was coming into being. This, it seems to me, is the modern interpretation to be made of his two laws. Hence the theories such as those of

16. Preobrazhensky's capitulation took place in 1928, but before that time he engaged in correspondence with Trotsky in which he indicated his differences with him, most particularly over China, permanent revolution, and the two stage process of revolution. He effectively re-adopted Lenin's earlier doctrine of two stages for the emergence of the socialist revolution, with the first stage being the democratic dictatorship of the proletariat and peasantry. In the case of China, this meant supporting an alliance with Chiang Kai-Shek, an alliance which led to the massacre of the Communist Party.
17. EA Preobrazhensky, *From the New Economic Policy to Socialism: A Glance into the Future of Russia and Europe*, London, 1973.

Charles Bettelheim and Ernest Mandel,[18] which base themselves on Preobrazhensky's original abstract theory, must inevitably only describe a pure transitional society, which is yet to come into existence. Trotsky did not formulate his thought in terms of the rigorous interaction of two laws, although we must presume he was not opposed to doing so.[19] Deutscher argues that Trotsky found Preobrazhensky's theory too abstract, but he does not explain what he means, although there is a certain rational kernel to Deutscher's view.[20] Trotsky did indeed formulate the relation between the market and planning as one of total antagonism,[21] in which one or the other must win. He argued that the NEP was a retreat

18. E Mandel, 'Ten Theses on the Social and Economic Laws Governing the Society Transitional between Capitalism and Socialism', *Critique*, no 3, p9; C Bettelheim, *Economic Calculation and the Forms of Property*, London, 1976, p131. Bettelheim does indeed recognise the effect of value on planning, which leads him to a formulation of a transitional law. It does not, however, lead him to a theory of the rise of a new social group on this basis.

19. In EH Carr and R Davies, *Foundations of a Planned Economy 1926-1929*, London, 1969, p630, the Trotsky archives are cited to show that Trotsky saw the two laws as a legitimate method, but was worried by their use to develop a theory of socialism in one country, as well as by the need to avoid the smear of trying to use the countryside as a colony. This, according to the source cited, is directed against the governing group rather than against Preobrazhensky. Indeed, Trotsky had earlier himself used the term of primitive socialist accumulation without any qualification on colonies or socialism in one country. The question was indeed one of use because it is clear that the theory was one of the present and not of what to do politically, so that it could in principle be used to justify what transpired, though only by the most cynical of bureaucrats. For Trotsky's use of the terms 'law' see 'The Soviet Economy in Danger', *Writings of Leon Trotsky 1932*, op cit, p278, where he refers to laws of the transition period, of capitalism and socialism.

20. I Deutscher, op cit, p238. Deutscher stresses Trotsky's speech at the Twelfth Party Congress, but in fact the term, as shown in note 4, had been used before, and not only by Trotsky and Smirnov, but by Preobrazhensky himself (*Vestnik Kommunisticheskoi Akademii*, no 2) and also by one D Kuzovkov, who wrote 'The Financial System in the Period of the Primitive Socialist Accumulation' (*Vestnik Kommunisticheskoi Akademii*, no 2). Preobrazhensky himself spoke of the unfortunate fact that Smirnov did not have the habit of writing (*Vestnik Kommunisticheskoi Akademii*, no 8, 1924). The essential point is that Deutscher may have a point in seeing Preobrazhensky as too abstract, but the formulation of the laws as laws in contradiction with one another and with primitive socialist accumulation was probably part of general currency, though possibly not as well expressed or put in the same way as Preobrazhensky. Trotsky recoiled not from Preobrazhensky, but from the political use that could be made of the theory during the time of Stalin and Bukharin.

21. Cf Trotsky's speech at the Twelfth Party Congress in April 1923, where he spoke of the necessity of having to defend the socialist (that is, state) territory tooth and nail against the centrifugal tendencies of private capitalist forces (XII S'ezd RKP, *Stenograficheskij Otchet*, op cit, p351). On page 343 he explicitly discussed the struggle between plan and market, speaking of the final victory being the liquidation of the market by the plan. His stages characterisation of the post-revolutionary period, characterising the NEP as a sharp retreat, is given post fac-

and a concession, from which it did follow that the law of value was opposed by planning. Hence, at this level, there can be no disagreement here between Trotsky and Preobrazhensky.

Trotsky, however, did speak of his suspicion of Preobrazhensky's formulation.[22] He agreed with the general view put forward by Preobrazhensky, but then said that he thought that it could give rise to an acceptance of socialism in one country. This was based on Preobrazhensky's discussion of primitive socialist accumulation, in which Preobrazhensky argued for ways of industrialising the country. What, however, does primitive socialist accumulation represent in Trotsky's thought? It has to represent more than a subsidiary aspect of the law of planning. It actually appears to represent, in Trotsky's view,[23] the whole period and stage, to use his words, during which the society acquires the basic requirements to plan with any degree of success. It is in fact the precondition for planning. It requires the raising of productivity and the level of culture as its primary aspects, but this has to be done at a primitive level through the exhortation of the party, and in struggle with the market forces. At the low level of the productive forces, the market is essential to control and measure the success of state industry. Unlike Preobrazhensky, Trotsky did not simply assimilate the law of primitive socialist accumulation to the law of planning. It represented for Trotsky the elements of proto-planning, or perhaps a period of organisation of political command which had to be exercised by the party representing the proletariat. It is here that Deutscher may have correctly grasped the difference between the two Left Oppositionists. Trotsky did not abstractly represent the law of primitive socialist accumulation as a law of planning, like Preobrazhensky, but rather saw the former as a process occurring at the time, which was facilitated by planning. In principle, however, Trotsky defined planning to include the response of the masses or democracy,[24] without which only the most imperfect planning could be occurring.[25]

> tum in 1929 in 'Preface to *La Révolution Defigurée*', *Writings of Leon Trotsky 1929*, New York, 1975, p119, where he spoke of the NEP containing the possibilities of dual power, which in fact was the next stage.
>
> 22. LD Trotsky, 'Notes on Economic Questions', *Challenge of the Left Opposition, 1926-27*, New York, 1980, p57.
> 23. Cf Trotsky's speech on the economy, XII S'ezd RKP, *Stenograficheskiy Otchet*, op cit, p351.
> 24. In his speeches, such as the two he made at the Twelfth Party Congress, and in the resolution put forward to the congress, the stress on democracy was put indirectly by saying that planning was not commanding, but was a combination of factors: leading, coordination, preparatory, sectoral agreement, etc. At that stage planning actually needed the market to determine its results. Later, in March 1933, he spelled out the details of democratic control over planning in terms of the masses' critical review of their collective experience, without which planning is impossible (LD Trotsky, 'Alarm Signal!', *Writings of Leon Trotsky 1932-33*, op cit, p96).

Trotsky and the Social Forces Leading to Bureaucracy

Trotsky's conception is of a transition period which goes through a number of stages, one of which is that of primitive socialist accumulation. The law of planning would itself have to go through a number of stages if there is any logic to this conception, and have its own history. It is this history that is absent in Preobrazhensky. He appears to have produced the most developed and profound economic theory of the transition period which politically was identical to the conceptions put forward by Trotsky at the time. In fact, it appears to be little more than a rigorous formulation of Trotsky's political economy, and this is where Deutscher goes too far in opposing Preobrazhensky, but on the other hand the latter was too rigorous in attempting to specify and arrange basic categories. The categories and laws in operation were in a process of formation, and Trotsky captured the process without establishing the political economy.

Perhaps any attempt to formulate a political economy at that time was doomed to capture only a part of the process, precisely because of the contradictoriness and the rapid change occurring. As a result, the less precise formulations of Trotsky were able to comprehend more of the reality. If we regard primitive socialist accumulation as a process and not as a law, then it becomes easy to accommodate the rise of an apparatus, and other elements in combination with it, as the overseer of this primitive socialist accumulation. Furthermore, planning then appears as a derivative of primitive socialist accumulation, and in the form which it did occur as a very defective planning, if it can be called that at all. Trotsky did not formulate his theory in this form, but the political attack on the concept of primitive socialist accumulation was such as to make the use of the term almost impossible. The importance of the discussion is only to bring out the tensions inherent in the thought of Trotsky. While we have contrasted the thought of Preobrazhensky and Trotsky, in fact both men used their categories in the manner of the other at different times. Preobrazhensky, after all, fought for the introduction of planning in 1923, while Trotsky in 1928-29 was able to incorporate a theory of the bureaucracy into his general outlook of market versus the workers' state. The point, however, is that while both aspects of the struggle of left versus right and the existence of another group arising precisely on the basis of the backwardness and isolation of the USSR were present in the thought of both men — and here Deutscher is on weak ground in attributing in any sense a theory of socialism in one country to Preobrazhensky[26] — the thought of Trotsky was sufficiently sup-

---

25. It is interesting to note that Trotsky said in 1933 that the Soviet economy was not planned but was a bureaucratic economy (LD Trotsky, 'The Degeneration of Theory and the Theory of Degeneration', *Writings of Leon Trotsky 1932-33*, New York, 1972, p224).
26. I Deutscher, op cit. Preobrazhensky explicitly repudiated such a viewpoint many times. This is made explicit in his series of articles in *Vestnik Kommunisticheskoi Akademii* in 1924.

ple to accommodate the incompatibility of the theory with the reality. Preobrazhensky was not able to do so at any time, which may indeed relate to the structure of his thought.

The Break Between Preobrazhensky and Trotsky

In 1928 the differences between Preobrazhensky and Trotsky took a clear form with Preobrazhensky supporting the concept of the democratic dictatorship of the proletariat and peasantry as against permanent revolution.[27] The difference between the two amounted to this. For Trotsky, in the transitional epoch, the struggle was between socialism and capitalism, and any additional intermediate stage could only be formal, and without any depth or length. By raising the possibility of a real existing stage other than a transitional form, Preobrazhensky effectively laid the basis for a stages theory of the USSR. Trotsky could not do so; he could not see Stalinism as a stage to socialism as have Bahro and various other East Europeans.[28] Stalin represented an unnecessary and counter-revolutionary deviation from socialism. In other words, the industrialisation of 1929 onwards was not a step towards socialism. For Trotsky, more was required than industrialisation and planning at a formal level. He pointed out time and again that planning would cease to exist without democracy.[29] For Trotsky, planning had as one of its essential components precisely the aspect which Stalin and Bukharin had virtually destroyed by 1927.

Before he capitulated to Stalin in 1928, Preobrazhensky also talked of the lack of the specific features of a socialist economy, such as the identification with the society as a whole, and the spontaneous sabotage by the workers of bad planning, but he did not consider the effect that lack of the democracy could have on the nature of planning and the society itself.[30] In fact, Trotsky only spoke explicitly

27. Preobrazhensky's letter was printed in the April 1936 issue of *The New International*.
28. R Bahro, *The Socialist Alternative*, London, 1978, p133.
29. Apart from 'The Degeneration of Theory and the Theory of Degeneration', *Writings of Leon Trotsky 1932-33*, op cit, there are the following: 'Where is the Stalin Bureaucracy Leading the USSR?', *Writings of Leon Trotsky 1934-35*, New York, 1974, p158; and again in January 1938, in 'Does the Soviet Government Still Follow the Principles Adopted 20 Years Ago?', *Writings of Leon Trotsky 1937-38*, New York, 1976, p127. In the first case he said that planning consisted of financial control plus democracy, and in the second case he said that democracy was the one and only conceivable mechanism for running a socialist economy, and he then went on to emphasise the importance of the disruptions occurring for the continued existence of planning. I have quoted this latter instance in my article in *Critique*, no 9, pointing out that the obvious conclusion is that, if one takes this viewpoint, planning no longer existed in the USSR.
30. Thus in the *New Economics* (p259) he spoke of the working class exerting pressure through

after he was expelled from the USSR, so that the comparison may be unfair to Preobrazhensky. Nonetheless, this comparison again highlights the basic point that both men did not consider the effect of having forms of planning without democracy. That Preobrazhensky should have discussed the negative effect of bad organisation on the workers, who then replied by working badly, is itself very interesting. Clearly, he must have realised that planning cannot be successful without the participation of workers, but he did not go on to consider the consequences of such so-called planning. In fact, even Trotsky did not take his theory to its logical conclusion before he died. If planning has two components — financial and democratic — as he argued, and one component is missing, one logically no longer has planning. Nonetheless, the fact that Preobrazhensky did not discuss this issue at any time, and certainly not with Trotsky in his correspondence, would seem to indicate that at the very least he saw the question less clearly than Trotsky.

The consequence of this view would have been far reaching, as it would have destroyed the workers' state argument put forward by Trotsky. The latter was predicated on the presence of two aspects — nationalisation and planning — one of which had thus ceased to exist. Just like Preobrazhensky, Trotsky refused to take the logical next step, but with less reason because he did develop a theory of bureaucratic control within the USSR. Indeed, he developed a theory of the origins of this bureaucracy from specific social groups, a theory which changed over time.

The Theory of Dual Power

Trotsky failed to draw the logical conclusions of his thought because he held to a new theory of dual power. Trotsky considered that there was a new stage of dual power in the USSR, that is, bureaucracy and proletarian power.[31] Dual power, as the term had been previously used, could not last for long, and consequently the damage done by the non-proletarian element could be the more easily undone than if the period had lasted a long time. In other words, Trotsky's view of the 1920s of the existence of dual power remained with him to the end, although in the modified form of the degenerate workers' state. The modification, that the workers' state was now degenerate, made it unnecessary to draw the logical conclusion that, if the system lasted a long period of time, dual power could not be said still to exist. With hindsight it is clear that, at the very least, Trotsky was

> consumption and through industrial sabotage. The English translation has 'go slows' for a Russian word implying industrial sabotage. The literal translation is probably something like dilatoriness, that is, working in a manner contrary to instructions.

31. See footnote 21.

wrong to avoid writing more about the destruction of the workers' state. Instead, he consistently characterised Stalin as a centrist, when there was in fact no right wing, and when indeed his own class analysis showed that he could not but fail to identify Stalin with the forces he saw as backing Bukharin in the final phase of the conflict in 1929.

The problem with Richard Day's analysis[32] — and his analysis is better than that of the usual academic — is that he has not correlated the economic forces with the class involved. For Trotsky, the primary question was not how to build up the Soviet Union, but how to maintain the survival of the workers' state as a workers' state. This required the implementation of certain measures which would strengthen the class forces supporting the workers' state, and ruled out the opposite factor, that is, support for the enemies of socialism whatever their economic abilities. Planning and industrialisation strengthened the working class in both size and power — as long as there was a workers' party — so that the imperfections induced by the deformations of the workers' state might be at least held at bay. In this sense, Trotsky was consistent even from the time of the argument around the militarisation of labour.[33] Deutscher provides an incorrect summary of Trotsky's views at the time.[34] Trotsky did not provide a global justification for the raising of productivity through force, but instead argued that force had existed as long as class society, and that the so-called free labour of the bourgeois period had a higher productivity than under previous formations. But the workers' state could not use the lies, the angels, and the prison warder and executioners of the previous orders. Its own apparatus, on the other hand, had not yet been built up, so that it had to use whatever is at hand: bonuses, centralised distribution with preference for priority sectors, and if necessary repressive measures.

The Semi-Asiatic Nature of Russia and the Development of Capitalism

Trotsky stated that the reason for these measures lay not only in the backwardness of a ruined Russia, but also in the backwardness of the socialist apparatus. The better it planned, the more the individual could relate to the society and state. One could see that things were working, and that he was beginning to obtain what he wanted. But the apparatus was itself bureaucratised in its very structure, and not just in its methods, so that a form of direct command had become necessary. The

32. RB Day, *Leon Trotsky and the Politics of Economic Isolation*, Cambridge, 1973.
33. See Deviatyi S'ezd RKP(b), *Protokoly*, Moskva, 1960, pp91ff, see particularly p98, where Trotsky discusses the question of force.
34. I Deutscher, op cit, p500.

commanding apparatus was the trade union. The interesting point about Trotsky's views at the time was not that he was in favour of force in principle, which is untrue, but that he saw the way out through planning and undercutting the bureaucratised apparatus.

In a sense, he never changed this point of view. Under war communism he was trying to use the direction of labour, on a planned basis, as a means of restoring the economy to a situation where there would be genuine planning. This involved the building up of the working class, and the introduction of working class norms to the peasantry. He was quite explicit about this. The alternative to the bureaucratic structure was direct political planning. With the NEP the situation obviously altered. It was in fact during the course of the NEP that he put forward, in bits and pieces, the question of the classes in the society. The key to Trotsky's views is given by his outline of the semi-Asiatic nature of pre-revolutionary Russia. This he took, as is well known, from Marx and Plekhanov. This led Trotsky, in his attack on Pokrovsky, to restate his view clearly formulated in his book on 1905.[35] Pokrovsky's view of Russian capitalism was certainly eccentric at best, and a kind of vulgar, mechanical Marxism at worst, but the two writers at least agreed on one fact: the importance of the Russian trader and merchant over a period of several centuries. Trotsky was led to deduce from this that it was not merchant capitalism but the primitiveness of Russian development which demanded a link among its villages precisely because of the absence of capitalism. The failure of the village to develop a differentiation between agriculture and artisan production and so to evolve into town and country, with the town dominating the countryside, meant that the countryside required the merchant to interrelate its different parts, and, in so requiring, invited its own domination not by the town but by the merchant.

The merchant, however, represented not just Russian trade but international trade, for he provided the village with its external markets and foreign supplies, which was inevitable, given the backwardness of Russian industry. As a result, the merchant could appear to the village as a considerable force. As long as the landlord and autocracy stood above the peasant, the merchant represented only one aspect of the regime, the more important only where the other aspects were of less significance. Trotsky gave the example of his own experience in Siberia, where quite obviously the merchant would be of the greatest importance. After the revolution, the autocracy and landlord ceased to exist, leaving the merchant with a higher degree of control than he would have had under other circumstances. It was this feature which remained in Trotsky's mind when he referred to the competi-

---

35. LD Trotsky, *1905*, London, 1972. See chapter 27, where he restated in 1922 with some development the view expressed in the first chapter.

tion and race between the state on the one hand, and the merchant private capitalist and village artisan on the other. This point is discussed in some detail in the previous chapter in this collection.

In Trotsky's speeches to the Twelfth Party Congress, the question of primitive socialist accumulation was raised both by name and in essence.[36] The line that Deutscher tries to draw between Preobrazhensky and Trotsky on this question did not exist. Both leaders believed in trying to hold on to the proletarian state as long as possible, and for this purpose foresaw the need to contain the challenge of capitalism. For this purpose the building of industry was absolutely essential. The subjection of the semi-Asiatic to the socialist mode of production was required in order to avoid the success of capitalism. However, this was not Preobrazhensky's formulation — it was only that of Trotsky. Thus for Trotsky the backwardness of Russia, its Asiatic character, created precisely the danger of the restoration of capitalism.[37] Although Trotsky never produced an argument of continuity in terms of the Asiatic mode of production, the latter was constantly in his mind. Thus he referred to Asiatic morality, and called the kolkhoz market an Asiatic bazaar.[38] From the point of view of Marxism, he was probably correct, but it is not of interest to go beyond the class question, except to note that he continued to his death to see the Asiatic mode of production as important in analysing the USSR ('Stalin was an Asiatic', he said in his biography of him).[39] Thus the geographical dispersion of the villages, the close link between the artisan and agriculture, and the farmers' need to sell over a wide area created the merchant and gave the trader his power. The more successful the NEP, the greater the potential power of this capitalist embryo, and thus the possibility of the artisan-merchant nexus establishing itself as an alternative to socialism. Trotsky did not believe that war communism had simply suppressed this axis, he thought that it had only been reduced in scope and in its rate of growth. He saw these factors as the essential part of the basic metabolism of the Russian economy. They could not be artificially transferred by force from country to town because it would be both an economic catastrophe and a political impossibility. There thus remained only a period of economic competition which involved the use of taxation measures to control their growth while not strangling them before the state could replace them. This was in fact primitive socialist accumulation. From this point of view it can be seen that even collectivisation did not solve the problem of capitalism arising, even after the defeat of the

36. See notes 4 and 21.
37. See his second speech at the Twelfth Party Congress, XII S'ezd RKP, *Stenograficheskyy Otchet*, op cit, p399.
38. LD Trotsky, 'The Soviet Economy in Danger', *Writings of Leon Trotsky 1932*, op cit, p276
39. LD Trotsky, *Stalin*, New York, 1967, p1.

Nepmen, kulaks, traders, etc. The basic backwardness and dispersion of Russia remained, and until this question was solved with the introduction of an industry of a higher productivity than that of the previous or existing merchant-artisan activity, capitalism would always have a potential. That is why Trotsky could not but maintain his previous perspective even after collectivisation. That is why he referred in the 1930s to capitalism coming through the pores of the society, and did not concede that socialism was itself being built, or that a return to capitalism was out of the question.

The Impossibility of Socialism in One Country and the Rise of the Bureaucracy

Trotsky's stress on the need for productivity in the USSR to be higher than anywhere else before socialism was assured must be seen in the context of the internal competition between the different social systems. Since Russia had never had a developed capitalism, the population did not have the developed anti-capitalist culture of the West, and hence Russian development had been faced with greater difficulties than the West. We have stressed Trotsky's view of the special semi-Asiatic nature of Russian society because it is so often ignored, and because it was indeed integral to his whole class viewpoint of the time. Needless to say, it is very different from the view of modern Asiatic theorists like Bahro and the German school.[40] He thus saw the pull to capitalism almost as primeval. Here in fact he was expressing the common viewpoint, held before the revolution, of the need for Russia to experience a capitalist development through the directly contrary viewpoint that while it did not require it (provided that socialism would come in the West), there was a powerful drive towards it, which had to be repelled. Thus socialism in a single country or a separate country was impossible. At most the enemy could be held at bay because the development required would proceed over decades and over a number of stages, during which socialism would have the possibility of success in the West.[41]

40. Bahro and the East German-derived school like Rudi Dutschke see the USSR as a variant of the Asiatic mode of production, which was certainly not Trotsky's view. See R Bahro, op cit, and R Dutschke, 'Against the Popes', *International Journal of Politics*, Summer-Fall 1980, Volume 10, nos 2-3, p203.
41. LD Trotsky, *The First Five Years of the Communist International*, Volume 2, op cit, p272; 'Theses of the Economic Situation of Russia from the Standpoint of the Socialist Revolution', December 1922, *Leon Trotsky Speaks*, New York, 1972, p137. The term is frequently used directly and indirectly, for example, in LD Trotsky, 'Towards Capitalism or Socialism', *The Challenge of the Left Opposition, 1923-25*, New York, 1975, p375; and in 1938 in *The Transitional Programme, Documents of the Fourth International*, New York, 1973.

In fact, this strand of his thought was not correlated with the other aspect — that of the rise of the bureaucracy and what it represented. As mentioned earlier, because he saw the struggle as a stage and not as two laws, Trotsky could allow of other aspects without encountering theoretical problems. While he was correct politically, it was at a cost to his economic theory, which he never resolved. From where did the bureaucracy come? Theoretically, it could only have come from capitalism, socialism, the previous modes of production, or some combination of them. Trotsky's theory of the transitional epoch had ruled out the possibility of the USSR being a new unique mode of production.[42] It is clear that it implied that the whole world was in transition, and that different stages and forms would come into existence, all of which would be unviable until socialism itself was reached. Logically, therefore, he should have argued that the bureaucracy came from the backwardness of Russia, the market relations existing before and after the revolution, married to the erection of a state required by the proletariat to defend itself. Indeed, by 1929 his views had come close to that view. He did not see Bukharin as a representative of the bourgeoisie, but rather the skilled intelligentsia and the petty proprietors.[43] He then stated very clearly, as against those who would wish to see the struggle between the left and right in technical terms, that Bukharin and the right wing might indeed have been correct in arguing that the course towards the capitalist farmer might work. This was true, but it was a woeful truth, for the fruits of such a course could only be capitalist:

'In 1924-26 only the first steps were taken towards staking everything on the capitalist farmer. Nevertheless, this led to an extreme growth of the self-assertion of the urban and rural petit-bourgeoisie, to its seizure of many lower soviets, to the growth of the power and self-confidence of the bureaucracy, to increased pressure upon the workers, and to the complete suppression of party democracy. Those who do not understand the interdependence of these facts are generally able to understand nothing in revolutionary policy. The course toward the capitalist farmer is absolutely incompatible with the dictatorship of the proletariat.'[44]

What is noteworthy about this quotation is both the total rejection of a technical economic solution, and the consequent insistence on a class approach. Trotsky then followed up with a continuation of the demand for industrialisation and planning. He argued that there was a connection between the policy of concilia-

---

42. See my 'Leon Trotsky's Political Economy of Capitalism' in this book.
43. LD Trotsky, 'Groupings in the Communist Opposition', *Writings of Leon Trotsky 1929*, op cit, p82.
44. Ibid.

tion to the petit-bourgeoisie and the growth of bureaucracy, and the resulting decay of democracy. Logically, this ought to have led to a theory of the rise of bureaucracy out of this environment. Indeed it did. He argued that the apparatus had been formed into its new bureaucratic and independent guise through the pressure on itself of the bourgeois or liberal intelligentsia, Nepmen, kulaks and petit-bourgeoisie of all varieties, the corruption of state functionaries, and, of great importance, the effect of the world bourgeoisie.[45] The party apparatus had thus been corrupted by the state apparatus operating in a hostile environment. Since this had arisen in the atmosphere of the NEP, it must, therefore, logically be said that it was the pressure of the bourgeoisie internally and externally that had created the bureaucracy. In other words, the bourgeois order had triumphed in throwing the revolution back, but it had not gone the whole way, and had had to produce a peculiar compromise. That compromise was Stalin and Stalinisation. The bureaucracy was therefore a peculiar victory for the right, and Trotsky kept quoting Ustrialov's support for Stalin as a harbinger of conservative and pro-capitalist tendencies.[46]

The Difficulties of a Turn to Capitalism

It was the strength of the left that Trotsky saw as one of the main reasons for the impossibility of a turn to capitalism. This led him to vacillate on the nature of the bureaucracy as an objective or subjective phenomenon.[47] Thus for Trotsky, the bureaucracy objectively represented a real counter-revolutionary phenomenon of the unity of the bourgeois forces with the party apparatus. On the other hand, he still entertained the view that it was also an ideological phenomenon, in which the party apparatus had been corrupted by bourgeois ideology. He spoke of the penetration of bourgeois thinking into the party as a negative force which might be counteracted, particularly by the Left Opposition. In fact it was this that led him to see the importance of the Left Opposition as crucial at that time. With hindsight, it is clear that Trotsky's view that the society could turn back to a socialist path, given the correct leadership, but that it would degenerate beyond repair if it continued along its then existing path, was over-optimistic. The bureaucracy, as Trotsky argued, had a social basis, and it could only be deflected from its anti-socialist project if it represented a social group with no historical task, or a social

---

45. LD Trotsky, *The Third International After Lenin*, New York, 1970, pp304-5.
46. LD Trotsky, *The Stalin School of Falsification*, New York, 1962, p141.
47. This comes out in clearest form in the LD Trotsky, 'The New Course', *Challenge of the Left Opposition, 1923-25*, op cit; and 15 years later in 1938 in *The Transitional Programme*. Trotsky saw the problem as one in which the objective elements were present.

group which had not yet entered its period of accomplishing its individual historical task. In both cases the bureaucracy represented a social group of a transition period which had only a very fleeting existence in it. Precisely because of its fleeting and transitory character, it could be influenced by subjective motivation. Hence it became possible to see history in terms of subjective betrayals, and indeed the whole epoch could be looked at as one of individual or group treachery.

This tension in Trotsky's thought existed both in terms of the nature of the bureaucracy and in terms of the transitional epoch. As time went on from the early 1920s to the end of the 1930s, it became clearer that what was once apparently group corruption and individual betrayal had developed an objective basis which was no longer related to any individual viewpoint. At all stages along this route oppositions developed, which argued in a mechanistic way that the elite group in the USSR was a distinct social group founded in production, whether capitalist or of a new type.[48] Trotsky always refuted them by maintaining his initial view of dual power and the dual origin of the bureaucracy in the October Revolution and in bourgeois influence. He never attempted to provide an economic theory rooting the elite in production even if in a dual form. Thus we return to the starting point.

Preobrazhensky attempted a theory of political economy, which ultimately failed as a theory of the USSR, although it was the best that was produced, because there was no theory of the role of bureaucracy. Trotsky, on the other hand, had a theory of bureaucracy, but he never anchored it in production. It is not enough to argue that he saw the bureaucracy as parasitic and wasteful, because this provides only a description of symptoms, and not a political economy. Ultimately, they both failed to produce the required theory because they could not foresee the longevity of the regime. This means, not the banality that they were too optimistic like all great revolutionaries, but that the task has continued to lie largely untouched, or has merely been scratched on the surface, to the present day.

---

48. LD Trotsky, 'Defence of the Soviet Republic', *Writings of Leon Trotsky 1929*, op cit, p271.

Trotsky in his study during a discussion with American visitors, 1940

Hillel Ticktin

Leon Trotsky's Political Economic Analysis of the USSR, 1929-40

Trotsky's Method

Trotsky's approach to the USSR was complex. In *The Revolution Betrayed* it was more journalistic and impressionistic than in his political economy of capitalism, or in his history of Russia. He also showed, however, a profundity in his understanding of the forces at work in Soviet society, particularly in his speech on the 'scissors crisis' at the Twelfth Congress of the Russian Communist Party in 1923, which remains unmatched.[1] In between, his many articles on the Soviet Union have provided the theoretical basis for practically every serious Marxist analysis of the Soviet Union.[2]

---

1. See Dvenadtsatyi S'ezd RKP/b, *Stenograficheskii Otchet*, Moscow, 1968, p313.
2. I am here excluding Maoist views as they lack any real basis other than support of Mao himself. Maoists either repeated a new class viewpoint which had already been formulated by Trotskyist proponents of state capitalism and bureaucratic collectivism, or else produced an obscurantism which was not only un-Marxist, but lacked any genuine meaning. Anarchists and anarcho-Marxists in their turn sometimes derived their theory from Trotskyism, as with Castoriadis, but more often produced a series of anti-state pronouncements which did little to further our understanding of the Soviet Union. Above all, most of the analyses of the Soviet Union have been bedevilled by a total failure to grasp its empirical reality and to marry it with an evolution of Marxist concepts. While this is true both of theories that were derived

It is impossible to produce a consistent theory of a rapidly changing entity. Trotsky captured the essence of the movement of the Soviet Union, but he failed to produce a theory of its nature. His writings are necessarily inconsistent. The basis of his argument is that a new social group had arisen and expropriated the proletariat, but because it had not overthrown nationalised property, this new social group was centrist in that it stood between capitalism and revolution. Trotsky failed to recognise the specificity of Stalinism. To call a social group 'centrist' gives it an importance and value above that of capitalism. Yet this same social group was responsible for acts of barbarism which exceeded those of Adolf Hitler and the Nazis. Trotsky recognised this point when he declared that Stalinism was politically worse than fascism.[3] The problem was that he still seemed to hold to the view that nationalised property somehow made the Soviet elite superior. In fact, his violent attacks on the ruling Soviet elite belie that viewpoint. The only conclusion that could be drawn was that Trotsky saw the overthrow of private property in the Russian Revolution as a crucial phenomenon, which determined all future history. Insofar as that elite embodied that overthrow, it was also part of the future. In a certain sense, however, the overthrow of private property, once performed, becomes irreversible. Although the particular nationalised property itself could revert to private ownership, large-scale nationalisation of property demonstrated that capitalism was transient, it could be overthrown, and that an alternative was therefore feasible. One can then argue that nationalised property is part of the epoch as a whole, and not just a feature of the USSR, as Trotsky also seemed to be arguing. The Soviet elite thus reveals itself to be reactionary and to have no special role in the future.[4]

The laws of the political economy of the USSR during the 1920s were explained by Preobrazhensky, who emphasised the conflict between planning and the market. In fact, the concept of two conflicting laws operating under the New

from those of Trotsky and those which were not, it is only the former that have shown any kind of potential for development. For a complete account of all known theories, see Marcel van der Linden, *Het Westers Marxisme en de Sovjet Unie*, Amsterdam, 1989.

3. LD Trotsky, *The Death Agony of Fascism and the Tasks of the Fourth International*, New York, 1964, pp50-1. The document was written by Trotsky as the programme of the Fourth International.

4. Trotsky spoke of the possibility of the bureaucracy privatising the nationalised concerns, but he did not appear to think that it would be successful in that endeavour in the 1920s: 'If Messrs Capitalists hope that capitalism will be reborn again in our country, they will be disappointed. For the resurrection of capitalism in our country, they would have to wait until the second coming of Christ.' (LD Trotsky, 'Speech in Honour of the Communist International', *The First Five Years of the Communist International*, Volume 2, New York, 1953, p218) This was in 1922. I have cited this instance in the next chapter in this book, in which I discuss this issue in more detail.

Economic Policy was derived from Trotsky's view of the forces of socialism fighting the forces of capitalism within the context of the NEP, as expressed in the interaction of plan and market. Nonetheless, Trotsky did not produce a theory that was based on his perceptions, and Preobrazhensky did.[5] In so doing, the strengths and weaknesses of these two people become apparent. Preobrazhensky was the most profound and courageous political economist of the Bolshevik party and the Left Opposition, but he lacked both the subtlety of Trotsky, and the historical understanding and the dialectical skill necessary to be a great political economist. Trotsky, on the other hand, was probably the most dialectical of all Marxist writers since Marx, but his work never delved sufficiently deeply into political economy itself. As a result, his method was profound, but was unable to reach the fundamental laws in operation.

The result was that both Trotsky and Preobrazhensky failed to grasp the full nature of Stalinism.[6] They saw Stalin as a centrist, standing between capitalist restoration in the person of Bukharin, and the proletarian revolution as expressed by the Left Opposition. To call Stalin and the bureaucratic elite 'centrist' is simply meaningless today. The Stalinist road was a path of its own, and it is this specificity and historical role which Trotsky did not understand.[7] Because he could not recognise the special historical role of Stalinism, he attributed to it a specifically political nature. This in turn meant that he saw Stalinism as a phenomenon which was largely subjective. On the other hand, Trotsky's work is full of insights, impressions and profound categorisations of the movement of Soviet reality. When he characterised Stalinism as worse politically than fascism, it was an insight which was as profound as any. Only now are we beginning to see the depths of the brutality of Stalinism, and it is clear that it was indeed worse than Hitlerite Germany. But Trotsky's characterisation was a political one, not a social and economic one.

The are three reasons why Trotsky's understanding of the USSR was relatively

---

5. See LD Trotsky, 'Notes on Economic Questions', *Challenge of the Left Opposition 1926-27*, New York, 1980, p57. In that article, written in 1926, Trotsky explicitly endorsed Preobrazhensky's laws, but expressed the fear that some people might use it for purposes of 'national socialism'.
6. The theoretical problem is that the two laws of which Preobrazhensky spoke did indeed interpenetrate and contradict each other, so providing two poles of a new entity. Logically, planning and the market stand in conflict, with one necessarily squeezing out the other. Hence Preobrazhensky provided the dynamic of a genuine transition period, and not of Stalinism. I argue this point in the chapter 'Trotsky and the Social Forces Leading to Bureaucracy'.
7. It must be emphasised that to say that Stalinism was a path of its own does not mean that it was a mode of production, but only that it established a temporary system which had its own life and laws.

limited. Firstly, he could not have been aware of the changes occurring in the USSR at the time, when all knowledge was so heavily controlled. Secondly, events themselves were moving so fast that the USSR appeared to be unformed. That is really what Trotsky was saying, and yet the nature of the USSR was to be unformed. To have understood that a society could have come into being, yet at the same time was never truly formed, that is to say, never established itself as a mode of production, and so swallowed up its own population in the process, was possibly superhuman.[8] Thirdly, Trotsky's greatness derived from his position in the political economic process. Once cast aside into exile, he became a mortal like all other mortals, and the lack of people with whom to discuss and interact could only cause his thought to decline. That does not mean, of course, that his thought was not profound in his last years, but only that it was below his previous level.

Trotsky's Problem

The overall outline of the USSR was already clear in theoretical terms by 1929. A new bureaucratic social group had taken power, and it was attempting to establish its own system of control. A number of questions then arose. Where did this new group come from? What was the objective basis of this bureaucratic elite in Soviet society? What were the laws of the operation of Soviet society, and what was its nature? The answer to the last question provided the basis for the determination of the longevity of the regime. There was a necessary corollary to the replies. The nature of the epoch would be determined by the answers to these questions. Trotsky in particular used the concept of the epoch.[9] He argued that the social democrats had rescued the bourgeoisie, and so the period 'stretched out to a whole historical epoch'.[10]

Trotsky's answer to these questions, however, was not clear. He appeared to regard the bureaucracy as a subjective phenomenon born of objective circumstances: 'The historical crisis of mankind is reduced to the crisis of the revolutionary leadership.'[11] The problem, of course, is that the subjec-

---

8. How are we to understand a statement like the following: 'Industry, freed from the material control of the producer, took on a supersocial, that is, bureaucratic character.' (LD Trotsky, 'The Degeneration of Theory and the Theory of Degeneration', *Writings of Leon Trotsky 1932-33*, New York, 1978, p224) A supersocial character implies that the bureaucratic form of which he spoke is really undefined. Otherwise he could just say that it takes on a new form.
9. 'But there still remains the character of the Soviet state, which does not remain at all unchangeable throughout the whole transitional epoch.' (LD Trotsky, 'The Degeneration of Theory and the Theory of Degeneration', *Writings of Leon Trotsky 1932-33*, op cit, p216)
10. LD Trotsky, *The Revolution Betrayed*, London, 1937, p62.
11. LD Trotsky, 'The Transitional Programme', *Documents of the Fourth International*, New York, 1973, p181.

tive/objective dialectic has to be formulated. But it was extremely difficult to do so. The reason, in principle, lies in the fact that the epoch itself was one of transition, as Trotsky correctly saw it. A transitional epoch from capitalism to socialism could only mean that there was a movement from the objective occurrence of events towards the socialist form of planning. In the intermediate period, organisation and administration of the economy and political life were bound to come to the fore. Hence, the subjective would play an increasing role in political life. But what role? Since there was neither planning nor the pristine spontaneous market, it was not at all clear.

In fact, without theorising it, Trotsky placed a stress on both aspects. He had, however, posed the question of the emergence of the bureaucracy, and had attempted to answer it. His answer was two-fold. On the one hand, the bureaucracy was the organ of the world bourgeoisie, or, in other words, the expression of the victory of the world bourgeoisie within the USSR.[12] On the other hand, it was also the immediate expression of the interests of the apparatus which had come into being under conditions of both scarcity and the market. It is, of course, obvious that the combination of relatively well-paid non-Marxist specialists, and party and state officials, who were appearing in positions of privilege and authority, even if they were not corrupt, represented a conservative force. Trotsky, therefore, did see the bureaucracy as an objective phenomenon: 'The Soviet bureaucracy, which represents an amalgam of the upper stratum of the victorious proletariat with broad strata of the overthrown classes, includes within itself a mighty agency of world capital.'[13] If carried through, this view ought to have led him to continue his analysis on an objective plane.

A new stage in the discussion was reached with Rakovsky's intervention in the debate. Trotsky considered that Rakovsky's letter to Valentinov of 2 August 1928[14] was 'exceptionally interesting and significant',[15] and it logically led to an

---

12. 'Stalin serves the bureaucracy and thus the world bourgeoisie.' (LD Trotsky, 'Not a Workers' and Not a Bourgeois State?', *Writings of Leon Trotsky 1937-38*, New York, 1976, p 65)
13. LD Trotsky, 'Problems of the Development of the USSR', *Writings of Leon Trotsky 1930-31*, New York, 1973, p219.
14. C Rakovsky, 'The "Professional Dangers" of Power', *Selected Writings on Opposition in the USSR, 1923-30*, London, 1980. Isaac Deutscher refers to the way in which Trotsky commended Rakovsky's work to others, in the second volume of his trilogy, *The Prophet Unarmed*, Oxford, 1959, p439. Deutscher sees Rakovsky's work as both more pessimistic than Trotsky, and also more sociological. He argues that Rakovsky saw the division in the working class as inevitable in any country or period. Gus Fagan, in his introduction to the Rakovsky collection, follows Deutscher. Both Deutscher's and Fagan's interpretations are tendentious. Rakovsky was certainly more incisive than Trotsky and possibly less optimistic, but there is no evidence that he had become so much a

analysis of the origins of the bureaucracy in terms of the market itself. Rakovsky had analysed the bureaucracy in a way which was novel for its time. He argued that it was a new social group. His argument was twofold. On the one hand, he pointed out in an analysis, which Trotsky specifically called superstructural,[16] that the taking of power automatically put the section of the workers who ruled in a privileged position. He talked of both material privilege and the corruption of power in itself. He then stressed the importance of educating the working class, but he also specifically spoke of its corruption by the nobility and the market. For Rakovsky, this degeneration of the working class could be mitigated through the correct leadership of the Communist Party, which, of course, was not forthcoming at that time. Furthermore, he specifically argued that 'we should have been prepared for the nefarious influence of the NEP, against the temptations and ideology of the bourgeoisie'.[17]

At that time, the question of the source of the degeneration was less necessary, since it was obvious that if the bureaucracy was the organ of the world bourgeoisie, it arose from the market.[18] Today, however, such a question is clearly posed. Even if Trotsky's view was clear, it has never been spelled out. What is needed is a discussion of the interaction between the NEP and the origins of the bureaucratic elite. Trotsky did make it clear that the bureaucratic apparatus merged with the 'bourgeois elements'.[19] The next question is why they did not introduce the market at the time. Trotsky did reply that they would have liked to, but they were unable do it.[20] What

liberal that he now argued that power automatically and inevitably corrupts, to the point where socialism could be prevented through the inevitable rise of a bureaucracy.

15. LD Trotsky, 'The Sixth Congress and the Opposition's Tasks', *The Challenge of the Left Opposition 1928-29*, New York, 1981, p261.
16. Ibid.
17. C Rakovsky, op cit, p134.
18. Trotsky said: 'In that period [that is, under Lenin] bureaucratic deformation represented a direct inheritance of the bourgeois regime and, in that sense, appeared as a mere survival of the past.' He then went on to say that the 'bureaucracy received new sources of nourishment'. (LD Trotsky, 'Not a Workers' and Not a Bourgeois State?', *Writings of Leon Trotsky 1937-38*, op cit, p67)
19. 'The capitalist element finds its primary expression in the class differentiation in the countryside and in the increased numbers of private traders. The upper layers in the countryside and the bourgeois elements in the city are interweaving themselves more and more closely with various components of our government and economic apparatus.' (LD Trotsky, 'Platform of the Opposition', *Challenge of the Left Opposition 1926-27*, op cit, p304)
20. LD Trotsky, 'Where is the Soviet Republic Going?', *Writings of Leon Trotsky 1929*, op cit, p48. Trotsky argued that there was a battle between the petit-bourgeois elements and Stalin, but also: 'This conservative layer, which constitutes Stalin's most powerful support in his struggle against the opposition, is inclined to go much further to the right, in the direction of the new propertied elements, than Stalin himself or the main nucleus of his faction.' (By the

were the conditions at that time which constrained the bureaucracy from introducing the market?

Trotsky's Critique

Trotsky's critique was composed of a number of elements — labour, the gains of the October Revolution, and planning — which are discussed in turn below. The result is quite complex.

Labour

Trotsky argued that the framework of the USSR remained nationalised property. This gave those who controlled the bureaucratic apparatus enormous strength, based on their ability to direct labour in the economy. This insight has unfortunately been largely lost sight of, outside of *Critique*. The stress on the control of an amorphous labour force goes straight to the heart of the matter, both methodologically and theoretically.

Methodologically this argument goes back to Marxist political economy and its starting point in human social labour and the specific form of that labour. Trotsky was implicitly arguing that human social labour in the USSR was not independently oriented, but was controlled, and hence the regime had enormous economic and social power. What he could not foresee was that the contradictions involved in such control would lead to the purges, labour camps and a grossly inefficient economy. He could see the advantages in terms of growth, and the disadvantages of the lack of democracy in terms of waste, but he did not foresee the scale of the killing and the enormity of the waste.[21] The fundamental problem was that he anticipated the rapid end of the bureaucracy, and so he had no need to produce a theory of the nature of its economy.[22] The question of the contradictions of the system is taken up below.

In methodological terms, the problem is that labour is obliged to have a form. Under capitalism it is abstract labour, under socialism it is directly social labour,

---

       term 'conservative layer', Trotsky was referring to 'the majority of this officialdom'.) From this point of view, there were two political forces which wanted the restoration of private property: those who held private property, that is to say, the property owning peasantry and the Nepmen, and large sections of the bureaucratic apparatus itself. Stalin did not choose that path. The same general attitude is taken in Trotsky's 'Preface to *La Révolution Defigurée*', *Writings of Leon Trotsky 1929*, op cit, pp118-22.

21.   He said that 'bureaucratism as a system became the worst brake on the technical and cultural development of the country' (LD Trotsky, *In Defence of Marxism*, London, 1966, p7).

22.   Ibid, p10.

under feudalism it is subsistence labour combined with a direct extraction of the surplus product, etc. What was it under Stalinism? Implicitly I have already answered the question — it is the form of no form.

Put differently, the question is one of the extraction of the surplus product, and the form under which it took place. It was clearly unique, as it was neither capitalist nor socialist. In fact, as I have argued elsewhere, it was because the extraction of the surplus product conflicted with the control over the labour process that the system malfunctioned, was inefficient, and gave rise to massive waste. Yet, this is no more than a statement that there was no historical form of social labour, but a stalemate between the social groups in the USSR, and an historical stalemate between the classes in the world. Trotsky, of course, insisted on the crucial role of labour productivity. He pointed out time and again that as long as productivity was lower than the rest of the world, the USSR would remain unstable.[23]

Trotsky's strength lay in his statements that the nature of the USSR was undetermined, and in his perception that it was the centralised control over labour which permitted the bureaucracy to rule. He specifically argued that 'the control of the surplus product opened the bureaucracy's road to power'.[24] His weakness lay in his inability to theorise these points to their logical conclusion.

The Gains of the October Revolution

Instead, misled by optimism and poor information, Trotsky still placed hopes on the preservation of aspects of the October Revolution. This led him to produce his formulation of the conflict in the USSR between the 'social revolution' still existing 'in property relations', on the one hand, and bourgeois norms of distribution on the other.[25] That such a conflict existed in the early days of the USSR was obvious, but that a bureaucratic apparatus would necessarily appropriate as much control as possible to itself over the means of production did not seem to enter Trotsky's discussion. In order to appropriate the surplus product, the bureaucracy had to assert control over the means of production and thus over labour and its product. But once that is said, there is no longer a conflict between production and distribution. Of course, if one argues that the working class in some sense remained in power, and the elite was confined by the structure itself, then Trotsky would have been right. This, of course, is what he did argue: 'Thus, in spite of monstrous bureaucratic distortions, the class basis of the USSR remains proletarian.'[26] The problem is that no elite would accept such structural con-

23. LD Trotsky, *The Revolution Betrayed*, op cit, p52.
24. LD Trotsky, *Stalin*, New York, 1967, p410.
25. LD Trotsky, *The Revolution Betrayed*, op cit, p237.
26. LD Trotsky, *Stalin*, op cit, pp405-6. In similar vein: 'In general and on the whole the new

trol. It would inevitably try to find ways of removing it. Indeed, Trotsky goes into some detail on precisely this point.

The whole essence of the discussion since the 1930s has really been around this question of the nature of the structural control, and the form in which the elite managed to liberate itself from the original form of the nationalised property. From one angle, such a division between production and appropriation is a nonsense, but looked at historically it has its own justification. If the working class were in power but could not run its own economy because it had neither the skills nor the experience, it would have to delegate authority to a bureaucratic apparatus. This, it could be argued, was the case in the 1920s, and this is precisely what Trotsky did argue, starting from the general principle that any transitional period involved a bourgeois state enforcing bourgeois norms of distribution on socialist property relations.[27] The problem, however, is to argue that the working class was still in power in however attenuated a sense in the 1930s. Nationalisation is not good enough as an argument. Here Trotsky's political view of Stalinism as centrism is crucial. If Stalin actually stood between the revolutionary left and capitalist restoration then he still embodied, in however distorted a form, the spirit of the October Revolution. If, on the other hand, Stalin represented a systemic if temporary change in control, which completely dispossessed the working class, then it could not be said that there was a difference between the form of control over the means of production and the form of distribution. They corresponded exactly.

The whole discussion was, of course, derailed by the primitive nature of the arguments of Bruno Rizzi, Max Shachtman and James Burnham. The only real argument against them is that they were unable to develop any theory whatsoever. They simply asserted that the USSR was a new mode of production with classes, but in no way did they try to understand the laws of motion of this new mode of production. For that reason it was easy for Trotsky to show them up. He had at least some understanding of the society, whereas they only had a slogan. Today, it is obvious that if it were a mode of production it ought to have lasted at least longer than six decades, which is not much more, after all, than Salazar's regime in Portugal, and no one would call that a mode of production. Trotsky, however, took their arguments very seriously, specifically arguing that there was neither a new class in the USSR nor a new mode of production. His arguments were in fact irrefutable in Marxist terms. A class must have a specific form of control over the surplus product, and Trotsky argued that the Soviet bureaucracy was too constrained to have developed a new method of pumping out surplus product. The

> economic base is preserved in the USSR, though in a degenerated form.' (LD Trotsky, 'The World Situation and Perspectives', *Writings of Leon Trotsky 1939-40*, New York, 1977, p156)

27. LD Trotsky, *The Revolution Betrayed*, op cit, p58.

privileges were hidden, and the bureaucracy was forced to implement planning, and hence to industrialise the country.

Planning

The major underpinning of Trotsky's analysis of the USSR was its planned nature, and indeed the whole debate hinges around the question of planning. Both he and the bureaucratic collectivists argued that the bureaucracy planned the economy, but the latter argued that planning was possible in this new social formation. That argument, however, broke with Marxism in that Marxists had argued effectively that planning was the antithesis of the market, and was thus the basis of socialism. Trotsky himself remained convinced of that. Indeed, he argued that planning was only possible on the basis of democracy.[28] Both sides of that debate were then locked into arguments which were incoherent. Had Trotsky completely abandoned the view that the USSR was planned, he would have been forced to conclude that the USSR was not a workers' state, and that there was no contradiction between production and distribution. Indeed, at one point he did explicitly say as much, writing in 1933: 'The Soviet economy today is neither a monetary nor a planned one. It is an almost purely bureaucratic economy.'[29] Trotsky thus embraced the contradiction in himself that the USSR was planned and yet was not planned, while not effectively recognising that fact.

On the other hand, the other side of the debate produced a mechanical statement which was simply wrong in Marxist terms. Trotsky found it easy to make mincemeat of them. Their work was obviously not dialectical in that they did not try to perceive the contradictions operating in the society. Nonetheless, the underlying point that Shachtman and others were trying to make was that the USSR could not be understood as socialist, or proto-socialist, towards which a workers' state viewpoint tended. Nationalisation of the means of production could give rise to a form which was exploitative. The problem was not that Trotsky disagreed. He explicitly stated that a social revolution would be required in the USSR.[30] He

---

28. 'The plan is only a working hypothesis. The fulfilment of the plan inevitably means its radical alteration by the masses whose vital interests are reflected in the plan.' (LD Trotsky, 'Planned Economy in the USSR, Success or Failure?', *Writings of Leon Trotsky: Supplement 1929-33*, New York, 1979, p296)
29. LD Trotsky, 'The Degeneration of Theory and the Theory of Degeneration', *Writings of Leon Trotsky 1932-33*, New York, 1978, p224.
30. 'Needless to say, the distribution of productive forces among the various branches of the economy and generally the entire content of the plan will be drastically changed when this plan is determined by the interests not of the bureaucracy but of the producers themselves... Certain of our critics (Ciliga, Bruno and others) want, come what may, to call the future

shifted from a standpoint of critical support that based itself on the view that it was a workers' state and hence it had to be defended against imperialist attack, to an uncompromising hostility to all the institutions of the USSR. After all, if the USSR was exploitative, why did it have to be defended? It really is not clear unless one was to argue that nationalisation in itself had to be defended. Today, with nationalisation implemented by the most conservative of regimes, no one would argue for the defence of a country simply on those grounds. This would be superfluous, as, after all, the simple argument that nations are entitled to their own destiny would suffice in order to argue for their defence. Indeed, Trotsky did argue in precisely this manner in 1940, when he said: 'When Italy attacked Ethiopia, I was fully on the side of the latter, despite the Ethiopian negus for whom I have no sympathy. What mattered was to oppose imperialism's seizure of this new territory. In the same way now I decisively oppose the imperialist camp and support independence for the USSR, despite the negus in the Kremlin.'[31] While such a view is consistent with a defence of the USSR as a workers' state, it actually renders otiose those grounds for its defence.

The question of exploitation or non-exploitation is a fundamental question. Trotsky rejected the view that 'there was a system of exploitation in the scientific sense of the term'.[32] He spoke of 'gangsterism', 'embezzlement and theft', and said that it was embezzlement and theft which was the main source of the income of the bureaucracy.[33] On the other hand, he found that 'from the standpoint of the interests and position of the popular masses it is infinitely worse than "organic exploitation"'.[34] The point that Trotsky was making was that the form of the extraction of the surplus product was one in which there was no system. Hence he spoke in the same paragraph of the 'absence of crystallised class relations'. This is what I have called a form of no form. The fact that the USSR lasted another half century makes it difficult to speak of something worse than exploitation, which is not exploitation. Seventy-five years of simple 'gangsterism' have to be explained. In other words, the very forms of which Trotsky was speaking could be said to have congealed to become a temporary system of its own kind. Trotsky was thinking of a mode of production rather than a temporary system, a concept which he did not entertain. It is clear that a mode of production did not evolve. It lasted too

      revolution social. Let us grant this definition. What does it alter in essence?' (LD Trotsky, *In Defence of Marxism*, op cit, p4)
31. LD Trotsky, 'Fragments on the USSR', *Writings of Leon Trotsky: Supplement 1934-40*, New York, 1979, p885.
32. LD Trotsky, 'The Bonapartist Philosophy of the State', *Writings of Leon Trotsky 1938-39*, New York, 1974, p325.
33. Ibid.
34. Ibid.

short a time, and this clear economic failure militates against that designation. In that sense, Trotsky was correct. Nonetheless, particular social relations did evolve, with particular relations between the ruling group and the workers. I have argued that we can continue his view along the following lines. We can say that the extraction of the surplus product by and for the 'bureaucracy' and its control of that surplus product was partially negated by the workers' continuing control over the labour process. The workers, however, did not control their product, and hence were exploited.[35] The fact that the USSR lasted another half century makes it difficult to speak of the absence of a system of exploitation.

According to Trotsky, the political economy of the USSR rested upon the question of planning and the ability to direct labour centrally. Put differently, he was arguing that the strength of the regime rested on its ability to plan the surplus product. Logically, when the control over the surplus product was removed, the regime would cease to have any historical justification, and would cease to exist. Since Trotsky did not foresee the regime lasting that long, he could not develop such a political economy. Instead, he saw the contradiction as a development of Preobrazhensky's laws governing the relationship between the market and the plan, with the process being transformed into bourgeois norms of distribution, a capitalist state and so a bourgeois bureaucracy, versus the continuation in some form of the October Revolution. Thus he wrote as early as 1933: 'The Stalinist system is exhausted to the end and is doomed. Its break-up is approaching with the same inevitability with which the victory of Fascism approached in Germany.' He then argued that Stalinism was like a parasite which had wound itself around the tree of the October Revolution, although: 'The October Revolution will yet know how to fend for itself.'[36]

If the laws governing the relationship between the market and the plan had been transformed in this manner, Trotsky was left with the question of the nature of the new laws that emerged from this transformation. What was the new political economy? Here Trotsky was left with merely a description of the abolition of the market in market terms. His fundamental error, which in one sense was very strange, was not to understand that the period of the form of no form could be the nature of the epoch itself. In the chapter in *The Revolution Betrayed* on the nature of inflation, he argued that the market was needed simply in order to have a measure of value and so a measure of costs. The argument, however, reflected a critique from the angle of the NEP, and failed to understand the nature of the Soviet econ-

---

35 For a more detailed account of the argument see my book, *The Origins of the Crisis of the USSR*, Armonk, 1992.
36 . LD Trotsky, 'The Degeneration of Theory and the Theory of Degeneration', *Writings of Leon Trotsky 1932-33*, op cit, p225

omy of the time. The point is that the Stalinist economy did indeed evolve into a non-market system, and it was the task of Marxists to analyse it.

As we remark elsewhere, Trotsky's mistake was that he did not realise that Stalinism could last for so long, relatively speaking. It could be said that the mistake was understandable, and was only a mistake with hindsight. Nonetheless, Trotsky admitted that he had made a mistake when he had earlier argued that Thermidor had not occurred.[37] Logically, he was on a trajectory of gradually admitting the reality of the formation of a system, which remained undefined, but was a system nonetheless.

The Nature of the System and its Overthrow: The Paradox of History

Trotsky discussed the possible overthrow of the Soviet Union, and moved from a position in 1922[38] where he argued that capitalism would never win, to a position where he said: 'A prolonged isolation would inevitably end not in national communism but in a restoration of capitalism.'[39] That statement, in *The Revolution Betrayed*, is then followed by a statement that the workers would fight for socialism. The clear implication is that restoration would not be easy, and that it would moreover require a revolution to accomplish it.[40] It would be easy to find many other quotations to show that Trotsky anticipated the move to capitalism, but expected the working class to hinder it and possibly block it.[41] In this respect, Trotsky has been proved correct in anticipating that the Soviet elite would move to capitalism, something which he actually saw as being inherent in its nature. At the same time, he was more optimistic than such a prognosis might imply because he expected strong working class resistance. This was not a pragmatic point. Since, as we have seen, Trotsky considered that the fact that capitalism was not restored under Stalin was partially due to the strength of the working class and the Left Opposition, he was compelled to argue that such opposition would continue to bar the way to capitalism.

Events have provided a true historical paradox, looked at from the point of view of Trotsky's prognosis. The Soviet bureaucracy has chosen to move to capitalism, and has abandoned the old Soviet Union, privatising practically everything

---

37. LD Trotsky, *In Defence of Marxism*, op cit, p6.
38. See footnote 4.
39. LD Trotsky, *The Revolution Betrayed*, op cit, p284.
40. Ibid.
41. In *The Revolution Betrayed* itself he declared: 'On the road to capitalism the counter-revolution would have to break the resistance of the workers.' (Ibid, p241)

of importance by 1995. The left and the workers apparently stand nowhere. There is indeed no left opposition and no mass workers' opposition. On the other hand, the very reason that the Soviet ruling group abandoned the Soviet Union was its fear of the potential of the working class to remove it, and it went, as it were, for a pre-emptive strike. Trotsky had provided the tools for analysing the end of the system. The crucial form of control held by the ruling group was that over labour. Once that began to go, the system was doomed. The flow of labour into production had ended by 1976. At that point, higher productivity, rather than additional labour, alone could raise production. The increase in the absolute surplus product had to be replaced by increases in the relative surplus product. The workers by that time were too strong and potentially too powerful to control. Hence the ruling group took the only way out left for them.

At the same time, the ruling group has not been able to introduce the market, and privatisation is often only formal. It is indeed the working class which is blocking true privatisation and the market. The ruling group, which is largely unchanged in the new non-Soviet order, is afraid to introduce mass unemployment and the necessary capitalist forms in case there is a social explosion. Inchoate, mute and underground nonetheless, the working class continues to act. Trotsky was right, but in a way that he could never have foreseen. The subjective, Stalinism, had become objective, and the subjective opposition had been totally wiped out. The world situation appeared to favour the capitalist road. A new movement had to be created, from the very beginning, with few internal cadres and under conditions where socialism looked utopian, even if desirable.

The Nature of the Epoch

Trotsky could have taken an alternative and more logical path. The crucial concept was the epoch itself. Although the epoch had been initiated by the October Revolution and then altered by the Stalinist counter-revolution, it had become detached from its parent, the USSR. If one proceeds from this point, then one can argue that it is the world which is in transition, and that this transition is caused by the movement of the laws of capitalism and the decline of value itself. Thus Trotsky had this to say: 'The sharpness of the social crisis arises from this, that with today's concentration of the means of production, that is, the monopoly of trusts, the law of value — the market — is already incapable of regulating economic relations. State intervention becomes an absolute necessity.'[42] In addition to the objective decline of capitalism, capitalism itself had been overthrown at least once,

---

42. LD Trotsky, 'Bonapartism, Fascism and War', *The Struggle Against Fascism in Germany*, Harmondsworth, 1975, p460.

in Russia. Whatever would happen to the USSR in the future, in a sense, could not alter the fact that capitalism had been overthrown. Thereby a conscious transition was placed on the agenda throughout the world, a transition, according to Trotsky, which had become prolonged because of social democracy. Of course, one would have to add that the prolongation of the transition gave rise to Stalinism, which, in its turn, delayed the onset of socialism still further.

What was omitted from much of Trotskyist thinking was the fact that the bourgeoisie was also conscious of its own decline. It could and did take countermeasures to ensure that it remained in power, even if for an historically limited time. After all, if the individual capitalist retained his capital until his death, he at least had achieved something. Delay is today the essence of the epoch. The bourgeoisie took on board the lessons of the October Revolution. It realised that it would have to make concessions to the working class in order to stabilise the situation. Nationalisation, growth, full employment, etc, have now become standard aims of reformist and Christian democratic governments. Even conservative governments have nationalised property and introduced forms of proto-planning, with France, Germany and Japan being obvious examples.

If the epoch itself now expresses the spirit of the October Revolution, only a complete reaction could return the world to what it was before the October Revolution. In this sense, the USSR is no longer important. Unless the working class the world over is prepared to return to mass unemployment and a low and static standard of living, no return is possible. In fact such a return is unthinkable for other reasons as well. The socialisation of the means of production has already enshrined the gains of the October Revolution. Thus even the United States has maintained growth and relatively low unemployment levels in large part because the whole nature of the modern capitalist class is dependent upon it. Arms production is the centrepiece of modern industrial production, and it cannot be eliminated without enormous disruption to capital itself. It is also a needs-based industry funded by the state, and it is in fact organised and planned over a long period of time. Plan periods, predictability and organisation are now watchwords of modern industry, which would not exist if growth had not become a feature of modern capitalism.

In other words, Trotsky did see the objective character of the epoch in terms of the decline of the law of value and the increased economic role of the state, but he did not foresee how far it could go, and that the bourgeoisie would use what instruments it could to retain power, even if they were the very tools required for the transition to socialism itself.

It is strange that Trotsky did not argue this point. After all, the concept of the transitional epoch is his own. It is not a question of a general automatic movement, but a simple understanding of the laws of motion underlying not one country, but the entire epoch. Yet although this is a logical extension of his view, he did not get there. He continued to maintain the view that Stalin was a centrist. The consequence was that Stalinism became a subjective phenomenon rather than having its own political economy. Furthermore, it appeared to be a largely Russian rather than an epochal phenomenon.

The Process at Work in the USSR

The market had really been abolished in the USSR. Furthermore, the concept of the conflict between the laws of the plan and of the market of which Trotsky and Preobrazhensky had spoken had omitted the actual result of such a conflict. Three results were possible: that the forces of the proletariat would win, that the forces of the market and thus the bourgeoisie would win, or there could be an interpenetration of the two laws themselves resulting in a new form of society. In principle, either planning would defeat the market, or the market would win, but if neither won then there would be neither one nor the other but degenerate forms of both, temporarily united in a society which had no historical form, but which had an historical existence. At one level Trotsky was actually struggling towards such a statement when he talked of the historical nature of the USSR being open.[43] At another level, he was still bound to the previous history of the NEP, seeing the USSR in terms of the conflict between the plan and the market.

Soviet theorists all argued in the early 1920s that primitive socialist accumulation was required in the USSR. Later, some identified the Stalinist process of industrialisation with primitive socialist accumulation. While Trotsky hailed the industrialisation of the USSR as a result of the elements of October, he did not call it primitive socialist accumulation. Indeed, any identification would have implied that the USSR was building socialism. When Trotsky criticised Preobrazhensky, he had referred to the possibility of using his analysis for purposes of building a national socialism.[44] Hence Stalin's industrialisation could not be called primitive socialist accumulation. Indeed, its highly contradictory nature, gross inefficiency and high levels of repression and killing were perhaps reminiscent of primitive capitalist accumulation. And yet it is not at all clear if there was an extraction of surplus product from the countryside. There was, of course, a shift of population from the countryside, although even that is called in question when the numbers killed in collectivisation and who died in the famines are added up. After all,

---

43. 'But let us bear in mind that the unwinding process has not yet been completed, and the future of Europe and the world during the next few decades has not yet been decided.' (LD Trotsky, *Stalin*, op cit, p406) See also LD Trotsky, *The Revolution Betrayed*, op cit, pp238-41.
44. See footnote 5.

would there really have been a shortage of labour in the absence of collectivisation? In that case, the process served no historical purpose at all, except to maintain the elite in power.

Trotsky saw the contradictions of the system, and he opposed the forms of collectivisation and so-called planning, but he still saw the system as showing the world the advantages of nationalisation and planning. At that time, of course, no other country had utilised those instruments. What he did not fully analyse was the nature of the system coming into being. Logic, however, could have driven him into the position of arguing that the Soviet bureaucracy was not only unable to implement planning, but could not return to the market, so it would be driven from pillar to post in the quest to find an inherently impossible solution. Indeed, I would argue that this position is the only one consistent with his theoretical thought.

Trotsky considered that the bureaucratised system had reached its limits. The bureaucracy constituted a brake on 'the demands of development'. For a time it was possible to develop, but already by the late 1930s, it could no longer do so. Hence the 'political convulsions' and the purges.[45] He therefore theorised the contradictions of the system. But he did so in an absolutist way, really failing to say more than that the forces of production were coming into conflict with the relations of production. That was true, but it remained so thereafter. What was missing was an explanation of the forms in which the conflict was taking place.

The Question of the Market Versus Planning

Trotsky argued very strongly in favour of the restoration of the market. This has misled Alec Nove and Richard Day into thinking that Trotsky was arguing for the market under socialism. This is simply a nonsense. Trotsky was arguing quite clearly that there would have to be a market in a transitional period between capitalism and socialism. Nonetheless, the market is the enemy of socialism. Thus: 'The ruble will become the most stable valuta only from that moment when the Soviet productivity of labour exceeds that of the rest of the world and when, consequently, *the ruble itself will be meditating on its final hour.*'[46] And again, Trotsky basically repeated Marx when he said: 'In a communist society the state and money will disappear. Their gradual dying away ought consequently to begin under socialism. We shall be able to speak of the actual triumph of socialism only at that historical moment when the state turns into a semi-state, and money begins to lose its magic power.' But he then goes on to say: 'Money cannot be arbitrarily

45. LD Trotsky, *In Defence of Marxism*, op cit, p8.
46. LD Trotsky, *The Revolution Betrayed*, op cit, p79.

"abolished", nor the state and old family "liquidated". They have to exhaust their historical mission, evaporate and fall away.'[47]

Of course, Trotsky was not likely to say anything else if he were a Marxist, since the contradiction between exchange value and use value is the basis of all Marxist political economy. It has only been the reformist Stalinists and social democrats who have ever argued anything else. It is pointless to take this part of Trotsky's argument further at this point because it is the ABC of Marxism, but what is more interesting is to look at what Trotsky was actually saying about the withering away of money and the market. He appears to be saying that money and the market must continue to be used until the demise of the transitional period to socialism. They have to wither gradually. (The terminology is not important since it is apparent that Trotsky has adopted not Marx's terminology, but that of the Soviet republic.) How can they be used by the proletariat? Trotsky does not really address this question. He had done so earlier in his 'scissors' speech, when he pointed out that there is an irreconcilable conflict between the market and planning.[48]

There are really two problems. The first is how the proletariat can use the market under the best conditions of the transitional period, and the second is the same question, but under the worst conditions, as it were. The latter was the case in the USSR, where the country stood alone in the capitalist world, and the economy was both backward and in ruins. At the same time, the proletariat was a tiny proportion of the population. In the first case, the proletariat could be assumed to be strong enough to deal with the problems which would arise out of a market economy. It would begin to phase out the market from the first day of taking power, even if it took some time completely to extinguish it. In the case of the USSR, however, the domestic market would inevitably be linked to international capitalism, and would therefore constitute a political enemy. Furthermore, the small size of the proletariat would make it easy for the growing market sector to displace the proletariat from power. That would be the political problem, which indeed Trotsky had pointed out much earlier in his 'scissors' speech.

There was also an economic problem which would be ameliorated in the case of an advanced country that was part of a wider socialist fraternity of nations by

---

47. Ibid, pp68-9.
48. Dvenadtsatyi S'ezd RKP/b, *Stenograficheskii Otchet*, Moscow, 1968, p313. Trotsky's speech at the Twelfth Party Conference on the 'scissors crisis' described the NEP as follows: 'The NEP is our recognition of a legal order for the arena of struggle between us and private capital.' Earlier he made it clear that the market was essential for all countries undergoing a transition to socialism. At the same time he made it crystal clear that it was the use of 'methods and institutions of the capitalist system' which would be phased out as quickly as the new socialist methods of planning, centralisation and accounting could be introduced (ibid, p310).

two factors: a high and rising standard of living and a high level of democracy. The problem would be ameliorated, but not removed. The economic problem is that the two sectors do not complement each other, but undermine each other. This was the essence of Preobrazhensky's argument, and again it is essentially a logical development of the contradiction between exchange value and use value into the transitional period. The basis of the market sector has to be exchange on the basis of value, which is precisely what Trotsky insisted was needed for planning in the USSR.[49] But the basis of value is abstract labour, whereas the basis of planning is democratic participation in decision making by the associated producers themselves. Abstract labour and democratic participation by labour cannot coexist. In the first case, we are talking of the alienated, controlled worker, whereas in the second case we are talking of the free worker, who will be increasingly engaged in creative labour, and whose interests as a human being take priority over production. Thus, from the point of view of value, women's labour must be reduced or paid less because they have to take time off to have children. From the point of view of the planned society, however, women's interests are primary, with production itself coming secondary. It is true that in the long run, women's labour will be much more productive under planning than under the forms of repression in capitalism, but in the transitional period this would take some time to show itself. Again, for instance, mining is an inhuman form of labour, and the planned sector would have to automate it to the maximum degree, or phase it out. On the other hand, the market sector might find it highly profitable to use cheap peasant labour.

The proletariat would have to remove crucial aspects of the law of value on taking power. It would have to eliminate unemployment and thus eliminate the reserve army of labour. It would have to introduce a minimum wage and standard of living. Under these conditions, the workers in the market sector would have less incentive to work hard, since they either could not be dismissed or would easily find another job. Quality of Soviet goods did indeed drop in all sectors in the post-revolutionary period, as compared with the same firms under Tsarism. Preobrazhensky's plaintive cry that the Soviet regime had neither the advantages of capitalism nor of socialism would be an inevitable concomitant of any transitional period.

To make matters worse, the kind of problem now being faced by cooperatives in the USSR is also inevitable. Where do supplies come from for the different sectors? They cannot, of course, be self-sufficient. If the market sector needed machinery from the planned sector, it would have to conform to the planned form. That is, it would have to place its orders with the central planners, in accordance with the needs of the

---

49. LD Trotsky, *The Revolution Betrayed*, op cit, p69-70.

planned economy. Under conditions of shortage, the planned sector could not have sufficient goods to leave it to wholesale trade and so to spontaneity, as it were. On the other hand, the planned sector could not simply place enormous orders with the market sector at random. There would have to be planned cooperation. The market sector would then chafe at the difficulty in obtaining supplies, and with selling to the state sector. The state sector would find, in its turn, that the market sector would charge it whatever it could get. If the market firm was a monopoly, it could overcharge the planned sector, while if there were competition, the monopoly of the state sector would permit it to squeeze the market sector.

Then, too, the whole question of pay would be enough to lead to a revolution. The private sector would be based on profits, and so the managerial staff would be very well off, while the planned sector would be based on need, so that pay would be planned as the maximum possible after meeting the needs of further investment. Managers in the planned sector would be less well paid than in the private sector. The result would be an increasing animosity between workers and the private sector managers, supervisors, skilled workers, etc. Indeed, the workers of the private sector would be bound to strike for higher pay, better conditions and more democratic participation in management. How could they be denied them?

There is no ready solution to these problems. They are inevitable, and were bound to be much worse in the conditions of the early USSR. In a developed society, the market sector would be quickly reduced in size and scope, but in a backward society this would not be possible.

The point is that Trotsky faced these problems, which were indeed raised in the 1920s, but he saw them only in the most general class form. Rather, at one point, he saw Stalinism as being the expression of the bureaucratic apparatus, which found itself in conflict with the growing petit-bourgeoisie of the 1920s. Stalinism then had to turn against its allies, the petit-bourgeoisie.[50]

From this perspective, it would be clear that socialism in one country is a complete nonsense. But what also follows is that Stalinism did not turn against money and the market by accident. The NEP could not possibly have lasted very long. It could only have been a holding operation. Logically, once that holding operation failed, some result had to eventuate. That result was Stalinism.

The Stalinist economy resulted, therefore, from the failure to introduce the planned economy. But the planned economy could not coexist with a market economy under the conditions of the USSR. On the other hand, the market economy demanded the abolition of the forms of urban organisation which had come into existence.

50. 'In the matter of the national surplus product the bureaucracy and the petit-bourgeoisie quickly changed from alliance to enmity.' (LD Trotsky, *Stalin*, op cit, p410)

Conclusion

Trotsky's analysis failed to foresee that the Stalinist economy could last for some time, although it was not a mode of production, and did not have classes. Nonetheless, it is possible to understand Stalinism using Trotsky's method and initial starting point. From this viewpoint, a Stalinist regime is necessarily both non-market and non-socialist. No reforms are possible. It must either disintegrate and be overthrown, or return to capitalism. The USSR had a limited life that was based on the expansion of the absolute surplus product, and it exhausted it.

This chapter has argued that Trotsky's political economy of the USSR was in process of formation. He provided a logical analysis which could be drawn out to provide a fuller political economy of Stalinism. At the same time, he himself could not do so, and his own views were less of a theory than a series of observations and insights. The crucial concept is that of the nature of labour and, following from that, the control of surplus labour. Trotsky's thought evolved over the period of 1929-40, but it is also internally inconsistent. This chapter has argued that Trotsky totally opposed the market, but argued for its retention and gradual phasing out in the transition period. His view of Stalinism as an economic entity was unformed. On the one hand, he saw it as a parasite, while on the other he viewed it as a socio-economic entity. He remained true to the end to the idea that Stalinism was centrist, and hence that there remained some aspect of the gains of October. On the other hand, his argument of 1940 for the defence of the USSR no longer relied on that point.

Trotsky's crucial concept was not that of a workers' state, but of the transition period. Logically, he could have argued that the transition period had incorporated the effects of the October Revolution in an irrevocable way.

Trotsky fishing off Vera Cruz, early 1940

Hillel Ticktin

Leon Trotsky's Political Economy of Capitalism[1]

Introduction

This chapter discusses Trotsky's political economy of capitalism. It argues that the two key categories that Trotsky uses are the concepts of the curve of capitalist development and the transitional epoch. It is not possible to separate entirely his political economy of capitalism from that of the USSR, but I have written a separate chapter on the latter. Only a number of aspects can be tackled in this chapter. A book or books would be required completely to reconstruct Trotsky's political economy of capitalism.

Method

Leon Trotsky is possibly the most dialectical of all Marxist theorists. He wrote on dialectics in a number of places,[2] but it is in his writings as a whole that one sees his dialectical method. It is enough to contrast Trotsky with Bukharin to show the

---

1. This is a revised version of the article that appeared in T Brotherstone and P Dukes (eds), *The Trotsky Reappraisal*, Edinburgh, 1992.
2. LD Trotsky, 'Philosophical Tendencies of Bureaucratism', *The Challenge of the Left Opposition, 1928-29*, New York, 1981, pp389ff; 'Dialectics and the Immutability of the Syllogism', *Writings of Leon Trotsky: Supplement 1934-40*, New York, 1973, pp399ff. His replies to Max Shachtman and James Burnham in the collection, *In Defence of Marxism*, London, 1966, are replete with paragraphs discussing aspects of the dialectic. See also Philip Pomper, *Trotsky, Notebooks of 1933-35*, New York, 1986.

enormous difference between a dialectical Marxist and a mechanical one.³ But this is really unfair to Trotsky, since Bukharin was actually an extreme example of a Marxist who failed to grasp the essence of Marxism.

It is clearer when comparing Trotsky to Lenin. Lenin's political economy is directed to a purpose. He shows the drive inherent in imperialism leading to war, and then argues that this is part of a declining capitalism. Both the inherent movement in capitalism and its degeneration into finance capitalism are dialectical concepts. What, however, is lacking in Lenin is an attempt to see the contradictions within capitalism and the interpenetration of those contradictions. His original work, *The Development of Capitalism in Russia*, argued convincingly but in unilinear form that the problem with capitalism is not one of markets.⁴ He then seems to argue that it is a question of proportionality. Lenin sees contradiction as part of reality, but he sees it as causing 'the decay and transformation' of capitalism, and not as the essence of movement itself. He therefore could not interrelate profits, disproportionality and markets. Lenin is right against the Narodniks, but wrong otherwise, since it is quite possible that the absence of a market could lead to the underdevelopment of a country. While writers have argued that Lenin changed after reading Hegel, and indeed his work on imperialism is a testament to that fact, he never went as far as Trotsky in incorporating dialectics into the basis of his thought.⁵

Whereas Trotsky looks for the forces at work, Lenin looks to a way in which those forces can be stopped. For Lenin, the dynamic appears to be a one way street, whereas for Trotsky there is an ebb and flow. Trotsky's approach is shown best in his *History of the Russian Revolution*, but it inspires his other work as well. In particular, his concept of equilibrium does not only stand in sharp contrast with that of Bukharin, but is the only dialectical description of the term. Trotsky described the dialectic as

3. LD Trotsky, 'Who is Leading the Comintern Today?', *The Challenge of the Left Opposition, 1928-29*, op cit, p203. Trotsky interprets the comments on Bukharin in Lenin's testament as effectively meaning that Bukharin was not a Marxist theoretician. See Richard Day, 'Dialectical Method in the Political Writings of Lenin and Bukharin', *Canadian Journal of Political Science*, Volume 9, no 2, June 1976, pp244-60.
4. VI Lenin, 'Razvitie Kapitalizma v Rossii' ('The Development of Capitalism in Russia'), *Pol'noe Sobranie Sochinenie*, Volume 3, Moscow, 1958, p48.
5. See M Löwy, 'From the *Logic* of Hegel to the Finland Station in Petrograd', in this collection. Löwy shows that Lenin adopted a more dialectical viewpoint after writing the *Philosophical Notebooks*. He argues that this then permitted him to agree with Trotsky's concept of permanent revolution. There can be no doubt of Lenin's understanding of Hegel and Marxist dialectics from that point (1915) onwards, but his writing never took on the necessary theoretical form or depth consonant with such an understanding. His major theoretical work, *Imperialism*, does not look at the movement of exchange value and use value and their interpenetration, leading to a new form of capital, finance capital, but assumes that the rise of finance capital is the coming into being of a parasitic form of capital.

follows: 'Marx's method is *dialectic* because it regards both nature and society as they evolve, and evolution itself is the constant struggle of conflicting forces.'[6] Trotsky saw equilibrium as a temporary containment of conflicting forces.

Trotsky's approach was organicist. He was explicit about this.[7] In other words, he saw society as comparable to a living organism, with its own coming into being, maturity and decline. Society has its own laws, which are different not only between societies, but also in the embryonic, mature and declining phases of the particular society. This is to be contrasted with the mechanical approach of Bukharin.

The problem with Trotsky's work is not his dialectic, but his own dialectical decline. He never produced a specific work on political economy prior to his exile in 1929, and when he had the time to do so, he could no longer do it. Trotsky's analysis remained at too general a level to be called a detailed political economy, but there was enough said to be able to construct one based on his approach. It is therefore of some merit to attempt to draw out the nature of Trotsky's political economy of capitalism by looking at his published writings.

Capitalist Equilibrium and Revolution

The concept of an equilibrium of forces under capitalism played a crucial role in Trotsky's thought. He saw capitalism constantly attempting to assert an equilibrium, which is constantly breaking down. This is in direct contrast to Bukharin, who saw the equilibrium as a state of rest. For Trotsky, the term is not one of a balance of forces. It is not derived from the metaphor of the physicists' balance, with two substances being weighed against each other. Instead, his concept involves the view that there are contradictory self-moving forces opposing each other, which are part of the society. As long as they can interact and not overwhelm the other, they move into and out of equilibrium. Equilibrium from this point of view is a state which is constantly being reached and broken until one or other of the poles of the contradiction loses its power and fails. How does this process occur?

Trotsky saw a revolution occurring either on an upturn, when the workers acquire confidence after previous defeats, or after a series of defeats and partial victories. Unlike other Marxists, Trotsky was specific about the conditions for working class consciousness; capitalism would continue until it is overthrown.

6. LD Trotsky, 'Presenting Karl Marx', in his *The Living Thoughts of Karl Marx*, New York, 1963, p16.
7. 'Just as the operation of the laws of physiology yields different results in a growing organism from those in a dying one, so the economic laws of Marxist economy assert themselves differently in a developing and a disintegrating capitalism.' (Ibid, p19)

In 1922 Trotsky produced a statement which is remarkable for its prescience:

'If we are told: "And where are the guarantees... that capitalism will not restore its equilibrium through cyclical oscillations?" then I would say in reply: "There are no guarantees and there can be none." If we cancel out the revolutionary nature of the working class and its struggle and the work of the Communist Party and of the trade unions... and take instead the objective mechanics of capitalism, then we could say: "Naturally, failing the intervention of the working class, failing its struggle, its resistance, its self-defence and its offensives — failing all this, capitalism will restore its own equilibrium, not the old but a new equilibrium; it will establish the domination of the old Anglo-American world in which the entire economy will pass into the hands of these countries, and there will be a temporary alliance between the United States and Great Britain, but presently this equilibrium will once again be disrupted."'[8]

Trotsky's View of Capitalism at the Third Congress of the Communist International

Trotsky's best discussion of political economy was in his speech to the Third Congress of the Comintern. In that speech he described the way in which the bourgeoisie had recovered, and had stabilised capitalism. From his understanding of contemporary capitalism, he was led to put forward the theory of capitalist development, which was later taken up by Kondratiev, in the form of a long-term cycle. It is, however, quite clear that Trotsky was proposing it because it was part of his understanding of capitalist stabilisation at that time. At the centre of his analysis is the category of accumulation, which is determined in large part by the political perception of the bourgeoisie. In other words, the capitalist class will not invest in productive capital unless it is guaranteed control over the working class. It is the job of the capitalist state to ensure this result. It requires some form of disciplining, such as wars and counter-revolution. Accumulation then appears as a result of both subjective and objective events.

Trotsky has been the only Marxist theorist to insist on the introduction of the subjective factor into political economy. He stood in stark contrast to theorists like Paul Mattick and Henryk Grossman who in their own ways tended to objectivise economic laws, and consider that capitalism would come to a natural end. Trotsky did not dwell theoretically upon this point, he simply used it. He was not counterposing his own Marxism to that of Marx, but simply using Marxism in his

8. LD Trotsky, 'Report on the Fifth Anniversary of the October Revolution and the Fourth World Congress of the Communist International', *The First Five Years of the Communist International*, Volume 2, New York, 1953, p201.

own way. When Roman Rosdolsky quoted Marx to the effect that capital constitutes its own barrier, Trotsky would not dissent. Indeed his later work made that abundantly clear.[9] Trotsky added a new dimension to political economy by arguing that the movement of capital had to be seen as part of the class struggle, and not just as an unconscious movement of rates of profit. On the other hand, he did not proceed to the point where all movements of capital were to be seen as a conspiratorial form, as some modern day theorists have seen it.[10]

In contrast to those theorists, Trotsky was looking at the control over capital rather than the form of control over labour.[11] He saw the form of capital itself and the struggle over its control as crucial. In other words, he adopted Hilferding's and later Lenin's formulation of finance capital as the modern form of capital.[12] The class struggle took on forms which originated from the subjectivity of the capitalist class itself, but became incorporated in the categories themselves. He was also arguing that the bourgeoisie needs a clear vehicle for its investment. It will not invest when it expects to have negative profits through obstacles deriving directly or indirectly from working class opposition.

At the same time there was no discussion in Trotsky's writings on the nature of capital accumulation itself. He did not discuss the falling rate of profit, and, although he did refer to the disproportionalities developing in capitalism and the problem of the market or underconsumption, he never produced an explanation of crisis. His discussion was more one of a general political economy which was

9. LD Trotsky, *The Living Thoughts of Karl Marx*, op cit.
10. See, as representative of this approach, Leo Tronti, *Workers and Capital, The Labour Process and Class Strategies*, London, 1976. He argues that collective bargaining and the labour contract 'are more relevant in this respect than just the birth of finance capital, the various "stages" of imperialism, the so-called "ages" of monopolies. Here we have the *labour history of capital* which is its actual history, and in front of which everything else is ideological legend, a dream of visionaries, the unconscious ability to mislead, or the wanted will to error on the part of the weak subaltern intellectuals.' (pp125-6) The contrast with Trotsky could not be more complete.
11. Both factors have their own validity. There is no evidence that Trotsky would have denied the forms of control over the labour process. This is investigated below.
12. Capital was seen as finance capital, with all the consequences which follow: 'If the complete subjection of the state power to the power of finance capital had led mankind into the imperialist slaughter, then through this slaughter finance capital had succeeded in militarising not only the state but also itself.' (LD Trotsky, 'Manifesto of the Communist International to the Workers of the World', *First Five Years of the Communist International*, Volume 1, New York, 1945, p22) In fact, Trotsky had already used the conception of finance capital in *1905*, which was written originally in 1908-09, and reconstructed in 1922: 'The new Russia acquired its absolutely specific character because it received its capitalist baptism in the latter half of the nineteenth century from European capital, which by then had reached its most concentrated and abstract form, that of finance capital.' (LD Trotsky, *1905*, New York, 1972, p50)

focused on the antagonisms between countries, and between labour and capital. Trotsky's perspective was much more one of looking at the nature of capitalist equilibrium and its disruption: 'To understand the mechanism whereby various aspects of the economy are brought into a state of relative balance, is to discover the objective laws of capitalism.'[13]

The problem with Trotsky's analysis is that it remained at too general a level to be called a detailed political economy; but there is enough said to be able to construct one on the basis of his approach. Trotsky did outline the possibility of a new equilibrium in which the capitalist class had recovered, and there would be an upswing over decades. His political economy is based entirely on his developmental theory, popularised by Ernest Mandel as the long wave theory. In fact, most people do not realise its importance to his analysis, simply regarding it as a part of his viewpoint. In fact, it is central to his overall theory.

The Curve Of Capitalist Development

Trotsky's argument on the development of capitalism was based upon the view that there is an overall tendency to decline or boom over longer periods than the immediate trade cycle.[14] He specifically alluded to the underlying causation. This could be wars, revolutions or more technical causes like expansion overseas and the introduction of new technology. Which of these two sets of causes was primary, or were they co-equal?

Trotsky considered the exogenous and usually political causes to be primary.[15] In his article contrasting Mandel and Kondratiev with Trotsky, Richard Day states that whereas Kondratiev saw the technical developments playing an independent role, for Trotsky they play a dependent role. In a remarkable rehabilitation of an

---

13. LD Trotsky, 'Manifesto of the Communist International to the Workers of the World', *The First Five Years of the Communist International*, Volume 1, op cit.
14. He put forward the conception in many places after the initial speech at the Third Congress of the Comintern. See LD Trotsky, 'Report on the World Economic Crisis and the New Tasks of the Communist International', *The First Five Years of the Communist International*, Volume 1, op cit, pp226-79; 'The Curve of Capitalist Development', *Problems of Everyday Life*, New York, 1973, pp273ff; and 'K voprosu o tendentsiakh razvitiya mirovogo khoziaiastvo', *Planovoe Khoziaistvo*, 1/1926, pp188-91, translated and reproduced below.
15. 'The acquisition by capitalism of new countries and continents, the discovery of new natural resources, and, in the wake of these, such major facts of "superstructural" order as wars and revolutions, determine the character and the replacement of ascending, stagnating, or declining epochs of capitalist development.' (LD Trotsky, 'The Curve of Capitalist Development', *Problems of Everyday Life*, op cit, p277)

old debate, Day has shown conclusively that Ernest Mandel's interpretation based on the theory of the long wave is incorrect.[16]

Kondratiev argued that there were long cycles, which were ultimately based upon a relation between savings and technology. Mandel, however, tries to combine the technological argument with one of 'exogenous' shocks. He asserts that there were three technological revolutions: firstly steam, then electricity, and finally the electronic-nuclear age.[17] This would mean that there were indeed long waves of development, whatever the initial driving force. Trotsky does not assert more than that there had been upturns and downturns, and he associates them very clearly with political events. The conclusive argument is probably the length of time of Trotsky's illustrative curve. His x-axis has 90 years without providing an upturn. This implied that only one curve had really ever existed. Alternatively, one might argue that there could be more if one projected capitalist development from before Napoleon, and took the post- Second World War era as the beginning of a new period. In such a case, however, it would be more proper to use Trotsky's usual terminology of epochs.

We can explicate the political economy as follows. Surplus value is extracted, re-invested and so turned into capital in distinct periods. In the upturn, the extracted surplus value is turned into productive capital, but in the downturn it is not. How could it not be? It can be turned, for instance, into finance capital and thus into circulating capital, and hence act parasitically on productive capital. Trotsky accepted the role of finance capital, giving it explicit prominence.[18] In other words, the 'curve of capitalist development' would then be dependent upon the extent of accumulation in productive capital.

The concept was also bound up with the decline of capitalism. Trotsky argued that as capitalism grows it develops the productive forces, but: 'In the epoch of capitalist decline, the productive forces are decomposing, as has been by and large the case in the epoch which began after the war, which has endured to this very day and which will continue to endure for a long time to come.'[19]

The overall argument can now be put together. Developing capitalism would tend to have long-term boom periods. A declining capitalism will have long-term

16 . RB Day, 'The Theory of the Long Wave: Kondratiev, Trotsky, Mandel', *New Left Review*, no 99, September-October 1976, pp67-92.
17 . E Mandel, *The Long Waves of Capitalist Development*, Cambridge, 1980.
18 . LD Trotsky, 'Manifesto of the Communist International to the Workers of the World', *The First Five Years of the Communist International*, Volume 1, op cit.
19 . LD Trotsky, 'Report on the Fifth Anniversary of the October Revolution and the Fourth World Congress of the Communist International', *The First Five Years of the Communist International*, Volume 2, op cit, p199.

downturns. At the same time, in both kinds of capitalism there can be the other part of the curve, but there are special reasons to explain this. The upturn at the end of the nineteenth century was due to the rise of imperialism, while the period of boom during and after the Second World War was due to the war and, subsequently, the new equilibrium which established control over the working class. Nonetheless, it is impossible to avoid the conclusion that the curve, which Trotsky discussed in respect of the period from 1789, relates both to the organic evolution of capitalism and to causes internal to accumulation. Most particularly, the capitalist class accumulates in a way and at particular periods which will ensure its returns. Curiously, this is a kind of mirror image of Keynesian subjectivism in relation to liquidity preference and the animal spirits of the stock exchange. As I have argued, there is a deliberate injection of the subjective view of the capitalist class.

The subjective aspect opens the way to the argument that the capitalist class may not understand its real interests, or alternatively may understand the epoch better than the workers. As a result, the leadership of the working class becomes absolutely crucial in the transitional epoch. Trotsky does argue that the problem is one of leadership, and although he does not actually draw the connection made above, it is an inescapable consequence of his argument.

Another conclusion applicable to the present time must also be drawn. The capitalist equilibrium is established when the class relations are favourable to the capitalist class over a period of time. Then a boom period can ensue. A declining capitalism will find it increasingly difficult to establish such an equilibrium. Hence it may be concluded that the capitalist class might fail to reach such a state, and there could then be long-term stagnation. In other words, the increasing strength of the working class might compel the capitalist class to eschew productive investment. The down swing might then not find an end.

It has been argued that there is no evidence of a long wave. There is now a considerable literature on the subject. Trotsky was not arguing, of course, for the kind of automatic movement often implied in the use of waves, but on Trotsky's argument, the evidence is amenable to mathematical modelling. The question is whether there is a period of relatively low accumulation followed by a period of relatively high levels of accumulation. The last 70 years quite clearly show precisely that tendency. The depression is followed by a war, a period of reconstruction, and relatively high growth, followed a period of relatively low growth, with mass unemployment. Of course, a look at some global average will lead to any conclusion, but this contradicts Marxism (and common sense) to do so. The point would be to choose the determining *productive* capital in the world, and to chart its course. Before 1920 or so that would be Britain, and after that period it would be the United States. In fact, Trotsky took the United Kingdom as his particular case. It is easy to show that odd countries bucked the trend, but that is neither here nor there.

The next stage would be to look at crucial companies in the particular country, and observe their behaviour. Thus for the United States one might look at Ford or General Motors. Again there is no point in looking at some general average because that shows very little. It is obvious that one could average out high profits in the big companies and very low profits in the small companies, and come to some absurd conclusion. Then if the determining companies show specific trends in accumulation, the case will be proven. What makes the statistical analysis very difficult is that bourgeois categories are not the same as Marxist ones.

Nonetheless, it should be clear that Trotsky's argument is not one of long cycles or waves of generalised upturn and downturn, but rather an organicist reading of economic history in which a capitalism in decline will tend to have an overall decline in its economy unless countermeasures are taken. In Trotsky's terms, if an equilibrium can be established in favour of the capitalist class then there can be an upturn, but once the equilibrium breaks down, the system itself begins to crash.

The whole question arises out of the need of Trotsky and the Bolsheviks to understand their own situation within the world economy, so that in the end Trotsky is really saying that cycles are neither here nor there. What is critical is whether the capitalist class can find a new strategy for maintaining and expanding capital. He answered that question in the negative for the 1920s, but argued that Marx had been wrong in 1848 because he did not understand that capitalism was on a generally rising tendency: 'If the capitalist world stood now before the possibility of a new organic boom, there would be a new economic equilibrium as the basis for the further development of the economic forces, and this would signify that we were finished as a socialist state.'[20]

My interpretation seems to be closer to Trotsky's actual thinking of the time. But it is not surprising that Kondratiev and Mandel should have taken him up differently because Trotsky does not explicate his own theory. The problem with Kondratiev and Mandel is not that they have introduced a technological component, but that they have made that component play either a primary role (Kondratiev), or at least a fundamental role in the movement of capital (Mandel). As a result they are able to see cycles, which Mandel, to differentiate his own view, calls a wave, which must have some necessity of their own. These waves must go up and down and so constitute a similar mechanism to the crisis. It is not at all clear that Trotsky would have wanted to argue that case. Put differently, the economic crisis does have an automaticity about it inasmuch that if the workers do

20. LD Trotsky, 'K voprosu o tendentsiakh razvitiya mirovogo khoziaiastvo', *Planovoe Khoziaistvo*, 1/1926, p199.

not take power equilibrium is restored through a reduction in wages and depreciation of capital. Trotsky's downward movement has no necessary reason to end. If it does come to an end, it will be due to a particular new class equilibrium that can be introduced like imperialism, Stalinism and fascism. No one can say that such so-called exogenous events are unlimited. I have referred specifically to the downturn because Trotsky argued that the almost cataclysmic events of the early 1920s were part of the overall decline of capitalism.

There is no reason why the word 'wave' should not be used as Mandel has done, as long as it is clear that the analogy with water or light is limited to a single wave. Alternatively, the waves could be regarded as empirical forms of the past, which have no necessary movement into the future. One could just as well, however, use an analogy with a man who had achieved his goal in life and then started to decline. There would be an upturn during his mature period, and a downturn as he entered his late middle age. This might be followed by a another upturn as the old man found a new equilibrium by entering a more rewarding job, but his powers would have clearly diminished. His influence might grow, but his ability could only decline, and in time, whatever upsurges he might have, the decline could only become increasingly important. It appears to me that Trotsky's crucial perspective was of a declining capitalism which was desperately seeking a way out of its old age. At certain periods it was able to find a temporary alleviation through imperialism, fascism, war, Stalinism and the Cold War, but the palliatives become ever more useless over time.

Trotsky and Crisis

The logic of the curve theory seems to lead to the view that the regular crisis is a secondary phenomenon. On the other hand, the driving causes of both the curve and the crisis are the same. Trotsky took the view that markets and disproportionality play crucial roles in the economy.[21] He argued that fixed capital is critical in crises, but that as Marx had written only hints on the subject, Hilferding had pieced it together.[22] Preobrazhensky, Lenin and Trotsky say little about the falling rate of profit. Trotsky, however, is insistent that crises are in the nature of capitalism, and that a depression is necessarily followed by a boom, until the working class itself takes power.

21. LD Trotsky, 'Report on the World Economic Crisis and the New Tasks of the Communist International', *The First Five Years of the Communist International*, Volume 1, op cit, pp226-79. He looks there at the problem of consumption and the disproportions between sectors and countries.
22. LD Trotsky, 'K voprosu o tendentsiakh razvitiya mirovogo khoziaiastvo', *Planovoe Khoziaistvo*, 1/1926, p188.

This leads to the conclusion that Trotsky saw capitalism as a system whose contradictions necessarily led it into crises, but those crises would tend to get worse in periods of decline and be less important in periods of boom. The key concept remains one of the crisis, but the evolution of capitalism determines its depth and importance. Trotsky insisted on the evolutionary aspect of capitalism, and the logic of Trotsky's position leads to the argument that crises can only grow deeper under capitalism, but not in a unilinear way.

Capitalism in the Introduction to *Capital*

Perhaps the most extensive exposition of Trotsky's views is set forth in his introduction to the Fawcett edition of an abridged edition of *Capital*.[23] The edition itself was put together by Otto Rühle. Trotsky's introduction puts *Capital* in the context of the contemporary global situation, which at that time was one of world depression. His own outline of Marxist political economy comes across as rigid and mechanical, which was in sharp contrast with his own dialectical work of the 1920s. He supported the view that capitalism would collapse, and was indeed already collapsing. He also was of the opinion that there was a theory of increasing misery which was validated by the empirical situation of the time. Even if these views were correct, they need to be argued out and theorised, and not simply buttressed by empirical evidence. The contrast between this dogmatic attitude to Marxist political economy and his own earlier views makes it impossible to synthesise his later work with his earlier speeches. The common thread lies in their support for the opposition to exchange value and, following from that, abstract labour.

Trotsky was insistent that socialism is not merely possible but is indeed inevitable. If there is a necessary development of human history and the world is not to be destroyed, then Trotsky is right. He elided, however, the whole question of working class defeat, and what would happen if the working class was defeated over a very long period of time. It looks very much as if Trotsky did not want to admit that the October Revolution had been defeated, even if he argued that there had been a counter-revolution. If the revolution had been defeated, then there would be not just a transitional epoch, but a whole epoch of defeat, which would determine the nature of that transitional epoch. That would then mean that it was necessary to retrench, and hold out for as long as the epoch of defeat itself lasted. It would mean that the left was obliged to devise ways of organising a strategic retreat.

The left at that time was small. Yet there were many disparate groups and

---

23. LD Trotsky, *The Living Thoughts of Karl Marx*, op cit.

many isolated left wing anti-Stalinist intellectuals. If it was an epoch of defeat, then the task would be to find a minimum common programme in order to conserve forces. On the other hand, if it was a temporary defeat that would be reversed within a few years, as Trotsky clearly believed, then the task became one of founding a pure socialist organisation in order to lead the coming working class upsurge. The cataclysmic view therefore buttressed Trotsky's perception of the political tasks of the time.

We can ask whether Trotsky's statements make more sense if we understand the assumptions outlined above. Clearly they do. The terminal crisis of capitalism would necessarily involve a disintegrating society, as he saw it, with a standard of living which would drop, if for no other reason than that the capitalist class would itself cease to accumulate if it could see no future for itself.

Trotsky was wrong in his assessment of Stalinism, and thus also in the nature of the epoch. He, who had seen the great importance of the subjective, was forced to rely on the mechanical movement of objective categories because the subjective expression of the working class had been defeated. He argued at the same time that the subjective was all-important, but he failed to see the new objective categories that had formed. Stalinism and social democracy were not just subjective doctrines. They had become an objective reality, and constituted the main obstacle to change. Trotsky's argument, however, was that they were subjective realities which could be defeated. This implicitly meant that they would be defeated by the movement of objective categories, and this would lead to the formation of new parties and new leaders, and thus a new subjective reality to replace the old. In other words, because he did not anticipate a whole epoch of defeat, he was not able to sketch out the underlying laws of contemporary capitalism.

Paradoxically, it is today, when Stalinism and social democracy are dying, that the subjective has become all important. The enormous obstacles that have stood in the way of the proletariat for the last 70 years are being swept away without anything being put in their place. The bourgeoisie is playing for all it is worth the tune that Stalinism is Marxism and the only feasible socialism. The speed of the socialist recovery will now depend on the ability of socialists to put forward a credible revolutionary programme.

Imperialism

Trotsky's concept of imperialism seems to be restricted to the view that the forces of production outgrow national boundaries, and capitalism is obliged to expand.[24]

24. 'Imperialist wars are nothing else than the detonation of the productive forces against the state borders, which have come to be too confining for them.' (Ibid, p49)

The national state becomes increasingly otiose and indeed a barrier to production itself. He did not flesh this out, although it is possible to see that his argument is different from that of Bukharin and Lenin.

Because he was dialectical he was not led into the Bukharinist simplicities of a supra-capitalism. Trotsky argued that two forces are at work, the national and the international. The necessity of the development of capital drives it to go beyond national boundaries, but not all industry does, so while the nation state itself continues to exist, it hinders the internationalist drive of modern industry. This may be seen in his description of the problems of Europe and the need for a United States of Europe.[25] He argued that while the forces of production demand an international base, they are not able to obtain it. Hence there is a conflict between nation states to establish the new international order.[26]

His description of the mechanism of imperialism is closely linked to his theory of combined and uneven development. He argues that capitalism has developed unevenly, and hence the more developed countries are quickly able to exploit the less developed ones. This process starts with the origins of capitalism itself.[27] His view is, therefore, close to that of Luxemburg in seeing imperialism and capitalism as one entity, and therefore differed from Lenin, who saw imperialism as a particular stage of capitalism. On the other hand, he adopted both the concepts of monopoly and finance capital from Hilferding and Lenin, but he did not apply it to the theory of imperialism.

Trotsky considered imperialism as consisting of the exploitation of one country by another. It is the exaction of tribute, which is used by the metropolitan country to build up its productive forces at the expense, therefore, of the colonial world.[28] At this point there is a problem since he appeared to be arguing that imperialism represents the movement of capital in its embryonic phases as well as in its declining phases. The argument that the forces of production have gone beyond the nation state is only sustainable in the late phase of capitalism. The lacuna in his argument can be made good by using the same divisions for imperialism as for capitalism, of early, mature and declining capitalism. Therefore a declining imperialism is one in which expansion beyond the borders of the nation state is necessitated by the forces of production having outgrown their national boundaries, whereas a rising imperialism goes beyond its national borders because the uneven

---

25. LD Trotsky, *Europe vs America: Two Speeches on Imperialism*, New York, 1971, p61.
26. 'The programme of so-called autarchy has nothing to do with going back to a self-sufficient circumscribed economy. It only means that the national base is being made ready for a new war.' (LD Trotsky, *The Living Thoughts of Karl Marx*, op cit, pp49-50)
27. Ibid, pp47-9.
28. Ibid.

development of national economies has permitted a more dynamic capital to exploit other less developed economies on a national basis. In the first instance, the nation state is in a process of disintegration, whereas in the second it is in the process of formation. Indeed we find Trotsky using another definition of imperialism which fits this description. In 1939 he defined imperialism as the expansionist policy of finance capital.[29]

The less developed country is then subject both to the law of combined development and to permanent revolution. In the first instance, it can skip economic stages by using the most advanced technique with all its social and political consequences, and in the second it finds that it cannot consummate its own bourgeois democratic revolution. Trotsky specifically points to the lack of an agrarian revolution in underdeveloped countries of his time.[30]

There has been a considerable debate around the continued applicability of permanent revolution because of the anti-colonial revolutions and the relative success of the so-called national liberation movements. While there can be no doubt that local elites have taken power in the underdeveloped world, it is difficult to argue that there are any such countries which have stable and genuine bourgeois democracies. Both the political and economic components appear to be lacking. Agrarian reform, where it has taken place, has been limited or punitive. It is hard to find a genuinely democratic process in the Third World which has lasted for more than a short period of time. The Stalinoid states such as Nicaragua, Ethiopia, Cuba, Angola, etc, have certainly not ushered in any form of democracy. Their agrarian reforms have had their own deformations. In any case, of course, Trotsky was arguing that the local bourgeoisie could not consummate the bourgeois democratic revolution, not that Stalinoid elites would not have their own specific programmes. However, even in the latter instance a strong case could still be made that Trotsky was right, as the concept of permanent revolution also argues that the revolution can only be permanent if it is part of a revolutionised world division of labour.

The whole argument, however, is subsumed into the general nature of the transitional epoch. It is in this period that attempts to consummate the bourgeois democratic revolution are linked to the failed proletarian revolution and thus to Stalinism.

---

29. LD Trotsky, 'Again and Once More Again on the Nature of the USSR', *In Defence of Marxism*, London, 1966, p31.
30. Ibid, p49.

The Transitional Epoch

The concept of the transitional epoch is Trotsky's own. I discuss the concept in relation to the USSR in another chapter. Trotsky argued that social democracy had saved capitalism, and a whole transitional epoch had evolved.[31] This was a transitional epoch between capitalism and socialism. Previous to arguing this he took the view that 'the epoch beginning with World War I and our revolution is the epoch of the socialist revolution'.[32] Preobrazhensky and Trotsky discussed the transitional period in the USSR, but the content of the transitional epoch for the world is another matter. It would not be going too far to state that the category of the transitional epoch is Trotsky's crucial invention. It contrasts with the Stalinist view of a general crisis of capitalism, or of the coexistence of two social systems.

Trotsky did not produce a political economy of the transitional epoch, but it may be pieced together. In the first place, the transitional epoch is a period when capitalism has been overthrown in a part of the world, but without the introduction of socialism itself. In the second place, capitalism continues to decline. In the third place, the subjective aspect plays a critical role, as both the leaders of social democracy and Stalinism are seen as saving capitalism during this period. It may therefore be seen as the period during which the old order is objectively declining, but the revolutionary forces of the working class have yet to defeat the old ruling class. It is, therefore, a period of partial victories and defeats: 'It is impossible to say how long the proletarian revolution will endure from its beginning to its termination: It is the question of an entire historical epoch.'[33]

In a certain sense, it is an extension of the concept of permanent revolution. Trotsky considered that the revolution could only be consummated when all the partial victories of the working class were made permanent through world revolution. The working class in the developed world is driven to go beyond the bourgeois democratic successes it achieves, if it wants those successes to last, while the workers in the parts of the world which cannot even have bourgeois democracy are doomed to a half-life until they can take power. The original concept of permanent revolution is a combination of two aspects. On the one hand, the revolution proceeds from one anti-government class to another: from the industrial bourgeoisie to the petit-bourgeoisie, and then from the petit-bourgeoisie to the

---

31. LD Trotsky, *The Revolution Betrayed*, London, 1937, p62.
32. LD Trotsky, 'Platform of the Opposition', *Challenge of the Left Opposition, 1926-27*, New York, 1980, p373.
33. LD Trotsky, 'Report on the Fifth Anniversary of the October Revolution and the Fourth World Congress of the Communist International', *The First Five Years of the Communist International*, Volume 2, op cit, p187.

working class. On the other hand, the demands of the workers begin from limited forms of pressure, which are conceded, to more important and global programmatic demands. Both aspects can be seen at work during the transitional epoch. The old landlords are swept away with agrarian reform, industry is expanded, nationalisation is extended, unemployment is reduced, and the standard of living is raised, but all these victories are constantly under threat because they undermine the capitalist system.

Trotsky did not take the next step and argue that the transitional epoch was one during which the decline of capitalism would also involve the increasing socialisation of production. This would logically lead to the reduction of the sphere of operation of the law of value. There would then be a conflict between increasing degrees of organisation of production and society on the one hand, and an increasingly beleaguered and transmuted law of value on the other. James Burnham, Max Shachtman and Victor Serge all pointed to aspects of this change, but in a primitive and sociological form, to which Trotsky reacted negatively because they appeared to be arguing that the administrators were actually taking over, whereas the law of value had clearly not been superseded.

The word epoch is used as a period of time during which a specific correlation of forces evolves to its natural end. Put differently, Trotsky saw capitalism and socialism as distinct modes of production, with their own laws, and hence with their own organic natures. They cannot be mixed. The evolution from one to the other involves the complete elimination of the form of the old mode of production — exchange value — and its replacement by the new form — planning. The two cannot function together. If they are placed together, then they have the disadvantages of both systems and the advantages of neither. A caterpillar is not a butterfly, and a caterpillar with wings will not fly, but a caterpillar can gradually transmute into a butterfly. I have argued this point in more detail elsewhere.[34] This leads to the theory of the transition period. The evolution of the forces of the working class to the point of victory ushers in the transition period as opposed to the transitional epoch.

Political Economy Of The Transition Period

'If Messrs Capitalists hope that capitalism will be reborn again in our country, they will be disappointed. For the resurrection of capitalism in our country, they would have to wait until the second coming of Christ.'[35] Thus spoke Trotsky in

---

34. See my 'Trotsky's Political Economic Analysis of the USSR', in this book.
35. LD Trotsky, 'Speech in Honour of the Communist International', *The First Five Years of the Communist International*, Volume 2, op cit, p218.

1922. The transitional period to socialism involves the gradual elimination of the market under the direction of the working class. Trotsky thought that the process was irreversible. That may now be questioned, although the jury is still out on the question. The crucial questions were discussed over time during the period of the NEP and later. These are the reconcilability of plan and market, the inherent drives involved in the process, and whether the process is indeed reversible. However, the political economy of the transition period is a different question to that of the political economy of capitalism, and I have discussed this question elsewhere.

The only point to be drawn out is the reinforcement of the previous discussion on Trotsky's organicism. He saw the market as part of capitalism, even if it had to be used for a temporary period, standing in total conflict with planning and democracy. Although Preobrazhensky spelled out some of the problems, Trotsky did not do so. Nonetheless there is no mistaking his approach. Two systems have their own quite different drives, and the idea of mixing them is ludicrous, like putting together cheese and curtains.

Fascism

Trotsky's concept of fascism is well known. His political understanding of fascism remains unsurpassed. Whereas the Stalinists insisted on regarding it simply as the rule of monopoly capital by force, after they had moved towards the popular front, Trotsky stressed the importance of the petit-bourgeoisie and the ability of the fascists to mobilise them. On this basis, where there was no petit-bourgeoisie, there would be no fascism. For Trotsky fascism was a specific phenomenon, whereas for the Stalinists it was a natural outcome of capitalism. Had the Communist Party of Germany heeded Trotsky and joined with the Social Democratic Party to halt Hitler, it is very probable that Hitler would not have come to power. In addition, many of Hitler's inventions from the one-party state to the role of the Führer had already been introduced by Stalin, and hence appeared as natural socialism when the National Socialists introduced them. The two features which the Stalinists refused to introduce into the discussion — Stalinism itself and the role of the petit-bourgeoisie — appear as critical for the understanding of fascism. Trotsky used the concept of totalitarian to apply to both states. Obviously the Stalinist conception of fascism could not use such a term.

The point of comparing the Stalinist conception with that of Trotsky is to illustrate the specificity and the power of Trotsky's view. Furthermore, the Stalinist view of fascism has remained extremely influential down to the present day. It is not usual in discussions of fascism to find reference to either of the two components discussed above, except in a cursory way. Either fascism is seen as the rule of such monopolists as Flick, Krupp and the IG Farben cartel, or it is seen as an unfortunate seizure of power by a populist grouping.

When one turns to the specific economic attitude that Trotsky takes to fascism, the picture is less clear. He saw fascism as a political formation which emerges and takes power in a period of declining capitalism: 'Fascism, which merely reduces to the utmost the limits of decline and reaction inherent in any imperialist capitalism, became indispensable when the degeneration of capitalism blotted out the possibility of maintaining illusions about a rise in the proletariat's standard of living.'[36] From this point of view, fascism is a means of maintaining the rate of profit by raising the rate of exploitation. For Trotsky, the bourgeoisie had to concede either to the aristocracy of labour, or else to the fascists. In either case, the capitalist class effectively made concessions in order to maintain the system. The fascists, however, were called on in the case of the less well off countries, as opposed to the 'imperialist democracies'. In this context, Trotsky is clearly only talking of the developed countries. Fascism, from this angle, serves to club the proletariat in order to force down wages.

Trotsky did not synthesise his earlier work on fascism with that of these remarks on its political economy. It could, of course, be argued that fascism arises with the two components given above in order to force down wages, when capitalism is in terminal crisis. In other words, in a period of capitalist collapse, with declining incomes and consequent instability, force is required to control the working class, and to restore profitability: 'The last word in the disintegration of monopolistic capitalism is fascism.'[37] Such force can only be introduced if there is a mass basis in the population for the regime, and the alternative, socialism, is discredited or impotent. It would have been better if Trotsky had argued that the alternatives were direct force or a division of the workers, with concessions by the capitalist class in either case, rather than fascism or the New Deal as the only options. It may be the case that Trotsky did not want to introduce complications into his introduction to *Capital*, but it is more likely that he wrote the introduction, under the stress of exile, without the necessary books, and with constant organisational and financial problems.

At all events, Trotsky argued that capitalism is in a state of terminal crisis, with disintegration setting in, and it turns either to fascism in the less well endowed developed countries, or to a New Deal type of reformism in the wealthier countries. If we project the argument onto a theoretical plane away from the context of the 1930s, then it would have to be argued that capitalism can only maintain itself by depressing wages, when in the midst of a depression. This view coin-

36. LD Trotsky, *The Living Thoughts of Karl Marx*, op cit, p26.
37. Ibid, p21.

cides with that of the bourgeois economists, particularly, though not exclusively, with the doctrines of the monetarists. Wages then can be forced down either by directly smashing the organisations of the working class, or by dividing the workers sufficiently to demoralise the entire class. Today it is difficult to see any way that the capitalist class could actually employ either means to drive down wages in the developed countries. The reason lies in the precondition for fascism, so well discussed by Trotsky: the existence of a mass petit-bourgeoisie. Both the peasantry and the small entrepreneur have declined in importance. The consequence is that the application of force in a developed country would have no mass support whatsoever.

The simple application of force to an industrialised country cannot achieve very much in political economic terms. If anything it would tend to speed up the organisation of opposition to capitalism, and it would very likely fail to secure a change in class relations at the level of the factory. Of course, a Chile-type solution is always possible, but that is the final solution, the liquidation of modern industry in order to maintain control. It is not really an option for more than one or two countries as the ruling class of the particular country must have an alternative country to invest its capital. Hitler did not liquidate industry. On the contrary, he built it up and reintroduced full employment. The success of fascism was its ability to use force to restore capital, even if it was at a price to the capitalist class.

I have argued here that Trotsky's conception of fascism was one which was specific to the time. His conception of fascism, as I have drawn it out, is one which explains its success and its concrete historical role. He did not, however, actually make the necessary connections, and he may not have produced the same argument. He also did not discuss the contradictions of fascism as fascism, as opposed to the general contradictions of capitalism.

Yet those contradictions stare at one on the pages that he writes. On the one hand the fascists are supported by the petit-bourgeoisie, while on the other their measures destroy that very layer. The fascist drive raises the rate of profit and develops industry, but that leads to an increasingly powerful working class, which demands a better deal. They are forced to war and a controlled economy, but continue to rule by force. The nature of production necessarily suffers. The quality of German goods deteriorated. Fascism is a temporary solution predicated on capitalism finding an alternative form of continued existence.

The Labour Process and Taylorism

In the past 20 years it has become fashionable to look at the form of control over labour as a key element in the domination over the worker. In this respect, Taylorism is seen as playing an historic role. As is well known, both Lenin and Trotsky welcomed the use of Taylorist methods in the early USSR, although both indicated that such methods were not in any way socialist. This apparent contradiction is seen by some as playing a determining role in the formation of Stalinism. In the case of Trotsky, an additional element is added. His support for the militarisation of labour and his opposition to the right to strike show his anti-worker attitude, it is alleged.[38]

These arguments are useful only as a background to a discussion of Trotsky's views of labour. Lenin and Trotsky both opposed Bogdanov and workerism.[39] Lenin had in 1902, in his *What Is To Be Done?*, explicitly attacked workerism, and he remained consistent in his opposition to it. Trotsky criticised Bogdanov for precisely this attitude. Along with most Marxists, he argued that the worker has no culture to preserve, he has only a slave culture, which must be overthrown. The working class takes power in order to abolish itself. The form of labour is abstract labour, which is the very expression of capitalist domination, and hence must be sloughed off. There are no positive values on the side of labour. Taylorism, in this context, serves to reinforce abstract labour. Hence the working class must explode abstract labour on taking power and so destroy Taylorism. Such is the logic of the argument, although Trotsky did not anywhere argue in that form.

However, workers who have not yet become the masters of the economy remain workers. There is therefore a transition period during which the worker must shift from being an object to becoming the subject. If he simply refuses to work or works badly, the whole economy suffers, and he cannot reach his goal of becoming the regulator of the economy itself. Hence the worker must remain the abstract labourer until such time as he can control the economy, and then by being the master of the economy itself he will have an incentive to work in a rational and socially planned way. He cannot, however, master production until production has reached a level sufficient to supply the basic needs of society. Until that time with the best will in the world and the highest level of democracy, the worker will remain dominated by the machine. Hence it is in the interest of the worker to function in a disciplined manner until such time as it becomes a self-discipline. That is why Trotsky took such an apparently harsh attitude to the workers. If we start from the labour theory of value it then follows that the nature

---

38 .   Reinhart Kossler and Mammo Muchie, 'American Dreams and Soviet Realities: Socialism and Taylorism, a reply to Chris Nyland', *Capital and Class*, no 40, Spring 1990, pp61-88. This article argues very persuasively that Taylorism was introduced early on in the USSR. The authors, however, assume an unbroken development of socialism in one country, and never consider the essential argument of Lenin and Trotsky that the base for an advance elsewhere in the world had to be maintained. Nor do they really take into consideration Lenin's and Trotsky's critiques of Fordism and Taylorism.

39 .   LD Trotsky, 'Leninism and Workers' Clubs', *Problems of Everyday Life*, op cit, p317.

of production depends precisely on the nature of labour and hence on the form of labour.

Trotsky argued concretely that the crucial question is poverty, which has to be overcome. This can only be done on the basis of 'mechanisation and automation, the finished expression of which is the conveyor. The monotony of labour is compensated for by its reduced duration and its increased easiness. There will always be branches of industry in society that demand personal creativity, and those who find their calling in production will make their way to them.'[40] He argued, in other words, that while the economy must be run on the principle of the conveyor, the worker gains by having a higher standard of living, improved work conditions, fewer hours of work and more creative labour.

From this point of view, Stalinism and Bogdanovism appear as the false friend of the worker. They accept the culture of the worker even if that means that workers work slowly and badly, and their standard of living is consequently low. Trotsky was no voluntarist or Maoist. Only through collective discipline could external discipline be overcome and be replaced by the mastery of production through self-discipline.

Conclusion

The form of capitalism which has existed for the last 50 years is based on the disciplining of the workers through Stalinism, social democracy and the constant threat of a return to fascism and depression. It has permitted an unprecedented growth of industry, and thus an upturn in the 'long wave'.

Trotsky's political economy did not foresee the future, and it did not describe all the contradictions of the time, but it is the best that was written. Its dialectical nature, its insights, hints and pregnant beginnings provide the basis for a modern political economy based on a theory of the decline of capitalism, which distinguishes between the terminal crisis he was describing and the decline of the law of value and, following from that, the conversion of laws of motion into laws of transition.

---

40. LD Trotsky, 'Culture and Socialism', *Problems of Everyday Life*, op cit, p244.

Trotsky in his study during a discussion with American visitors, 1940

Politics, Philosophy and Culture

Lynne Poole

Lenin and Trotsky: A Question of Organisational Form?

Introduction

Despite having been organisationally separated from Lenin since the Second Congress of the Russian Social Democratic Labour Party in 1903, on the eve of the October Revolution Trotsky found himself within the upper echelons of the Bolshevik party, espousing a vision of radical social change which appeared fully to complement that of his long time adversary.

In an attempt to explain Trotsky's apparent change of heart regarding the Bolshevik organisational form, theorists have tended to utilise Isaac Deutscher's convergence model,[1] inspired by the post-revolutionary writings of Trotsky himself. Advocates of this model argue that Trotsky, finally realising his errors, came to embrace Lenin's organisational line, as laid out in *What Is To Be Done?*, after the February Revolution of 1917. In addition, it is argued that during this same period Lenin himself embraced Trotsky's theory of permanent revolution. Thus, these two revolutionaries came together under the Bolshevik banner after years of bitter polemicising and division. Tony Cliff, following this same pattern (though from a partisan viewpoint), sums up Trotsky's embrace of Bolshevism as follows: 'Trotsky... for some 14 years refused to accept Lenin's concept of the party, which

---

1. I Deutscher, *The Prophet Armed*, London, 1954, p256.

he wholeheartedly embraced only in 1917...'[2] In a similar vein, Baruch Knei-Paz attributes Trotsky's joining the Bolsheviks to his coming to terms with the central importance of 'purely political devices' in revolutionary social change and the lure of power.[3]

Insofar as these analyses do not recognise Lenin's changing organisational position but rather emphasise Trotsky's mistakes, especially with regard to the party, they are inadequate. It is the aim of this chapter to challenge this model, and, in doing so, argue that it was in fact Lenin who, in the light of the revolutionary events of 1905, re-evaluated his organisational position, and thus essentially closed the organisational gap between himself and Trotsky.

In arguing from a position which refutes any major *organisational* divergence between Lenin and Trotsky from 1905 onwards, it is necessary to explain why Trotsky did not join the Bolshevik party at this time. Hence, it is the second aim of this chapter to demonstrate that from 1905 onwards, Lenin and Trotsky remained separated primarily as a result of non-organisational differences, most importantly Trotsky's factional conciliationism, Lenin's rejection of the theory of permanent revolution, the nature of the coming Russian revolution, and its relation to the international situation. The importance of these differences varied over time, and as some were resolved others developed and took on greater significance. Hence from 1905 to early 1917, the two remained separated despite their informal organisational reconciliation.

In order to analyse the non-organisational differences which kept Lenin and Trotsky apart, it is necessary to consider their political and theoretical relationship within the context of the factional struggle between the Bolsheviks and the Mensheviks. Despite the two struggles being in no way conflatable, the relationship between Lenin and Trotsky can only be understood in the context of the history of the RSDLP, as the struggle between the Mensheviks and the Bolsheviks consistently had an effect on the relationship between these two revolutionaries. Hence, throughout this chapter reference will be made to the development of factional divisions and reconciliations insofar as they are related to the position of Lenin vis-à-vis Trotsky. Finally, it is important to note that this chapter will primarily draw on the pre-1917 writings of Trotsky wherever possible, whilst avoiding much of the defensive work Trotsky produced in response to Stalin's attacks, in which Trotsky appeared, in my view, to be overly concerned to demonstrate his credentials as a Leninist, thus both underplaying and distorting the differences between himself and Lenin in the period prior to the October Revolution.

2. T Cliff, *Trotsky 1879-1917: Towards October*, London, 1989, p78.
3. B Knei-Paz, *The Social and Political Thought of Leon Trotsky*, Oxford, 1978.

Lenin's Early Thinking

The 'Draft Programme of the Social Democratic Party' of 1895 set out Lenin's view of the developing struggle between Russia's young proletariat and the capitalist class in this early period.[4] Here Lenin argued that the struggle often takes an isolated, economic form in its first stages, but develops into a class struggle with political aims as the economic battle increasingly brings workers into conflict with the state. In fighting for improved conditions, the workers naturally begin to question the nature of the social structure and the role of the state and government. They thus come to understand more clearly the nature of their oppression. Lenin at this time recognised that political or revolutionary consciousness could spontaneously develop through economic struggle. In the true Marxist sense, the worker could become conscious insofar as he acted politically. The Lenin of 1895 perceived a link between the strike and political consciousness, and he recognised a real potential for workers to reach consciousness through their own actions and analysis. There is, then, at this time no role for the party, or more specifically the socialist intelligentsia, in the bringing of consciousness to the workers from outside.

However, the failure of the 1895-96 strike wave to win any notable advance left Lenin questioning the potential of economic and hence trade union struggle, and thus marked the beginning of an evolution in Lenin's thinking, with particular regard to the role of the political party. Indeed, as Antonio Carlo argues,[5] in Lenin's analysis of the limits of such struggles presented in his 'The New Factory Law', one can see the beginnings of a commitment to an organisation united in struggle as the method through which to squeeze more adequate concessions from the employers.[6]

The significance of the party for Lenin in this period was increasingly its perceived potential to extract political results from the economic struggle, thus preventing the government from watering down economic concessions after the chaos had subsided. Hence, in 'The Tasks of the Russian Social Democrats', Lenin emphasised the practical importance for political advance of an autonomous workers' party rooted in the factories.[7] However, it is clearly the case that at this time Lenin gave something like equal weight to the economic and political aspects of the struggle. Equally clear from this work is Lenin's continued focus on the

---

4. VI Lenin, 'Draft Programme of the Social Democratic Party', *Collected Works*, Volume 2, Moscow, 1964.
5. A Carlo, 'Lenin on the Party', *Telos*, no 17, Fall 1973, p7.
6. VI Lenin, 'The New Factory Law', *Collected Works*, Volume 2, op cit, p302.
7. VI Lenin, 'The Tasks of the Russian Social Democrats', *Collected Works*, Volume 2, op cit.

spontaneous nature of workers' struggle and political consciousness. However, in the period of stagnation after 1897, Lenin took his re-evaluations of 1895-96 a stage further. He argued that the division between the working class movement and socialism (or its theorisation) was damaging; the movement needed theoreticians, and that meant principally the intelligentsia. He therefore argued for the fusing of 'socialism with the working class movement in a single social democratic movement' in order to facilitate the transformation of the class struggle of the workers into the conscious struggle of the proletariat to emancipate itself.[8] In this way, then, Lenin elevated the political struggle and its organisational forms above those of the economic struggle. In fact, Lenin began to argue the position most clearly illustrated in *What Is To Be Done?*, that theoretical socialism, and therefore the intelligentsia, is the source of proletarian consciousness. Essentially, in this period characterised by extreme autocratic political repression and the rise of 'revisionism', Lenin deemed the workers to have less potential to develop political consciousness through spontaneous economic struggle. He thus advocated the formation of a strong vanguard party of professional revolutionaries to organise politically and lead the struggle. This period of reorientation culminated in 1902 with the publication of *What Is To Be Done?* in which Lenin finally subordinated the economic to the political struggle. Thus, we see the first example of Lenin's thinking undergoing an evolution in the face of new objective conditions.

The 1903 Congress

Before focusing in more detail on the content of Lenin's new vision, as laid out in *What Is To Be Done?*, and Trotsky's critique of this work, it is necessary briefly to summarise the events which both led to the split at the Second Congress of the RSDLP, and provided the context for the organisational debate which subsequently followed between Lenin and Trotsky.

It is clear that whilst the party as a whole came to the 1903 Congress verbally committed to replacing the loose federation of disparate groups which made up the social democratic movement with a centralised Marxist party,[9] its unity did not hold up in the face of Lenin's clash with Martov over the question of party membership.[10] Neither Trotsky nor the group which became known as the minority or Menshevik

---

8. VI Lenin, 'A Retrograde Trend in Russian Social Democracy', *Collected Works*, Volume 4, Moscow, 1972, p257.
9. This was most clearly illustrated by the party's general united opposition to the Jewish Bund's call for autonomy within the party.
10. The contentious paragraphs on party membership are cited in VI Lenin, 'One Step Forward, Two Steps Back', *Collected Works*, Volume 7, Moscow, 1977, p244.

faction could accept Lenin's organisational vision. Indeed, in his *Report of the Siberian Delegation*, Trotsky, supporting the Menshevik position, argued that Lenin's schema did not take account of those organisations, already formed through struggle and increasingly influential among the workers, which carried out work alongside the RSDLP, but did not officially belong to it. Trotsky insisted that it was neither acceptable nor prudent to set up an organisation based on a formal blueprint yet independent of the political reality of the period in which it would function. Rather, it was necessary continuously to adapt the structure of the organisation to the movement of the time, as it actually existed and developed. In this way, then, Trotsky anticipated the 'theory of organisation as a process' commonly attributed to Rosa Luxemburg.[11] Trotsky then went on to argue that Lenin's formalism separated the party from other forms of organised opposition, concluding that rather than excluding these groups, the Central Committee would do better to work alongside them, and thus attempt to influence them.[12] Choosing to support Martov's position over that of Lenin, Trotsky thus argued for the primacy of the educative argument over organisational formalism and rigidity.

It is clear that the break between the Mensheviks and the Bolsheviks over the organisational question marked the beginning of the split between Lenin and Trotsky, who at this juncture supported opposing tendencies.[13] This organisational division between the two deepened over the coming months, Trotsky's *Our Political Tasks* being published in 1904.

11. See A Carlo, 'Trotsky and the Party', in this book.
12. LD Trotsky, *Report of the Siberian Delegation*, London, 1980, p22.
13. It is interesting to note that in 1901 Trotsky had written in favour of a strong Central Committee at the head of the revolutionary party, and had even gone so far as to suggest that local organisations refusing to recognise its full powers ought to be cut off from the party, although only in exceptional cases. Unfortunately, it would appear that this document no longer exists, and thus one is forced to rely mainly on Trotsky's own references to it, principally in his *Report of the Siberian Delegation*. Here Trotsky argued that this position was arrived at in a period when he was essentially cut off from all practical work, and thus in the light of experience he could reject it in favour of the position laid out in *Our Political Tasks* which was more based on reality. Whilst this appears, in my view, to be the best explanation one can attain, given that the document itself is missing, it has in fact been refuted by a number of commentators, perhaps most importantly Cliff, who argues that Trotsky's position of 1901 is indeed his 'true' position. Hence, Trotsky's public attack of Lenin at the 1903 Congress and in his *Our Political Tasks* is seen simply as the result of his personal friendship and indeed reverence for such as Martov, rather than a principled disagreement with Lenin's organisational schema of 1902. Furthermore, this allows Cliff to argue that Trotsky's embrace of Lenin's organisational form in 1917, though belated, was both wholehearted and natural given his true position, masked by polemics and personalised posturing, as laid out in 1901. Of course, in my view, this interpretation can be dismissed as both inadequate and misinformed.

Trotsky's Critique of *What Is To Be Done?*

In *What Is To Be Done?* Lenin set out to define the principles of party organisation appropriate to the contemporary conditions existing in Russia, more specifically the illegality of oppositional party organisation. Furthermore, as has already been suggested, Lenin sought to argue that the potential for the proletariat to develop class consciousness if left to its own devices was limited, and that this had important implications regarding both the essential functions of the RSDLP in the revolutionary process, and the form that the party must take in order to be most effective. It is clear that for the Lenin of 1902 worker-led spontaneity, taken by itself, would result in nothing more than trade union consciousness. The proletariat, being naturally limited to trade union consciousness, needed the party, or more specifically the socialist intelligentsia making up its ranks, to bring socialist consciousness to it from without.[14] If the party failed in this task, bowing to the dictate of working class spontaneity, it would simply fail the class and hinder the social democratic movement. Indeed, Lenin went on to clarify the central point, citing Kautsky in support of his position, that the vehicle for developing consciousness beyond the confines of trade unionism is the radical socialist intelligentsia.[15]

However, it will be argued here that Lenin's view that the working class alone can develop only trade union consciousness is spurious. In forwarding this position, Lenin incorrectly conflated 'consciousness' and 'theory'. History does indeed illustrate that socialist theory has exclusively been developed by the intelligentsia, as Lenin alluded to himself.[16] The very fact that workers work in production implies that they will have limited energies to devote to the task of theorising. But social democratic consciousness is not the same as the theoretical doctrine of social democracy, the former being developed outside the realm of the intelligentsia. More specifically, socialist consciousness can indeed come from the workers themselves, given that their interests are determined by the objective conditions of their class position. Hence, insofar as the proletariat acts politically, engaging in class struggle, it can in and of itself develop a socialist consciousness. Even if one accepts that the party has an important role to play in the fight for socialism, as indeed Trotsky does at

---

14. It is important to note that Lenin was clearly referring to the proletariat as a whole when he made these arguments, and not just that of Russia. This is illustrated, for example, when he wrote in *What Is To Be Done?*: 'The history of all countries shows that the working class, exclusively by its own effort, is able to develop only trade union consciousness...' (VI Lenin, 'What Is To Be Done?', *Collected Works*, Volume 5, Moscow, 1977, p375)
15. Kautsky is quoted in VI Lenin, 'What Is To Be Done?', *Collected Works*, Volume 5, op cit, pp383-4.
16. VI Lenin, 'What Is To Be Done?', *Collected Works*, Volume 5, op cit, p422.

this time, it is not the task of that party to provide the proletariat with an awareness of its interests through theory, so much as to assist it in the fulfilment of those interests, which the proletariat can recognise through its own political actions, through the coordination of class struggle. Following Marx, Trotsky, in his *Our Political Tasks*, made the essential point when he wrote:

'Marxism teaches that the interests of the proletariat are determined by the objective conditions of its existence. These interests are so powerful and so inescapable that they finally oblige the proletariat to allow them into the realm of its consciousness, that is, to make the attainment of its objective interests its subjective concern. Between these two factors — the objective fact of its class interest and its subjective consciousness — lies the realm inherent in life, that of clashes and blows, mistakes and disillusionment, vicissitudes and defeats. The tactical farsightedness of the party of the proletariat is located entirely between these two factors and consists of shortening and easing the road from one to another.'[17]

Indeed, how can one accept that the intelligentsia is the bringer of consciousness when it does not share the objective position of the proletariat? In accepting this position as the correct one, Lenin appears not only to break with Marx, but, in Trotsky's view, to cheat history by attempting to substitute the party's intelligentsia for the conscious proletariat.

Returning to Lenin, it is clear that given his assumptions regarding the limits of 'unassisted' proletarian consciousness as laid out in *What Is To Be Done?*, he was able to insist — and this is absolutely central — that the revolutionary party must by necessity embrace the services of the socialist intelligentsia if the proletariat is to be provided with its socialist consciousness.[18] However, having refuted Lenin's claims regarding the necessity for the intelligentsia to bring to the workers social democratic consciousness from without, it was subsequently possible for Trotsky to deny the necessity of such a central role for the intelligentsia within the proletarian party itself.[19] Indeed, while maintaining that the intelligentsia does have a role in the party, albeit more limited, Trotsky argued for the more familiar mass party which consists principally of workers who themselves have the role of po-

17. LD Trotsky, *Our Political Tasks*, London, 1980, p75.
18. At this point Lenin was careful to emphasise that the inclusion of the socialist intelligentsia as central players within the social democratic party did not exclude the broader mass of workers from participation. He argued that workers had a part in creating socialist ideology, but as theoreticians rather than as workers.
19. Carlo presents an excellent critique of Lenin's position on the intelligentsia's role in bringing consciousness to the proletariat through the party, see his 'Lenin on the Party', op cit, pp17-18.

litical actors and organisers, rather than the role of theoreticians. He thus argued against the notion of an intelligentsia-dominated party.[20]

One can summarise so far that while Trotsky saw an important role for the intelligentsia, in terms of theoretical development of social democracy and even as actors within a socialist party itself, he did not accept the inflated role that Lenin ascribed to them. Furthermore, Trotsky, in my view correctly, refuted the central Leninist notion of the limited potential of unchecked proletarian consciousness. He saw more potential in workers' spontaneity than Lenin at this time, and denied that without the radical intelligentsia the workers would be entirely lost to bourgeois ideology. Rather he believed that the workers themselves were not only capable of attaining consciousness independently through political struggle, but could lead the revolution from the front in the form of a workers' vanguard organised into a mass proletarian party.

Having presented Trotsky's critique of Lenin's views regarding the limits of spontaneous proletarian consciousness and its implications for the role of the intelligentsia in the social democratic party, it is now possible to take up the second though intimately related issue, that of the organisational form.

Firstly, it is important to be clear that from the outset Lenin argued against the appropriateness of the form of the German Social Democratic Party for Russia, insisting that the notion of a mass party was unattainable where parliamentary democracy was not yet in place.

Secondly, though not entirely unrelated, Lenin argued that given the Russian conditions of autocracy, it was not possible to wage a political struggle in the same way as the workers would wage an economic struggle, that is through mass participation and in public. Rather, as has already been suggested above, Lenin proposed that the RSDLP should ideally consist of a small 'professional revolutionary' core which would work to organise the class struggle from within a secret organisation. He argued for a social democratic party in Russia which would rigorously incorporate the principles of centralism and discipline in order to match the centralism and discipline of the interior ministry, and thus succeed in its aims.[21] Clearly, while Lenin attempted to emphasise the potential participation of the masses in the revolutionary social democratic party, arguing that 'our first and most pressing duty is to help to train working class revolutionaries who will be on

---

20. LD Trotsky, *Our Political Tasks*, op cit, p55.
21. Lenin used the German example to illustrate that 'without the "dozen" tried and talented leaders (and talented men are not born by the hundreds), professionally trained, schooled by long experience, and working in perfect harmony, no class in modern society can wage a determined struggle' (VI Lenin, 'What Is To Be Done?', *Collected Works*, Volume 5, op cit, p461).

the same level *in regard to party activity* as the revolutionaries from amongst the intellectuals',[22] he appeared consistently to undermine the importance of the mass party as traditionally conceived by Marxists.

Herein lies the source of Trotsky's discomfort. Lenin had characterised the form of the 'ideal' party as one which was small and secret, with a group of 'professional revolutionaries' at its core. Furthermore, it was their function to lead the struggle against the existing regime. However, for Trotsky, such an organisational form had within it inherent dangers if allowed fully to develop.

Firstly, Trotsky charged Lenin with inviting 'substitutionism'. He argued that this core of 'professional revolutionaries', which in essence would form the leadership of the social democratic movement, themselves would become the centre of the movement's socialist consciousness. All the workers outside the party, and even those within it, would be relegated to the position of at best technical functionaries. Hence, the party in effect would find itself above the proletariat, acting in its name, but separated from it. Trotsky believed this would deny the proletariat its own historic role. Moreover, he went on to argue that while it was necessary to confront tyranny at all levels, as indeed Lenin himself argued,[23] it was the proletariat itself which was obliged to do this under the leadership and guidance of the most advanced section of the working class, which would ideally be organised into a proletarian mass party. This was not the same as the party, dominated by intellectuals, carrying out these tasks on behalf of the workers and then informing the latter of these actions at a later date, for example through the social democratic paper. Trotsky clearly argued that the form of the party laid out in *What Is To Be Done?* would lead to the substitution of itself for the conscious proletariat. However, he insisted that this substitutionism would not be tolerated by the workers themselves. They would break away from the party, and carve out their own path.[24] Hence, Trotsky feared that in blinding himself to the threat of substitu-

22. VI Lenin, 'What Is To Be Done?', *Collected Works*, Volume 5, op cit, p470.
23. In *What Is To Be Done?* Lenin argued that struggle in the economic sphere of society is insufficient by itself to advance the social democratic cause. He asserted that the party must seek comprehensively to expose the autocracy, its abuses, oppression and violence, no matter what class is affected, and in doing this draw the masses into political struggle on the widest basis possible. He was clear that while social democracy includes the struggle for reforms it is not entirely reducible to this. On the contrary, most important is the demand for an end to the autocratic regime, and the subordination of the struggle for reforms to the wider struggle for freedom and socialism.
24. It is important to note that whilst he wrote of how in theory Lenin's organisational methods would lead to 'the party organisation "substituting" itself for the party, the Central Committee substituting itself for the party organisation and finally the dictator substituting himself for the Central Committee', it would be a mistake to attribute to Trotsky a prophetic quality in this particular case as do so many of Trotsky's commentators. This is because Trotsky had

tionism, Lenin would succeed in not only destroying the RSDLP as it was developing at that time, but also in discrediting and bringing down the social democratic movement as a whole, thus leaving the proletariat to its own devices — that is, without organisational form or adequate leadership. What was necessary for Trotsky, then, was the extension of the base of the party to include more workers, who would actively participate in political struggle and maintain their roots in, and close contact with, the proletariat; the vanguard was obliged to be more closely linked to the class by a mass party membership. Theory on its own was just theory. For it to be meaningful and useful to the workers it had to be integrated with their political action and experience as it occurred in reality.

The second charge that Trotsky levelled at Lenin and the Iskraists was that of sectarianism; an over-emphasis on the battle for control of the intelligentsia, and the neglect of the most important of its tasks, that of politically educating and shaping the masses, and developing close organisational links with the revolutionary class. In succumbing to sectarianism, the Iskraists had forwarded the notion of a very specific discipline, one which required no less than the subordination of oneself to the Central Committee and the programme written by that committee. Trotsky attacked this conception of discipline, arguing that to insist that party dissidents remain quiet in the name of discipline would be to fail to see the worth of internal debate. Indeed, such discipline for Trotsky 'crushes the vital interests of the party' as it would prevent internal debate, and hence encourage complacency by the party leadership, who as a result were protected from being asked to justify their actions or prescriptions.[25] This in itself was dangerous given that it decreased the need for the committees to base themselves on the workers; they had in essence found themselves a new base, that of the 'principles of centralism'.[26] The party's potential for 'degeneration' was therefore heightened, and this is essentially Trotsky's third criticism of Lenin's proposed form of the party. However, this potential threat of degeneration was made even more real given Lenin's response to the charge that his proposed party format was undemocratic. Indeed, on the issue of democracy, Lenin insisted that the argument against this format on the grounds of its flouting of democratic principles (its lack of elections and public accountability, for example) was a sterile one as it ignored the central importance

        already asserted that if such a tendency towards substitutionism was to take any tighter grip on the party, the working class would move away from it and carve out its own independent course. The party would then lose its social base and disintegrate.
25 .   LD Trotsky, *Our Political Tasks*, op cit, p99.
26 .   Ibid, p93. Note that here Trotsky was referring to Lenin's form of centralism rather than the general principle of centralism per se. Trotsky's conception of centralism was bound up with the maximum local autonomy that unity allowed for, and could not be separated from the principle of democracy.

of Russian conditions, that is, the persistence of autocracy. He argued that a social democratic party functioning in conditions of Russian autocracy could not be democratic simply because it had to be effective, that is to say, secret. Moreover, Lenin argued that any threat of a degeneration into self-interest was guarded against by the very fact that the party leadership consisted of 'professional revolutionaries' who had 'a lively sense of their responsibility'.

This argument was clearly entirely inadequate, and reduced the principle of democratic accountability to mere blind faith. Indeed Trotsky inferred as much when he asked why a proletarian party member should be content in the knowledge that a 'professional revolutionary' above him was supervising things, and had everything in order.

In summary, it has been argued here that Lenin conceived of a social democratic party which would have at its centre a small core of 'professional revolutionaries', drawn principally from the intelligentsia, at least in the first instance, which would be organised into a highly disciplined, highly centralised format appropriate for the task of pushing the proletariat into political action. In response to this schema, laid out by Lenin in *What Is To Be Done?*, Trotsky highlighted a number of problems. He pointed to the dangers of substitutionism, the tendency to slide into sectarian squabbling, and a lack of concern for internal party democracy. He therefore prescribed that the strong Central Committee, which for Trotsky as well as Lenin was seen as a necessary inclusion, be tempered by a broadly-based rank and file movement which would play a central rather than peripheral role in party life. He thus looked to a centralism governed by scrupulous democratic arrangements made possible only if social democracy remained essentially a mass movement. Furthermore, he attacked Lenin for attempting to control the proletariat from above rather than harnessing its spontaneous growth of consciousness, and maintaining organisational roots within the class itself. Trotsky favoured the maximisation of local autonomy, and the reduction of the central bodies to functions of coordination, rather than prescription. For Trotsky, the principle of centralism could not be separated from the principles of democracy and maximum proletarian participation without there being disastrous effects for the whole social democratic movement. If the party failed to educate and mobilise the class by seeking to take the shorter route of substitutionism, it would be forever dragging the class behind it.

By the end of 1904 the organisational divisions between Lenin and Trotsky were clear. Lenin's analysis of the Russian class struggle at the turn of the century had taken him away from his position of 1895. Moreover, it had led to a split within the social democratic movement, with Trotsky responding with his critique of Lenin in the form of *Our Political Tasks*. However, the revolutionary events of 1905 saw a rapid development of the class struggle which culminated in

Lenin once again shifting his organisational position in response to the new conditions in Russia during this period. This time Lenin's re-evaluation brought him much closer to Trotsky.

Events Lend Weight to Trotsky's Conception of the Party

How did Lenin's organisational view develop in the period of upturn marked by the events of 1905? Whilst it is beyond the scope of this chapter to offer a detailed account of the 1905 Revolution itself,[27] it is necessary briefly to summarise those events which, in my view, precipitated Lenin's organisational reassessment.

In the first instance, the events of 1905 were characterised by a largely spontaneous outburst by the masses in response to Bloody Sunday. Most importantly in this context is the fact that this spontaneous outburst had a political character, and was accompanied by a series of strikes and demonstrations. The repression which followed these outbursts gave rise to a period of relative calm, although sporadic incidents of unrest were still apparent. However, in October an all-Russian political strike erupted, its participants presenting demands for an eight-hour day, widespread civil liberties, and the convening of a constituent assembly. Out of this political strike, and more specifically the revolutionary workers' council of self-management, grew the Petersburg Soviet. Trotsky argued that this Soviet was purely class-founded, spontaneously rising, and incorporating unorganised, scattered workers into its non-sectarian, non-party-controlled activities. It sought to coordinate and spread the strikes, and in doing so increasingly came to the forefront of the political struggle.[28]

The people's Soviet and indeed the revolution itself were defeated, not least by the issuing of the October Manifesto, and by the level of repression the state was prepared to administer. However, the importance of the events of 1905 in terms of their effect on Lenin (and in a different way on Trotsky) cannot be underestimated. The experience of 1905 demonstrated to Lenin the positive potential of mass self-activity and spontaneous proletarian initiative. Furthermore, these events demonstrated the central importance of the mass strike, and re-emphasised the connection between economic and political struggle which Lenin himself had played down since the late 1890s. Lenin responded by re-evaluating his own position on these issues in the light of both the events of 1905 and the organisational changes forced by the rapid influx of new members into the RSDLP, which resulted from the revolutionary upturn.

The changes seen in Lenin's analysis can be broadly divided into three areas:

27. See Trotsky's first hand account, *1905*, New York, 1972.
28. See ibid, especially chapter 8.

Lenin's re-evaluation of spontaneity and the working class's potential to act in a politically conscious way independently; the rise of the soviets as a spontaneous class-based organisational form and its relation to the party; and the changing form of the RSDLP in conditions of increased political freedom and the radicalisation of the working class as a whole. Each change, as I will demonstrate, brought Lenin ever closer to Trotsky's organisational orientation.

Let us first look at Lenin's re-evaluation of mass spontaneity. Having seen the masses act independently of the RSDLP leadership, Lenin was essentially forced to rehabilitate working class spontaneity as a politically important factor in revolution. The need for the party to push the masses from without seemed to Lenin less important than he had thought it in 1902. Moreover, at this juncture, Lenin recognised the potential for workers' self-initiative, their organisational abilities and the use of the general strike as a revolutionary tool.[29] He felt more confident to 'rely fully and solely on the free initiative of the working masses themselves'.[30]

This re-evaluation of mass spontaneity, coming in the light of the spontaneous development of an organisational form, the soviet, revolutionary in its aims yet outside of party control, brought Lenin broadly into line with Trotsky. Furthermore, it gave rise to a positive evaluation by Lenin of the soviet itself, and thus marked another shift towards that position held by Trotsky.

At this time, then, both Lenin and Trotsky believed the party and the soviet to be equally necessary in the revolutionary struggle[31] (although many of Lenin's Bolshevik comrades did not agree).[32] Moreover, both were against the adherence of the soviet to a single social democratic party programme — a move that would in effect represent the elevation of the party over the soviet — whilst at one and the same time assigning the party an influential role within the soviet.

Marcel Liebman correctly sums up the position when he argues that Lenin was ultimately in favour of taking part in the soviet, while trying to increase its links with the party in terms of political activity as he recognised the soviet's ultimate organisational weakness, that is, its lack of a central authority.[33] Indeed, Lenin

29. VI Lenin, 'Revolutionary Days: The First Steps', *Collected Works*, Volume 8, Moscow, 1977, p117.
30. VI Lenin, 'Our Tasks and the Soviet of Workers' Deputies', *Collected Works*, Volume 10, Moscow, 1972, p27.
31. Carlo, in his 'Trotsky and the Party', is correct to dismiss Broué's claim that Trotsky and Lenin remained at odds regarding the soviet.
32. For example, Bogdanov, an Old Bolshevik, took up an anti-soviet position on the grounds that such a non-party organisational form would challenge the social democratic party, perhaps becoming the nucleus of activity aimed against it. He thus called for the soviet to accept party authority and its programme, or face the withdrawal of party support.
33. M Liebman, *Leninism Under Lenin*, London, 1975. The first all-Russian congress of soviets

argued for social democrats to form tight groups within the soviet in order to direct it in accordance with party activity, and thus maximise the influence of social democracy over the class.[34] Essentially for Lenin, as for Trotsky, the soviet was a means of connecting the party more closely to the class. It did not render the party superfluous, and it remained of great importance, especially in terms of the ideological leadership that it could provide.

Thirdly, how was the party itself actually changed in the wake of 1905? Clearly, in this revolutionary period the party in the form it took in 1902 seemed increasingly to lag behind the masses. If the leadership was to keep abreast of class action, it would have to increase its organisational links with the masses; the vanguard with the class. Indeed, Lenin not only fully recognised this,[35] but he also accepted the need to incorporate into the struggle the ideas of party sympathisers who had not formally adopted the party programme. The idea was to encourage a broader alliance by increasing the points of contact that the party had with these individuals and organs, and thus increase its influence over them. Thus, one can again see the parallels in Lenin's schema in 1905 with that laid out by Trotsky when the latter wrote in 1906: 'The revolutionary character of the epoch does not allow us to work systematically to create a broad and stable organised basis for the party. In the period of upsurge, the huge mass of the proletariat is drawn into the movement. In order to master it politically, the party has to resort to the mediation of broad, non-party organisations.'[36]

Numerically, membership did in fact increase substantially in this period,[37] forcing a more democratic and flexible party structure, especially given the parallel liberalisation of the regime. As Lenin argued, the influx of new members, increasingly from a variety of social layers rather than principally from the socialist intelligentsia, required new organisational forms.[38] The organisational reform advocated by Lenin in this period was also identified by him as the precondition for the

was not held until 1917. Note also that in 'Our Tasks and the Soviet of Workers' Deputies', Lenin called for an all-Russian political centre, but argued that the soviets would be too narrow a base.

34. VI Lenin, 'A Tactical Platform for the Unity Congress of the RSDLP', *Collected Works*, Volume 10, op cit.
35. For example, Lenin wrote: 'We must considerably increase the membership of all party-connected organisations in order to be able to keep up to some extent with the stream of popular revolutionary energy which has been a hundred-fold strengthened.' (VI Lenin, 'New Tasks and New Forces', *Collected Works*, Volume 8, op cit, p217)
36. LD Trotsky, 'A Letter to PB Axelrod', *Journal of Trotsky Studies*, Glasgow, no 2, 1994, p127.
37. Liebman quotes the membership figures as 8400 in January 1905, 34 000 in spring 1906 and 46 000 in 1907 (M Liebman, *Leninism Under Lenin*, op cit, p47).
38. VI Lenin, 'The Reorganisation of the Party', *Collected Works*, Volume 10, op cit, p34.

application of the elective principle which would itself ensure the participation of all party members in party decision-making. In 'The Reorganisation of the Party' Lenin explained how under new conditions, with increased political liberties, the elective principle should become the aim. Hence, he concluded that at this time, as conditions began to change, it was both appropriate and necessary for the party to prepare for the development of a legal apparatus whilst still maintaining a clandestine organisational nucleus. Such a view was first expounded by Lenin as early as June 1905.[39]

Again, then, there was a clear shift in Lenin's position which brought his conception of the party closer to that of Trotsky, emphasising the need for a mass membership and a body of aligned supporters to link more closely the party vanguard (which both Trotsky and Lenin continued to support throughout) to the class as a whole. Lenin now envisaged a party which would be increasingly under the sway of the workers themselves, who would form a majority and be able to exercise their influence to the maximum with the application of the elective principle. There would therefore be a decrease of absolute committee powers and Central Committee control, with the congress being the new more broadly-based seat of control. Moreover, in this period the principles of democratic centralism were outlined as a means of making local organisations the principle organisations of the party, increasing the autonomy of regional sections of the party and the freedom to criticise within the party, albeit within the framework of unity of action,[40] and putting into practice the right of minorities not only to exist within the party structure, but freely to express their views.[41] So, we see in 1905 an evolution of Lenin's thought, in particular with regard to organisational questions, which essentially brought him theoretically closer to Trotsky. This is not to say that Trotsky did not also respond to new conditions, but rather to emphasise that the principle movements regarding this issue were to come from Lenin. We are thus left in this period with a situation in which both Lenin and Trotsky were now essentially in agreement over the question of increased party membership, increased working class influence within the party, and an increasingly flexible, more democratic party structure within which this could take place. The inflow of new party mem-

---

39. VI Lenin, 'Two Tactics of Social Democracy in the Democratic Revolution', *Collected Works*, Volume 9, Moscow, 1972, p89.
40. 'The principle of democratic centralism and autonomy for local party organisations implies universal and full freedom to criticise, so long as this does not disturb the unity of a defined action; it rules out all criticism which disrupts or makes difficult unity of action decided upon by the party.' (VI Lenin, 'Freedom of Criticism and Unity of Action', *Collected Works*, Volume 10, op cit, p433) Note that according to Lenin it is the congress which has the power to decide when criticism must cease in the interests of unified party action.
41. They were written into the party rules in 1903-04, but became a reality only in 1905-06.

bers on a huge scale ended the restricted advocacy embodied in *What Is To Be Done?*.[42]

The Disunity of the Bolsheviks and the Mensheviks' Swing to the Left

At this juncture it is important to note that whilst Lenin moved closer to Trotsky regarding the organisational question, his own party faction, on the whole, did not. This is important, as the seriousness of Lenin's response is illustrative of his commitment to this revised organisational schema.

The old Bolsheviks, who remained at this point committed to Lenin's organisational schema as laid out in *What Is To Be Done?*, and who had worked in clandestine conditions prior to 1905, found the transition to a more open party form difficult. They were essentially conservative and pro-stability, rejecting inner-party democracy more than changing Russian conditions dictated as necessary. Hence, at the Bolshevik congress in 1905, there was a serious confrontation between the supporters and opponents of change. The division was so important to Lenin that he felt it necessary formally to dissociate himself from the views of these comrades over this question.[43]

Given that this period led Lenin to re-evaluate his organisational orientation, one would expect that the revolutionary upturn, marked by the events of 1905, would also influence the Menshevik position, and indeed it did, though Trotsky himself had a key role to play in this.

Whilst the organisational disputes of 1903 in some ways grew out of and indeed masked the underlying programmatic differences that existed between the Bolsheviks and the Mensheviks, Trotsky had at this juncture chosen to align himself with the latter on the organisational question, despite his fundamental disagreements with their stance on class allegiances and the potential for proletarian hegemony in the coming bourgeois revolution.[44] However, these programmatic differences with the Mensheviks were sufficiently important for Trotsky to break from the faction as early as 1904,[45] though he still

---

42. In 'Should We Boycott the Duma?' and 'Reorganisation of the Party', *Collected Works*, Volume 10, op cit, Lenin wrote for the first time of a mass party in terms of both membership and structures.
43. VI Lenin, 'Our Tasks and the Soviet of Workers' Deputies', *Collected Works*, Volume 10, op cit.
44. See A Pantsov, 'Lev Davidovich Trotskii', *Soviet Studies in History*, Summer 1991, p14.
45. Deutscher notes how at the end of September 1904 Trotsky's 'Open Letter to Comrades' announced his break with the Mensheviks. Whilst not published in *Iskra*, its contents, in particular Trotsky's criticisms of Fyodor Dan, were in part reflected in his private letter to Yuli

cooperated with them practically. In *My Life* Trotsky wrote of how in 1905, whilst not formally a member of either faction, he worked consistently with the Bolshevik Krasin and local Menshevik groups who both supported non-participation in the first Duma.[46] In late 1905, a period of radicalisation, the Mensheviks came increasingly under the programmatic influence of Trotsky, dismissing the bourgeoisie as essentially counter-revolutionary, and supporting a seizure of power and the setting up of a provisional revolutionary government. The revolutionary period from early 1905, in my view, demonstrated Trotsky's underlying agreement with the Bolsheviks on the most important of these programmatic questions even in 1903, as, given the events of 1905 and Lenin's organisational reorientation, Trotsky found himself dragging the Menshevik faction towards the Bolsheviks' programmatic position.

With the Bolsheviks, and Lenin in particular, forced to reassess the organisational needs of the class struggle in the light of the spontaneous evolution of the soviet, and the Mensheviks being increasingly influenced leftwards by both Trotsky and the events of 1905, the stage was set for the Unity Congress in the spring of 1906 at which the issue of factional reconciliation would be top of the agenda. The organisational relaxation of Bolshevism, the swing to the left by the Mensheviks, and the new conditions of Russian political life, allowed the two factions to come together not only programmatically but also around such issues as the elective principle within the united party.[47]

It is important, however, to note, as indeed Lenin himself did, that some programmatic differences remained between the Bolsheviks and Mensheviks even at this time of supposed unity. They included disagreements over the question of standing candidates in the Duma elections,[48] and subsequently the attitude to-

---

Martov and Vera Zasulich. At a closed conference, which he attended, the issues Trotsky had raised were discussed, and it was decided that the emigré Menshevik organisation be disbanded. This formal decision, whilst not carried out, did serve to free Trotsky from the organisational discipline and ties of Menshevism.

46. LD Trotsky, *My Life*, New York, 1970.
47. Deutscher writes: 'Both Lenin and Martov now admitted that their passionate controversies had been storms in so many emigré teacups. The disputes over the prerogatives of the Central Committee and the conditions of membership had referred to the clandestine type of organisation. The party had since emerged from the underground and it conducted its activities in broad daylight. For the first time its members could vote and elect their leading bodies without fear of the Okhrana. Lenin no less than Martov was anxious that the committees be elected from below and not appointed from above.' (I Deutscher, op cit, p136)
48. The Bolsheviks supported the use of the Duma as a platform for agitation, whilst boycotting its elections. In contrast, the Mensheviks supported the standing of candidates despite recognising the bankruptcy of the Duma. See VI Lenin, 'Should We Boycott the Duma?', *Collected Works*, Volume 10, op cit.

wards an armed uprising,[49] and were to prove ultimately irreconcilable. Still, most important at this juncture are not the disagreements that continued to exist between the Bolsheviks and Mensheviks (although the importance of these differences become more relevant to this chapter in the years of reaction, as I shall demonstrate), but rather the differences which continued to exist between Trotsky and Lenin. As I have already suggested, these differences were neither organisational in form, nor were they the same issues as those which still separated Lenin from the majority of the Mensheviks. Indeed, at this time the main issue dividing Lenin and Trotsky was essentially Trotskyist in nature — the theory of permanent revolution. It is to this theory that we must now turn.

Lenin, Trotsky and the Theory of Permanent Revolution

In order to compare and contrast the views of Lenin and Trotsky on the coming revolutionary form and its principle actors, it is necessary, in the first instance, to summarise those aspects of Trotsky's theory of permanent revolution deemed particularly pertinent to this debate.

The central importance of the theory of permanent revolution in this context is that it places the proletariat at the head of the bourgeois revolution. In *1905* Trotsky first recognised that the proletariat had a leadership role in the coming revolution, arguing that it would play the part played by the bourgeoisie down to 1848, given its potential for hegemony over the peasantry and the inherent weakness of the bourgeoisie.[50] For Trotsky, 1905 demonstrated the potential strength of the proletariat, which would, in his view, be fully realised in the coming upturn. Furthermore, Trotsky argued that whilst the overthrow of the proletariat and the peasantry by the bourgeoisie would limit the scope of the revolution, if the proletariat succeeded in maintaining its hegemony and broke out of national confines, then the revolution could become the prologue to a world revolution.[51] The proletariat must in this situation enter into a process of permanent revolution in order to survive; proletarian hegemony in the bourgeois revolution forces permanent revolution on the working class.

In *Results and Prospects* Trotsky reiterated this position outlined in *1905*, but went further to develop the idea that, once in power, the proletariat would neither want nor be able to limit its goals to those of the bourgeois revolution. Here Trot-

---

49. Some Mensheviks supported the constitutional route offered by the Duma.
50. For a full discussion on the decreasing role of the bourgeoisie and subsequent increasing importance of the proletariat in the bourgeois revolution, see chapter 3 of Trotsky's *Results and Prospects*, New York, 1978.
51. LD Trotsky, *1905*, op cit, p289.

sky concluded that the result would be a temporary dictatorship of the proletariat (supported by the peasantry) existing until the European revolution came to the aid of Russia, enabling the proletariat to complete its socialist tasks.[52]

The task of the proletariat, then, is one of permanent revolution: to push the boundaries of reform, promoting an increasingly radical programme which does not stop at the bourgeois democratic stage, but goes over to socialist measures, and in addition forces direct and immediate support in the form of a European revolution. Of central importance here is Trotsky's assertion that while the revolution begins at the level of nation, it is completed, indeed can only be completed, at the international level. The system of economy is a world system; there is an international division of labour, and a world market which dominates national markets. Productive forces have outgrown national boundaries.[53] National revolution can only be a link in the international chain.

Whilst the question of why the theory of permanent revolution was applicable to backward countries is an interesting one, it is beyond the remit of this chapter to consider this question in any detail. Suffice it here to note that in his writings on the 1905 Revolution and, indeed, permanent revolution, Trotsky looked at the peculiarity of Russian historical development. He noted its 'comparative primitiveness and slowness'. He explained this peculiar development as being a result of two major factors: the grafting on of capitalism by the state, and Russia's dependence on foreign capital. What is important to the argument here are the implications this peculiar development of Russian capitalism had for the evolution of Russian class forces. A 'grafted on' capitalism which is overly dependent on foreign capital and is without organic roots would result in a retarded and abnormal development of the bourgeoisie. It would essentially produce a bourgeoisie without cultural or social-historical roots, and thus no developed consciousness of itself as a class. Furthermore, a bourgeoisie existing under peculiar Russian conditions would, for Trotsky, do well out of the autocracy, and would thus have little quarrel with it; its revolutionary potential would, therefore, be hugely diminished. Moreover, the specific development of Russian 'capitalism' would serve to create an urban working class virtually overnight. This was peculiar in a number of ways, as was demonstrated by the Russian working class, which did indeed result. This proletariat would not develop gradually, and it would be concentrated in large factories, utilising advanced technology from the developed West despite its immaturity — the most important forms of production were dependent on it. Fur-

---

52. In his introduction to the German edition of *The Permanent Revolution*, Trotsky argued that the national dictatorship of the proletariat should be strengthened economically until the European socialist revolution comes to its aid.
53. As illustrated in 1914 by the beginning of the Great Imperialist War

thermore, given the size and nature of the bourgeoisie, the proletariat would enjoy a strength disproportionate to its size and age. Given this state of affairs, Trotsky was able to argue that it may well be possible for the proletariat of a backward nation like Russia to come to power sooner than that of an advanced country. In this way, then, Trotsky denied that the dictatorship of the proletariat is in some way automatically dependent on the technical development and resources of a country. Trotsky did not directly link the question of the development of the forces of production to the ability of the proletariat to assume power. He argued: 'Between the productive forces of a country and the political strength of its classes there cuts across at any given moment various social and political factors, of a national and international character, and these displace and even sometimes completely alter the political expression of existing economic relations.'[54]

This, indeed, was for Trotsky the case with Russia. The lack of a developed, politically powerful bourgeoisie and the existence of a centralised autocratic state meant that the proletariat was very powerful — the only class that could take up the revolutionary cause in Russia. However, it is crucial to note that the possibility of a proletarian dictatorship in a backward country was underpinned by the need to solve the agrarian question — a task that only the proletariat could take on successfully.

Finally, before going on to contrast Trotsky's theory with the position held by Lenin, it is essential to give a brief mention to the 'law of uneven and combined development' on which, in an important sense, the theory of permanent revolution rests.

The law stated that as industrialisation was 'grafted' onto Russia's natural economic stem rather than developing organically, old economic and social forms would not die away, resulting in the coexistence of these old and new forms. Subsequently, the contradictions of uneven development would be severe. Such developmental contradictions, of course, gave rise to instability and an acceleration of social disintegration, especially given the autocracy's resistance to corresponding changes in social relations. Indeed, the state could not hold on indefinitely. However, there is another central dimension to this law. Due to the peculiar development of Russia, and, in particular its use of high level technique, the model of 'capitalism' in Russia differed from that in, for example, Western Europe, and, hence, there was a strange potential for Russia to develop beyond what one would expect politically, that is, to engage in permanent revolution. For Trotsky, then, backwardness was the source of social change and upheaval, and it gave rise to a peculiar revolution of backwardness.

---

54. LD Trotsky, *Results and Prospects*, op cit, p197.

Lenin and the Russian Revolution

How does this position compare with that of Lenin? It is clear that due to the retarded development of the bourgeoisie and its alliance with the autocracy, Lenin saw the possibility of the peasantry and the proletariat potentially forging an alliance against the autocracy. Trotsky, of course, agreed with this formulation. However, the two disagreed over both the nature of that alliance and the political conclusions that one could draw. Trotsky emphasised the heterogeneity of the peasantry, isolated in rural localities away from the towns, and subsequently suffering from localism and disorganisation. Hence, he drew the conclusion that, as a social group, it was incapable of being a leading force in the coming revolution, as the history of all revolutions had shown. Rather, the peasantry had a great, indeed vital, supporting role to the proletariat's hegemonic role — the latter would widen its social base to the peasantry in order to consolidate its power.

In contrast, Lenin was more optimistic about the possibility of an independent peasant party. He believed that if the peasants were drawn into the political struggle they could be politicised, form a peasant union (the embryo of a peasant party), and participate in the soviet. Despite his optimism, though, Lenin, like Trotsky, did not believe that the peasantry itself could attain a hegemonic role in the revolution.[55] However, he did insist that the dictatorship of the proletariat and peasantry represented the victory of the peasantry led by the proletariat.[56] Herein lies the essential difference between Lenin and Trotsky. Whilst Lenin saw the peasantry, led by the proletariat, coming to power for the achievement of the minimum programme,[57] and then retreating into opposition against the bourgeoisie, Trotsky insisted that the proletariat, supported by the peasantry, must itself take power and push the boundaries of reform to achieve socialism itself, though in the context of a European revolutionary upheaval.

Insofar as Lenin expected the proletariat and peasantry voluntarily to relinquish power having achieved the minimum programme, Trotsky, in my view correctly, dismissed Lenin's position as nonsense. He thus made the distinction between Lenin's 'dictatorship of the peasantry and the proletariat' and his own 'dictatorship of the proletariat supported by the peasantry'. Essentially, then,

---

55. Lenin wrote that 'the peasantry, in the mass, tends to come under the leadership of the revolutionary and republican party' (VI Lenin, 'Two Tactics of Social Democracy in the Democratic Revolution', *Collected Works*, Volume 9, op cit, p99).
56. VI Lenin, 'The Historical Meaning of the Inner-Party Struggle in Russia', *Collected Works*, Volume 16, Moscow, 1977.
57. The minimum programme consisted of pushing the bourgeois revolution to its limits, thus achieving the maximum freedom possible within the bourgeois framework.

Lenin made the mistake of accepting the two-stage revolutionary schema as relevant to the Russian situation.

However, whilst Lenin's rejection of permanent revolution appeared to be complete in April 1905 when he wrote 'a too rapid a transition to the maximum programme is simply absurd',[58] it is clearly not that straightforward. Even at this time Lenin was prepared to concede that it was possible to 'make the Russian political revolution the prelude to the socialist revolution in Europe'.[59] Thus he implied an acceptance of the view that the transition period between the two revolutions could potentially be shortened. Moreover, at the end of 1905 Lenin argued that the counter-revolution may be threatened by the awakening of the European proletariat which may come to Russia's assistance by preparing for the socialist revolution.[60] Indeed, whilst writing on the land question in the same period, he argued that one could not have a definite plan regarding this issue, as a number of scenarios may present themselves, and he was clear that the ultimate aim was 'uninterrupted revolution'.[61]

We can see, then, that whilst Lenin essentially rejected permanent revolution and its inherently internationalist stance, the seeds of his acceptance of this theory appear already to be visible. At the very least, it would appear that Lenin considered there to be enough common ground between himself and Trotsky on the nature of the coming revolution and its primary actors to see a potential for cooperation.[62]

So far, it has been argued here that the differences between Lenin and Trotsky on the organisational question effectively disappeared as Lenin re-evaluated his position in the wake of the 1905 Revolution. However, the two were still destined for separation as during this period a new point of departure developed regarding the nature of the coming revolution and its primary actors. Whilst Lenin appeared to be somewhat open to the ideas presented by Trotsky in his theory insofar as he shared his pessimism regarding the bourgeoisie and viewed the proletariat as the hegemonic class in the coming revolution, he was not to be entirely convinced of the theory per se until early 1917. Indeed, as will now be demonstrated, the division between Lenin and Trotsky was unfortunately to be accentuated in the period

58. VI Lenin, 'The Revolutionary-Democratic Dictatorship of the Proletariat and Peasantry', *Collected Works*, Volume 8, op cit, p297.
59. Ibid, p303.
60. VI Lenin, 'The Stages, the Trends and the Prospects of Revolution', *Collected Works*, Volume 10, op cit, p92.
61. VI Lenin, 'Social Democracy's Attitude to the Peasant Movement', *Collected Works*, Volume 9, op cit, pp236-7.
62. Deutscher writes: 'Lenin twice emphatically acknowledged that in advocating an alliance of workers and peasants Trotsky was on common ground with the Bolsheviks.' (I Deutscher, op cit, p78)

of reaction, during which the irreconcilable split between the Menshevik and Bolshevik factions would lead the two revolutionaries to differ on a much more important issue — that of conciliationism.

Reaction, Disintegration and Division

The conciliatory years of social democracy, characterised not least by the Unity Congress in 1906, were to be short lived. By mid-1907 the period of reaction had set in. Repression increasingly began to displace the new found freedoms of the upturn, with Stolypin effectively restoring the autocratic conditions of past years, and overseeing a new reign of terror. The Second Duma was dissolved in July 1907 by Stolypin, who then introduced a new electoral law, drastically restricting the suffrage, disenfranchising even many of the liberals, and hence rendering the Third Duma something of a more moderate, right-liberal affair. Having originally been a proponent of reform, Stolypin had attempted to disarm the populace and then introduce controlled political and social reform from above, including an insurance scheme for workers, increased civil rights, and access to education and a local government (Zemstvo) expansion, with the support of the liberal Guchkov. However, he did not have a free hand with which to implement these reforms, managing only to implement his agricultural reforms of 1906 and 1910, whilst falling short in all other areas in the face of severe programmatic restrictions enforced by the Upper House, led by Durnovo. This period was marked by increasing levels of repression and the restriction of freedoms which culminated in the assassination of Stolypin in 1911, and thus the end of liberal-government cooperation for good. The Fourth Duma was doomed to be even more conservative than its predecessor, and indeed took Russia into the First World War.

The effects of the period of reaction on the class struggle and, in particular, the RSDLP were significant. The Russian-based leadership of the movement effectively disintegrated, with many of its members going into exile.[63] In addition, many of the bourgeois intellectuals left the party in a disheartened state.[64] Moreover, the membership of both the Bolshevik and Menshevik factions suffered considerably as a result of the downturn and, more specifically, class demoralisation.[65] In terms of local committees there was a rapid decrease in their functioning, and, crippled by the stagnation, retreat and then near collapse of the revolutionary

---

63. Lenin himself left Russia at the end of December 1907.
64. See A Carlo, 'Lenin on the Party', op cit.
65. Cliff is incorrect to refer to the party as a mass party throughout — the collapse in 1907 of the social democratic movement being a good example of how the party did not consistently warrant this label. In applying this label indiscriminately, he downplays the evolution of Lenin's organisational position and the effects of objective and subjective conditions on the state of the party.

movement, the party was unable to hold a congress in the years immediately after 1907. It was the Mensheviks who suffered the most severe disintegration, this being reflected in their organisational and tactical stance during the period that followed. However, the Bolsheviks too were not without their problems, with the force of circumstances causing internal divisions.

The period 1907-12, then, was characterised by, on the one hand, the Bolsheviks' struggle against the new right-oriented Mensheviks, and, on the other, the struggle of the Leninist section of the Bolsheviks against Bogdanov, who was expelled from the party in 1909. The latter of these two struggles is not of great concern in this context. In contrast, however, the struggle between the Mensheviks and Bolsheviks represented a resurrection of old feuds, and is central to the changing relationship between Lenin and Trotsky.

In 1903 there was clearly a general agreement between social democrats on the need for the party to form alliances with the democratic liberals, whilst at one and the same time educating the masses about their specific class interests. However, by the end of 1904, as the liberals established themselves as an increasingly powerful political force, a divergence of the Menshevik and the Bolshevik positions became ever more apparent, with the Bolsheviks increasingly viewing the Zemstvo campaign as essentially counter-revolutionary. In this way, the divisions of 1903, principally around organisational issues, had widened to incorporate the contentious issue of the nature and extent of class alliances in the coming revolution. The events of 1905, of course, convinced Lenin further of the essentially counter-revolutionary credentials of the liberals, though he did separate the petit-bourgeois section from the liberal monarchist section of the bourgeoisie,[66] arguing that only the former possessed democratic aspirations. So, whilst the two factions of the RSDLP were drawn together through the struggles of 1905, they remained latently but inherently separated by their attitudes to liberal class alliances. Thus, as soon as the period of upturn waned, the fragile unity was displaced by heated controversies over such issues as participation in the Duma, the potential for a future revolutionary upsurge, and the nature of its leadership. It was these tactical differences which emerged between the two factions that underpinned the new organisational disputes that characterised the period of 1907-12.[67]

The Mensheviks, suffering a rapid decrease in membership, believed the revolutionary upsurge to be defeated, but balked at the idea of returning to the underground. They seized upon the opportunities still remaining for a degree of legal work, and thus

66. Here we can see the beginnings of Lenin's proletariat-peasantry alliance in the form of the democratic dictatorship.
67. VI Lenin, 'On Bolshevism', *Collected Works*, Volume 18, Moscow, 1972.

called for a commitment to an open party form.[68] This was the position of the Menshevik majority, a position which was to be strongly contested by the Bolsheviks, especially Lenin, who viewed such a stance as essentially bourgeois.[69] Indeed, Lenin argued that in rejecting the need for a clandestine party nucleus and illegal activities, the Liquidationists were in effect rejecting the resolutions of December 1908 on tactics and organisation, and the decisions made at the plenary meeting of January 1910. They were conflating the need for legal work with the need for a legal organisational form.[70] Moreover, Lenin argued that to dissolve the illegal party nucleus was to diminish the revolutionary vanguard, and thus force the movement to rely increasingly on reformism — a completely unacceptable proposal. In contrast, Lenin argued for a combination of legal and illegal work (the consolidation of a clandestine party nucleus as a stable centre) in the period of downturn,[71] as indeed did Trotsky.[72] Clearly, Lenin did not view this stance as representing a return to the pre-1905 party form, as he considered that since that period the links between the underground party and the masses had greatly improved as a result of the upturn characterised by the Revolution.[73] Lenin thus called for a systematic exposure of Liquidationism and its organisational separation from the RSDLP. In his 'Introduction to the Pamphlet *Two Parties*', he took Kamenev's line, arguing that the Liquidators represented a different movement, separate from the RSDLP, and aiming to displace it with a legally existing federation, or, as Lenin termed it, a 'Stolypin Labour Party'.[74] These events and the formation of the Bolshevik party in Prague in 1912 represented the culmination of a series of programmatic divisions which developed rapidly in this period.

68. It is important to note that for many of the Mensheviks the party in its old form had been destroyed in the wake of Tsarist repression. Hence, the fact that there was no longer a real party in the shape of an integral organised hierarchy was sufficient grounds for those, such as Potresov, to deny the charge of 'Liquidationism' (Potresov, writing in *Nasha Zarya*, no 2, 1910, is quoted by Lenin in his paper 'Controversial Issues: An Open Party and the Marxists', *Collected Works*, Volume 19, Moscow, 1977).
69. This charge of reformism and bourgeois collaboration was seen by Lenin to be supported by the Menshevik position regarding participation in the Second Duma.
70. VI Lenin, 'The Illegal Party and Legal Work', *Collected Works*, Volume 18, op cit; see also 'Controversial Issues: An Open Party and the Marxists', *Collected Works*, Volume 19, op cit.
71. VI Lenin, 'Resolution of the Conference of the Extended Editorial Board of *Proletary*', *Collected Works*, Volume 16, op cit; see also 'The Fifth (All-Russian) Conference of the RSDLP', *Collected Works*, Volume 15, Moscow, 1977.
72. Paul LeBlanc cites Trotsky's article in his *Pravda* as proof of his support for Lenin's position, that is, a combination of legal, open work and a clandestine, illegal party nucleus (P LeBlanc, *Lenin and the Revolutionary Party*, New Jersey, 1990, p176).
73. VI Lenin, 'To the Social Democrats', *Collected Works*, Volume 18, op cit.
74. VI Lenin, 'Resolution Adopted by the Second Paris Group of the RSDLP on the State of Affairs in the Party', *Collected Works*, Volume 17, Moscow, 1972, p218.

Lenin and Trotsky: A Question of Organisational Form?

How did this difficult period of repression and subsequent political division (which appeared to take the form of an organisational disagreement, but in reality was merely a symptom of the underlying programmatic divisions which existed between the two factions) affect the relationship between Lenin and Trotsky? It has already been demonstrated that Lenin and Trotsky not only shared the view that a clandestine party nucleus supplemented by legal activities was the way forward for the party, but also that they were of a similar opinion on many tactical questions. Furthermore, it is clear that Trotsky played no part in the Duma participation debate within the Bolshevik faction. However, despite this, Lenin increasingly attacked Trotsky during this period. Now, whilst Lenin did indeed disagree with Trotsky on the theory of permanent revolution, he had done so since 1906 without having to attack Trotsky to such an extreme degree. Moreover, I have demonstrated that their differences on the nature of the coming revolution were in fact insufficient to keep them irreconcilably divided, especially given their agreement on the need for a proletarian-led revolution.[75]

There must, therefore, be an added dimension outside of their differences in respect of permanent revolution. Of course, it has been widely argued that the organisational question remained a contentious issue between the two right down to 1917. However, it has also been shown here that the revolutionary events of 1905 essentially resolved the organisational divisions which had dominated the 1903 Congress. Whilst it could be argued that the period of reaction had forced a degree of change in Lenin's thinking and party practices,[76] it must be recognised that the period 1912-14 saw a renewed period of struggle and an accompanying relaxation of the Bolshevik party once more, with an increased utilisation of legal channels of resistance (strikes, political mobilisations and so on). Furthermore, Trotsky himself had come to realise through the experience of 1905 that the democratic, mass party in its perfect form could not be achieved under autocratic conditions, especially in periods of extreme downturn in the class struggle.[77] Moreover, whilst concerned to minimise the influence and control of the committeemen,[78] there is no evidence to suggest that Trotsky remained other than relatively confident that

---

75. I Deutscher, op cit, p78.
76. Liebman argues quite convincingly that the return to objective conditions of repression resulted in an increasing imposition of the party line, a decrease in the rights of minority groups, and a partial reversion to the pre-1905 organisational forms insofar as the party once again became small, centralised and disciplined, with an emphasis of the merits of organisation in and of itself, and an increase in the strength of the central institutions over autonomous local committees.
77. LD Trotsky, 'In Defence of the Party', *Journal of Trotsky Studies*, no 2, 1994, p143.
78. Cliff argues that the aim of Trotsky's *Pravda* was in part to break the influence of the committeemen in the Bolshevik faction.

come the 'fresh political upturn' the remaining excesses of Bolshevism would be smoothed out.[79]

It appears to be the case that whilst the objective conditions of Russian society throughout this period forced a partial return to old party ways, this was offset to some degree by the upturn in the class struggle in 1912, and remained only a marginal issue in terms of Trotsky's relationship with Lenin at this juncture. Hence, having rejected both the organisational issue and the question of permanent revolution as the main force behind Lenin's polemic, we are still left with the question of what exactly led Lenin to instigate a vicious polemic against Trotsky.

In order to answer this question one must look at the context in which the polemic took place, that is, the irreconcilable splitting of the Menshevik and Bolshevik factions. Clearly, the principle point of departure between Lenin and Trotsky in this period was their different stances with regard to the Mensheviks. It has already been argued above that Lenin took an unequivocal stand towards the Mensheviks regarding their rejection of revolutionary tactics. He saw the battle for unity as totally lost, and thus sought to consolidate the Bolshevik wing of the revolutionary party, writing off the Mensheviks once and for all. Trotsky on the other hand, whilst in no way supporting the Liquidationism of the Mensheviks, still believed it was possible to work with both factions of the party. He sought to play down their differences, seeing them as purely technical difficulties that could be overcome, so that unity could be established. At the very least, Trotsky did not want to break all ties with the Mensheviks, as he still believed that a new upturn would unite the two factions in actions as had been the case in 1905. Trotsky had not yet accepted the bankruptcy of Menshevism, as Lenin had, and, indeed, would not do so until the beginning of the First World War. For Lenin, then, this conciliationism demonstrated Trotsky's lack of understanding with regard to the tactical differences between Bolshevism and Menshevism.[80]

In my view, Lenin was actually correct on this issue. It would seem logically to be the case that an essentially reformist group has no real points of contact with a revolutionary group. Indeed, to a large extent both the Mensheviks and Bolsheviks appeared to accept this split as unavoidable. However, Trotsky still saw room for cooperation. In essence, he did not seem fully to appreciate the programmatic differences between the two groups, and, if he did, failed to attribute sufficient importance to these differences in terms of the potential for united action. Therefore, Trotsky was to remain separated from Lenin principally over the issue of conciliationism and, perhaps of less importance, the issue of permanent revolution. The

---

79. LD Trotsky, 'In Defence of the Party', op cit, p147.
80. VI Lenin, 'Disruption of Unity Under Cover of Unity', *Collected Works*, Volume 20, Moscow, 1977.

result was an intense polemical battle between the two so severe that they appeared to be further from each other than they had ever looked before, with Lenin, in particular, exaggerating the problem of permanent revolution perhaps beyond the level necessary,[81] and blinding himself to the weakness of his own position, that is his advocacy of the democratic dictatorship of the proletariat and the peasantry.

Preparing the Ground for Unity

It has been argued that the principal division between Lenin and Trotsky in the run-up to the 1905 Revolution was one of organisation. Whilst this particular issue was resolved during the period of revolutionary upheaval, other non-organisational conflicts were to develop between Lenin and Trotsky, most significantly over the issue of conciliationism and the theory of permanent revolution with its inherent internationalism. How were these contentious issues resolved in the run-up to 1917?

The period 1912-14 saw an increase in working class activity after the prolonged downturn of 1907.[82] Whilst this upturn threatened to strengthen social democracy in Russia, the declaration of war in 1914 and the subsequent rise of social patriotism, characterised by the abandonment of internationalism, threatened the very foundations of that social democratic movement. The development of this tendency had a profound effect on Lenin, who made it his overriding concern to break social patriotism, and to distance the Bolsheviks from the Second Internationalists who supported this chauvinist position. It was in this context that Lenin was finally to realise that the fate of Russia was intrinsically linked with developments in Europe. He thus abandoned his earlier position as laid out in *Two Tactics*, writing: 'The task confronting the proletariat of Russia is the consummation of the bourgeois democratic revolution in Russia in order to kindle the socialist revolution in Europe.'[83]

Lenin's reorientation with regard to this issue did, of course, have serious implications for his two-stage revolutionary schema. If the fate of Russia was indeed linked to the coming international socialist revolution, insofar as events in Russia could ignite socialist revolution elsewhere,[84] and Russia itself was part of the

81. For example, Lenin described Trotsky's permanent revolution as 'absurdly left' (VI Lenin, 'Disruption of Unity Under Cover of Unity', *Collected Works*, Volume 20, op cit, p346). Note also that, in my view, Carlo is overstating the division between Lenin and Trotsky regarding permanent revolution and the nature of the revolutionary dictatorship.
82. See M Liebman, op cit.
83. VI Lenin, 'Several Theses', *Collected Works*, Volume 21, Moscow, 1972, p402.
84. Note that Lenin did not believe that Russia could lead the socialist revolution.

world system, it was quite possible for the Russian revolutionary upheaval to overstep the boundaries of the bourgeois revolution. Indeed, for Lenin, natural societal development acting alongside the new conditions of imperialist war could lead to a general socialisation of production, which would enhance that international socialist development.[85] What is important is that the role of the European proletariat now became central to Lenin's analysis.[86]

Robert Daniels notes the importance of Lenin's internationalist reorientation when he highlights how many 'leftists' returned to the Bolshevik fold around the issue of internationalism during this period, and especially at the Bolsheviks' Sixth Congress.[87] Moreover, it is clearly the case that this reorientation was no less important for Trotsky, whose theory of permanent revolution depended on an internationalist stance.

However, Trotsky did not join the Bolsheviks at this stage, given that several other issues still separated him from Lenin. For instance, whilst his position now incorporated a more internationalist viewpoint, Lenin had not yet fully accepted Trotsky's theory of permanent revolution. At this time Lenin saw the consummation of the bourgeois-democratic revolution in Russia by the proletariat as the spark which, along with the imperialist war, would ignite the socialist revolution in Europe. What he did not accept, however, was the permanent or uninterrupted nature of that revolutionary transformation in Russia. He did not realise the extent to which the bourgeois and socialist revolutions would merge into a single, continuous process.[88]

Before turning to look in more detail at how this particular difference of opinion between Lenin and Trotsky was to be resolved in the run-up to the October Revolution, it is necessary firstly to consider the effect that the outbreak of war had on Trotsky, particularly with regard to the issue of internationalism.

It will be recalled that one of the central issues which continued to separate Trotsky from Lenin after the virtual resolution of their organisational differences in the period from 1905 was that of conciliationism. Trotsky had consistently taken a conciliationist position with regard to the Mensheviks, despite distancing himself both organisationally and programmatically from the Menshevik faction. Indeed, it has already been stressed that on many of the most fundamental programmatic questions Trotsky was closer to Lenin than he was to Menshevism.

---

85. See VI Lenin, 'Imperialism: The Highest Stage of Capitalism', *Collected Works*, Volume 22, Moscow, 1977, p205.
86. See VI Lenin, 'Meeting of the Central Committee of the RSDLP(B)', *Collected Works*, Volume 26, Moscow, 1977, p192.
87. RV Daniels, *The Conscience of the Revolution*, Cambridge, 1960, chapter 1.
88. VI Lenin, 'Several Theses', *Collected Works*, Volume 21, op cit, p402-3.

What was important, then, in terms of the war and internationalism was not that Trotsky had radically developed his existing position on the nature of the revolution, as had been the case with Lenin, but that, on the contrary, Trotsky had been forced, in the light of support of the Menshevik majority for social patriotism, finally to abandon his conciliationist position. The Mensheviks' abandonment of internationalism in this period of wartime demonstrated to Trotsky their absolute bankruptcy as a revolutionary force. Hence, it appears to be the case that whilst Lenin was developing his internationalist stance, Trotsky was writing off the Mensheviks for not developing theirs. He thus fully grasped the impossibility, in fact the undesirability, of a compromise over the issue of programmatic principle.[89]

So far, I have demonstrated the convergence of Lenin and Trotsky over the issues of internationalism and anti-conciliationism. However, it is important to note that what has not been suggested is that the two now held identical positions regarding the war — they quite plainly did not.[90] However, their differences were not sufficient to override their shared antipathy for social patriotism and its Menshevik advocates.

Returning now to the issue touched upon above, that is the implications of Lenin's internationalist reorientation in terms of his analysis of the nature of the coming revolution, it has already been suggested that in this period Lenin was increasingly convinced that the bourgeois and socialist revolutions in Russia would be very close together. However, it appears to be the case that this acceptance did not extend to the idea of permanent revolution, and thus the total fusion of the two revolutions, until the beginning of 1917. Whilst it is clear that Lenin identified the Russian bourgeois revolution as the prologue to the coming European revolution as early as October 1915, it is not until the third of his 'Letters From Afar' that Lenin began fully to grasp the logic of his own position, and move increasingly towards a full acceptance of Trotsky's theory of permanent revolution. Here, he called for the spreading of the soviets in particular, given that they were organisations of the proletariat, armed insurrection and soviet rule. Furthermore, he called for the displacement from political power of the bourgeoisie by the proletariat. Whilst Lenin remained cautious, claiming that such measures would not constitute socialism,[91] in the last of his letters he talked of the democratic dictator-

---

89. See Deutscher's citation of Trotsky's writing in *Nashe Slovo* as evidence of his change of heart regarding the Mensheviks (I Deutscher, op cit, p253).
90. Lenin supported the conversion of the imperialist war into a revolutionary civil war, a position labelled 'defeatism'. In contrast, Trotsky held a position of 'pacifism', arguing that war of any kind was damaging insofar as it adversely affected the economy. Lenin himself noted this difference as late as 1917, see *Leninski Sbornik*, Volume 4, p301.
91. VI Lenin, 'Letters From Afar', *Collected Works*, Volume 23, Moscow, 1977, pp329-30.

ship taking 'further steps towards control of the production and distribution of the basic product, towards the introduction of "universal labour structure"'.[92] This de facto acceptance of Trotsky's permanent revolution was further reiterated in what became known as *The April Theses*,[93] where Lenin wrote: 'It is not our immediate task to "introduce" socialism, but only to bring social production and the distribution of products at once under the control of the soviets and workers' deputies.'[94] This surely implies an immediate building towards socialism in an international context of socialist revolutionary upheaval, and, hence, represents an acceptance of Trotsky's theory.

Trotsky wrote in his *History of the Russian Revolution* that the events of early 1917 forced Lenin to accept the theory of permanent revolution. Indeed, as Liebman notes, Lenin's writings in the early part of 1917 represent a resolution by Lenin of his previous, untenable position — proletarian leadership in the coming Russian revolution, but the restriction of the revolution's aims resulting from the imposition of bourgeois democratic boundaries, which logically meant that the party, or social democracy as a whole, would be forced into the position of holding the masses back once in power in order to prevent them spontaneously engaging in a permanent revolutionary process as they became aware of their own true interests.[95] In fact Trotsky himself made a similar point in his *History*, when he argued that in not seeing the peasants as socialist allies, cooperation with them could only mean that the proletariat would eventually have to give up its socialist aspirations. This, for Trotsky, was the essential weakness of Lenin's position prior to his acceptance of the theory of permanent revolution.

To sum up so far, Lenin's acceptance of permanent revolution in the face of the new reality meant that Lenin and Trotsky were reconciled on the remaining three issues of contention that had existed since 1905. However, whilst Lenin's acceptance of Trotsky's theory may have bridged the last major gap between the two revolutionaries, it did little for the cause of unity within the Bolshevik party itself. The old Bolsheviks remained attached to Lenin's old two-stage revolutionary theory in the same way that they had remained attached to the pre-1905 party form. They accused Lenin of abandoning Bolshevism for Trotskyism.[96]

The reason why Lenin revised his previous position despite Bolshevik opposi-

---

92. Ibid, p341.
93. VI Lenin, 'The Tasks of the Proletariat in the Present Revolution', *Collected Works*, Volume 24, Moscow, 1974.
94. Ibid.
95. For a discussion of whether or not Lenin actually rejected the theory of permanent revolution as late as suggested here, see M Liebman, op cit.
96. I Deutscher, op cit, p256.

tion lay in the renewal of working class spontaneity in the new period of upturn. Even in its new form, the party, with its large cautious right wing, held back the spontaneous initiative of the masses. Indeed, Lenin himself recognised that this period was characterised by a mass which was '100 times more leftwards' than its leaders.[97] Thus, in accepting permanent revolution, Lenin responded to the realities of 1917, that is, the heightened spontaneous struggle of the masses and the centrality of the soviets in this struggle, as in 1905.[98]

In agreement with Lenin now on the major questions of the time — internationalism, the theory of permanent revolution and anti-conciliationism with the Mensheviks — Trotsky was thus able to write a letter in solidarity with the Bolsheviks in the wake of the July Days. In it he argued: 'The fact that I am not connected with *Pravda* and am not a member of the Bolshevik party is not due to political difference, but to certain circumstances in our party history which have now lost significance.'[99] The way, then, was almost clear for Trotsky to join the Bolshevik party.

Trotsky joins the Party

In order fully to understand the nature and extent of the negotiations which took place over the issue of Trotsky joining the Bolshevik party, it is necessary to present a brief outline of the Bolshevik party as it stood in early 1917, and, in doing so, identify both the changes that had taken place since 1903, and the problems still remaining.

Whilst the party of 1917 has been popularly identified with that of 1903, in reality Bolshevism had undergone a radical transformation. This was in part a result of the huge increase in party membership after the February Revolution, which fed the fires of inner-party democracy. This can be illustrated by the relative autonomy of local organisations, which not only enjoyed a degree of freedom in the interpreting of Central Committee directives, but also gave voice to the minority groupings within their own organisations.

Indeed, an indication of the level to which this change of spirit within the party was a result of the changing composition of the party at all levels can perhaps be gleaned from the figures themselves. Thomas Rigby argues that on

97. VI Lenin, 'Titbits for the "Newborn" Government', *Collected Works*, Volume 24, op cit, p364.
98. This is demonstrated further in Lenin's 'State and Revolution', *Collected Works*, Volume 25, Moscow, 1974. Here Lenin ascribes a central political control role to the soviets, and makes little mention of the party.
99. LD Trotsky, 'Statement of Solidarity with the Bolshevik Leaders', *Documents of Russian History, 1914-17*, London, 1927, p461.

the eve of the collapse of Tsardom, the Bolsheviks had 23 600 members. Moreover, by April 79 000 members was the estimate, growing to somewhere around the 200 000 mark by October. Whatever the precise figures, it is clear that at this time only about one out of 20 members had been in the clandestine organisation — the others had come in during the period of transformation and expansion.[100]

It is clearly the case that in 1917 the central organisation was weak and poorly adapted to the large increase in the party's activities and membership,[101] and that local and regional organisations not only wished for but enjoyed a large degree of freedom regarding decision and policy making. Such a tendency towards autonomy reflected the realities of the new political life characterised by workers' initiative and spontaneity, though there did, of course, remain a degree of unity and cohesion within the Bolshevik party. In terms of organisational transformation, it would appear that there was a large degree of democratisation and a loosening of central control, which, added to the changes seen in the years from 1905, resulted in the decreasing influence for the old Bolsheviks and their old formulas, and the elevation of the notion of the party as a living organisation. Hence, Trotsky was able to talk of de-Bolshevisation.

In *My Life* Trotsky claimed that the party of 1917 was greatly transformed. Lenin had appealed to the masses for support against party leaders, launching a systematic fight against the old Bolsheviks and their adherence to the old, rigid theories and tactics, and supporting a programme which grew out of an analysis of real conditions. Hence, when Trotsky arrived in Russia on 4 May 1917 to find that his comrades in the Mezhraiontsa[102] were considering joining the Bolsheviks, and that Lenin had essentially triumphed over the right wing of his party, he was open to negotiations regarding his membership of the Bolshevik party.

From Lenin's notes on the meeting of Bolshevik and Mezhraiontsa leaders on 10 May, it is clear that Trotsky and his comrades were invited to join the party and offered editorial status and positions on the organisation committee of the forthcoming party congress. Furthermore, at this meeting Trotsky expressed his

---

100. TH Rigby, *Communist Party Membership*, Princeton, 1968, p59. Rigby claims that one week before the seizure of power Sverdlov reported to the Central Committee that the party had 400 000 members. Four weeks later reports to the Seventh Congress placed the number at 300 000. Subsequent recalculation gave rise to the figure of 115 000 in January 1918. He concludes that whilst the figure of 400 000 may be seen as an exaggeration, it is reasonable to assume 20 000 plus the underground to be only a fraction of the membership of 1917.
101. See M Liebman, op cit.
102. The Mezhraiontsa (Inter-District Group) was a temporary organisation of socialists who were neither Bolsheviks nor Mensheviks, and who were united in their opposition to the war and social patriotism, see I Deutscher, op cit, p255.

agreement with the issue of the Bolsheviks and Mezhraiontsa unifying 'insofar as Russian Bolshevism internationalises itself'.[103]

However, Trotsky was not only clear at this meeting that 'it is impossible to demand of us a recognition of Bolshevism', but also that he could never call himself a Bolshevik, particularly given that it was 'undesirable to stick to old labels',[104] old divisions had been resolved, and Lenin's party had undergone a process of de-Bolshevisation. Trotsky thus proposed the fusing of all internationalist left groups into a newly named party at a joint congress. In fact, in *The April Theses* Lenin himself had not only demanded the setting up of a commune state and a new International, but had, like Trotsky, also argued for the changing of the party's name, and he suggested the Communist Party as a suitable alternative. As Liebman suggests, Lenin realised that the Bolshevik party was vastly different from that organisation that had existed before the revolution. Indeed, on his return to Russia, he too called for a change of name.

Clearly, Lenin was in support of changing the name of the Bolshevik party as he himself had been convinced of de-Bolshevisation since 1905, when he essentially refuted his own schema of 1902 in the face of Bolshevik resistance to change.[105] Indeed, at the end of September Lenin wrote a document to the Petrograd soviet praising Trotsky's internationalist stance and his work among the Mezhraiontsa in support of a merger under such terms. Moreover, in March 1918 he got agreement from the party as a whole.

Some Conclusions

It has been the central aim of this article to challenge the generally accepted view that Lenin and Trotsky were separated by the organisational question from the writing of *What Is To Be Done?* until the eve of the October Revolution. At the centre of this challenge is the premise that whilst the evolution of Lenin's organisational thinking from 1895 to 1902 did indeed result in the organisational break between him and Trotsky, the events of 1905 led him further to revise his position, and, in doing so, essentially to end that division.

This period of revolutionary upheaval resulted not only in the theoretical unity of Lenin and Trotsky over the issue of organisational form, but also in the transformation of the RSDLP into a more democratic, broader based and less centrally controlled party form. Although the years of downturn witnessed a slight

103. These notes have been reproduced in *Leninski Sbornik*, Volume 4.
104. Ibid.
105. LeBlanc disagrees with this view, arguing rather that Lenin supported a name change as a means of dissociating the Bolsheviks from the Second International.

organisational regression on the part of Lenin and the Bolsheviks, this was largely a reaction to the decline of the party by Tsarist repression, rather than a return to the principles of *What Is To Be Done?*.

Having dismissed the organisational explanation, I have argued that the principle issues separating Lenin from Trotsky from 1905 onwards were the theory of permanent revolution and its inherent internationalism, and Trotsky's conciliationism with regard to the Mensheviks. Thus, when the developments of the Russian situation and the outbreak of the First World War led to the resolution of these differences, the way was cleared for Trotsky and Lenin to unite within a single party — a most pragmatic outcome in view of the revolutionary events of the period.

Trotsky at a picnic, early 1940

Antonio Carlo

Trotsky and the Party

From *Our Political Tasks* to the October Revolution[1]

I

Our Political Tasks is not among the most easy of Trotsky's works to read. This is so, firstly, because its literary style is not Trotsky at his best, and so difficulties of interpretation arise. Secondly, it is difficult to situate the work historically within the monumental political and literary achievements of the great Russian revolutionary — especially since he renounced this work during the years of exile. He said: 'I wrote a brochure in 1904, *Our Political Tasks*, in which I developed some views on the question of organisation quite similar to those of Rosa Luxemburg... nonetheless all my later experience has shown me that in this controversy Lenin was right against Luxemburg, and against myself.'

So Trotsky repudiated his closeness to the positions of Luxemburg, whom he came to regard as a spontaneist during his years of exile. These statements of Trotsky's have given sustenance to the thesis, maintained by a number of historians (with Isaac Deutscher leading the field), that in 1917 Lenin accepted Trotsky's theory of permanent revolution, while Trotsky in turn accepted the Bolsheviks' theory of organisation, abandoning his youthful spontaneism in the process.[2] I think that this view is simplistic and wrong, if for no other reason than that, as we have tried to show elsewhere, after 1905 Lenin's views on organisation underwent a

1. This article first appeared in *Critique*, no 7, 1976.
2. I Deutscher, *The Prophet Armed: Trotsky 1879-1921*, Oxford, 1979, pp256-7.

radical change which brought him close to Rosa Luxemburg. This was not just a modification, or a richer elaboration of the organisational views of the *Iskra* period, as some, like Pierre Broué and Roger Garaudy, have maintained, but in fact an effective abandonment of those views.[3]

If we accept this premise, the entire relationship between Trotsky and Lenin on the problem of organisation merits a radical re-examination. This is what we intend to do, attempting in the process to crack a few historical nuts that may be represented roughly by the following questions. Firstly, what was the background against which the debate on organisation and the break between Lenin and Trotsky developed and matured? Secondly, why, after Lenin's shift of position in 1905, did the positions of the two revolutionaries, now almost identical, remain artificially apart until 1917? Thirdly, why did Trotsky himself give fuel to the view, objectively false, that he accepted the Leninist thesis, whereas the course of political and historical events was actually quite different?

II

The political situation of the Russian working class between 1890 and 1900 was characterised by the existence of social democratic circles which encouraged the emerging proletariat in its struggle. These activities were craft-oriented, and were organised, at best, by cadre still lacking broad experience, with few means, and lacking extensive ties with the rest of the vast country. Lenin was later to speak of this 'primitivism', which in its turn *nourished* the tendency to confine the struggle to the local, immediate and restricted situation of the factory — economism.[4] Today, however, we can see in hindsight that it would have been very difficult, given the conditions in Russia at the time, for the proletariat to have pursued its development without passing through some such phase, marked by the strong presence of 'economism', even if only briefly. Indeed, broad political discussion reaching beyond the walls of the factory would have required a stronger and more conscious working class which was capable of asserting itself as a hegemonic force in Russian civil society.

But a working class still politically green and only recently emerged from the peasantry, could not attain such a level all at once. It is understandable, therefore, that in its initial stages it was sensitive only to those problems which affected it in a direct and tangible way — the struggle around jobs. It is not surprising that economism, of which Lenin himself was one of the most advanced opponents,

3. See below, section IV; P Broué, *Le Parti Bolchevique*, Paris, 1977, pp30-31.
4. VI Lenin, 'What Is To Be Done?', *Collected Works*, Volume 5, Moscow, 1970, pp441ff.

should have dominated unchallenged until 1895-96.[5] It took the experience of defeats, and the growth of the proletariat brought about by the rapid development of industry in Russia, to compel the movement to pose the problem of moving on to a more advanced stage.

The first occasion for rethinking was provided by the failure of the great economic strikes of 1895-96. In the following year, 1897, Lenin, in two essays of major importance, was the first to pose the problem of politicising the struggle, a process without which even the economic goals would not be achieved.[6] Lenin clarified and radicalised this position in his later writings, and won the concurrence of many leading social democrats in exile, who were waging a fundamental struggle in the columns of *Iskra* against the old backward tendency of Russian social democracy. This backwardness, of course, tended to outlive the circumstances in which it had originally arisen, and indeed not all of those circumstances had changed. *What Is To Be Done?*, published in 1902, initially encountered no criticism from the Iskraists. At the Second Congress of the Russian Social Democratic Labour Party in 1903 there were few signs of battle, and the *Iskra* group seemed to retain cohesion throughout the first stages. This unity, however, eventually fell apart over the famous question of the conditions for party membership. As has been pointed out, by Deutscher for example, the seemingly marginal importance of this problem concealed a fundamental disagreement between those who wanted a solid party of experienced revolutionaries — Lenin and the Bolsheviks — and those who wanted a more open mass party analogous to the Western social democratic parties, which to a certain extent prefigured the legalist and reformist organisation of the post-autocracy period — Martov and the Mensheviks. This was the disagreement that split the party into two wings. Trotsky, however, who joined forces with the Mensheviks (with whom he remained only for one year), merits a separate discussion.

Trotsky was not a crypto-reformist, and this is shown both by his quick break with the right which occurred in the following year, and by the role he played in 1905. It was no coincidence that his positions brought him close to Luxemburg, whose criticisms of Leninism were certainly not reformist. No doubt the harshness with which Lenin treated Vera Zasulich and Pavel Axelrod (to whom Trotsky was quite close) did offend the young, combative 'Pen', but only with the effect of inducing him to clarify a number of critical positions, initially perhaps only latent, which Trotsky was not alone in holding in the RSDLP, as we shall see.

To understand the origins and the substance of the Lenin-Trotsky dispute at the Second Congress, we will have to return to the *Report of the Siberian Delega-*

---

5.   A Carlo, 'Lenin on the Party', *Telos*, no 17, pp3ff.
6.   Ibid, pp7ff.

tion, which Trotsky published immediately following the Second Congress, and which prefigured in broad outline the themes developed in *Our Political Tasks*. This text is of major importance in that it precedes Luxemburg's 'Organisational Questions of the Russian Social Democracy'[7] by one year, and anticipated the general theoretical discussion, although less profoundly, less calmly and without her polemical balance. Trotsky writes:

'If beforehand, during the "economist" period, these comrades could not or would not link the particular industrial interests they served with the general tasks of class politics, which they ignored, today, in the "political" period, they show themselves incapable of linking the tasks of the revolutionary political struggle (which they basically recognise only formally) with immediate, daily demands, in particular, the limited demands of specific trades. If beforehand, in the period of "dilettantism", they could not or would not link up in their consciousness the local detailed tasks with the need to create a central fighting apparatus common to the whole party; now, at the height of "centralism", they make a complete abstraction, in their considerations and resolutions about this apparatus, *of all the practical complexity and concrete character* of the tasks the party must carry out, tasks with which the organisational apparatus must conform, tasks which alone permit the existence of this apparatus. This is why, to go ahead a little, unilinear "centralism", that is the purely formal centralism put forward by Lenin, found its warmest supporters in certain ex-"economists". They were the ones who turned out to be the *hardest* "Iskraists".'[8]

As we can see here, Trotsky indicts economism for its corporatist limitations, as well as those theoreticians who postulated a consciousness wholly external to the relations and struggle within the factory — Lenin, in *What Is To Be Done?* — and he blamed the latter for the sin of abstraction. The solidly materialist assumption underlying such an argument is that a class cannot achieve consciousness solely on the basis of its specific social practice, dictated to it by the position it occupies in society; that is why Lenin's argument, divorced from the material situation of the proletariat, is abstract: in reality the 'politicians' had not surmounted the position of the economists, but had overturned it only mechanically, so to speak.

Trotsky further maintains that the form of organisation is not given a priori, but is a variable which is dependent on the politics that are its raison d'être. There you have, in a nutshell, the theory of organisation as a process, commonly attributed to Luxemburg.

---

7. Republished under the title 'Leninism or Marxism', in R Luxemburg, *The Russian Revolution and Leninism or Marxism*, Ann Arbor, 1961.
8. LD Trotsky, *Report of the Siberian Delegation*, London, nd, pp19-20.

The argument about the 'abstract nature' of the position of the 'politicians' was taken by Trotsky from a letter from a comrade that appeared in *Iskra* no 3 (later to be cited more extensively in *Our Political Tasks*), in which we find assertions analogous to that of Trotsky, and again antedating Luxemburg. Since this letter was published, it presumably expressed a real critical current within the RSDLP, so that Trotsky could write: 'Yes! The congress was the triumph of the "political tendency" in programme and tactics, and of the "centralist" tendency in organisation. But this same congress showed that for many comrades "politics" and "centralism" still only have *a purely formal meaning*, that they are only the empty antithesis of "economism" and "dilettantism".'[9]

Trotsky, therefore, anticipating Luxemburg's thesis, and hence independent of it, makes himself the spokesman of a current within the RSDLP that was critical of both the spontaneism of the economists and the abstract political agitationism of the 'politicians'.

III

Let us now quote from *Our Political Tasks*:

'In reality, our organisation long since ceased to subject itself to the requirements and needs of the "trade union" struggle, in particular of the form the fight frequently takes on: the strike. In the course of our struggle against "economism", to which we have opposed the practice of "political denunciations" on every occasion, not only have we completely unlearned the art of leading strikes, but we have begun to suspect all "trade" struggles in general, considering that they are not "politically sound".

'At the beginning of the new century, announced in Russia by such noisy events, the demonstration had already replaced the strike as a central means of struggle of local work. In a whole series of towns the activity of the committees began to be limited to preparing a street demonstration, in the course of which all — or nearly all — the forces of the committees were involved in organising an action which in fact was not always all that flamboyant. But a demonstration without a precise object, the demonstration against the existing regime "in general", the demonstration for its own sake, lost all its power of attraction once it ceased being a novelty... In the towns where demonstrations had already taken place, the masses were not so keen on facing the bayonets, bullets and nagaika (the Cossack lash) just to sing revolutionary songs and wave the red flag. Demonstrations will only rise up again... if they come out of the application of richer and more com-

9. Ibid, p18.

plex methods for integrating the masses into the sphere of matters of living political interests.'[10]

In my opinion, this extensive quote captures the central point of *Our Political Tasks*, and fits in well with the *Report of the Siberian Delegation* written a year earlier.

Trotsky thus criticises the fact that, whereas formerly there had been strikes devoid of any political content, now there were demonstrations devoid of any bearing on reality. In each case, the working class remained politically isolated. The real problem, on the other hand, was to raise political consciousness through daily struggle, otherwise the party would end up like the Polish Socialist Party, which had been reduced to an organisation that did nothing but produce printed matter. It is extremely interesting in this context to see the assessment that Trotsky makes a few pages later of how the economists proceeded practically; the concrete example he uses is the great strikes at Odessa in 1896. The economists worked with and among the masses, organising meetings and assemblies, discussing the details of the strike, and analysing their real concrete ability to resist the owners, preparing solidarity funds, etc.

The wrong approach? Certainly not; but one which must be taken up and integrated into a broader political perspective. Trotsky gives a symptomatic example as testimony to the totally unproductive practical course of action that the party was now pursuing in the political phase. In 1904 a Congress for Trade and Vocational Education met at St Petersburg. It was, in fact, a bourgeois assembly, which was to demand the overthrow of the autocracy, but would instead be dissolved by it. When the members of the party committee told the workers of the dissolution, one of them got up and said: 'And now what do we do?' Indeed the question of what attitude to take towards the congress had been reserved for the elite of the committee, so that when the workers finally got to know about it after the event, their reaction was naturally one of bewilderment: 'And what do we do now?'

Trotsky says that the party should have acted quite differently. As soon as they learned of the congress, they should have organised meetings and assemblies of workers to explain the event, and to encourage a broad debate about the possibility of presenting a list of political demands from the St Petersburg proletariat to the congress. The presence of police repression was no objection. That had existed in 1896 as well, and then it did not prevent the mass work of the economists. There were two possible reactions — either the congress (that is, the bourgeoisie) would accept it, and the proletariat would find itself at the vanguard of the struggle against Tsarism; or it would reject it, and then the politically ambiguous position

10. LD Trotsky, *Our Political Tasks*, London, nd, pp44-5.

of the bourgeoisie would have been clear to all. Either way, something would have been gained, for the proletariat would have been directly involved politically. Whereas what actually happened was that the whole opportunity was lost, and everything passed without issue. Trotsky pursues his criticism of 'substitutionism' implacably:

'The system of political substitutionism, exactly like the system of simplification of the "economists", proceeds — consciously or not — from a false and "sophistical" understanding of the relationship between the objective interests of the proletariat and its consciousness. Marxism teaches that the interests of the proletariat are determined by the objective conditions of its existence. These interests are so powerful and so inescapable that they finally oblige the proletariat to allow them into the realm of its consciousness, that is, to make the attainment of its *objective* interests its *subjective* concern. Between these two factors — the objective fact of its class interest and its subjective consciousness — lies the realm inherent in life, that of clashes and blows, mistakes and disillusionment, vicissitudes and defeats. The tactical farsightedness of the party of the proletariat is located entirely between these two factors, and consists of shortening and easing the road from one to the other...

'The greater the distance separating the objective and subjective factors, that is, the weaker the political culture of the proletariat, the more naturally there appear in the party those "methods" which, in one form or another, only show a kind of passivity in the face of the colossal difficulties of the task incumbent upon us. The political abdication of the "economists", like the "political substitutionism" of their opposites, are nothing but an attempt by the young Social Democratic Party to "cheat" history.'[11]

The party's necessary function as a driving force is thus neatly shielded against any suggestion of spontaneism; we are shown only that the party can and must develop the subjective factor on the basis of the objective factor — the real life situation of the proletariat. This, however, is not a simple forward moving, mechanical, unilinear process; it is a process marked by advances and retreats, disappointments and defeats — the dialectical process. To accuse Trotsky of being mechanistic on the basis of the short phrase at the beginning of the cited passage (working class consciousness will assert itself, sooner or later) is going too far; if there is any mechanistic thinking here it is due to the revolutionary optimism that has been the stock-in-trade of every great revolutionary. Actually, Trotsky appreciated quite well that the process is contradictory and complex, and in need of the party's

11.   Ibid, pp74-6.

active intervention, and this puts him in a position quite different from that of the economists, including the young Lenin. Up until this point Trotsky has only developed and specified the positions he put forth in the *Report* of the preceding year. There is one point, however, on which the work from 1904 shows signs of a direct influence of Luxemburg's famous article published shortly before, namely, where Trotsky, using almost the same words as Luxemburg, repeats the charge that Lenin wanted to impose a barracks discipline on the party, and forgot that social democratic centralism must not be a copy of the centralism of the capitalist factory, since the one is the expression of the discipline of a politically autonomous class, and the other is in general in the service of capitalist class interests.

In other words, a revolutionary party cannot be a 'social democratic factory'. An organisation aiming at the overthrow of capitalism cannot copy its organisation and division of labour, which are not at all neutral. So far, Trotsky's reasoning is flawless, but just at this point a contradiction appears in his argument: 'Without fear of betraying my "bourgeois intellectual psychology", I affirm firstly that the conditions which impel the proletariat into concerted, collective struggle are not to be found in the factory, but in the general social conditions of its existence...'[12]

Thus, impelled by the need to correct Lenin, Trotsky plays down the importance of factory conditions, to which he had given a central role up until then in *Our Political Tasks*. In that work, he had reproached the party for agitating around issues that were too general, and for neglecting strikes and occupational struggles, and he played up the activities of the economists which had been closely geared to factory struggles. However, 'the general social condition of the proletariat' becomes an empty abstraction if life in the factory is downgraded, since it is precisely this which is the source of the proletariat's alienated general social condition; factory life carries its influence beyond the factory — for example, a worker's leisure time is used to restore his labour power, and hence is a function of labour time and factory conditions. Unquestionably, the proletariat must challenge the capitalist organisation of labour. But to say that the party must not be a 'revolutionary factory' does not mean downgrading the important, and indeed indispensable, role in shaping political consciousness of economic struggles arising from antagonisms within the factory.

The reason for the appearance of this sudden contradiction in Trotsky's argument can be explained, I think, by the vehemently polemical style used by political protagonists at this period (which reflected the explosive social situation), who quite often took abrupt turns in order to follow and combat the polemical twists of their opponents' arguments. Thus, Lenin, confronted with the avalanche of

12. Ibid, pp102-3.

criticism of his views after the Second Congress, would find himself saying in *One Step Forward, Two Steps Back* that he had not underestimated factory relations since social democratic centralism had its roots in the centralism of the capitalist factory (which of course is not immune to the original criticisms). Trotsky clearly meant the first part of *Our Political Tasks*, in which strikes and occupational struggles are upgraded, to be an explicit or implicit polemic against Lenin's *What Is To Be Done?*, in which these elements are played down. The second part, on the other hand, takes up the battle against *One Step Forward, Two Steps Back*, where Lenin again stresses (with a dose of instrumentalism) factory relations. At this point Trotsky, still a young and relatively inexperienced polemicist, takes an abrupt, awkward and unforeseen turn in trying to follow polemically the zigzags of Lenin's argument, and ends up contradicting himself.

Despite this marginal lapse, this work of Trotsky's (which also outlines an historical interpretation of various extremely interesting highlights of the RSDLP) must be considered an important and quite timely work, judging from the quoted passages.

IV

In two articles published, as it happened, almost on each other's heels in April 1970, Marcel Liebman and I defend the position that Lenin made a radical shift in 1905 in his views regarding the party's relationship to the masses,[13] a shift which I think lasted until the beginning of 1919.[14]

To see this, one need only read the following two excerpts from Lenin typical of many others of a similar tone from the same period: 'It was not some theory, not appeals of the part of someone, or tactics invented by someone, not party doctrine, but the force of circumstances that led these non-party mass organs [the soviets — AC] to realise the need for an uprising, and transformed them into organs of an uprising.'[15] And further: 'The whole history of the Russian revolution [of 1905 — AC] shows that all the powerful upsurges of the revolutionary movement began only on the basis of such mass economic movements.'[16]

The autonomous revolutionary capacity of the masses — that is, a capacity that does not depend on the outside prompting of the *What Is To Be Done?* brand of

13. A Carlo, op cit, pp23ff; Marcel Liebman, 'Lenin in 1905', *Les Temps Modernes*, April 1970, and in English in *Monthly Review*, no 6, 1970.
14. A Carlo, op cit, pp29ff.
15. VI Lenin, 'The Dissolution of the Duma and the Tasks of the Proletariat', *Collected Works*, Volume 11, Moscow, 1972, p125.
16. VI Lenin, 'Draft Resolution for the Fifth Congress of the RSDLP', *Collected Works*, Volume 12, Moscow, 1972, p142.

theory — is clearly affirmed, and the resurgence of the revolutionary movement is linked to economic demands. At the same time, Lenin tries to give a more flexible and democratic structure to the party.[17] We must ask, then, why despite such a radical turn which aligns him with Trotsky and Luxemburg, Lenin remained at odds with his great adversary until 1917. Are historians like Pierre Broué right when they say that Lenin's inability to understand the soviets remained one of the key points in the split between the two? I should say definitely not.

Both Liebman and I drew attention to the fact that Lenin, in a letter to the Bolshevik newspaper in 1905, called on the party to undertake a radical revision of its negative attitude towards the soviets, pointing out that they were revolutionary bodies of prime importance that had to be joined without demanding in advance that they accept the social democratic programme, and that the party's own actions had to be rooted in the initiative and critical judgement of the masses.[18]

The real reason for the lasting split is therefore to be sought elsewhere. First of all, the letter sent by Lenin to the newspaper was not published — it first came to light in 1940 — so that one of the major documents with which Lenin initiated a brief but sharp struggle to impose the new pro-soviet line on the party leaders in Russia (Krasin and Bogdanov) remained unknown. Secondly, Lenin's volte face did not remain merely an idea just because of the silent opposition of the literati to the proletarianisation of the party[19] — the end of the soviets with the failure of the 1905 Revolution made it difficult to implement the new line. The result was that to many people the Bolsheviks' approach seemed in large measure to have remained just as it was during the period of the political circles.

Finally, if in 1905 the rupture between Lenin and Trotsky had in certain respects been objectively healed, in others it grew perceptibly deeper. At the time, Lenin was defending the notion of the democratic dictatorship of the workers and peasants, while Trotsky was putting forth his quite different notion of permanent revolution. A polemic therefore developed between the two on this key point, and in the overheated and confused atmosphere of retreat that prevailed, this could only aggravate the old differences. Lenin and Trotsky, therefore, remained unaware that they had come to see eye to eye on the problems of organisation, and it was not until 1917 that this agreement was able to find a political form.

By then the situation was changing radically. The gravity of the world crisis and the bankruptcy of the Second International in 1914 forced Lenin to reconsider

17. A Carlo, op cit, p25.
18. M Liebman, op cit; A Carlo, op cit, p23.
19. See L Amodio, 'Il contrasto Lenin-Rosa Luxemburg sulla organizzazione del partito', *Quaderni piacentini*, no 21, p11.

many of the past political blueprints which had quite often been linked to the positions of the 'centre' in the Second International.[20] In particular, the theory of the 'democratic dictatorship' was a leftist version of the theory of revolution by discrete stages (first the bourgeois, then the proletarian), which, with some variations, was typical of the dominant currents in the Second International, and had been accepted by Lenin.[21] The view to which Lenin came was that Russia would be unable to salvage the bourgeois stage because of the weakness of the local bourgeoisie, and that that phase could only be carried through by the workers and peasants. But the gravity of the world crisis which had exploded into an imperialist war was, as Lenin argued in *Imperialism* in 1916, the political expression of the seriousness of the contradictions within the system, and necessitated a re-evaluation of past policy. In the interim, the February Revolution broke out in Russia, the soviets reappeared, and the people wanted such simple things as bread, peace and land. These, however, were unattainable within a bourgeois democratic system, since the tremendous crisis rending imperialism was also removing any room for manoeuvre within the system, so that in order to give any concrete answer to the minimal demands of the masses, it was necessary to go beyond the framework of the bourgeois capitalist world. The socialist revolution was the order of the day, and Lenin's *April Theses* sanctioned his de facto conversion to the theory of permanent revolution.

On the other hand, the strong resurgence of the soviets allowed Lenin to take up again, and to develop, his positions on the soviets during 1905-07. Once again, they would not be accepted peacefully by the party, or rather by its leaders, since the members were with Lenin. In the end, however, Lenin's line would prevail, and the Bolsheviks would be the only organised political force capable of upholding the concept of a proletarian seizure of power in the face all other recognised forces (aside from the ambiguous, tardy and transitory alliance with the Left Socialist Revolutionaries). The ground was now cleared for Trotsky and the other independent social democrats to merge with the Bolsheviks. This, of course, would not happen all at once — you do not overcome 15 years of ferocious polemic and misunderstanding in a matter of a few weeks — but on the eve of October, Lenin and Trotsky would be on the same side.

V

If our foregoing argument is correct, then clearly the thesis that in 1917 Lenin and Trotsky underwent a reciprocal self-criticism, 50-50, is untenable. Even with regard to the problem of organisation, Lenin referred back to Trotsky's position; or,

---

20. See George Haupt, *Lenin e la seconda internazionale*, Roma, 1969.
21. VI Lenin, *Gli anni della reazione e della ripresa rivoluzionaria*, Roma, 1950, pp202-4.

to put it more precisely, the causes that had prevented them from bringing to light the convergence of views which had actually taken place in 1905 no longer operated. Nevertheless, in a certain sense it is wrong to say that Lenin accepted Trotsky's view; he had arrived at certain conclusions independently, on the basis of his own political experience, and without being overly concerned with the problem of theoretical primogeniture.

This said, one last problem remains. How and why did Trotsky repudiate these positions on organisation, which by 1917 had become the legacy of the entire Bolshevik leadership? To understand the development and efforts of Trotsky after 1919, we shall have to look briefly to the historical situation of Russia after 1919. In 1917 *The April Theses* and *State and Revolution*, with their focus on the soviets rather than on the party,[22] expressed the profound ties between the party and the masses, of which it was an integral part.

However, the situation was to get worse. The war and the economic crisis destroyed the best elements of the proletariat, which by 1920 had been reduced to a few hundred thousand harried and politically declassed members. Those of the best elements of the working class who survived were removed from production, and placed in administrative positions. Thus the last remaining members of the vanguard, separated from their class and from the terrain of production which they knew, became mere functionaries of the state; a state which, by this time, was absorbing increasing numbers of petit-bourgeois elements from the old state apparatus, because the dramatic situation that existed made it imperative that decisions be made and carried out, no matter how. All this was compounded by the unreliable nature of the peasantry in the specific Russian situation, the petit-bourgeoisie, and the imperialist encirclement which required an iron vigilance. The party, which was becoming more and more inseparable from the state, found itself in the position of having to nurture a society in disarray, in prohibitive historical conditions, without a mass base, with a politically passive proletariat socially reduced to little more than a cipher, and totally isolated in a hostile world.

These were the circumstances that caused the Bolsheviks to change their political perspective. From this time on they were increasingly to identify the dictatorship of the party with the dictatorship of the proletariat — substitutionism — and to view mass organisations like the unions as mere transmission mechanisms.[23]

This turn, historically conditioned, affected the entire leadership from Lenin and Trotsky to Stalin and Zinoviev, the Workers Opposition being the sole exception. Indeed, at the start it was Trotsky himself who took the hardest positions, in

22.   A Carlo, op cit, pp29ff; Ralph Miliband, 'Lenin's *State and Revolution*', *Socialist Register 1971*, London, 1971.
23.   A Carlo, op cit, pp33ff.

his celebrated brochure *Terrorism and Communism*. Trotsky's own self-criticism of this work, which he was later to make, concerned its extreme conclusions, not the premise from which they flowed, namely, that the dictatorship of the proletariat coincided with the party dictatorship. This premise was not up for discussion. Trotsky's entire polemic against Stalin in 1923-27 revolved only around the party, which was degenerating and needed to be revitalised, and which was becoming increasingly cut off from the masses. Even the most libertarian document of that epoch, the celebrated *Platform of the Joint Opposition*, which was a kind of summing up, written mainly by Trotsky and Zinoviev, is of this character.[24] Thus we read that the party has the power and must criticise and correct its own mistakes undauntedly — it must reintroduce workers' democracy everywhere, in the soviets, in the trade unions, and in the party itself. But to whom are these exhortations addressed? Trotsky and Zinoviev tell us when they paint a detailed and documented but disturbing picture of the situation in the party and of its social composition, giving the reader the distinct impression that the workers' party has no more than a name and a past. In practice, then, the demand amounts to calling for a restoration of workers' democracy to a party that is no longer a workers' party.

The Opposition omits totally any discussion of a 'cultural revolution' that would pit the masses against the leadership and bureaucratised middle layers of the party. We do not mean to say that there was any real possibility of such an occurrence at the time; there was not, for bureaucratisation had progressed so far by 1923 that a challenge to it from within Russia would have been very difficult. We wish only to emphasise a basic historical limitation of the platform that had been imposed by circumstances, but which was all the more material for that very reason.

To be sure, in 1927, on the tenth anniversary of the revolution, the Opposition tried to make a mass appeal again, but, as Deutscher describes so well, the crowd that marched by, silent and orderly, moved onwards indifferent to the group of leftist activists who, with their own banners and posters, were engaged in clashes with the police. This episode shows the totally distant and passive attitude of the masses towards the struggle for power; this was a struggle that had been going on for years within the party, in which even the Opposition had accepted a party-oriented conception. Deutscher further points out that the slogans could only have been comprehensible to party members, illustrating how through years of a party-centred praxis the Opposition itself had lost its ability to address the masses. No wonder then that this episodic, desperate and awkward effort failed.[25]

24. LD Trotsky and others, *The Platform of the Joint Opposition*, London, 1973. See also LD Trotsky, 'The Platform of the Opposition', *The Challenge of the Left Opposition, 1926-27*, New York, 1980, pp301-94.
25. I Deutscher, *The Prophet Unarmed: Trotsky 1921-1929*, Oxford, 1978, pp372-6.

During his years in exile Trotsky would maintain his party-centric approach — which had been shared by the entire Bolshevik leadership by 1919-20 — and when the Fourth International was founded, it would become The Party.

It is hard to see how the situation could have been different. Positions such as those of Rosa Luxemburg, the young Trotsky, and Lenin in *State and Revolution* arise on the eve or during periods of major social upheavals when the masses are quickened to autonomous activity. Trotsky's years of exile, on the other hand, corresponded to a phase in which the regressive tendencies that began to appear in 1919-20 had become consolidated and ossified. The Chinese revolution had ended in a sea of blood, in Europe the working class was on the defensive, and the spectre of fascism loomed large. In the Soviet Union, the bureaucracy had won out. The interludes in France and Spain in 1936 were too brief, were quickly brought under control, and were squelched.

In 1904 Trotsky noted that during periods of retreat the party tended to substitute itself for the masses, and play tricks with history. This prophesy was later to prove true for himself and the Fourth International, which was to identify itself as the revolutionary consciousness of a proletariat which on its own terms was social democratic or Stalinist.

There we have the reason for Trotsky's repudiation of his writings of 1903-04, and the legend that in 1917 he accepted Lenin's *Iskra* theses, etc.

Therein also we see the ambiguous and limited nature of Trotsky's criticism of Stalinism and his analysis of the social nature of the Soviet Union. It is a criticism that touches the effects and not the causes of the phenomenon, and remains bound by a conception of the relations between the party and the masses that had matured in 1919-20 and 1923-24, and was shared by both Trotskyists and Stalinists alike, although the former rejected its ultimate consequences. Only a few isolated intellectuals tried to go beyond this conception (Bruno Rizzi, for example) by seeking the real causes of the degeneration of the Soviet Union, but in doing so assumed a position that was too far ahead of the level of the masses; they therefore remained isolated, and did not even carry the modest weight of the Fourth International. We do not mean to say that Trotsky's critique was useless because it was only partial and limited by prohibitive historical factors. Indeed, a good amount of the truth can be gleaned from Trotsky's criticism (for to criticise the effects of a phenomenon does not mean that one is criticising nothing), and these insights were to serve as an obligatory point of reference and point of departure for succeeding generations on their way towards much more radical positions.

VI

Let us now sum up. Firstly, in 1903-04 Trotsky set forth a series of positions that to a large degree anticipated Luxemburg, and which were the expression of a real tendency within the RSDLP. Secondly, the disagreement with Lenin on the problem of organisation was overcome de facto in 1905-07, but because of a complex series of historical circumstances, the reconciliation with Lenin did not take place until 1917, and then most certainly not on the basis of the positions enunciated in *What Is To Be Done?*. Thirdly, in 1919-20 the Bolshevik leadership adopted a relatively bureaucratic position which Lenin and Trotsky also shared. Trotsky would essentially stick with that position even during the period of his criticism of Stalin. Fourthly, Trotsky's rejection of his writings of 1903-04 during this period expressed the abandonment of positions which by that time seemed questionable even to him, but which, far from being mistaken, were still alive and relevant.

Trotsky in his study during a discussion with American visitors, 1940

Stephen Dabydeen

Trotsky, the United States of Europe and National Self-Determination

Introduction

Trotsky's revolutionary career divides easily into his pre-revolutionary anti-Bolshevik and the post-revolutionary Bolshevik periods, the turning point being his rapprochement with Lenin and Leninism in mid-1917. It has been said that this momentous change of outlook and allegiance was the result of a trade-off with Lenin, in which the latter accepted Trotsky's idea of permanent revolution, while Trotsky in turn agreed to Lenin's conception of the revolutionary party.[1] Whether this is so is open to discussion. What is not open to dispute is the great gulf between them prior to 1917. This is vividly depicted in their frequent and violent denunciations of each other's positions during the prewar years. Trotsky started hostilities with his notoriously vehement and penetrating critique of Lenin's theory of revolutionary organisation set out in *What Is To Be Done?* and in speeches at the Second Congress of the Russian Social Democratic Labour Party.

---

1. See, for example, Ernest Mandel, *Trotsky: A Study in the Dynamic of his Thought*, London, 1979, p20.

Lenin was excoriated as a 'caricature Robespierre', demagogic and malicious, and his proposed reconstruction of the party was dismissed as 'the practice of organised mistrust [which] demands an iron fist'. Trotsky's *Our Political Tasks* more rigorously elaborated his famous charge of 'substitutionism' against Lenin's 'Jacobin' system: at its head will emerge a 'dictator' substituting himself for the Central Committee and ultimately for the party and the people.[2] The imputation to Lenin of an obsessively Blanquist design for power is the thematic core of Trotsky's assessment in these pre-October years.

From the other side, Lenin constructed a persisting image of Trotsky and his activities which was the exact opposite. His typical and recurrent criticisms ran as follows: 'Trotsky... possesses no ideological and political definiteness... [he freely flits]... from one group to another.'[3] 'It is impossible to argue with Trotsky on the merits of the issue, because Trotsky holds no views whatever. We can and should argue with confirmed liquidators and otzovists... in his case the thing to do is to expose him as a diplomat of the smallest calibre.'[4] Recalling the character created by his favourite novelist, M Saltykov-Shchedrin, in 1911 Lenin even referred to his opponent as 'Judas Trotsky'.[5] Lenin's unflattering view of Trotsky also emerges in his essay of 1914 on self-determination. 'Trotsky', Lenin averred, 'has never yet held a firm opinion on any important question of Marxism. He always contrives to worm his way into the cracks of any given difference of opinion and desert one side for the other.'[6]

Two questions naturally arise, and may be briefly considered here. The first is about the large analytical bases, spanning a range of theoretical and strategic issues, on which these uncomradely comments rest as superstructures — the tips, as it were, of two icebergs moving towards collision (and eventual coalescence) in the darkness of Russia's political backwardness. Those issues, as we might infer from the passages above, concerned the nature of the coming Russian revolution, the organisation for implementing it, the role of the peasantry and of Western proletarian aid, the conception of imperialism, and socialist participation in Russian (autocratic) politics. On these questions there was genuine rational disagreement between Lenin and Trotsky — for example, to Trotsky's programme for perma-

2. Baruch Knei-Paz's *The Social and Political Thought of Leon Trotsky*, Oxford, 1978, pp183ff, gives a convenient summary of Trotsky's earliest criticisms of Lenin.
3. VI Lenin, 'Disruption of Unity Under Cover of Outcries for Unity', *Collected Works*, Volume 20, Moscow, 1977, p331.
4. VI Lenin, 'Trotsky's Diplomacy and a Certain Party Platform', *Collected Works*, Volume 17, Moscow, 1977, p362.
5. VI Lenin, 'Judas Trotsky's Blush of Shame', *Collected Works*, Volume 17, op cit, p45.
6. VI Lenin, 'The Right of Nations to Self-Determination', *Collected Works*, Volume 20, op cit, pp447-8.

nent revolution Lenin opposed his concept of the revolutionary dictatorship of the proletariat and peasantry; and while Trotsky tended to underline the peasants' incapacity to organise and act independently, Lenin wanted to make use of the 'historically real and progressive historical content' of peasant socialism (as in his letter of 1909 to Skvortsov-Stepanov). There were also important specific differences over the attitude and tactics of Russian social democrats towards current political questions and alliances.[7]

The second question relates to the validity and fairness of the charges and counter-charges each man flung across the great divide within the RSDLP. Here a curious feature may be observed — each seemed to be accusing the other of sins he was apt to commit himself, while claiming virtues which he did not practise as consistently as he believed. We can reasonably argue in fact that they had more in common, before their convergence in 1917, than they and later historians were able to perceive. For Trotsky was as strict a centralist and disciplinarian as Lenin, and his concept of permanent revolution can be criticised for its corporate or collective Blanquism. Lenin on his part was more democratically inclined, out of 'moral' and prudential considerations, than Trotsky was willing to allow. On the other hand, it was more than a little ironic that Lenin should accuse Trotsky of a penchant for intrigue, petty diplomacy and opportunism. An eye for the main chance and a degree of 'flexibility' were prerequisites for success among the various fluid and scheming groups of Russian social democrats, as the instructive failure of Martov (and arguably of Trotsky himself) testifies. On theory, too, it was Lenin who did not hesitate to 'change his mind' or 'break new ground' (according to one's viewpoint) when the situation demanded. He did so in 1905-06 (especially on agrarian policy), in 1914, 1917 and again in 1921. The scale of convergence beneath the thick polemical cover gives credibility to Lenin's answer in July 1917, when asked what still kept him and Trotsky apart, that it was 'ambition, ambition, ambition'.[8]

Lenin and the United States of Europe

One issue, however, which really did keep Lenin and Trotsky apart during the First World War was the famous slogan of the United States of Europe. It has particular relevance for us because it arose out of deeper differences over the national question, and therefore makes a convenient point of entry for a discussion of

---

7. See VI Lenin, 'The Aim of the Proletarian Struggle in Our Revolution', *Collected Works*, Volume 15, Moscow, 1977, p370; 'The Historical Meaning of the Inner-Party Struggle in Russia', *Collected Works*, Volume 16, Moscow, 1977, p374, for his views on the main issues here.
8. I Deutscher, *The Prophet Armed: Trotsky 1879-1921*, London, 1954, p256.

Trotsky's ideas in that area; it incidentally throws more light on what we have said about Lenin's readiness to alter policies (here, in pursuit of a national Russian revolution), and on Trotsky's more steadfast and consistent stand on the necessity for international action.

The search for slogans that would rally support for a Russian revolution and at the same time express genuinely socialist ideals took up much of Lenin's energies in the early months of the war. The first formulation of such devices was in September-October 1914, when his group called for 'socialist revolution' in Western Europe, 'a democratic republic' in Russia, 'the conversion of the present imperialist war into a civil war... [as] the only correct proletarian slogan', and 'the formation of a republican United States of Europe'.[9] The difficulties involved in slogan-making were clearly illustrated in the case of the most notorious — the call to turn the imperialist war into a civil war. It was soon brought home to Lenin that this concept not only made him vulnerable to damaging accusations that he was anti-Russian and indifferent to the suffering of Russian soldiers, but was acting as an agent of German imperialism. He was obliged to respond, and he gradually toned down 'civil war' from being a positive good to being 'the lesser evil', while proclaiming in December 1914 his 'true' patriotism and national pride as a Great Russian.[10] 'Civil war' thus became 'revolutionary defeatism', and Lenin carefully refrained, as Deutscher has noted, from calling on his followers to engage in positive sabotage of the Russian war effort.[11]

The slogan of the United States of Europe first appeared in a set of theses on the war which Lenin presented to a group of Bolsheviks in Berne in the first week of September 1914. He wrote as one of their immediate slogans, 'propaganda for republics in Germany, Poland, Russia, etc, and for the transforming of all the separate states of Europe into a republican United States of Europe'.[12] A month later in his manifesto, 'The War and Russian Social Democracy', Lenin announced:

'The formation of a republican United States of Europe should be the immediate political slogan of Europe's social democrats. In contrast with the bourgeoisie, which is ready to "promise" anything in order to draw the proletariat into the

9. VI Lenin, 'The War and Russian Social Democracy', *Collected Works*, Volume 21, Moscow, 1977, pp33-4.
10. VI Lenin, 'On the National Pride of the Great Russians', *Collected Works*, Volume 21, op cit, pp102-6.
11. I Deutscher, op cit, p236.
12. VI Lenin, 'The Tasks of Revolutionary Social Democracy in the European War', *Collected Works*, Volume 21, op cit, p18.

mainstream of chauvinism, the social democrats will explain that this slogan is absolutely false and meaningless without the revolutionary overthrow of the German, the Austrian and the Russian monarchies.'[13]

It will be noticed that the slogan of a United States of Europe was intended to answer an assumed desire on the part of European workers for transnational cooperation (to stop present and future fighting), and to counter bourgeois exploitation of such sentiments. There was, however, an internal difficulty or contradiction in Lenin's scheme, between the call, on the one hand, for a United States of Europe and the aim, on the other, of overthrowing the Russian and Austrian empires, where self-determination, another slogan, would be both cause and effect in the process of secession. The difficulty was that a united Europe was really twice as far away as 'revolutionary overthrow' made it seem, since unification would only come about after self-determination had led to secession and a period of independent statehood for the former 'oppressed' nationalities. As this point emerged, it was not surprising that the slogan of the United States of Europe lost favour and survived only a few months as part of Bolshevik propaganda and policy. It was in effect jettisoned by the conference of foreign Bolsheviks in March 1915 when it was announced that 'on the question of the "United States of Europe" slogan the discussion was purely political, it being decided that the question be deferred pending a discussion in the press of the *economic* aspect of the matter'.[14] Four months later Lenin published the article which ended his party's involvement with that slogan.

By early 1915, therefore, Lenin was beginning to have serious doubts about the slogan of the United States of Europe. But it was not until August 1915 that he published his full reconsideration of the whole issue in the article 'On the Slogan for a United States of Europe', which was to become a crucial document in the later Stalin-Trotsky struggle. It therefore bears close examination.

Lenin began by noting 'the one-sided political character' of the debates on the United States of Europe proposals, and the neglect of its 'economic side... of the most important question of its economic content and meaning'. Somewhat paradoxically, he proceeded to defend the validity of the slogan of the United States of Europe as a purely political concept: 'To argue against such a [political] approach to the question while remaining entirely in the field of political analysis... is entirely erroneous', he declared. This was a reaffirmation of his steady commitment to the importance and autonomy of politics, political forms and political action,

13.   VI Lenin, 'The War and Russian Social Democracy', *Collected Works*, Volume 21, op cit, p33.
14.   VI Lenin, 'Conference of the Foreign Sections of the Bolsheviks', *Collected Works*, Volume 21, op cit, p158.

and underlined his favourable assessment of truly bourgeois democratic political ideals and institutions. We should note two elements in Lenin's positive evaluation of politics. The first was the idea of (bourgeois) democracy as a precondition of socialism: '... political changes of a truly democratic nature (we recall that the proposal of the United States of Europe depended on the prior "revolutionary overthrow" of the reactionary autocracies in Germany, Austria and Russia) can never obstruct or weaken the slogan of socialist revolution. On the contrary, they always make it nearer and widen the basis for it, drawing into the socialist struggle ever new strata...' The second element pertained to the non-economic dimensions of the process of socialism: 'Political revolutions', he reiterated, 'are inevitable in the course of a socialist revolution, which must not be looked upon as a single act, but must be considered as an epoch, a number of stormy political and economic upheavals, a most sharpened class struggle, civil war, revolutions and counter-revolutions.' This conception was of pivotal importance in Lenin's thinking. Therefore, he concludes, the slogan of the United States of Europe 'is entirely impregnable as a political slogan', that is, as a slogan for the democratic revolution which was a necessary condition for socialist change.

If that is the case, we may not unreasonably enquire, why discard the slogan at all? Lenin's answer added up to a definition of the limits and constraints on the autonomy of politics, his view of its ultimate dependence on 'economic content and meaning'. The United States of Europe was envisaged as a democratic entity, but however radical its democracy, he considered that it would still be circumscribed by the bourgeois capitalist economic framework, that is, to use the terms of Lenin's own characterisation of contemporary conditions, by the imperialist stage of capitalism. It was, he argued, this specific and ultimate form of capitalism and its imperatives that proponents of the slogan of the United States of Europe had tended to overlook. If we understand the concept 'United States' to include an idea of 'unification' and the idea of a 'state', the requirements or desiderata of imperialism could and would accommodate a 'state element' of a particular (conservative) nature, but would not tolerate for long the Europe-wide 'unification' which the left wing socialists had in mind. In Lenin's words, 'from the point of view of the economic conditions of imperialism, that is, capital exports and division of the world... the United States of Europe under capitalism is either impossible or reactionary'.[15]

Lenin validated the 'impossibility' part of this thesis by outlining what was a succinct preview of the theory of imperialism which he was then developing and would present more fully the following year. In the 'epoch of the highest capitalist

---

15. VI Lenin, 'On the Slogan for a United States of Europe', *Collected Works*, Volume 21, op cit, pp339-43.

development', he wrote, capital had become 'international and monopolistic, [and] the world has been divided among a handful of great powers'. Under capitalism 'only force is possible as the basis, the principle of division' — one cannot divide the income otherwise than in proportion to power, and power inevitably changes in the course of economic development. With capitalism, which is private property in the means of production and anarchy in production, 'equal economic progress of the individual concerns, or individual states, is impossible... and no other means for periodically re-establishing destroyed equilibrium are possible outside crises in industry or war in politics'. Uneven capitalist development meant that 'war is no contradiction to the foundations of private property... it is a direct and inevitable development of those foundations'. This Clausewitzian formula — Lenin was immersed in the works of the German military theorist at this time — signified that a United States of Europe, which was in fact the goal of the ultra-imperialists' strategy for dividing colonies 'justly', was an impossible dream. ('Dream', it is interesting to note, recurs as Lenin's frequent criticism of his left opposition's policies.)

He conceded that 'temporary agreements between capitalists and states are possible', but insisted that such a temporary union of the states of Europe would necessarily be deeply reactionary (the second part of his thesis), and totally unsuited to socialist aims or strategy, because its raison d'être was the desire, firstly, to combine against the proletariat and socialism in Europe, and, secondly, to preserve a backward and stagnating European economic hegemony in the colonial world against the more dynamic and dissatisfied emergent capitalisms of the USA and Japan: 'On the present day economic basis, that is, under (European) capitalism, the United States of Europe would mean an organisation of reaction for thwarting the more rapid development of America... The days when the cause of democracy and socialism was associated with Europe alone have passed forever.'

Having disposed of the question of the United States of Europe, Lenin could logically have ended his article at this point, but he felt it necessary to go on to deal with Trotsky's further reference to the United States of the World. It was in the course of criticising this idea, *not* the slogan of the United States of Europe, that Lenin made some of his most resonant and fateful remarks about socialist prospects. The United States of the World, he says, will become a reality 'only when the full victory of communism will have brought about the total disappearance of any state, including its democratic form'; in this sense the concept relates to the very distant future, not to any practical contemporary concern. 'As a separate slogan, however', Lenin continued, 'the United States of the World would hardly be a correct one, first, because it merges with socialism; second, because it might be wrongly interpreted to mean that the victory of socialism in a single country is impossible; and it may also create misconceptions as to the relations of such a country to the others.'[16]

This celebrated, even notorious, passage is explained by Lenin in a short paragraph.[17] The 'erroneous interpretation' he had in mind, but did not explicitly describe, was the view that the concept of the United States of the World entailed the notion of the simultaneity of the Russian and European revolutions; the 'misconceptions' created by this view included quietism, or, more precisely, the international socialist version of Lenin's oldest enemy, 'tail-endism', with its proposal (implied rather than stated by Lenin here) that socialists in one country should wait until all other countries were ready to start the revolution before themselves acting.

In Lenin's mind, the main theoretical weapon against such errors was the thesis that 'unequal economic and political development is an absolute law of capitalism'. It followed from this, against the 'simultaneity idea' which Trotsky may fairly be said to have championed, that 'the victory of socialism is, at the beginning, possible in a few capitalist countries, even in one, taken separately'.[18] This of course became the locus classicus of subsequent disputes where the theory of socialism in one country was claimed to have been first propounded authoritatively. We may sound a cautionary note and argue that Lenin's expression of the 'theory' was tentative and qualified, as the words 'beginning', 'possible' and 'even in one' indicate. More important, this single sentence on socialism in one (or a separate) country was not further explained, but was directly followed, in the rest of the paragraph, by Lenin's elucidation of his anti-quietist, anti-tail-endist, policy for the hypothetical first socialist regime.

Lenin's policy aim for that isolated socialist country was to use it as a base to spread the revolution immediately and uninterruptedly against the states that had not yet gone over to socialism: 'After expropriating the capitalists and organising their own socialist production, the victorious proletariat of that country will arise *against* the rest of the world — the capitalist world — attracting to its cause the oppressed classes of other countries, stirring uprisings in those countries against the capitalists, and in case of need using even armed force against the exploiting classes and their states.'[19] Lenin further suggested that the main rationale for the political

16. Ibid, p342.
17. At this point we should bear in mind that 'socialism' refers to the 'lower stage' of communism, as Marx defined it in his *Critique of the Gotha Programme*, and which will give way to 'full communism'. Lenin includes the revolution itself and its immediate reconstructive aftermath in his consistent and precise usage of 'socialism'.
18. VI Lenin, 'On the Slogan for a United States of Europe', *Collected Works*, Volume 21, op cit, p342.
19. Ibid.

form of the new socialist regime, the dictatorship of the proletariat, was 'more and more [to] concentrate' the forces of the socialist nation or nations for 'prolonged and stubborn struggle' against the capitalist states.[20] The overall impact of this militant policy statement was to modify considerably, reinforcing the verbal qualifiers noted, Lenin's 'anti-simultaneity' conception of socialism in one country, and so to bring his outlook much closer than is usually recognised for his pre-1917 period to Trotsky's conception of permanent or uninterrupted revolution. Whether the differences which undoubtedly remained between them, conveniently but misleadingly encapsulated in the phrase 'socialism in one country', are central or marginal was and is a matter for reasonable debate.

Trotsky and the United States of Europe

Unlike Lenin's tactical-propagandist adoption of this slogan, Trotsky's call for a United States of Europe grew logically out of his theory of 'the permanent character of revolution in an imperialist epoch', and of 'the subordination of belated national revolutions to the revolution of the proletariat'.[21] In November 1914, in articles which later formed the book *War and the International*, Trotsky called for the self-determination of subject nations, not as an end but as the means to their freely joining an international socialist system:

'In the present historical conditions, the proletariat is not interested in defending an anachronistic national "fatherland", which has become the main impediment to economic advance, but in the creation of a new, more powerful and stable fatherland, the republican United States of Europe, the foundation for the United States of the World. To the imperialist blind alley of capitalism, the proletariat can oppose only the socialist organisation of world economy as the practical programme of the day.'[22]

Notable here is Trotsky's characteristic emphasis on productive-technological needs and possibilities as the prime cause of historical change. A few months later, in February 1915, he brought into his argument the crucial political factors working for the viability of the concept of the United States of Europe when he asserted that 'the war was breaking up the nation-state, and was also destroying the

20. Ibid.
21. LD Trotsky, *History of the Russian Revolution*, New York, 1967, Volume 3, p56. See the whole later passage, which argues like earlier ones that a national revolution is 'a necessary link' in the struggle of the international proletariat.
22. Cited in I Deutscher, op cit, p214.

national basis for revolution', thus creating the conditions for simultaneous and interdependent socialist revolution in Europe.

Trotsky responded to Lenin's criticism directly and forcefully in the second part of an article in April 1916 entitled 'The United States of Europe'. We shall look first at his specific rebuttal of Lenin's argument, and then move on examine its general theoretical grounding in Trotsky's concept of self-determination:

'The only concrete historical consideration against the slogan of the United States of Europe was formulated by the Swiss *Social Democrat* [that is, Lenin] as follows: "The unevenness of economic and political development is the unconditional law of capitalism." From this the Swiss *Social Democrat* draws the conclusion that the victory of socialism is possible in one country, and that it is needless, therefore, to make the dictatorship of the proletariat in each isolated state conditional upon the creation of the United States of Europe.'[23]

Trotsky's further refutation rested on his crucial revision of Lenin's basic law of uneven capitalist development. He wrote: 'That the capitalist development of various countries is uneven is incontestable. But this unevenness is itself extremely uneven.' In concrete terms, the capitalist levels of England, Austria, Germany or France are not the same, but 'compared with Africa and Asia all these countries represent capitalist "Europe", which is ripe for social revolution'. Trotsky seemed to be moving towards an idea of 'socialism in one continent' in place of Lenin's 'socialism in one country'.

His further criticisms of Lenin's position showed up the thin line between opportunism and orthodoxy for revolutionary social democrats as they sought to utilise the war for their own purposes. On the one hand, Trotsky conceded to Lenin that 'it is necessary to repeat the elementary thought that no single country must "wait" for the others, lest the idea of parallel international action be supplanted by the idea of procrastinating international inaction'. He urged that revolutionaries should begin and continue the struggle on 'our own national soil',

---

23. This and following quotations, LD Trotsky, 'The United States of Europe' (early 1916), part 4 of the pamphlet *Programma Mira*, which consists of a series of articles published in January-April 1916. It is included in his collection *Voina i Revolyutsia*, part 2, 1923, pp459-82. It is this version which is used and referred to in the present discussion. (The *Programma Mira* is also to be found in Trotsky's *Sochineniya*, Volume 3, part 1, pp70-93.) I have quoted mainly from the translation made by John G Wright, entitled 'The Programme of Peace', which was published in the May 1942 issue of *Fourth International*, the journal of the US Socialist Workers Party, by Ceylonese Trotskyists in the booklet *What is a Peace Programme?*, Colombo, 1956, and in the Summer 1984 issue of *Permanent Revolution*, the journal of Workers Power, the British section of the League for a Revolutionary Communist International.

without waiting for others, in the certainty that their struggle will spark revolution in other countries. But he stuck to his central point that 'it is hopeless to think... that revolutionary Russia can maintain herself in the face of conservative Europe, or that a socialist Germany could remain isolated in a capitalist world'.

On the other hand, Trotsky at the same time (and more sharply) interpreted Lenin as going beyond this elementary truth about the initiating role of single countries, and 'succumbing to the same national narrowness that forms the content of social patriotism'. It was a startling accusation which bracketed Lenin, the scourge of the chauvinists, in the same category as Vaillant, Lensch, Chernov et al, who had sought to justify the defence of their respective nation on the grounds that it alone was the representative and champion of true socialist ideals. Trotsky went on to identify the precise element in Lenin's 'socialism in one country' which vitiated his attempt to 'view the prospects of social revolution within national frameworks'; he noted 'that in social patriotism there is, in addition to the most vulgar reformism, a national revolutionary messianism which regards its national state as chosen for introducing to humanity, "socialism" or "democracy", be it on the grounds of its industrial development or its democratic form and revolutionary conquests'. Any such defence, Trotsky declared, of 'the national base of the revolution' undermined proletarian internationalism and the revolution itself, 'which cannot begin otherwise than on the national basis, but which cannot be completed on that basis owing to the present economic and political-military interdependence of the European states... The slogan, "the United States of Europe", expresses this interdependence...'

In alleging a national-messianic factor at work in Lenin's abandonment of the United States of Europe proposal, Trotsky, we believe, undoubtedly had in mind Lenin's apparently ambivalent article of December 1914, 'On the National Pride of the Great Russians'. There Lenin, as if to affirm his Great Russian credentials, had eulogised the revolutionary democratic and socialist achievements of the Great Russian nation. Trotsky detected a further self-contradiction in Lenin's standpoint, between its alleged messianism and its clear rejection of defencism: 'If the problem of socialism were compatible with the framework of the national state, then it [socialism] would thereby become compatible with national defence.' In other words, if Lenin really believed that socialism could be established in, say, Russia, then he was logically bound to concede the necessity and the social democratic legitimacy of the defence of Russia against its enemies. The validity of 'socialism in one country' implied the validation of 'this messianism, bound up with the programme of national defence'.

There was a bitter double irony in this criticism, the full force of which can only be appreciated if we remember that 'national defence' was the hallmark of Second International socialism's 'treachery' and 'social chauvinism' in the eyes of Lenin and his revolutionary left wing comrades. Trotsky himself had on a previous page counterposed to 'the conservative defence of the antiquated national fatherland ', the 'creation [and presumably the defence] of a new higher "fatherland" of the revolution, republican Europe'. Secondly, and more important, Trotsky was correct in drawing out the implication of national defencism from the doctrine of socialism in one country, but was mistaken in thinking that he was thereby convicting Lenin of incoherence, for (excluding any reference to messianism) Lenin's policy of revolutionary defencism (the defence of the socialist Russian state, created by a democratic revolution) was presented as self-consistent and logical in essentially the same terms as Trotsky was using in his inferential argument here.

It was not only by immanent analysis, bringing to light dubious presuppositions and internal contradictions, that Trotsky sought to refute Lenin's rethinking on the idea of the United States of Europe, but also by head-on disagreement. He admitted the force of Lenin's main conclusion, that in the existing conditions of imperialist war (though their definitions of imperialism did not coincide) a unification of Europe would be at most partial and at best reactionary, since it would be in the form of a 'compulsory military tariff union' against 'the weak and backward peoples, and especially against their own working classes'. But against 'certain opponents of the programme of the United States of Europe' (that is, the Leninists) who focused on its 'reactionary monarchist-imperialist content', he boldly counter-attacked by asserting that 'it is precisely this prospect that provides the most graphic testimony in favour of the revolutionary viability of the slogan of the United States of Europe'. What, he asked in his best rhetorical manner, would be the best slogan for the European workers in the likely eventuality of such a reactionary union? Would it be the dissolution of the reactionary United States of Europe, and 'the return of all peoples under the roof of isolated national states', with the restoration of national tariffs, national currencies and social legislation, etc? Utilising a basic distinction, he argued that the revolutionary-proletarian programme could only be 'the destruction of the forced, anti-democratic form... and the preservation and consolidation of the foundations' of such imperialist unification. This fundamental point he put more uncompromisingly in a later passage: 'If the capitalist states of Europe succeeded in merging into an imperialist trust, this would be a step forward as compared with the existing situation, for it would first of all create a unified, all-European material base for the working class movement.'

It is instructive to compare Lenin's pessimism of will with Trotsky's optimism of intelligence at this juncture, one year or so into the war. In Lenin's mind, as we have noted: 'Europe as a whole denotes economic stagnation... under capitalism, the United States of Europe would signify an organisation of reaction to retard

America's more rapid development'.[24] Trotsky, on the other hand, saw even such a Europe as a decisive 'step forward', a structure uniquely ripe for conversion to a 'European Republican Federation' and then, without delay, ready for the revolutionary transition to a socialist United States of Europe. Trotsky combined in one passage his antipathy to Lenin's socialism in one country and demotion of Europe's revolutionary prospects, when he wrote: 'Europe is not only a geographic term, but a certain economic and cultural-historical community. The European revolution does not have to wait for the revolutions in Asia and Africa, nor even in Australia and America.'[25] And as we reflect on that first sentence, which is entirely consonant with Trotsky's general outlook, we begin to suspect that his description of a European 'community' is a subtle reconceptualisation of the continent as one nation or country containing and transcending the conventional component 'nations' such as Russia, Germany and England. We can go further and articulate what was the latent meaning of Trotsky's words; that it was this 'Europe-as-one-nation' which was the appropriate subject of Lenin's strategy of self-determination whose result would be really 'socialism in one country writ large', on a continental scale. The constituent 'nations' (in the ordinary sense) would then be conceived as the real subjects of Trotsky's own theory of self-determination which was designed and intended to facilitate at most a limited and temporary movement towards Lenin's idea of 'socialism in one country'.

Trotsky and Self-Determination

Trotsky's main argument against self-determination was 'that the national state has outlived itself — as a framework for the development of the productive forces, as a basis for the class struggle, and thereby also as a state form of the proletarian dictatorship'. Of these three categories, the first, the development of the productive forces, is given primacy and an emphasis which is typical of Trotsky's Marxism, in which 'production technology' needs and forces are sometimes described as if they constituted a determining, autonomous, teleonomic entity with the capacity to evaluate, and adopt or reject, political superstructures. Forms of the state, and concepts and structures of national self-determination were to be assessed in relation to the inexorable historical drive towards higher productivity, so that the system of independent national states (and therefore the right of each nation to independent statehood), which at one stage aided and assisted productive-economic growth,

---

24. VI Lenin, 'On the Slogan for a United States of Europe', *Collected Works*, Volume 21, op cit, p342.
25. This and following quotations, LD Trotsky, 'The United States of Europe', *Programma Mira*, part 4, op cit.

might at a later stage become a fetter on further development, and would need to be reconstructed or discarded. In this interpretation, the complex concept of the 'nation state' was reanalysed by Trotsky, and the 'state' component was expanded near to its breaking point, while the 'nation', the apparently more durable, probably permanent, entity, was given a new self-image.

The article 'The Right of Nations to Self-Determination', written in 1915-16, is the clearest presentation of Trotsky's position on this central and controversial question. He admitted the right of nations to self-determination as a 'democratically unquestionable right' on two somewhat different grounds. It was, firstly, a weapon in the struggle for a genuine (socialist) 'peace without annexations', and against imperialist war. Trotsky noted that self-determination in this sense was the historical bourgeois conception (which Lenin recognised) of the right of nations to separate national states ('the meaning of self-determination is the cancellation of existing states... state and economic decentralisation'). It was also the logical and effective 'internal' ideological riposte against imperialism, which Trotsky conceived as 'by its very nature expansive and aggressive', and 'aiming at the extension of state borders, at the compulsory incorporation of weak states... and the acquisition of new colonies'.[26]

However, as an exterior weapon against imperialist activities (aggrandisement, exploitation, war), this bourgeois conception of self-determination, historically attested and theoretically validated, was in Trotsky's mind limited and already obsolescent. Firstly, self-determination was claimed and exercised by the Great Powers themselves, who used it to justify the imposition of their will on weaker countries; in this way it had come to mean 'my might is my right'. Secondly, this right of self-determination could only be exercised by means of a referendum, and Trotsky's criticism here was (and remained) that 'this obligatory democratic response will... remain purely formal. It does not tell us anything about the real possibilities, ways and means of national self-determination under the modern conditions of capitalist economy.'

Most significant was his third reason, which takes us to the heart of Trotsky's argument. The conventional concept of self-determination tended towards the 'dismemberment of present states', 'economic decentralisation', the fragmentation of existing economic-political amalgamations into small, separate, national states. Trotsky asserted that such an outcome cannot and should not be accepted or promoted by socialists. In the first place, the facts were against it: 'the powerful centralist tendencies of imperialism, which has at its disposal the state organisation and its military power', will ensure that any 'new state boundaries will not be de-

---

26. This and following quotations, LD Trotsky, 'The Right of Nations to Self-Determination', *Programma Mira*, section 3.

cided on the basis of the national principle, but on the basis... of military forces'. More important than sheer military power was the inevitable direction of capitalism. Trotsky made this point in a parable or metaphor which is remarkable for its conciseness and penetration. If, he said, by a miracle Europe were to be partitioned again into fixed national states (through bourgeois self-determination), the national question would not thereby be solved: 'the very next day after this "just" national redivision, capitalist expansion would resume its work', creating conflicts, 'wars and new acquisitions in gross violation of the national principle' in all cases where that principle cannot be upheld by force of arms. 'It would all give the impression of inveterate gamblers being forced to divide the gold "justly" among themselves in the middle of the game, in order to start the same game all over again with redoubled frenzy' — and with the same outcome — a few big winners and many small losers.

Trotsky's argument flowed on towards its decisive turn: if, on the one hand, national self-determination meant and could only mean one thing — the historical bourgeois right to a separate national state, and if, on the other, imperialism was the unique, inevitable and natural development of capitalism, then socialists should despair, since the alternatives they faced would be futile heroics for the sake of national states doomed to obsolescence, or 'passive submission' to inevitable imperialist centralisation.

Trotsky moved to dissolve the dilemma by redefining the major terms of the syllogism: national self-determination was not essentially and eternally political, to be realised only in the formation of a national state, nor was imperialism the unique and inescapable form of the highest phase of capitalism. To put it concisely, Trotsky argued that the nation had become in the modern epoch an essentially cultural entity, as compared to the previous era when its economic-political nature was primary; and that imperialism was not (as the Leninist view had it) capitalism in its most developed 'natural' form, but an avoidable perversion of its highest stages. Buttressing these redefinitions was Trotsky's central theorem about 'the irresistible and deeply progressive tendency of modern economic life towards a planned organisation throughout our continent, and further all over the globe'. In the light of such reasoning, he urged socialists to shed no tears over even the imperialist crushing of separatist aspirations, and offered them a compensatory formula for an alternative, viable, non-Leninist concept of national self-determination.

Obsolete national states and distorted imperialist centralism did not invalidate respectively nationality and centralism. Dealing with the problem of the nation, Trotsky started with his key definition: 'A national community is the living hearth of culture, as the national language is its living organ, and these will still retain their significance through indefinitely long historical periods.' Social democrats, he went on, want and have the obligation to 'safeguard to the national community its freedom of development (or dissolution) in the interests of material and spiritual culture. It is in this sense that we have taken over from the revolutionary bourgeoisie the democratic principle of national self-determination as a political obligation' — meaning an obligation on the part of the centralised state, not on its component nations, to provide for national freedom of self-expression. We can expect, from the emphasis on culture and the context of imperialist expansion, that Trotsky's concept of self-determination would be a variation of the Austro-Marxist programme for national cultural autonomy; the rights of national groups as such cannot be allowed to go beyond such autonomy and demand the right to secede and set up independent states. 'The right of national self-determination', he insisted, 'cannot be excluded from the proletarian peace programme, but it cannot claim absolute importance. On the contrary, it is delimited for us by the converging [unifying], profoundly progressive tendencies of historical development.' (Lenin, too, we recall, had stressed the non-absolute nature of the social democrats' commitment to self-determination up to secession, but on political-strategic grounds, not Trotsky's economic-historical basis.)

The self-determination of nations must be one counterweight to imperialist centralisation which enslaved weak peoples and crushed 'the hearths of national cultures'. On the other hand, the proletariat cannot allow the national principle to hinder the progressive tendency towards larger and more integrated economic areas: 'From the standpoint of historical development and of the tasks of social democracy, the tendency of modern economy is fundamental, and it must be guaranteed the fullest opportunity of accomplishing its truly liberationist historical mission: to construct the united world economy, independent of national frames, state and tariff barriers...' Trotsky concluded his argument with the following conspectus on self-determination: 'Poles... Serbians and other small weak European nations not yet annexed may be reinstated or set up for the first time in the national configurations towards which they gravitate; above all they will be able to remain within these configurations and freely develop their cultural existence only to the extent to which as national groupings they will cease to be economic groupings, will not be bound by state borders, will not be separated from or opposed to one another economically.' Nations now split by and placed among different states can, of course, only be unified if those state boundaries are abolished, but they will only be able to survive and prosper within a single state framework enlarged 'as an economic but not as a national organisation, until it embraces the whole of capitalist Europe'. We may now see the sense and meaning of Trotsky's apparently paradoxical statement that 'the state unification of Europe is clearly a prerequisite of the self-determination of great and small nations of Europe'.

Trotsky, Europe and the Nation

It will be useful here to examine more closely Trotsky's idea of the political and economic unification of Europe which alone could offer the possibility of real 'national cultural existence' to all nations. It will have a federal structure, as one might expect from Trotsky's general sympathy with the Austrian Bauer-Springer constitutional principles. He declared that only a European federative republic can 'put flesh and blood' into the right to self-determination. Secondly, it will be a 'democratically united' Europe freed from state and tariff barriers, as opposed to the predatory, anti-democratic integration being enforced by imperialist war. Thirdly, it will be revolutionary in the radical-democratic sense, and therefore transitional towards the united, socialist world economy. The meaning of 'revolutionary' at this point in Trotsky's career will become clear when we analyse a passage in which he distinguished his self-determination concept from that of fellow (or rival) social democrats.

The touchstone for social democrats on the national question, from Marx and Engels onwards, had been Polish independence, and it is not surprising that Trotsky should use it to distinguish his viewpoint from that of Lenin. He criticised (without naming him) Lenin's stand in favour of Poland's political self-determination in contemporary circumstances. Trotsky argued that the 'independence of Poland... outside the European revolution' was not possible, given the 'immediate dependence of national self-determination of weak peoples on the (democratised) collective European regime'. Lenin's scheme was obliquely characterised as 'utopian'. Trotsky's second target was the German socialist chauvinists or ultra-imperialists (Lensch, Cunow), who had argued that imperialist expansion and integration had made the principle of national independence merely 'reactionary romanticism', clearly obsolete in any of its meanings, cultural, political or economic. The third group whose position he rejected were 'the simplifiers in our revolutionary camp' who had asserted that the principle of national independence [in the sense of cultural autonomy, Trotsky should have added] 'is realisable only under socialism and who thereby rid themselves of the necessity of giving a principled answer to the national questions which have been posed point blank by the war'. This seems unduly harsh on a group, which a footnote identified as 'the Polish (Rosa Luxemburg, Radek, etc) and the Dutch (Pannekoek) leftists', with whom Trotsky worked and thought closely on a range of important questions, especially against the Leninist fraction. The Polish left opposed Poland's unification and independence because it was espoused by nationalistic parties and also because it had been made obsolete by Poland's economic integration into Russian capitalist development. Trotsky was anxious to present a standpoint that combined recognition of the integration of the whole of Europe (and not only in the 'Poland-Russia' economic area), and acknowledgement of the enduring fact and value of national (cultural) consciousness.

At the centre of Trotsky's proposed solution to Europe's national questions lay his theory of imperialism, a phenomenon which he described 'as by its very nature both expansive and aggressive'. Trotsky, however, thought that it was the aggressiveness or violence of the expansion, rather than the expansionist drive in itself, that had made imperialism so overbearing and repugnant: 'The programme of violent unification of Europe is just as characteristic of German imperialism as it is the tendency of French imperialism...' We observed above that Trotsky saw imperialism as a perversion (or, more aptly, an abortion) of the natural industrial-capitalist evolution towards more centralised and planned economics. His clearest and most concise statement of this idea was as follows: 'Imperialism is the capitalist-thievish expression of this tendency of modern economy to tear itself completely away from the idiocy of national narrowness, as it did previously with regard to local and provincial confinement.' Trotsky identified the root of this distortion in political-historical rather than economic-theoretical causes: normal bourgeois-industrial processes had been, so to speak, hijacked by 'the powerful opposition of the landed and capitalist classes in whose hands the tariff apparatus, joined with that of militarism (without which the former means nothing), constitutes an indispensable weapon for exploitation and enrichment'. Trotsky emphasised the role of landowners and financial interests, and more generally, the narrow, selfish ambition of the less advanced and more backward-looking sectors of the national economies, which were ever ready to use military power and 'artificial' tariff barriers to block the flow of peaceful competitive market activities towards 'natural' economic concentration and centralisation. (Trotsky may be said to have anticipated in essentials Joseph Schumpeter's famous theory, published some years later, of imperialism as social atavism.) At this juncture, he was not concerned to discuss in greater detail the historical origins of imperialism, only to underline its deleterious consequences for economic productivity, and for conventional forms of self-determination.

Unlike Lenin, Trotsky did not believe that 'imperialism' (its social and economic structures, its war-matured consciousness) represented the eve of the socialist revolution, the last stage of capitalism which socialism could directly replace and build on without pause or delay. Such a base, in his view, could only be the industrial capitalist mode of centralisation, which had been developing until it was overthrown and displaced by violence-permeated, partial and reactionary imperialist centralism. Although lacking in detail, there is to be found in his wartime writings enough material to give us Trotsky's picture of that apparently lost paradise of industrial-capitalist centralism, the consolidation of the bourgeois 'urge towards unifying the European market'.

The mechanisms for such a process would have been the institutions of classical, free trade, liberal internationalism, indicated in the following passage: 'To bourgeois politics, the destruction of "internal" European customs houses is an insurmountable difficulty, but without this the interstate courts of arbitration and international law codes will have no firmer duration than, for example, Belgian neutrality.' On the basis of such legal machinery might have been built a common market quite different from 'the halfway complete and consistent economic unification of Europe coming from the top by means of an agreement of the capitalist governments'. Again in contrast to the imperialist oppression of weaker nations, the democratic nature of the industrial bourgeoisie's 'progressive' unification would have been evident and effective in the real 'autonomy of [European] nations' which would have accompanied and mediated that process.

The defeat of the bourgeoisie by the combined class forces making up imperialist reaction had meant, in Trotsky's view, the dominance of the imperialist models of European economic integration, with decisive negative consequences for economic efficiency, democratic practice and socialist prospects. It was, therefore, absolutely necessary to destroy imperialism and rehabilitate the bourgeois model in its essentials, but this could only be accomplished by revolution. Here we come to the pivotal point in Trotsky's argument: the bourgeoisie being now too demoralised to act, it fell to the proletariat to complete the bourgeois revolution, and to unify Europe democratically: 'Hence it is that the economic unification of Europe which offers colossal advantages to producer and consumer alike, in general to the whole cultural development, becomes the revolutionary task of the European proletariat in its struggle against imperialist protectionism and its instrument, militarism.'

To Trotsky's mind, then, the first proletarian revolution would therefore be a 'bourgeois (radical bourgeois) revolution', with the aim of creating an efficient capitalistic economy that would be capable of producing the materially wealthy society which the second proletarian revolution, the socialist revolution proper, would push forward to socialist construction. The idea of the proletariat having to complete the bourgeoisie's revolution against the bourgeoisie, or rather to renovate the bourgeois machinery of production, was not unique to Trotsky — it was also the controlling concept in Lenin's system, but while Lenin held it to be suitable only for the Russian situation, Trotsky more audaciously applied it to the whole European economic area:

'The programme of the European [proletarian] revolutionary movement would be: the destruction of the compulsory, anti-democratic form of the coalition [that is, imperialist unification], and the preservation and extension of its foundations, in the form of the complete abolition of tariff barriers, unified legislation, especially labour laws, etc. In other words, the slogan "the United States of Europe" — without monarchies and standing armies — would... become the unifying and guiding slogan of the European revolution.'

European Federation and Cultural Autonomy

We should pause to distinguish three propositions which Trotsky tended to run together in his uninterrupted line of thought. Firstly, that the victory of the proletariat over imperialism will install the Europe-wide dictatorship of the proletariat; secondly, that the task of this proletarian state will be to implement the bourgeois-type unification of Europe; and, thirdly, that this essentially 'economic union of Europe' will be the basis for the subsequent socialist revolution and reconstruction. The complex combination of these ideas is to be seen, for example, in statements such as the following: '... over against the conservative defence of the antiquated national fatherland we place the progressive task, namely, the creation of a new higher "fatherland" of the revolution, republican Europe, whence the proletariat alone will be enabled to revolutionise and to reorganise the whole world.'

In Trotsky's estimate, a united republican Europe (a fortiori, the Europe of imperialist warmongers) would not be immediately ripe for socialist revolution, but would have to experience further increases in productivity and efficiency, made possible only by capitalist-type unification, which Marxists have always taken to be a necessary condition for socialist construction. This sort of regime was usually labelled transitional, but it is more usefully and precisely called revolutionary-democratic, the ultimate stage in the evolution of bourgeois industrial capitalism. Owing to circumstances unforeseen by the classical theorists, it would come after an 'imperialist' interval, and just before socialism. Trotsky saw such an order as both terminal and transitional: 'Between our present social condition [imperialism] and socialism there lies an extended period of social revolution, that is, the epoch of the open proletarian struggle for power, the conquest and application of this power with the aim of the complete democratisation of social relations, and the systematic transformation of capitalist society into the socialist society.' That statement was not merely rhetorical, but described the exact sequence of processes Trotsky envisaged, firstly, the social democratic conquest of power from the imperialists in the first revolution (as we call it), then the pushing of bourgeois democracy to its real limits which are far more extensive than existing practice suggested, and thirdly, the transition to socialism by means (as the next sentence indicates) of the 'expanding experiments of the proletarian regime and socialist reforms', which will at some point constitute the second, properly socialist, revolution.

We must now consider the nature of European unity, for which the social democratic revolution designed to restore and complete capitalist-industrial-democratic forms can and should aim. Trotsky usually referred to the United States of Europe, as in these statements: 'The United States of Europe is the slogan of the revolutionary epoch into which we have entered... The United States of Europe — without monarchies, standing armies and secret diplomacy — is therefore the most important integral part of the proletarian peace programme...', and (in his concluding sentence): 'The United States of Europe represents the form — the only conceivable form — of the dictatorship of the European proletariat.'

We noted that two fundamental factors led Trotsky to this construct — the irresistible processes of centralisation and expansion, and his linguistic-cultural concept of the nation. Imperialism was implicitly defined in Trotsky's scheme of things as centralism dictated by and subservient to (ultra) nationalistic politics (or political nationalism); against this specific form, his United States of Europe would be both a weapon and an alternative. However, closer inspection shows that Trotsky used the formula of the United States of Europe to convey two distinguishable forms or stages which, in our interpretation, tacitly corresponded to the two types or stages of the proletarian revolution. In the short term, he had in mind unification in the form of federation, and he consistently referred to 'a European Federative Republic' as the immediate aim of the revolution after or as part of the overthrow of imperialism. There are three or four passages in this sense — for example, 'the conversion of the imperialist trust into a European Republican Federation'. In the medium term, there would follow the more rigorously centralised 'state unification of Europe' which he envisaged as the mature constitutional form for full 'economic union of Europe', corresponding to what we described above as his continent-wide variant of 'socialism in one country'.

Trotsky did not explicitly defend or explain his proposed federal structure, but we may suggest some of the considerations that must have entered his mind. Firstly, in aligning himself with the theorists who supported cultural national autonomy as the sufficient expression of self-determination, he would naturally have been drawn to their further demand for federal state systems to replace the existing multinational empires. He felt no need to go into the detailed institutions of the European Federation since he probably comprehended it as patterned on the general lines of the Austrian proposals developed a decade earlier by the Austro-Marxists Renner and Bauer. On a different level, it is also not improbable that Trotsky intended a further and deliberate snub against Lenin, whose dislike for federalism, in both party and state organisation, had already been made plain in numerous articles, and whose preference was strongly in favour of the break-up of the Eastern empires into various successor nation states, rather than any federation of the nationalities in place of the ancien régime.

The federal scheme also possessed a certain logistical fitness in the immediate context of Trotsky's own argument for European economic union. For the old established historic nations of Europe, like France, England and Germany, it would represent a 'step down' from their now obsolescent nation state, and involved, in Trotsky's implicit argument, a not intolerable transfer of some sovereignty (in economic affairs mainly) to the central authority, while retaining autonomy and self-respect in other spheres. On the other hand, for the hitherto oppressed, stateless, 'non-historic' nations, federation would be a 'step up', from subjection and fragmentation to equal and secure national identity and autonomy in the sense that mattered most, their language and culture. Trotsky may be thought of as envisaging a gradual convergent movement of both groups towards equality, and towards cultural autonomy for all nations 'under the roof of a democratically unified Europe freed from state and tariff barriers'. We refer to one last passage which summarises Trotsky's thinking at this point in his career to substantiate our interpretation of a two-stage unification (reflecting the two-stage revolution engineered by the party of the proletariat): 'The founding of a stable regime of proletarian dictatorship would be conceivable only if it extended throughout Europe, and consequently in the form of a European Republican Federation. The state unification of Europe, to be achieved neither by force of arms nor by industrial and diplomatic agreements, would in such a case become the unpostponable task of the triumphant revolutionary proletariat.'

There is one other response from Trotsky to Lenin's critique of the slogan of the United States of Europe, which is of interest here. In Trotsky's earliest references to the 'republican United States of Europe', it was not clear whether this was to be a radical bourgeois-democratic or a social democratic entity. Lenin's critique had demonstrated the impossibility or regressiveness of the former concept (that is, of a united, democratic, imperialist Europe), but he had not similarly ruled out meaningful democratic revolutions in individual states. Trotsky seemed to have accepted this point, and moved to clarify his own revolutionary scheme. 'The democratic, republican union of Europe', he acknowledged, 'is possible only... by means of revolts... in individual countries, with the subsequent confluence of these upheavals into a collective European revolution.' The victorious European revolution, he continued, 'no matter how its repercussions may be fashioned in the various countries, can, in consequence of the absence of other revolutionary classes, transfer power only to the proletariat. Thus the United States of Europe represents the only conceivable form of the dictatorship of the European proletariat.' Here Trotsky was restating his early concept, with a weaker emphasis on the 'simultaneity' and uniformity of revolutions. The United States of Europe would come at the end of the first revolution, not as a precondition of the revolution. He thus deflected Lenin's strictures against the notions of a democratic United States of Europe and a socialist United States of the World by proposing in effect the slogan of a socialist United States of Europe, 'socialism in one continent'.

'We have every reason to hope', he had declared, 'that during the course of the present war a powerful revolutionary movement will be launched all over Europe. It is clear that such a movement can only succeed as a general European one. Isolated within national borders, it would be doomed to failure.' Addressing himself directly to Lenin's main ambition and anxiety, he wrote: 'The salvation of the Russian revolution lies in its propagation all over Europe... and if in one of the European countries the proletariat should snatch the power out of the hands of the bourgeoisie, it would be bound, if only to retain its power, to place it at once at the service of the revolutionary movement in other lands.' Nearly everything here would have been agreeable to Lenin, except perhaps Trotsky's characteristic and (to Lenin) probably reckless readiness, in prophetic words, to 'place power [that is, revolutionary Russia's power] at once at the service' of other revolutionary movements.

Trotsky at a picnic, December 1939

Michael Löwy

From the *Logic* of Hegel to the Finland Station in Petrograd[1]

'A man who talks that kind of stupidity is not dangerous.' (Stankevich, a socialist, April 1917)

'That is raving, the ravings of a lunatic!' (Bogdanov, a Menshevik, April 1917)

'They're mad dreams...' (Plekhanov, a Menshevik, April 1917)

'For many years the place of Bakunin in the Russian revolution has remained vacant; now it is occupied by Lenin.' (Goldenberg, an ex-Bolshevik, April 1917)

'On that day [4 April], Comrade Lenin could not find open sympathisers even in our own ranks.' (Zalezhsky, a Bolshevik, April 1917)

'As for the general scheme of Lenin, it seems to us unacceptable in that it starts from the assumption that the bourgeois-democratic revolution is ended, and counts upon an immediate transformation of this revolution into a socialist revolution.' (Kamenev, in an editorial in *Pravda*, organ of the Bolshevik party, 8 April 1917)

Such was the unanimous reception accorded by the official representatives of Russian Marxism to the heretical theses which Lenin had presented first to the crowd massed in the forecourt of the Finland Station in Petrograd from the top of an ar-

---

1. This article first appeared in *Critique*, no 6, 1976.

moured car, and then, on the morrow, to the Bolshevik and Menshevik delegates of the Soviet: *The April Theses*. In his celebrated memoirs, Sukhanov (a Menshevik, later to become a Soviet functionary), testifies that Lenin's central political formula — 'All power to the Soviets' — 'echoed like a thunderclap from a clear blue sky', and 'stunned and confused even the most faithful of his disciples'. According to Sukhanov, one leading Bolshevik had even declared that 'the speech [of Lenin] had not sharpened the differences within the social democracy, but had, on the contrary, suppressed them because there could be only agreement between the Bolsheviks and Mensheviks in face of Lenin's position!'.[2] The *Pravda* editorial of 8 April confirmed at the time that impression of anti-Lenin unanimity; according to Sukhanov: 'It seemed that the Marxist rank and file of the Bolshevik party stood firm and unshakeable, that the mass of the party was in revolt against Lenin to defend the elementary principles of the scientific socialism of the past; alas, we were mistaken!'[3]

How are we to explain the extraordinary storm which Lenin's words raised, and this chorus of general condemnation that came down on them? Sukhanov's simple but revealing description suggests the reply.

Lenin had done just that — he had *broken with* the 'scientific socialism of the past', with a particular way of understanding the 'elementary principles' of Marxism, a way which was, to some extent, common to all currents of Marxist social democracy in Russia. The perplexity, the confusion, the indignation or the scorn with which *The April Theses* had been received at one and the same time by Menshevik and Bolshevik leaders are only the symptoms of the radical break they imply with the Second International's tradition of 'orthodox Marxism' (we refer to that of the ruling current, and not to that of the radical left; Rosa Luxemburg, etc), a tradition for which materialism (mechanical, deterministic, evolutionary) was crystallised into a rigid and paralysing political syllogism: Russia is a backward, barbarous, semi-feudal country. It is not ripe for socialism. The Russian revolution is a bourgeois revolution. QED.

Rarely has a turn in theory been richer in historic consequences than that inaugurated by Lenin in his speech at the Finland Station in Petrograd. What were the *methodological sources* of that turn? What were the *differentia specifica* in method compared with the canons of the Marxist orthodoxy of the past?

Here is Lenin's own reply, written in a polemic directed *precisely against Sukhanov* in January 1923: 'They all call themselves Marxists, but their conception of Marxism is impossibly pedantic. They have completely failed to understand what is decisive in Marxism, namely, its revolutionary dialectics.'[4] *Its revolutionary dia-*

2. N Sukhanov, *The Russian Revolution of 1917*, Paris, 1965, pp39, 140, 142.
3. Ibid, p143.
4. VI Lenin, 'Our Revolution', *Collected Works*, Volume 33, Moscow, 1976, p476.

lectic — here, in a nutshell, is the precise point of Lenin's *break* with the Marxism of the Second International, and to some extent with *his own 'past' philosophical consciousness*. Beginning on the morrow of the First World War, the break was nourished by a return to the Hegelian sources of Marxist dialectics, coming to a head in the monumental, 'mad', 'raving' challenge of the night of 3 April 1917.

I. 'Old Bolshevism' or 'Past Marxism': Lenin pre-1914

One of the chief sources of Lenin's political thinking prior to 1914 had been Marx's *The Holy Family* of 1844, which he had read and summarised in a notebook in 1895. He had been particularly interested by the chapter headed 'Critical Battle Against French Materialism', which he described as 'one of the most valuable in the book'.[5] Now, this chapter constitutes the *only* writing of Marx in which he 'clings', in *non-critical* fashion, to the French materialism of the eighteenth century, which he presents as the 'logical basis' for communism. The quotations drawn from this chapter of *The Holy Family* provide one of those shibboleths which make possible the identification of 'metaphysical' materialism in a Marxist current.

On the other hand, it is a clear and well-known fact that Lenin was, at that time, greatly influenced *in his philosophical outlook* by Plekhanov. While being *politically* more flexible and radical than his master, who, after the 1903 break, became the principal theoretician of Menshevism, Lenin accepted certain fundamental ideological premises of Plekhanov's 'pre-dialectical' Marxism and his strategic corollary — the *bourgeois* nature of the Russian revolution. With this 'common basis' it is not difficult to understand how, despite his severe and intransigent criticism of the 'tailism' of the Mensheviks in regard to the liberal bourgeoisie, he had been able to accept from 1905 to 1910 several attempts at reunification of the two factions of the Russian social democracy. Moreover, it was at the moment of his closest political rapprochement with Plekhanov (against liquidationism in 1908-09) that he wrote *Materialism and Empirio-Criticism*, a work in which the philosophical influence of the 'father of Russian Marxism' can be seen and read.

What is remarkable and altogether characteristic of Lenin prior to 1914 is that the Marxist authority to whom he often referred in his polemic against Plekhanov was none other than Karl Kautsky. For example, he finds in an article by Kautsky of 1906 on the Russian revolution 'a direct blow aimed at Plekhanov', and he underlines enthusiastically the coincidence of the Kautskyist and Bolshevik analyses: 'A bourgeois revolution, brought about by the proletariat and the peasantry in

5.   VI Lenin, 'Conspectus of *The Holy Family*', *Collected Works*, Volume 38, Moscow, 1972, p41.

From the *Logic* of Hegel to the Finland Station in Petrograd

spite of the instability of the bourgeoisie, this fundamental principle of Bolshevik tactics is wholly confirmed by Kautsky.'[6]

A close analysis of Lenin's main political text of this period, *Two Tactics of the Social Democracy in the Democratic Revolution* of 1905, reveals with extraordinary clarity the *tension* in Lenin's mind between his rich, revolutionary realism and the limitations imposed on him by the straitjacket of what was called 'orthodox' Marxism. On the one hand, we find in it illuminating and penetrating analyses of the incapacity of the Russian bourgeoisie to lead successfully a democratic revolution, which can be carried out only by an alliance between the working class and peasantry exercising their revolutionary dictatorship; he even speaks of the *leading role* of the proletariat in this alliance, and, at times, seems to put his finger on the idea of an uninterrupted transition towards socialism — this dictatorship 'will be unable (without a series of intermediary stages of revolutionary development) to affect the foundations of capitalism'.[7] With this little parenthesis, Lenin opens a window on the unknown country of the socialist revolution, only to close it immediately to return to the closed area circumscribed by the limits of orthodoxy. These limits we find in numerous formulae in *Two Tactics*, where Lenin categorically reaffirms the bourgeois nature of the Russian revolution, and considers that 'the idea of seeking salvation for the working class in anything save the further development of capitalism is reactionary'.[8]

The main argument he offers to develop this thesis is the 'classic' theme of 'pre-dialectical' Marxism — Russia is not ripe for socialist revolution:

'The degree of Russia's economic development (an objective condition) and the degree of class consciousness and organisation of the broad masses of the proletariat (a subjective condition, inseparably bound up with the objective condition) make immediate and complete emancipation of the working class impossible. Only the most ignorant people can close their eyes to the bourgeois nature of the democratic revolution which is now taking place.'[9]

---

6. VI Lenin, 'Preface to the Russian Translation of Karl Kautsky's Pamphlet *The Driving Forces and Prospects of the Russian Revolution*', Collected Works, Volume 11, Moscow, 1972, p411.
7. VI Lenin, 'Two Tactics of the Social Democracy in the Democratic Revolution', Collected Works, Volume 9, Moscow, 1972, p56.
8. Ibid, p49. On the previous page we read: 'Marxists are absolutely convinced of the bourgeois character of the Russian revolution. What does that mean? It means that the democratic reforms in the political system, and the social and economic reforms that have become a necessity for Russia, do not in themselves imply the undermining of capitalism, the undermining of bourgeois rule; on the contrary, they will, for the first time, really clear the ground for a wide and rapid, European, and not Asiatic, development of capitalism; they will, for the first time, make it possible for the bourgeoisie to rule as a class.'
9. Ibid, p28.

The objective determines the subjective; the economy is the condition of consciousness: here, in two phrases are the Moses and the Ten Commandments of the materialist gospel of the Second International which weighed upon Lenin's rich, political intuition.

The formula which was the quintessence of prewar Bolshevism — 'old Bolshevism' — reflects within itself all the ambiguities of the first Leninism: 'the revolutionary dictatorship of the proletariat and the peasantry'. Lenin's profoundly revolutionary innovation (which marks it off radically from the Mensheviks' strategy) is expressed in the flexible and realistic formula of *workers' and peasants' power*, a formula of 'algebraic' character (as Trotsky put it), where the specific weight of each class is not determined a priori. On the other hand, the apparently paradoxical term '*democratic dictatorship*' is the shibboleth of orthodoxy, the visible presence of the limitations imposed by 'past' Marxism: the revolution is only democratic, that is, *bourgeois*, a premise which, as Lenin wrote in a revealing passage, 'flows necessarily from the whole of Marxist philosophy', that is to say, Marxist philosophy as conceived by Kautsky, Plekhanov and the other ideologists of what it was agreed to call at the time 'revolutionary social democracy'.[10]

Another theme in *Two Tactics* which testifies to the methodological obstacle created by the *analytical* nature of that Marxism, is the explicit and formal rejection of the Paris Commune as a model for the Russian revolution. According to Lenin, the Commune went wrong because it was 'unable... [to] distinguish between the elements of a democratic revolution and a socialist revolution', because it 'confused the tasks of fighting for a republic with those of fighting for socialism'. Consequently, 'it was a government such as ours [the future provisional revolutionary government — ML] should not be'.[11] We shall see later that this is precisely one of the nodal points around which Lenin was to undertake, in April 1917, the heartbreaking revision of 'old Bolshevism'.

II. The 'Break' of 1914

'It's a fabrication of the German High Command', declared Lenin when they showed him the copy of *Vorwärts* (the organ of the German social democracy) with the news of the socialist vote for the war credits of 4 August 1914. This fa-

---

10. The only (or almost the only) exception to this iron rule was Trotsky, who was the first in *Results and Prospects* (1906) to go beyond the dogma of the bourgeois-democratic nature of the future Russian revolution; he was, however, politically neutralised by his organisational conciliationism.
11. VI Lenin, 'Two Tactics of the Social Democracy in the Democratic Revolution', *Collected Works*, Volume 9, op cit, pp80-1.

mous story (like his stubborn refusal to believe that Plekhanov had supported the 'national defence' of Tsarist Russia) illustrates at one and the same time the illusions Lenin held about 'Marxist' social democracy, his astonishment when confronted with the failure of the Second International, and the abyss that was opening between himself and the 'ex-orthodox' who had become social patriots.

The catastrophe of 4 August was for Lenin striking evidence that something was rotten in the state of Denmark of official 'orthodox' Marxism. The political bankruptcy of that orthodoxy led him, therefore, to a profound revision of the philosophical premises of the Marxism of Kautsky and Plekhanov: 'The failure of the Second International in the first days of the war incited Lenin to reflect on the theoretical foundations of so great a betrayal.'[12] It will be necessary one day to retrace the precise track which led Lenin from the trauma of August 1914 to the *Logic* of Hegel, scarcely a month after. The simple desire to return to the sources of Marxist thought? Or a clear intuition that the methodological Achilles' heel of the Marxism of the Second International was the non-comprehension of the dialectic?

Whatever the reason, there is no doubt that his vision of the Marxist dialectic was profoundly changed by it. Evidence of this is the text itself of the *Philosophical Notebooks*, and also the letter he sent on 4 January 1915, shortly after having finished reading *The Science of Logic* on 17 December 1914, to the editorial secretary of Granat Publishers to ask if 'there was still time to make some corrections [to his 'Karl Marx'] in the section on dialectics'.[13] And it was by no means a 'passing enthusiasm' as, seven years later, in one of his last writings, 'On the Significance of Militant Materialism' of 1922, he called on the editors and contributors of the party's theoretical journal *Under the Banner of Marxism* to 'be a kind of "Society of Materialist Friends of Hegelian Dialectics"'. He insists on the need for a 'systematic study of Hegelian dialectics from a materialist standpoint', and proposes even to 'print in the journal excerpts from Hegel's principal works, interpret them materialistically, and comment on them with the help of examples of the way Marx applied dialectics'.[14]

What were the tendencies (or at least, the attempts) in the Marxism of the Second International which gave it its pre-dialectical character?

In the first instance, primarily, the tendency to efface the distinction between Marx's dialectical materialism and the 'ancient', 'vulgar', 'metaphysical' material-

12.   R Garaudy, *Lénine*, Paris, 1969, p39.
13.   Ibid, p40.
14.   VI Lenin, 'On the Significance of Militant Materialism', *Collected Works*, Volume 33, op cit, pp233-4. This is very contemporary today when attempts are being made once more to write off old Hegel on Lenin's authority.

ism of Helvetius, Feuerbach, etc. Plekhanov, for example, could write these astonishing lines: 'In Marx's *Theses on Feuerbach*... none of the fundamental ideas of Feuerbach's philosophy are refuted; they merely amend them... the materialist views of Marx and Engels have been elaborated in the direction indicated by the inner logic of Feuerbach's philosophy!' What is more, Plekhanov criticised Feuerbach and the French materialists of the eighteenth century for having too... idealist an outlook in the domain of history.[15]

Secondly, the tendency, which flows from the first, to reduce historical materialism to mechanical economic determinism in which the 'objective' is always the cause of the 'subjective'. For example, Kautsky untiringly insists on the idea that 'the domination of the proletariat and the social revolution cannot come about before the preliminary conditions, as much economic as psychological, of a socialist society are sufficiently realised'. What are these 'psychological conditions'? According to Kautsky, 'intelligence, discipline and an organisational talent'. How will these conditions be created? 'It is the historical task of capitalism' to realise them. The moral of history: 'It is only where the capitalist system of production has attained a high degree of development that economic conditions permit the transformation, by the power of the people, of capitalist property in the means of production into social ownership'.[16]

Thirdly, the attempt to reduce the dialectic to Darwinian evolution, where the different stages of human history (slavery, feudalism, capitalism, socialism) follow a sequence rigorously determined by the 'laws of history'. Kautsky, for example, defines Marxism as 'the scientific study of the evolution of the social organism'.[17] Kautsky had, in fact, been a Darwinian before becoming a Marxist, and it is not without reason that his disciple Brill defined his method as 'bio-historico-materialism'.

Fourthly, an abstract and naturalistic conception of the 'laws of history', strikingly illustrated by the marvellous pronouncement of Plekhanov when he heard the news of the October Revolution: 'But it's a violation of all the laws of history!'

Fifthly, a tendency to relapse into the *analytical* method, grasping only 'distinct and separate' objects, fixed in their differences: Russia-Germany; bourgeois revolution-socialist revolution; party-masses; minimum programme-maximum programme, etc.

15. GV Plekhanov, *Fundamental Problems of Marxism*, London, nd, pp21-2. 'Marx's theory of cognition is directly derived from Feuerbach's. If you like, we can even say that, strictly speaking, it is Feuerbach's theory... given a profounder meaning in a general way by Marx.'
16. K Kautsky, *The Social Revolution*.
17. K Kautsky, *The Agrarian Question*. Plekhanov, on the other hand, had, at least in principle, criticised vulgar evolutionism, basing himself on Hegel's *Science of Logic*.

It is clearly understood that Kautsky and Plekhanov had carefully read and studied Hegel, but they had not, so to speak, 'absorbed' and 'digested' him into their preceding systems of evolutionism and historical determinism.

How far did Lenin's notes on (or about) Hegel's *Logic* constitute a challenge to pre-dialectical Marxism?

In the first instance, Lenin primarily insists on the philosophical abyss separating 'stupid', that is, 'metaphysical, undeveloped, dead, crude' materialism from Marxist materialism, which, on the contrary, is nearer to 'intelligent', that is, dialectical, idealism. Consequently, he severely criticises Plekhanov for having written nothing on Hegel's *Great Logic*, 'that is to say, *basically* on the dialectic as philosophical knowledge', and for having criticised Kant from the standpoint of vulgar materialism rather than in the manner of Hegel.[18]

Secondly, he acquires for himself a dialectical understanding of causality: 'Cause and effect, ergo, are merely moments of universal reciprocal dependence, of (universal) connection, of the reciprocal connection of events...' At the same time, he approves the dialectical process by which Hegel dissolves the 'opposition of solid and abstract of subjective and objective, and destroys their one-sidedness'.[19]

Thirdly, he underlines the major difference between the vulgar evolutionist conception and the dialectical conception of development: 'the first [development as decrease and increase, as repetition] is lifeless, pale and dry; the second [development as a unity of opposites] alone furnishes the key to the "leaps", to the "break in continuity", to the "transformation into the opposite", to the destruction of the old and emergence of the new'.[20]

Fourthly, with Hegel, he struggles 'against making the concept of *law* absolute, against simplifying it, against making a fetish of it', (and adds: 'NB for modern physics!!!'). He writes likewise that 'laws, all laws, are narrow, incomplete, approximate'.[21]

Fifthly, he sees in the category of sum-total, in the development of the entire ensemble of the moments of reality, the essence of dialectical cognition.[22] We can see the use Lenin made immediately of this methodological principle in the pamphlet he wrote at the time, *The Collapse of the Second International*; he submits to severe criticism the apologists of 'national defence' — who attempt to deny the imperialist character of the Great War because of the 'national factor' of the war of the Serbs against Austria — by

18. VI Lenin, 'Conspectus of Hegel's *Science of Logic*', and 'Conspectus of Hegel's *Lectures on the History of Philosophy*', *Collected Works*, Volume 38, op cit, pp179, 278, 277.
19. Ibid, pp159, 187, 260.
20. VI Lenin, 'On the Question of Dialectics', *Collected Works*, Volume 38, op cit, p360.
21. VI Lenin, 'Conspectus of Hegel's *Science of Logic*', *Collected Works*, Volume 38, op cit, p151.
22. Ibid, pp157-8.

underlining that Marx's dialectic 'correctly excludes any isolated examination of an object, that is, one that is one-sided and monstrously distorted'.[23] This is of capital importance, since, as Lukács says, the reign of the dialectical category of sum-total brings the revolutionary principle into science.

The isolation, fixation, separation and abstract opposition of different moments of reality are dissolved in part through the category of sum-total, in part by the statement of Lenin's that 'the dialectic is the theory which shows… why human understanding should not take contraries as dead and petrified, but as living, conditioned, mobile, interpenetrating each other'.[24]

Obviously, what interests us here is less the study of the philosophical content of the *Notebooks* 'in themselves' than their *political consequences*. It is not difficult to find the red thread leading from the methodological premises of the *Notebooks* to Lenin's theses of 1917; from the category of sum-total to the theory of the weakest link in the imperialist chain; from the interpenetration of opposites to the transformation of the democratic revolution into the socialist revolution; from the dialectical conception of causality to the refusal to define the character of the Russian revolution solely by Russia's 'economically backward base'; from the critique of vulgar evolutionism to the 'break in continuity' in 1917; and so on, and so on. But what is most important is quite simply that the critical reading, the materialist reading of Hegel, had *freed* Lenin from the straitjacket of the pseudo-orthodox Marxism of the Second International, from the *theoretical limitation* it imposed on his thinking. The study of Hegelian logic was the instrument by means of which Lenin cleared the theoretical road leading to the Finland Station in Petrograd. In March-April 1917, freed from the obstacle represented by pre-dialectical Marxism, Lenin could, *under the pressure of events*, rid himself in good time of its *political corollary*: the abstract and rigid principle according to which 'the Russian revolution could only be bourgeois because Russia was not economically ripe for a socialist revolution'. Once he crossed the Rubicon, he applied himself to studying the problem from a *practical, concrete and realistic* angle: what are the measures, constituting in fact the transition towards socialism, that could be made acceptable to the majority of the people, that is, the masses of the workers and peasants?

III. *The April Theses* of 1917

The truth is that *The April Theses* were born in March, more exactly, between 11 and 26 March, that is to say, between the third and fifth 'Letters from Afar'. Close

---

23. VI Lenin, 'The Collapse of the Second International', *Collected Works*, Volume 21, Moscow, 1977, p235.
24. VI Lenin, 'Karl Marx', *Collected Works*, Volume 21, op cit, p23.

analysis of these two documents (which, by the way, were not published in 1917) allows us to grasp the very movement of Lenin's thought. To the main question — can the Russian revolution take transitional measures towards socialism? — Lenin replies in two ways; in the first (Letter 3) he questions the traditional answer, in the second (Letter 5) he gives a new reply.

Letter 3 in itself contains two juxtaposed moments in unresolved contradiction. Lenin describes certain concrete measures in the sphere of control of production and distribution which he considers indispensable for the advance of the revolution. He first underlines that these measures are *not yet socialism*, or the dictatorship of the proletariat; they do not go beyond the limits of the 'revolutionary democratic dictatorship of the proletariat and the peasantry'. But he immediately adds this paradoxical short passage which clearly suggests a doubt about what he has just said, that is, an explicit questioning to the 'classical' theses: 'It is not a matter of finding a theoretical classification. We would be committing a great mistake if we attempted to force the complex, urgent, rapidly developing practical tasks of the revolution into the Procrustean bed of cut and dried theory...'[25]

Fifteen days later, in the fifth Letter, the abyss has been crossed, the political break consummated: 'In their entirety and in their development, these steps [control of production and distribution, etc] will mark the transition to socialism, which cannot be achieved in Russia directly, at one stroke, without transitional measures, but is quite achievable and urgently necessary as a result of such transitional measures.'[26] Lenin no longer refuses to make a 'theoretical classification' of these measures, and he defines them not as 'democratic' but as transitional to socialism.

Meanwhile, the Bolsheviks in Petrograd remained loyal to the old schema (they were trying to lay the Russian revolution, that unmanageable, unconquered and liberated maid, in the Procrustean bed of a petrified theory...), and were sitting tight in prudent silence. *Pravda* of 15 March even gave conditional support to the Provisional (Cadet!) Government 'to the extent that it fights the reaction and counter-revolution'; according to the frank statement of the Bolshevik leader Shliapnikov, in March 1917, 'we agreed with the Mensheviks that we were passing through the period of the breakdown of feudal relations, and that in their place would appear all kinds of "freedoms" proper to bourgeois regimes'.[27]

One can understand, then, their surprise when the first words Lenin addressed at the Finland Station in Petrograd to the crowd of workers, soldiers and sailors, were a call to struggle for the socialist revolution.[28]

25.   VI Lenin, 'Letters From Afar', *Collected Works*, Volume 23, Moscow, 1974, p330.
26.   Ibid, p341.
27.   LD Trotsky, *The History of the Russian Revolution*, London, 1977, pp302, 305.
28.   See F Somilov, 'Memoirs of Lenin', in *Lénine tel qu'il fut*, Moscow, 1958, p673. Cf also the

On the evening of 3 April, and on the next day, he revealed *The April Theses*, which produced, according to the Bolshevik Zalezhsky, a member of the Petrograd Committee, *the effect of an exploding bomb*. Moreover, on 8 April this same Petrograd Committee *rejected Lenin's theses by 13 votes to two, with one abstention*.[29] And it must be said that *The April Theses* were to some extent a *retreat* from the conclusions already reached in the fifth of the 'Letters from Afar'; they do not speak explicitly of the transition to socialism. It seems that Lenin, in face of the astonishment and perplexity of his comrades, was forced to moderate his words somewhat. In fact, *The April Theses* do speak of the *transition* between the first stage of the revolution and the second, 'which must give the power to the proletariat and the layers of the poor peasants', but that is not necessarily in contradiction with the traditional formula of the old Bolshevism (except for the mention of the 'layers of the poor peasants' instead of the peasantry as a whole, which is clearly very significant) since the content of the tasks of this power (democratic only, or already socialist?) is not defined. Lenin even underlines that: 'It is not our *immediate* task to "introduce" socialism, but only to bring social production and the distribution of products at once under the *control* of the Soviets of Workers Deputies.'[30] — a flexible formula where the character of the content of this 'control' is not defined. The only theme which, at least implicitly, is a revision of the former Bolshevik conception is that of the state-commune as a model for the Republic of Soviets, and for two reasons; firstly, traditionally, the commune had been defined, in Marxist literature, as the first attempt at *the dictatorship of the proletariat*; and, secondly, Lenin himself had characterised the commune as a workers' government

---

stenographic notes of Lenin's first speech taken by the Bolshevik Bonch-Bruevich at the railway station: 'You must struggle for the socialist revolution, struggle to the end, till the complete victory of the proletariat. Long live the socialist revolution!' (G Golikov, *La Révolution d'Octobre*, Moscow, 1966)

29. LD Trotsky, op cit, chapter 14. Cf EH Carr, *The Bolshevik Revolution*, Volume 1, London, p77: 'Nobody had yet contested the view that the Russian revolution was not, and could not be, other than a bourgeois revolution. This was the solid and accepted framework of doctrine into which policy had to fit. Yet it was difficult to discover within this framework any cogent reason to reject out of hand the Provisional Government, which was indubitably bourgeois, or at least a transfer of power to the Soviets, which were essentially proletarian, or — least of all — to denounce the quest for a "democratic" peace and preach civil war and national defeat. It was left to Lenin, before the eyes of his astonished followers, to smash the framework.' Cf also the testimony of the Bolshevik Olminsky, quoted by Trotsky (op cit, p335): 'The coming revolution was to be only a bourgeois revolution… That was an obligatory premise for every member of the party, the official opinion of the party, its continual and unchanging slogan right up to the February Revolution of 1917, and even some time after.'

30. VI Lenin, 'The Tasks of the Proletariat in the Present Revolution', *Collected Works*, Volume 24, Moscow, 1977, p24.

which had wished to carry through *simultaneously a democratic and a socialist revolution*. That was why Lenin, prisoner of 'past Marxism', had criticised it in 1905. For the same reason, Lenin, the revolutionary dialectician, *took it as a model* in 1917. The historian EH Carr is, therefore, correct in underlining that Lenin's first articles after his arrival in Petrograd 'implied the transition to socialism, though it stopped short of explicitly proclaiming it'.[31] Explication was to be made during the month of April, in proportion as Lenin won the rank and file of the Bolshevik party to his political line. It was made especially around two axes: the revision of 'old Bolshevism' and the perspective of the transition to socialism. The major text on this subject is a small pamphlet — not well known — *Letters on Tactics*, composed during 8-13 April, probably under the pressure of the anti-Lenin editorial in *Pravda* on 8 April. There we find the key phrase which summarises the historic turn Lenin made, and his definitive, explicit and radical break with what had become outlived in the 'past Bolshevism': 'The person who *now* speaks only of a "revolutionary democratic dictatorship of the proletariat and the peasantry" is behind the times, consequently, he has in effect *gone over* to the petit-bourgeoisie against the proletarian class struggle; that person should be consigned to the archive of "Bolshevik" pre-revolutionary antiques (it may be called the archive of "old Bolsheviks").'[32] In this same pamphlet, while defending himself against wishing to introduce socialism 'immediately', Lenin declares that the Soviet power would take 'steps... towards socialism'. For example, 'control over a bank, the merging of all banks into one, is *not yet* socialism, but is *a step towards* socialism'.[33]

In an article published on 23 April, Lenin defined in the following terms what distinguished the Bolsheviks from the Mensheviks; while the latter are 'for socialism, but it is too early to think of it or to take any immediate practical steps for its realisation', the former think the 'soviets must immediately take all possible practicable steps for its realisation'.[34]

What does 'possible practicable steps' for the realisation of socialism mean? For Lenin, it means especially *the measures that can receive the support of the majority of the population*. That is, not only of the workers, but also of the peasant masses. Lenin, freed from the theoretical limitation imposed by the pre-dialectical schema — 'the going-over to socialism is objectively unrealisable' — is now occupied with

---

31. EH Carr, op cit, p82.
32. VI Lenin, 'Letters on Tactics', *Collected Works*, Volume 24, op cit, p45. Lenin adds: 'Is this reality covered by Comrade Kamenev's old Bolshevik formula which says that "the democratic revolution is not completed"? It is not. The formula is obsolete. It is no good at all. It is dead. And it is no use trying to revive it.' (p50)
33. Ibid, p53.
34. VI Lenin, 'Political Parties in Russia and the Tasks of the Proletariat', *Collected Works*, Volume 24, op cit, p97.

real, political-social conditions to ensure 'steps towards socialism'. So, in his speech to the Eighth Congress of the Bolshevik party (24-29 April), he poses the problem in a realistic and concrete way:

'What we should talk about, however, are concrete steps and measures. We cannot be for "introducing" socialism — this would be the height of absurdity. We must preach socialism. The majority of the population in Russia are peasants, small farmers who can have no idea of socialism. But what objections can they have to a bank being set up in each village to enable them to improve their farming? They can say nothing against it. We must put over these practical measures to the peasants in our propaganda, and make the peasants realise that they are necessary.'[35]

The 'introduction' of socialism, in this context, means the immediate imposition of socialism 'from above', against the will of the majority of the population. Lenin, on the contrary, proposes getting the support of the peasant masses for certain concrete measures, of an objectively socialist character, taken by the soviet power (with workers' leadership). To within a few degrees, this conception is astonishingly like that defended by Trotsky since 1905: 'The dictatorship of the proletariat supported by the peasantry' that effects the *uninterrupted* going over from the democratic revolution to the socialist. So, it is not by chance that Lenin was regarded as a 'Trotskyist' by the 'old Bolshevik' Kamenev in April 1917.[36]

Conclusion

There is no doubt that *The April Theses* represent a 'break' in theory and policy with the prewar tradition of Bolshevism. That said, it is nonetheless true that, to the extent that Lenin had since 1905 preached the revolutionary alliance of the proletariat and the peasantry (and the radical deepening of the revolution *without* or even *against* the liberal bourgeoisie), the 'new Bolshevism', born in April 1917, is the true heir and legitimate child of the 'old Bolshevism'.

On the other hand, if it is undeniable that the *Philosophical Notebooks* constitute a philosophical break with the 'first Leninism', it must be recognised that the methods *in action* in the political writings of pre-1914 Lenin were much more 'dialectical' than those of Plekhanov or Kautsky.

---

35. VI Lenin, 'Report of the Central Committee', *Collected Works*, Volume 24, op cit, pp241-2.
36. See LD Trotsky, *The Permanent Revolution*, New York, 1974, Chapters 3 and 4. It should not be forgotten, on the other hand, that for Lenin as much as for Trotsky, there was an 'objective limit' for socialism in Russia, to the extent that a completely socialist society — abolition of classes, etc — could not be established in an isolated and backward country.

Finally, and to avoid any possible misunderstanding, we in no way wish to suggest that Lenin 'deduced' *The April Theses* from Hegel's *Logic*... The theses are the product of revolutionary, realistic thinking in the face of a new situation — the world war, the objectively revolutionary situation it created in Europe, the February revolution, the rapid defeat of Tsarism, the massive appearance of the soviets. They are the result of what constitutes the very essence of the Leninist method — *concrete analysis of a concrete situation*. The critical reading of Hegel helped Lenin to free himself from an abstract, cut-and-dried theory that was *an obstacle to this concrete analysis* — the pre-dialectical pseudo-orthodoxy of the Second International. It is in this sense and in this sense only that we can speak of the theoretical journey that led Lenin from the study of the *Great Logic* in the library at Berne in September 1914, to the challenging speech that 'shook the world', launched for the first time on the night of 3 April 1917 in the Finland Station in Petrograd.

David Gorman

The Political Economy Of Defeat

Leon Trotsky and the Problems of the Transitional Epoch[1]

In his article on Trotsky's political economy of capitalism, Hillel Ticktin has presented a compelling analysis of the central category of Trotsky's thought, the transitional epoch. Although it was the basis of Trotsky's political practice from 1922 onwards, it has not previously been discussed in a critical manner. In contrast to the dogmatic certainties expressed in more orthodox circles, Ticktin's approach is refreshingly open and questioning. It is, indeed, a fine example of the kind of critical approach that will be necessary if Trotskyism is to reorient itself to the realities of the coming period. For this reason his argument deserves serious consideration.

For Ticktin, the category of the transitional epoch is 'Trotsky's crucial theoretical innovation'.[2] It is 'the period during which the old order is objectively declining but the revolutionary forces of the working class have yet to defeat the old

1. Earlier versions of this paper were presented at the Conference of Socialist Economists in Leeds in July 1994, and in debate with Hillel Ticktin and Mick Cox ('Trotsky, Trotskyism and the Transitional Epoch') at Conway Hall, 30 September 1994. An extended version appears in *Radical Chains*, no 5. Thanks to Gordon Alderson, Mick Cox, Rob Delaney, William Dixon, Mark Etkind, Alun Francis, Mike Neary, Annie Pike, Bob Shepherd, Hillel Ticktin and Lisa Ward for comments and criticism.
2. H Ticktin, 'Trotsky's Political Economy of Capitalism', in T Brotherstone and P Dukes (eds), *The Trotsky Reappraisal*, Edinburgh, 1992, p226, and reproduced in this volume.

ruling class'.[3] While acknowledging that 'Trotsky never produced a political economy of the transitional epoch', Ticktin argues nevertheless that 'it may be pieced together'. In Ticktin's account, it has three aspects: 'In the first place, it is a period when capitalism has been overthrown in a part of the world, without the introduction of socialism itself. In the second place, capitalism continues to decline. In the third place, the subjective aspect plays a crucial role as the leaders of both social democracy and Stalinism are seen as saving capitalism in this period.'[4] For Ticktin: 'Trotsky's crucial perspective is one of a declining capitalism desperately seeking a way out of its old age. At certain periods it was able to find a temporary alleviation through imperialism, fascism, war and Stalinism/Cold War, but the palliatives have become ever more useless over time.'[5]

Ticktin claims that Trotsky was 'the only Marxist theorist to put the subjective into political economy', analysing 'the movement of capital' as 'part of the class struggle and not just as an unconscious movement of rates of profit'.[6] This, for Ticktin, is one of the major strengths of Trotsky's understanding of the transitional epoch. He also draws a clear distinction between Trotsky's 'dialectical work of the 1920s', and the more 'rigid and mechanical' approach of the later 1930s, and speaks of Trotsky's 'dialectical decline'.[7] This enables him to separate the category of the transitional epoch from the catastrophist perspectives contained in *The Transitional Programme*. For Ticktin, the key formulation of Trotsky's political economy of transition is found in his 'Report on the World Economic Crisis and the New Tasks of the Comintern', which he presented at the Third Congress of the Communist International in July 1921. By stressing this account and downplaying the importance of *The Transitional Programme*, Ticktin is able to offer an apparently strong foundation for a revitalised Trotskyism that transcends the legacy of the Fourth International.

Ticktin's view is carefully argued, and if correct has important political implications. In what follows, however, I intend to challenge Ticktin's distinction between the dialectical Trotsky of the 1920s and the mechanical Trotsky of the Fourth International. In particular I want to show that while subjective and objective factors were indeed present in Trotsky's formulations of the early 1920s, he did not theorise them as two aspects of a unified whole, but tended always to separate them.[8]

3. Ibid, p225.
4. Ibid.
5. Ibid, p223.
6. Ibid, p218.
7. Ibid, pp217, 223.
8. This understanding of subjective and objective is common on the left, and follows from a view of commodity fetishism that I have analysed in 'The Myth of Working Class Passivity',

While this separation is obvious in *The Transitional Programme*, it is also present in the 'Report' of 1921. The result is that the catastrophism of *The Transitional Programme*, which Ticktin eschews, is also present in Trotsky's initial formulations of the category of the transitional epoch. I would argue further that if there is a break in Trotsky's theoretical development, it occurred earlier, probably between 1919 and 1920. It is only in the period before 1921 that Trotsky put forward the kind of analysis in which subjective and objective factors were unified. It was precisely this kind of analysis that Trotsky abandoned after 1921 when he came to formulate a theory of the transitional epoch.

There has been much talk about going back to Trotsky. For some this means going back to *The Transitional Programme*, which is believed to have been betrayed. For Ticktin, by contrast, the need is to go back to Trotsky in a much more critical spirit, and appropriate only those aspects of his thought that hold up to scrutiny. I want to argue, however, that there can be no going back in the sense of returning to the supposedly firm foundations of the past in order to build on them for the future. Because Trotskyism is part of the ideological heritage of the left, it is necessary to examine Trotsky's writings in a critical light, but this does not mean that we will necessarily find in them a firm basis for understanding the present.

The Development of the Theory

Trotsky's understanding of transition was formed in the period after the October Revolution, and must be understood in that context. He had initially seen transition in terms of a spontaneous upsurge of the proletariat leading directly to the seizure of power, but by 1922 he had begun to speak of a transitional 'epoch'. This conception was given its best known formulation in 1938 in *The Transitional Programme*, but its essential features had been established by 1922. It was a view that stayed with him for the rest of his life.

From the summer of 1917 and up to and including 1919, Trotsky's perspective was one of an immediate conquest of power by the proletariat. Like Lenin, he argued that the imperialist war had demonstrated that the productive forces could no longer develop within their capitalist form. Russia was the weakest link in the capitalist chain, and the Russian Revolution merely the starting point for the world socialist revolution. The basis for the new society was already present objectively in the collapse of the existing society and the development of statised property, and subjectively in the form of the workers' soviets. The statisation of eco-

Radical Chains, no 2, 1990, and 'Franz Jakubowski: Consciousness and Political Economy', *Radical Chains*, no 3, 1991.

nomic life was a fact: 'Today the one and only question is: who shall henceforth be the bearer of statised production — the imperialist state or the state of the victorious proletariat?'[9] The period of transition would be short.

The expectation of a short transition period persisted despite the defeat of the Hungarian Soviet, and numerous setbacks in Germany, including the disastrous March Action in 1921. The tempo of revolutionary development had been slower than expected, and capitalism had survived the crisis of the immediate postwar years, and was even experiencing a further period of boom. But this did not mean that the revolution had been defeated. Long-term capitalist recovery could be ruled out. Every step capital took to restore its equilibrium only disrupted its conditions of equilibrium still further. Revolution was still on the immediate agenda.

By 1922 Trotsky's optimism had become less pronounced. While he still argued that capitalism was in decline and that its overthrow in the USSR represented an important gain for the world proletariat, he was also forced to acknowledge that the revolutionary process was being impeded. Renewed capitalist crisis had not led to radicalisation, and the Comintern had made little headway. Centrist groupings, such as the German Independent Social Democratic Party, which only the previous year had been moving to the left, were now drifting to the right. The revolution would thus be 'a question of an entire historical epoch'.[10] In this epoch, in which socialism was both an objective possibility and a real necessity, what held back revolution was the subjective factor.

Starting from the assertion that capitalism was in decline and could therefore be overthrown, Trotsky's analysis seems to offer a firmer basis for revolutionary intervention than most of its rivals. It explains the role of reformism in holding back the revolution, but argues that as capitalism declines the productive forces begin to decompose, and the space for reform becomes ever more limited. While this forces the working class to struggle against capitalism as a whole, it does not make socialism inevitable. Recognising that there is no automatic breakdown or general crisis of capitalism followed by the immediate introduction of socialism, the theory thus seems to recognise the difficult and protracted nature of the transition. By placing human subjectivity at the centre of the process, it seems to place our fate in our hands, and thus to underpin a revolutionary orientation to the problems of the present.

Within actually existing Trotskyism, however, the recognition of the impor-

---

9. LD Trotsky, *The First Five Years of the Communist International*, Volume 1, New York, 1972, p23. For a critique of Lenin's understanding of transition, see W Dixon and D Gorman, 'The Hidden Political Economy of the Left', *Radical Chains*, no 3, 1991.
10. LD Trotsky, *The First Five Years of the Communist International*, Volume 2, London, 1979, p187.

tance of subjectivity has translated into an emphasis on the party as bearer of consciousness that in many ways is incompatible with the supposed commitment to proletarian self-emancipation. Belief that the objective conditions for revolution have matured, and that subjective conditions have merely to be pushed into effect, has resulted in explanations which exist at a merely subjective level. Tied in with a lack of success, this has only bred intolerance and sectarianism. It also raises doubts about a return to Trotsky. Is there indeed a Trotsky to return to who is free of the catastrophism of the Fourth International?

Consciousness and Political Economy: Trotsky in 1919

Lying behind Trotsky's revolutionary optimism in the period from 1917 to 1919 was an understanding of the political economy of capitalist development which recognised the interaction of subject and object. In an article written in 1919, 'En Route: Thoughts on the Progress of the Proletarian Revolution',[11] Trotsky offered an explanation of the uneven development of the European revolution which presented the international movements of capital, in particular the export of finance capital, as a response to the movement of the working class.

The high level of class struggle in France in the 1870s 'kept the French bourgeoisie constantly on guard, and compelled it to go over early to the export of finance capital'. In this way it was able to check the growth of new and revolutionising forms of industrialism within France itself.[12] This helped to check the progress of the class struggle in France, but only at the cost of exporting the revolution to Russia: 'Nurtured under the high pressure of foreign finance capital, Russian capitalism in the course of a few decades gave form to a million-headed working class, which cut like a sharp wedge into the milieu of all-Russian political barbarism.'[13] The internationalisation of capital in the late nineteenth century had reduced internal antagonisms only by intensifying international antagonisms, which eventually broke out in the form of imperialist war. Imperialist war disrupted an already shaky capitalist equilibrium, and pushed the proletariat towards revolution. The revolution broke out first in Russia precisely because it was the weakest link in the capitalist chain. It was this emphasis on the role of the class struggle in mediating transitions from one form of accumulation to another that explains Trotsky's optimism in the period immediately after the October Revolution.

In this instance, Trotsky's analysis can be seen as combining objective and subjective elements, or rather distinguishing the two aspects within the whole. At the

---

11. LD Trotsky, *The First Five Years of the Communist International*, Volume 1, op cit, pp50-63.
12. Ibid, p54.
13. Ibid, p57.

same time, however, in analysing the internal regimes resulting from the export of finance capital, Trotsky fell back on a crudely quantitative theory of imperialism which tended towards a separation of subjective and objective conditions:

'Fearful of the growth of the French proletariat in size and power, the French bourgeoisie preferred to export its capital and to reap profits from Russian industrial enterprises: the task of curbing the Russian workers was therewith unloaded on the Russian Tsar. In this way the economic might of the French bourgeoisie also rested directly on the labour of the Russian proletariat.'[14]

Through this 'usurious imperialism', the French bourgeoisie was able to divide and contain the French proletariat. The British bourgeoisie, too, was able 'to separate the top labour layer from the bottom strata, creating an aristocracy of "skilled" labour and instilling into it a trade union caste spirit'.[15] The power and resilience of the English bourgeoisie rested 'on the exploitation not only of the English proletariat, but also of the colonial toiling masses', giving it the flexibility of offering 'rather far-reaching concessions to its native proletariat', while at the same time 'exerting pressure' on it by using the colonies as a reserve army of labour.[16]

We see here, alongside a profound analysis of the interaction of subjective and objective in the historical process, a tendency also to split them. His understanding of the forces preventing the generalisation of the Russian Revolution was much weaker than his understanding of why the revolution had broken out first in Russia. Reformism, in this analysis, was based primarily on the ability of capital to make quantitative concessions out of imperialist superprofits. Once this material basis was gone, there could be no basis for reformism, and hence no reformism.

In the years after 1921, when Trotsky began to focus on the failure of the revolution, it was this cruder side of his thought which came to dominate. After 1921 Trotsky came more and more to treat objective and subjective as distinct spheres. In doing so he effectively identified the objective conditions with the social whole, a view which presupposed a theory of materialism in which ideas were mere reflections of objective reality. This inevitably had consequences for his conception of practice. We shall examine what led to this separation in thought, and what the consequences were.

14.   Ibid, p61.
15.   Ibid, p52.
16.   Ibid, p61.

Equilibrium: Crisis and Boom

The category of the transitional epoch has its roots in Trotsky's understanding of capitalist decline, and this in turn was rooted in his understanding of capitalist 'equilibrium' and the 'curve' of capitalist development. These categories were first fully formulated in July 1921 in Trotsky's 'Report on the World Economic Crisis and the New Tasks of the Communist International'.[17]

Capitalism, Trotsky argued, 'lives by crises and booms, just as a human being lives by inhaling and exhaling'.[18] This cycle of boom and crisis constitutes the basic equilibrium of capitalist society, one that is constantly disrupted and restored. The economic equilibrium is the basis of a political equilibrium through which social tensions and antagonisms are contained within limits, and they thus serve to advance the development of the productive forces, rather than to hinder this development. Once this equilibrium begins to collapse, however, the productive forces begin to decompose. Capitalism is in decline.

The period of boom that followed the First World War had led social democrats, Mensheviks and even some within the Bolshevik party itself — Bukharin for example — to argue that capitalist equilibrium, which had been disrupted by the war, had now been restored. They foresaw a long period of renewed expansion and prosperity in which the possibility of revolution could be discounted.[19] For Trotsky, by contrast:

'The fact that capitalism continues to oscillate cyclically after the war signifies only that capitalism is not yet dead, that we are not dealing with a corpse. Crises and booms were inherent in capitalism at its birth; they will accompany it to its grave. But to determine capitalism's age and general condition — to establish whether it has matured or whether it is in decline — one must diagnose the character of the cycles. In much the same manner the state of the human organism can be diagnosed by whether the breathing is regular or spasmodic, deep or superficial, and so on.'[20]

In judging the political situation, the cycle of boom and crisis was not the most important factor to be considered.

---

17. Ibid, pp174-226.
18. Ibid, p200.
19. See RB Day, *The 'Crisis' and the 'Crash': Soviet Studies of the West (1917-1939)*, London, 1979, pp42-51.
20. LD Trotsky, *The First Five Years of the Communist International*, Volume 1, op cit, p200.

The Curve of Capitalist Development

Underlying the cyclical oscillations of the business cycle was a more fundamental trend that Trotsky designated 'the curve of capitalist development'. The development of the productive forces of capitalism could be delineated graphically by drawing a curve, the axes of which defined, on the one hand, the development of the productive forces, and, on the other hand, the movement of history. This curve would be 'a composite of two movements: a primary movement which expresses the general upward rise of capitalism, and a secondary movement which consists of the constant oscillations corresponding to the various industrial cycles':[21] 'In periods of rapid capitalist development the crises are brief and superficial in character, while the booms are long-lasting and far reaching. In periods of capitalist decline, the crises are of a prolonged character, while the booms are fleeting, superficial and speculative. In periods of stagnation the fluctuations occur upon much the same level.'[22]

In the course of a boom the productive forces expanded; during crises they contracted. So long as the expansion of the productive forces in each boom more than compensated for their destruction in the course of each crisis, the productive forces of capitalism would continue to develop. But this need not be the case. The 138 years that had followed the American War of Independence, for example, could be divided into five distinct epochs of capitalist development, characterised by the nature of the series of cycles in each period. Firstly, in the period from 1781 to 1851, the development of the capitalist economy, measured in terms of output, trade figures, and so on, had been marginal: 'the development is very slow; there is scarcely any movement observable'.[23] In the second period, from 1851 to 1873, 'the curve of development rises steeply'. This epoch of capitalist expansion was followed, from 1851 to approximately 1894, by 'an epoch of depression' in which trade stagnated. A fourth period, characterised by conditions of boom, lasted from 1894 to 1913. Then, from 1914, came a fifth period, 'the period of the destruction of capitalist economy'.[24]

The Theory of Capitalist Decline

Following the scheme of development outlined in the 'Preface' to Marx's *Contribution to the Critique of Political Economy* of 1859, Trotsky argued that by 1913 the social relations of capitalism had become fetters on the further development of the productive forces: 'There obtains today not alone in Europe but on a world scale a

21. Ibid, pp200-1.
22. Ibid, pp201-2.
23. Ibid, p201.
24. Ibid.

situation which permits us, from the standpoint of Marxism, to say with complete assurance that the bourgeois system has completely drained itself. The world productive forces cannot develop further within the framework of bourgeois society.'[25] This was indicated by imperialist war: 'With the imperialist war we entered the epoch of revolution, that is the epoch in which the very mainstays of capitalist equilibrium are shaking and collapsing.'[26] With the collapse of the complex equilibrium of capitalist society, 'the basic premise for the revolution is given'.[27]

In the course of the First World War the balance of economic power had shifted to America, and this led some to argue that the USA held out hope for the revival and further development of capitalism. Trotsky acknowledged that by comparison with Europe, the USA had 'passed through a development of a diametrically opposite character. She has meanwhile enriched herself at a dizzy pace.'[28] But in Trotsky's view, the US economy had grown only by catering for the war needs of Europe. Now, with the decline of the European economies, American capitalism too was faced with disaster:

'For four-odd years Europe became converted into a sheet of fire fed not only by Europe's income but by her basic capital, while the American bourgeoisie warmed its hands at the flames. America's productive capacity has grown extraordinarily, but her market has vanished because Europe is impoverished and can no longer buy American goods. It is as if Europe had first done everything in her power to help America to the topmost rung and then pulled the ladder out.'[29]

While the living standards of American workers had undergone 'undeniable improvement', 'today and in the next period American workers will not have the means for automobiles and silk shirts'.[30] The possibility of a prolonged period of capitalist recovery could thus be ruled out. Capital could not restore the conditions of its equilibrium:

'If we grant — and let us grant it for a moment — that the working class fails to rise in revolutionary struggle, but allows the bourgeoisie the opportunity to rule the world's destiny for a long number of years, say, two or three decades, then assuredly some sort of new equilibrium will be established. Europe will be thrown violently into reverse gear. Millions of European workers will die from unemployment and malnutrition. The United States will be compelled to reorient itself on the world market, reconvert

25. LD Trotsky, *The First Five Years of the Communist International*, Volume 2, op cit, p3.
26. LD Trotsky, *The First Five Years of the Communist International*, Volume 1, op cit, p174.
27. LD Trotsky, *The First Five Years of the Communist International*, Volume 2, op cit, p4.
28. LD Trotsky, *The First Five Years of the Communist International*, Volume 1, op cit, pp193-4.
29. Ibid, p196.
30. Ibid, p97.

its industry, *and suffer curtailment for a considerable period.* Afterwards, after a new world division of labour is thus established in agony for 15 or 20 or 25 years, a new epoch of capitalist upswing might perhaps ensue.'[31]

But, Trotsky added, 'this entire conception is exceedingly abstract and one-sided. Matters are pictured here as if the proletariat had ceased to struggle. Meanwhile, there cannot even be talk of this if only for the reason that the class contradictions have become aggravated in the extreme precisely during recent years.'[32]

To restore its economic apparatus, capital would be forced to 'exert stronger and stronger pressure upon the working class'.[33] This would, however, force the proletariat to resist, and it was the task of the Comintern to extend these struggles into a general anti-capitalist offensive. Despite the postwar boom and the failure of the European working class to take power so far, Trotsky was able to conclude in 1921 that 'the world situation and the future perspectives remain profoundly revolutionary'.[34]

The Political Economy of the Transitional Epoch

It was only after 1921 that Trotsky actually developed a political economy of decline. Once elaborated, however, it would be the constant basis to his political practice. Both his conception of decline, and his theory of the transitional epoch, were developed in a period in which reverses to the revolutionary movement had made impossible any simple hope for the continuation of the Russian Revolution. They mark, then, an important point in the theoretical orientation of the movement to the defeat of 1917.

In Trotsky's writings, the transitional epoch appears as an extension of the epoch of decline. The decline of capitalism had removed the objective barrier to socialist revolution, but although revolution had broken out across Europe, it had only been successful in Russia. The fate of the dictatorship of the proletariat in Russia thus depended on the progress of the world revolution. This dictatorship was transitional to socialism, but socialism itself had not been and could not be introduced. Capitalism was a world system, and without its overthrow worldwide the proletarian dictatorship in the USSR could not survive; the possibility of capitalist restoration was real.

Although there was no objective barrier to socialist revolution, the perspective of a spontaneous upsurge and a short transition period had been shown to be false. Writing in July 1921, Trotsky claimed that at the time of the First Congress of the Comintern in 1919 'many of us reckoned — some more, others less — that the spontaneous onset

31. Ibid, p211.
32. Ibid.
33. Ibid, p209.
34. Ibid, p226.

of the workers and in part of the peasant masses would overthrow the bourgeoisie in the near future'.[35] The bourgeoisie had survived. The war and the revolutionary upheavals that accompanied and followed it had 'confronted the bourgeoisie with the terrible threat of destruction', and this had 'rendered its instinct of class self-preservation sensitive in the extreme'.[36] Indeed, Europe and the world as a whole were now 'passing through a period which is, on the one side, an epoch of the disintegration of the productive forces of bourgeois society, and, on the other side, an epoch of the highest flowering of the counter-revolutionary strategy of the bourgeoisie'.[37] The struggle for socialism would be harder, more protracted, than anticipated.

Given that the objective conditions had been achieved, Trotsky's explanation for a protracted transitional epoch rested, and had to rest, on subjective explanations. By 1922 Trotsky had come to recognise that it was 'impossible to say how long the proletarian revolution will endure from its beginning to its termination. It will be a question of an entire historical epoch.'[38] The 'ill-starred character' of the transitional epoch was determined by the fact that 'the bourgeoisie is no longer capable of ruling while the working class is still incapable of seizing power'.[39] What held back the revolution was the fact that the working class had not yet rid itself of reformist prejudices. Hence in the transitional epoch, consciousness, or the 'subjective factor', was crucial.

This idea of a contradiction between the objective conditions for revolution and the immaturity of the subjective factor was one that many on the left shared with Trotsky in the early 1920s. However, whereas with the ebbing of the revolutionary wave someone like Anton Pannekoek came to reassess his understanding of the objective features of the epoch, Trotsky did not, and this served to confirm a separation of objective and subjective. This treatment of an a priori separation of the subjective from objective conditions meant that Trotsky was limited in his understanding of the role of both social democracy and Stalinism in holding back the revolution. He could only understand the role of social democracy and Stalinism in subjective terms: in effect as a crisis of leadership.

Social Democracy, Stalinism and Betrayal

In 1917, on the eve of the October Revolution, Trotsky had argued that the 'bureaucratised socialist parties' had been revealed by the imperialist war to be 'at

---

35. LD Trotsky, *The First Five Years of the Communist International*, Volume 2, op cit, p8.
36. Ibid, pp4-5.
37. Ibid, p6.
38. Ibid, p187.
39. Ibid, p256.

variance with the requirements of further development'.[40] He did not regard them as a serious obstacle to revolution. In fact, however, the revolution suffered a number of setbacks. In Germany, Luxemburg and Liebknecht were murdered by the Freikorps, and the workers' councils handed back power to the bourgeois state in the form of the social democratic government. Further revolutionary upsurges occurred in which the radical workers' councils movement played a crucial role, but still the hold of the bourgeoisie was not dislodged. The Comintern itself, through its opportunistic orientation towards social democracy, played a crucial role in obstructing the emergence of a revolutionary alternative.[41]

Trotsky did recognise that social democracy had a played a role in ensuring the survival of capitalism in the interwar period: 'Social democracy saved capitalism...'[42] What was lacking, however, was an adequate understanding of the nature of that role. There was, in Trotsky's view, no objective basis for the survival of social democracy. Under conditions of capitalist decline it could no longer carry out its task of 'reconciling the workers to capitalism by means of reforms'.[43] A sustained period of reform was generally impossible. Social democracy could offer only sops and bribes that could not be of lasting significance. Its survival was explained by reference to subjective factors and conditions.

Initially, Trotsky identified these with the mistakes of the young and inexperienced parties of the Comintern: 'Despite the disastrous political conditions existing for it, the social democracy has been able, thanks to the aid of the communist party, to retain the great bulk of its following, and has up to the present escaped with considerable, to be sure, but nevertheless only secondary losses.'[44] After the seizure of power in Germany by the Nazis, however, Trotsky concluded that the Comintern was guilty not just of error, but of betrayal. It was the sectarian attitude of the Comintern towards the German Social Democratic Party that had made the Nazi victory possible. In *The Transitional Programme*, therefore, he spoke of the 'definite passing over of the Comintern to the side of the bourgeois order'.[45] As in the case of social democracy, however, Trotsky offered a merely subjective explanation of the counter-revolutionary role of Stalinism.

---

40. LD Trotsky, 'What Next?', *What Next and Other Writings from 1917*, London, 1988, pp30-1.
41. B Shepherd, 'Anton Pannekoek and the Theory of the Transition', *Radical Chains*, no 2, 1990.
42. LD Trotsky, *The First Five Years of the Communist International*, Volume 1, op cit, p231.
43. LD Trotsky, 'What Next? Vital Questions for the German Proletariat', *The Struggle Against Fascism in Germany*, New York, 1971, p143.
44. LD Trotsky, 'Germany, the Key to the International Situation', *The Struggle Against Fascism in Germany*, op cit, p122.
45. LD Trotsky, *The Transitional Programme*, London, nd, p13.

The Fourth International and the Crisis of Revolutionary Leadership

Trotsky's orientation to the Comintern was consistent with his understanding of the epoch in which: 'The objective prerequisites for the proletarian revolution have not only "ripened"; they have begun to get somewhat rotten... It is now the turn of the proletariat, that is, chiefly of its revolutionary vanguard. The historical crisis of mankind is reduced to the crisis of the revolutionary leadership.'[46] For the Fourth International, the strategic task was one of 'overcoming the contradiction between the maturity of the objective revolutionary conditions and the immaturity of the proletariat and its vanguard'.[47] The proletariat was confronted by a situation in which 'there can be no discussion of systematic social reforms and the raising of the masses' living standards; when every serious demand of the proletariat and even every serious demand of the petit-bourgeoisie inevitably reaches beyond the limits of capitalist property relations and of the bourgeois state'.[48]

Social democracy had divided its programme into two parts: a 'minimum programme' of immediate social reforms achievable under capitalism, and a 'maximum programme' of social revolution. While this was feasible in a period of capitalist ascendancy, in its epoch of decline capitalism could grant no further reforms, and had even to dismantle those won in the earlier period. Hence, what was necessary was a series of 'transitional demands'. The essence of these demands was 'contained in the fact that ever more openly and decisively they will be directed at the very bases of the bourgeois regime'.[49] A programme of transitional demands would constantly escalate and exacerbate the revolutionary situation, and drive the working class towards revolution: 'Not one of the transitional demands can be fully met under the conditions of preserving the bourgeois regime.'[50]

The Second World War, the Postwar Boom and the Crisis of the Fourth International

Writing shortly after the outbreak of the Second World War, Trotsky argued that the war itself 'attests incontrovertibly to the fact that society can no longer develop on the basis of capitalism. Thereby it subjects the proletariat to a new and perhaps decisive

---

46. Ibid, p8.
47. Ibid, p14.
48. Ibid, p15.
49. Ibid, p16.
50. Ibid, p40.

test.'⁵¹ It would test 'not only the stability of the existing regimes but also the ability of the proletariat to replace them'.⁵² On the one hand, the war might, as Trotsky firmly expected, provoke revolution. This would pave the way for socialism and the regeneration of soviet democracy in the USSR. On the other hand, if capitalism was not overthrown, the result would be 'the further development of monopoly capital, its further fusion with the state and the replacement of democracy wherever it still remained by a totalitarian state'.⁵³ Should the proletariat seize power in the advanced capitalist countries only to surrender it to a privileged bureaucracy, Trotsky concluded: 'Then we would be compelled to acknowledge that the reason for the bureaucratic relapse is rooted not in the backwardness of the country and not in the imperialist environment, but in the congenital incapacity of the proletariat to become a ruling class.'⁵⁴

The war did not lead to the collapse of capitalism, nor did it result in a successful revolution. As capitalism began to take off into the long postwar boom through the incorporation of social democracy, and Stalinism consolidated and expanded its hold over Eastern Europe, the raison d'être of the Fourth International collapsed. An already weak and divided movement, it splintered and disintegrated into mutually antagonistic sects, all of which claimed to hold the 'spotless banner' of the real Fourth International.

Objectivity, Subjectivity and the Need for the Party

The case for the party as the bearer of consciousness had already been stated by Lenin in 1902. But after 1917 Lenin's prescriptions acquired a renewed urgency. Trotsky's primary emphasis was on the ripeness of the objective conditions for revolution, and the need to bring subjectivity into line: 'The class, taken by itself, is only material for exploitation. The proletariat assumes an independent role only at that moment when from a social class *in itself* it becomes a political class *for itself*. This cannot take place otherwise than through the medium of a party. The party is that historical organ by which the class becomes class conscious.'⁵⁵

The tendency was thus, more and more, for the subjective factor to be identified with the party: 'The role of the subjective factor in a period of slow, organic development can remain quite a subordinate one... But as soon as the objective prerequisites have matured, the key to the whole historical process passes into the hands of the sub-

---

51. LD Trotsky, *In Defence of Marxism*, London, 1971, p10.
52. Ibid, p17.
53. Ibid, p10.
54. Ibid, p11.
55. LD Trotsky, 'What Next? Vital Questions for the German Proletariat', *The Struggle Against Fascism in Germany*, op cit, p163.

jective factor, that is, the party.'[56] Explanation of historical development had been reduced to the subjective level, underwriting a political practice of intense activism, frantic party building and constant injunctions to work harder to exploit every revolutionary possibility. It also resulted in a siege mentality which sealed off party activists from the outside world; by separating objective and subjective conditions, and placing the onus of history on an isolated subjectivity, Trotsky had made the programme of Trotskyism impervious to criticism. Because the objective conditions for revolution were ripe, all that held back the revolution was the subjective factor. From this there was an easy slide into treating attempts to reassess the objective situation as a sign of false consciousness, confusion, and the influence of reaction.

Social Democracy, the New Deal and the Postwar Boom

Trotsky did recognise that the outcome of the Second World War would 'undoubtedly have a decisive significance for our appraisal of the modern epoch as the epoch of proletarian revolution'.[57] 'If contrary to all probabilities the October Revolution fails during the course of the present war, or immediately thereafter, to find its continuation in any of the advanced countries, and if, on the contrary, the proletariat is thrown back everywhere and on all fronts, then we should doubtless have to pose the question of revising our conception of the present epoch and its driving forces.'[58] We cannot say how Trotsky would have responded to postwar developments had he lived to see them. However, an adequate understanding of these developments would have required him to question his separation of objective and subjective; it would have required fundamental theoretical reorientation.

In the 1920s Trotsky had argued that to restore its productive apparatus, capitalism would be forced to cut wages and intensify work. Existing concessions could only be short-term solutions. Capitalism had reached its limits, and there could be no epoch of reform. Reforms merely intensified the already existing economic chaos, and to restabilise itself capital would have to eradicate them. The European proletariat would not, however, accept such sacrifices: 'It demands a high standard of living, which is in direct contradiction to the objective possibilities of the capitalist system. Hence the strikes and uprisings; hence the impossibility of the economic reconstruction of Europe.'[59]

From Trotsky's perspective, the bourgeoisie was able at most to make only short-term concessions and provide 'sops' and 'bribes' to particular sections of the working

---

56. LD Trotsky, *The Third International After Lenin*, New York, 1970, p84.
57. LD Trotsky, *In Defence of Marxism*, op cit, p17.
58. Ibid, pp17-18.
59. LD Trotsky, *The First Five Years of the Communist International*, Volume 1, op cit, p255.

class in order to split the proletariat. These sops and bribes could not be transformed into reforms; bourgeois society would be forced rather to repress. 'When the bourgeoisie resorted after the war to throwing sops to the working class, the conciliators obsequiously converted these sops into reforms (the eight-hour day, unemployment insurance, and so on); and discovered — amid the ruins — the era of reformism.'[60] This is exactly what Trotsky denied was possible. Already in 1921, he argued, the world was passing through an epoch, not of reform, but of 'counter-revolution'.[61] This formal opposition of reform and counter-revolution misses the crucial point: reform was itself the centre of counter-revolution.

Even Roosevelt's New Deal of the late 1930s did not lead Trotsky to reassess his position. Trotsky thus ruled out the possibility of capital finding a variety of ad hoc solutions that could give it a renewed lease of life. More importantly, he discounted the possibility that social democracy and the New Deal might already be playing a very important role in the long-term stabilisation of class relations. The 'sops' and 'bribes' offered by social democracy and the 'fictitious achievements'[62] of the New Deal were in fact a mitigation of the conditions of absolute poverty, they were interventions in the process of class formation which changed its conditions. Through various initiatives, capital was already reforming the objective conditions of existence of the class struggle. It was this that Trotsky's separation of subjective and objective obscured.

The administrative impulse within social democracy adapted it well to the role of administering the needs of the working class in an epoch of failed revolutions. The development of social democratic forms of social and economic regulation breathed a new lease of life into bourgeois society. With the development of the Keynesian form of centralised state economic administration after the Second World War, moreover, capital was able to harness the energy of proletarian needs, via formal recognition, in the interests of its own self-expansion. The productive forces did not collapse, but were developed to a previously unparalleled extent. Social democracy was not a merely subjective phenomenon, but a real social movement that enabled the adaptation of the political economy of bourgeois society.[63] For the Fourth International, the need for revolution was premised on the impossibility of reform; once this premise was removed, revolutionary Trotskyism had only two options. Either it dissolved itself into social democracy where it spent its energy in the administrative regulation of the working class, or it remained outside where for 50 years it proclaimed the imminent collapse of capitalism.

60. Ibid, p223.
61. Ibid.
62. LD Trotsky, *The Living Thought of Karl Marx*, London, 1946, p26.
63. This understanding of social democracy draws on William Dixon, 'The Leopard in the Twentieth Century', *Radical Chains*, no 4, 1993. See also Hillel Ticktin, 'The Political Economy of Class in the Transitional Epoch', *Critique*, no 20-21, 1987.

For Trotsky there were two possible alternatives. Either capitalism would continue to decline until the working class took power and introduced socialism, or capitalism would succeed in restabilising itself in its pristine form and usher in a new phase of development. In fact neither prognosis has turned out to be true. If decline is identified, as Trotsky identified it, with the decomposition of the productive forces, then for the whole of the period of the long postwar boom, capitalism was no longer in decline. But this does not mean that capitalism had restored its equilibrium, and begun again to develop the productive forces in the way that Trotsky described in his discussion of the curve of capitalist development. For the revolutionary upheavals of 1917 to 1923 were indeed a watershed in capitalist history, although not in the way that Trotsky (or anyone else) understood it. The period of revolution punctuated the transition to a new form of capital accumulation, based on the incorporation of social democratic reformism into the basic structure of capitalist society. The subjective factor interpenetrated with the objective conditions of accumulation, and transformed them.

The Theory of Transition and the Experience of Defeat

It was only after the defeat of the revolution that Trotsky began to try to elaborate a theory of transition. His understanding of transition was shaped, informed and conditioned by the collapse of the revolution. At the back of his mind lay the fate of the Russian Revolution itself.

A theory of transition must include a description or account of movement from one form of society to another. In Trotsky's account such movement is absent. Instead, what he offers is the absence of movement, a condition of stalemate, the mutual ruination of the contending classes. His theory of transition looks more like a description of defeat. What Trotsky had described was a system that could not develop any further, and not a process of transition from one social system to another. In the early 1920s he had argued that the imperialist war had revealed that capitalism could no longer develop the productive forces. This meant that revolution was necessary. But insofar as capital could not defeat the working class, and the working class could not impose its rule, there was no reason why humanity should break out of the existing order. The resistance of the working class prevented the recovery and further development of capitalism, but that was all. Barbarism was in fact the most likely outcome. Indeed, the conditions that Trotsky identified as the objective conditions for socialism look more like those of barbarism:

'The economic prerequisite for the proletarian revolution has already in general achieved the highest point of fruition that can be reached under capitalism. Mankind's productive forces stagnate. Already new inventions and improvements fail to raise the level of material wealth. Conjunctural crises under conditions of the social crisis of the whole capitalist system inflict ever heavier depredations and sufferings upon the masses. Growing unemployment, in its turn, deepens the financial crisis of the state and undermines the unstable monetary systems. Democratic regimes, as well as fascist, stagger on from one bankruptcy to another.'[64]

Is There a Future for Trotskyism?

Trotsky's undeniable insight was that in the period after the First World War it was equally impossible for capital to reimpose its rule and for the working class to abolish it. This is an insight that should not be overlooked. On the other hand, it was one that he shared with others, notably left communists such as Anton Pannekoek, Otto Rühle and Herman Gorter. Furthermore, like them, he was unable to transform this insight into a convincing account of the political economy of a transitional epoch, and this is because of the catastrophist theory of decline on which it was based. A theory of decline which stresses the collapse of the productive forces is unable to bear a theory of transition which presupposes years and even decades of stalemate. Such a theory is unable to generate an understanding of the particular forms through which this stalemate is mediated. The category of the transitional epoch could only have been fleshed out and given determinate content by abandoning the theory of decline.

Trotsky was probably the most sophisticated Marxist theorist of the twentieth century. His attempt to deal with the political economy of transition was serious and more far-reaching than that of any of his rivals, but like them he was fighting with effects and not with causes. His real strengths lay in his early recognition that it is through struggle itself that the categories of capital are developed. That he rapidly lost this perspective in his attempt to come to terms with the defeat of the revolution is a central part of his tragedy, for he was thus rendered unable to achieve a full understanding of that defeat. Trotsky's writings cannot provide a firm foundation for an understanding of the present epoch, and the most perceptive analyses of the epoch are in fact beyond Trotskyism, whatever its authors might think. Trotsky reflected the conditions of his time more adequately than he analysed them, and this, more than anything, has been the material basis of his real success.

---

64 .   LD Trotsky, *The Transitional Programme*, op cit, p7.

Alan Wald

Literature and Revolution

Leon Trotsky's Contributions to Marxist Cultural Theory and Literary Criticism[1]

Professional Critics and Professional Revolutionaries

The contributions of Leon Trotsky to twentieth century literary and cultural theory are unique among what is generally regarded as 'literary criticism' in the advanced capitalist nations of the West today. By and large, literary criticism in countries such as the United States of America and those of Western Europe is the product of scholars affiliated to colleges and universities, or, in some cases, of journalists writing in mass media publications.[2] The seeming preponderance of 'Marxist' criticism outside the former Soviet bloc and existing post-capitalist societies (in which Marxism is still the official state ideology) is of the 'Western Marx-

---

1. A longer version of this essay appears in the *Journal of Trotsky Studies*, no 2, 1994.
2. In a relatively few cases, a self-employed individual, a full or part-time industrial or agricultural worker, or a salaried left wing political activist, may contribute substantial cultural criticism to a paper, journal or political organ that is independent of universities or business corporations.

ist' variety;[3] that is, often written from an arm-chair, and accordingly divorced from organisational commitment.[4] Thus, whatever the personal political views of the majority of the university and business-employed cultural critics, and whatever their social and political commitments might be, the bulk of the literary criticism they produce is filtered through a system of powerful institutional constraints.[5]

It is also noteworthy that critical practice never occurs in a vacuum, but is significantly conditioned by the everyday life experience of the critic. Again, in the USA and Western Europe, the critic is most often a teacher who is obliged for an income to have his or her work judged acceptable by a private or state educational institution, or else by a privately-owned publication where there is always the threat that he or she might be dismissed or denied future assignments. Moreover, he or she usually inhabits an environment of economic peers with similar cultural, social and even 'racial' features.[6]

In contrast to these 'professional critics', Leon Trotsky was a professional revolutionary. Even on those occasions when he received payment for writing, he did not regard literary activity as a specialised area of intellectual labour articulated through the network of institutions upon which his livelihood depended. Rather, writing cultural criticism was one aspect of his efforts to build a political movement based on his understanding of the main trends of contemporary history. Therefore, any evaluation of his contributions in the area of literary and cultural criticism must be rooted in an understanding of his central preoccupations and political objectives at various moments in his career.

These moments can be grouped roughly within three broad periods. The first is the pre-revolutionary period, dating from his initial literary essays around the turn of the century to the Bolshevik seizure of power in 1917. Writings of these years include youthful journalistic appraisals of Tolstoy, Ibsen and Gogol. A distinctive feature of his early method is readily apparent through his frequent assertion that every author has a crystallised psychology resulting from social conditions.

---

3. See Perry Anderson, *Considerations on Western Marxism*, London, 1976.
4. In Western Europe, the number of academic literary critics with a Marxist party affiliation is minuscule; it would be surprising to find as many as a dozen in the USA.
5. In the USA and Western Europe, these constraints are in the form of academic journals, university and commercial publishing houses, professional organisations, networks of 'readers' who evaluate their colleagues on behalf of various administrative bodies, and, often in the truly decisive positions, bureaucrats worried about the budgets of universities and periodicals — and who are frequently ignorant of the subtleties of the discipline. Useful insights into the complicated situation of literary criticism in the academy can be found in Richard Ohmann, *Politics of Letters*, Wesleyan, 1987.
6. For example, although the population of people of colour in the USA is approximately 20 per cent, literature teachers prior to the recent decade were 99 per cent white.

A second phase comes in the first five years following the Russian Revolution, prior to the onset of Trotsky's struggle against Stalin in 1923-24. These years witnessed the greatest fecundity of Trotsky's cultural work, punctuated by the publication of his famous *Literature and Revolution* in 1923, as well as *Problems of Everyday Life* in 1924. In these writings he vigorously and boldly sought to theorise a relationship between the cultural legacy of bourgeois society and the politico-cultural tasks of the epoch of the transition to socialism. Trotsky also promoted in these works a critical method based on the assertion of social judgements independent of artistic forms. This produced some brilliant results in practice, but the method is problematic on a theoretical plane due to its separation of content from technique.[7]

The third phase of Trotsky's writing begins with his exile from the Soviet Union in 1929, and lasts until his assassination in August 1940. In these years, he carried out the unpleasant but necessary task of documenting and analysing the effects of Stalinism on Soviet culture. Episodically, he also assessed a number of recent novels — the genre he preferred above all — and recorded diary notations of other readings. After 1933 Trotsky was increasingly active in seeking to draw writers and artists to the new revolutionary movement that became the Fourth International in 1938.[8] As such, his perspective underwent several important changes. Most significantly, he promoted for the first time a frankly 'libertarian' cultural view, calling for an 'anarchy' of literary production.[9] This is a decided improvement over the ambiguities of his formulation of 1924 for the relation of the state to various artistic groups and tendencies, 'while holding over them all the categorical criterion, *for* the revolution or *against* the revolution, to give them complete freedom in the sphere of artistic self-determination'.[10]

---

7. Such a schism has fallen in disfavour among more rigorous Marxist critics since the publication in 1974 of Fredric Jameson's *Marxism and Form*.
8. See the excellent studies in the following issues of *Cahiers Léon Trotsky*: 'Trotsky et les intellectuels des états unis', no 19, September 1984; 'Trotsky et les écrivains français', no 25, March 1986; and 'Trotsky, la littérature et les écrivains', no 47, January 1992.
9. The exact quotation is: 'If, for the better development of the forces of material production, the revolution must build a *socialist* regime with centralised control, to develop intellectual creation an *anarchist* regime of individual liberty should from the first be established. No authority, no dictation, not the least trace of orders from above.' (emphases in original) See 'Manifesto: Toward a Free Revolutionary Art' in Paul N Siegel (ed), *Leon Trotsky on Literature and Art*, New York, 1970, p117. The manifesto was signed by André Breton and Diego Rivera, but Trotsky wrote most of it.
10. LD Trotsky, *Literature and Revolution*, Ann Arbor, 1960, p14.

The Evolution of an Aesthetic

As in the case of Lenin, Franz Mehring and Rosa Luxemburg — not to mention Marx and Engels themselves — the early literary criticism produced by Trotsky was animated more by a 'Marxist sensibility' than by a systematic set of propositions. Moreover, this sensibility was derived from a profound assimilation of the first principles of historical materialism. Unlike the written texts of later debates that came to characterise literary discussions among Marxists of the Third International during the Stalin era, there are in Trotsky no long quotations from the famous writings of the 'founding fathers'. For one thing, the anthologies of excerpts and aphorisms of Marx and Engels on literature and art that are today familiar to all students of the subject were simply not available at that time. However, the major biographical sources agree that Trotsky, from the time he set his mind to it, had a special aptitude for Marx and Engels' method of historical, social, philosophic and economic analysis.[11] Moreover, as George Novack observes, 'Trotsky never claimed originality for his theoretical and political positions'; rather, he sought to apply classical Marxism with breadth and subtlety.[12]

Trotsky's two essays on Tolstoy, in 1908 and 1910, exemplify this approach. His method, like that of his mentors, tends to favour realist literature and to seek the social basis of imagery and characterisation. It was also a method that adamantly resisted the conflation of 'political' and 'artistic' judgements even as a social evaluation was provided. His first study, 'Tolstoy: Poet and Rebel', commences in characteristic fashion by refracting the social origins of the novelist through his personality. Trotsky concludes that while Tolstoy intellectually would not defend feudal relations in practice, he was nevertheless 'emotionally bonded' to that system where 'everything hinges on cycles of nature', and where 'one lives by hearing and obeying'.[13] Sharing the judgement of bourgeois critics, Trotsky declares *War and Peace* to be 'best and unsurpassed'. His three evaluative criteria are worth noting, for they are premised on an unabashed Hellenocentrism that may strike us as naively dated today.

Firstly, the novel incarnates the 'anonymousness of life and its sacred irresponsibility' in the character of Karatayev. Secondly, Tolstoy radiates a 'Homeric calm

---

11. See, for example, the sections on Trotsky's youth in Baruch Knei-Paz, *The Social and Political Thought of Leon Trotsky*, Oxford, 1978; Isaac Deutscher, *The Prophet Armed*, New York, 1963; and Edmund Wilson, *To the Finland Station*, New York, 1940.
12. G Novack, 'Introduction' to LD Trotsky, *Problems of Everyday Life and Other Writings on Culture and Science*, New York, 1973, p11.
13. All quotations from this essay can be found in LD Trotsky, 'Tolstoy: Poet and Rebel', *Leon Trotsky on Literature and Art*, op cit, pp127-41.

and Homeric love of children'. Thirdly, Tolstoy achieves characterisation through a unity of 'inner necessity' and 'harmony' resulting in an 'aesthetic pantheism'. The end result is incisively characterised by Trotsky as the creation of an 'agricultural aesthetic' bonded 'back to the Pentateuch and Illiad'. Thus Trotsky, like Marx and Engels before him, uncritically accepts inherited notions of aesthetics from the nineteenth century version of the Western tradition.[14] What is new and distinctive is Trotsky's ability to infuse these with the perspective and sensibility of historical materialism, which he brilliantly blends with a detailed knowledge of the Russian social formation.[15]

The second study, 'On Tolstoy's Death', written by Trotsky in Vienna shortly after the event, establishes a contradiction between Tolstoy's 'organic' ties to an unacceptable ruling class culture and his 'moral affinity' to socialist thought.[16] In his impressively-researched book, *The Social and Political Thought of Leon Trotsky*, Baruch Knei-Paz aptly summarises the literary values established by Trotsky in this essay; 'a liberal attitude in principle to all literature, an openness to the artistic merits of creative work without regard for the author's political views', but one that is also always asking 'the utilitarian question: what does it matter from the perspective of socialism?'.[17] Another enduring feature Trotsky establishes in his early work is a non-intrusive, dialectical mode of argumentation. Characteristically, he will first state the viewpoint of an opponent, and then reformulate the issue on a different basis — usually with some impressive twist. At its most effective, the method moves the reader from one view to another. However, it is crucial to realise that within the new view is embedded a dynamic tension stemming from the residue of the earlier proposition reinterpreted in the fresh context.

Art and Society

The second phase of literary criticism, occurring in the years immediately following the Russian Revolution, was indubitably Trotsky's most productive. But its achievement was significantly flawed by Trotsky's failure to foresee the main trend in Soviet society — the appearance of a bureaucratic tyranny led by Stalin that would subvert and negate Trotsky's entire literary projections for the future

---

14. That version is now in the process of unravelling through the impact of works such as Martin Bernal, *Black Athena*, New Brunswick, 1989.
15. It would be hard to surpass Norman Geras' remarkable discussion of the young Trotsky's writings in 'Literature of Revolution', in the collection *Literature of Revolution: Essays on Marxism*, London, 1986, pp217-67.
16. Quotations from this essay can be found in *Leon Trotsky on Literature and Art*, op cit, pp143-7.
17. Knei-Paz, op cit, p462.

of the USSR. It was not until 1937 that he would be able fully to come to grips with this phenomenon in the chapter 'Culture and the Soviet Bureaucracy' in *The Revolution Betrayed: What Is the Soviet Union and Where Is It Going?*. Trotsky's writings of the early 1920s, especially *Literature and Revolution* (originally a series of articles in *Pravda* that he wrote over two summers),[18] were produced under the impact of the immediate post-revolutionary events of social transformation and civil war. His overriding concern is to rework the complex tension between a view of art as an independent category of aesthetic experience, and the recognition of all culture as essentially ideological (that is, implicitly or explicitly bearing a political message).[19]

Perhaps surprisingly from a contemporary Marxist perspective, Trotsky argues that the claims of the artist are entirely irrelevant to the multiple functions of the work of art itself. On the one hand, regardless of what the reader or viewer might think about a work of art, it must exist within history and bear a relationship to history. He uses deliberately provocative terms to characterise the socially dependent nature of art, such as 'social servant' and 'utilitarian'.[20] On the other hand, the techniques attributed by Trotsky as ones intrinsic to art are in no way reducible to politics. He maintains that art is characterised by at least six traits. It finds the necessary rhythm of words for 'dark and vague moods'; brings thought and feeling 'closer or contrasts them, one with the other'; enriches the 'spiritual experience' of the individual and the community; refines feeling, rendering it more 'flexible' and 'responsive'; enlarges the volume of thought 'in advance and not through the personal method of accumulated experience'; and educates 'the individual, the social group, the class and the nation'.[21]

In sum, Trotsky's view is clearly that art is not 'pure'. Yet, to deny the 'purity' of art from a Marxist view is not to deny its autonomy, praxis or expansive dimension, rendering it a mere instrument of message. If anything, Trotsky seems to conceive of art as 'technique' — devoid of a particular content. Simply put, Trotsky regards art as a technique of articulating moods, formulating diverse relations between thought and feeling, expanding and enriching emotions, and educating us prior to empirical experience in some sort of preparatory way.

Upon this foundation, Trotsky sought to elaborate the tasks of Marxism in re-

---

18. The second part of *Literature and Revolution* consists of Trotsky's essays penned during 1908-14, yet to be translated into English. In this present essay, the first part is treated as a book in itself.
19. A fine study of Trotsky's views on the relation between art and ideology can be found in Cliff Slaughter, *Marxism, Ideology and Literature*, London, 1980, pp86-113.
20. *Leon Trotsky on Literature and Art*, op cit, pp30-1.
21. Ibid, p30.

gard to art as he saw them in the post-revolution era. In this local application of his theory, Trotsky demands a kind of 'scientific' investigation into the 'social roots of the "pure" as well as the tendentious art'.[22] That is, rather than '"incriminate" a poet with the thoughts and feelings which he expresses', Trotsky aims to focus on questions such as the following. To which order of feelings does 'a given artistic work correspond in all its peculiarities'? What are the 'social conditions of these thoughts and feelings'? What is their location in the 'historic development of a society and of a class'? What literary heritage has 'entered into the elaboration of the new form'? Under the influence of 'what historic impulse have the new complexes of feelings and thoughts broken through the shell that divides them from the sphere of poetic consciousness'?[23]

When Trotsky explores these issues in assessing writers such as Kliuev, Yessenin, Pilnyak, Blok and Mayakovsky, the result can be characterised as something of a balancing act. He never fails to offer complicated, detailed and individualised investigations full of verve and wit; yet these are directly set against his insistence on 'the subsidiary role which art plays in the social process'.[24]

One must conclude that if Trotsky holds art to be a realm of 'techniques' involving emotions, feelings, thoughts and perceptions, Marxism must be apprehended as a method appropriate to the understanding of the social roots that nourish the various techniques. In particular, it follows that the Marxist critic should be equipped to tell us what produces the content and the form exhibited in art. Such a charge is particularly complex and demanding when it comes to suggesting to what social order the content and form correspond, and what drives new human emotions into the realm of poetic expression.

By mid-career Trotsky had established the fundamental terrain of his cultural theory. From a Marxist view, art is subsidiary to social process. Yet art is simultaneously a category dealing with specialised techniques, and is therefore semi-autonomous, and not immediately reducible to political coding.

The Masterwork

The brilliance and relevance of *Literature and Revolution* and the related essays of the early 1920s stem from much more than Trotsky's mere articulation of a classical Marxist stance on art and society. Indeed, it is hard to think of another book in world history with an equivalent agenda of complex and burning issues. Among the questions he addresses are the following:

22. Ibid.
23. Ibid, pp30-1.
24. Ibid, p31.

- How does a social revolution affect literature? Does it help literature, hinder it, advance it, retard it or derail it?
- How do writers relate to the revolutionary process? Can a revolution be accurately grasped and communicated in literature? Are special literary forms necessary to express the revolutionary process?
- How should leaders of a revolutionary government evaluate the literature that grows out of a revolution? Should revolutionaries try to influence literature by encouraging certain schools?
- How should censorship be used in order to defend a revolution? Where should the line be drawn?
- How should one formulate one's expectations for the kind of literature one should expect to appear in the short run as well as the long run, following a successful revolution and the inauguration of a transitional period?

Trotsky uses pre- and post-revolutionary Russia as the laboratory in which to explore these and similar issues. He proceeds from a study of the literature existing in the period before the unsuccessful 1905 Revolution, and concludes with a utopian vision of the literature that he hopes will eventually emerge from the communist leadership of the 1917 Revolution, along the way covering just about every conceivable stopping point.

For example, his initial chapter, 'Pre-Revolutionary Art', encompasses developments in four main areas. He starts with a survey of the literature emerging before 1905, the first great upheaval in modern Russia, which consists in the main of the writing of nobles and peasants. He then turns to the bourgeois literature appearing in what he calls the 'intra-revolutionary period', between 1905 and the 1917 Revolution. The next period is marked by the literature of the counter-revolutionaries who fled Russia because of the revolution (the emigrés); and the last theme taken up is the literature of the counter-revolutionaries who remained inside Russia.

His second chapter, 'The Literary Fellow Travellers of the Revolution', analyses the work produced by writers obviously more sympathetic to the revolution than the counter-revolutionaries. The word 'fellow traveller' has acquired a variety of meanings over the years. It was also discussed by Trotsky in 'Class and Art', a speech made in 1924 to the press department of the Central Committee of the Communist Party of the USSR.[25] Trotsky applies the term to writers who approve of the abstract goals of the Russian Revolution, but who are not ready to go all the way with the revolutionaries to achieve them.

In his third chapter, Trotsky moves even closer to the revolution through a

---

25. It appears in ibid, pp63-82.

consideration of Alexander Blok, a writer whom he regarded as partly forming a bridge between the fellow travellers and the October Revolution. The fourth and fifth chapters discuss two movements — Futurism and Formalism — that try to interact with the revolution. The sixth chapter analyses the school of proletarian culture and art, one of the literary schools that is actually a conscious part of the revolution. The seventh chapter presents Trotsky's recommendations for communist policy regarding literature. The eight and concluding chapter contains Trotsky's projections and predictions as to the kind of art he believes the revolution will ultimately produce upon completion — when all classes have been abolished, and when communism has been established in the USSR.

From the outset, Trotsky applies his dialectical 'Marxist sensibility' to the topic. For example, he affirms the priority of the material and social over the cultural by emphasising that if communists had not fought against the counter-revolution and carried out a reorganisation of society, there could not even have been a debate over the various cultural policies of the USSR. Moreover, he adds that there will be no opportunity for the debate to continue if the severe economic problems besetting the USSR in the wake of the Civil War are not resolved. Then, in a characteristic inversion of perspective, Trotsky is equally emphatic that merely establishing a new state and organising an egalitarian economy is no guarantor of the achievement of socialist goals. According to Marxist theory, he argues, each new revolution in class relations ultimately produces unique changes in the form and content of art and culture. Therefore, until the USSR has developed a new socialist science, culture and art, one cannot say that a socialist society has been achieved. This is the essence of his aphorism, 'the development of art is the highest test of the vitality and significance of each epoch'.[26]

Trotsky then deepens this claim by being equally adamant that one cannot achieve a new socialist art or culture through declaring it by fiat or by conducting laboratory experiments. It is first necessary to create a successful society as a whole: 'Only a movement of scientific thought on a national scale and the development of a new art would signify that the historic seed has not only grown into a plant, but has even flowered.'[27]

Viewed with the hindsight of 70 years, one of the more striking features of *Literature and Revolution* is the degree to which it anticipates Gramsci's familiar adage: 'Optimism of the will, pessimism of the intellect.'[28] This could hardly be clearer than in Trotsky's scathing critique of the state of Soviet literature at the

26. LD Trotsky, *Literature and Revolution*, op cit, p9.
27. Ibid.
28. For the detailed discussion of Gramsci's concepts of optimism and pessimism, see A Gramsci, *Selections From the Prison Notebooks*, New York, 1971, pp173-8.

time. It is especially important to note his view that no particular school or group has as yet proposed a viable or appropriate literary response to the revolution: 'If a line were extended from the present art to the socialist art of the future, one would say that we have hardly now passed through the stage of even preparing for its preparation.'[29]

The Exile Period

Of interest in Trotsky's criticism in the 1920s and the 1930s is his attitude towards the experimental literature now known as modernism. An important aspect of his assessment of this genre is his longstanding opposition to the dominance of any particular literary school, regardless of the political claims of its adherents. The danger of supporting a particular literary trend is further underscored by his belief that the culture of the revolutionary movement of his day was at a very primitive stage. Thus Trotsky's basic sympathy for tradition, and for the realist genre of fiction, was balanced on principle by an openness to all art forms, and a demand for tolerance for the greatest degree of experimentation: 'Poets, painters, sculptors and musicians will themselves find their own approach and methods, if the struggle for freedom of oppressed classes and peoples scatters the clouds of scepticism and of pessimism which cover the horizon of mankind.'[30]

Nevertheless, despite all that has been made of Trotsky's collaboration of the late 1930s with André Breton, and some passing references to psychoanalysis in his own criticism, there is little evidence that Trotsky read many surrealist or other avant-garde works. His comments on modernist works, such as *Journey to the End of Night* (1933), reveal his traditional preoccupations, such as the refraction of national culture through language: 'Céline's style is subordinated to his receptivity of the objective world. In his seemingly careless, ungrammatical, passionately condensed language there lives, beats and vibrates the genuine wealth of French culture, the entire emotional and mental experience of a great nation, in its living content, in its keenest tints.'[31] On the other hand, in his exile, Trotsky appears to be more insistent than ever in identifying potential links implicitly existing between the more rebellious forms of art and rebel politics:

'Living creativeness cannot march ahead without repulsion away from official tradition, canonised ideas and feelings, images and expressions covered by the lacquer of use and wont. Each new tendency seeks for the most direct and honest contact

---

29. LD Trotsky, *Literature and Revolution*, op cit, p12.
30. *Leon Trotsky on Literature and Art*, op cit, p114.
31. Ibid, p193.

between words and emotions. The struggle against pretence in art always grows to a lesser or greater measure into the struggle against the injustice of human relations. The connection is self-evident: art which loses the sense of the social lie inevitably defeats itself by affectation, turning into mannerism.'[32]

Does this alter in any significant way his stance on the relation of political commitment to artistic practice? His original view was that, within limits, it is permissible to urge certain values and perspectives on the artist. The danger is in attempting to provide precise leadership for the arts, and in transgressing boundaries of areas not appropriately the terrain of Marxism. As I quoted earlier:

'The Marxian method affords an opportunity to estimate the development of the new art, to trace all its sources, to help the most progressive tendencies by critical illumination of the road, but it does not do more than that. Art must make its own way and by its own means. The Marxian methods are not the same as the artistic.'[33]

This meant in practice that while a political party might protect and assist artistic movements, it should in no way endorse a literary circle in competition with other literary circles.

However, what was new by the mid-1930s was that Trotsky began to put a special premium on the current within modernism drawn to the left — most notably the French surrealists and dissident communists gravitating towards *Partisan Review* magazine in the USA.[34] In his famous *Manifesto: Towards a Free Revolutionary Art*, written in collaboration with Breton, Trotsky appears to regard left wing modernism as the highest form of art, which he refers to simply as 'true' art: 'True art, which is not content to play variations on ready-made models but rather insists on expressing the inner needs of man and mankind in its time — true art is unable not to be revolutionary, not to aspire to a complete and radical reconstruction of society.'[35]

In this context, Trotsky speaks of a category of 'independent revolutionary art'. Politically, the category meant militantly anti-capitalist, anti-fascist and anti-

32. Ibid, p201.
33. Ibid, pp55-6.
34. For studies of Trotsky's relations with surrealists, see Marguerite Bonnet, 'Trotsky et Breton'; and Gérard Roche, 'La Rencontre de l'Aigle et du Lion', *Cahiers Léon Trotsky*, no 25, March 1986, pp5-18, 23-46. An analysis of Trotsky's associations with the *Partisan Review* group is central to my *The New York Intellectuals*, Chapel Hill, 1987.
35. *Leon Trotsky on Literature and Art*, op cit, p117.

Stalinist — but specifically excluding the view that equated Stalinism with fascism. In other words, a political trend compatible with Trotskyism, but much broader, reaching out to anarchists, left social democrats, independent communists, and others drawn to the left whose ideas were not so well formed. In 1938 Trotsky sought to unite such forces in the International Federation of Independent Revolutionary Art, and it seems probable that his writings at that time were modulated to appear more attractive to the existing radical modernist milieu, although he was clearly enthusiastic about Diego Rivera's art. In any event, the beginning of the Second World War in September 1939 truncated Trotsky's efforts to unite revolutionary artists.

Conclusion and Caveat

In summary, Trotsky's contributions to literary and cultural theory, of which *Literature and Revolution* comprises the central moment, must be grasped as an evolutionary project with some incomplete parts, gaps and (sometimes implicit) self-corrections. His youthful writings constitute an impressive application of basic Marxist principles to mainly Russian texts and events. In mid-life, under the impact of new circumstances created by the Russian Revolution, there occurs a creative leap to original and enduring contributions. Finally, with the writings of the last decade of his life, Trotsky enters a period of adjustment and reworking of earlier propositions in light of the unanticipated triumph of Stalinism, and the exigencies of building a new international revolutionary movement under the difficult conditions of the 1930s.

Trotsky's extraordinarily rich body of writing on culture must be regarded as a component of the foundation for contemporary Marxist criticism, especially as it relates to two urgent concerns. The first is that the evolution of Trotsky's writings up to and including *The Revolution Betrayed* of 1938 helps explain what occurred in the cultural realm under the name of 'Marxism' in the USSR. While the record is clear that a potentially liberatory doctrine became the rationale for political domination and control of the arts, Trotsky's work demonstrates both the authentic character of the potential that was crushed, as well as the heroic legacy of an effort to defend artistic integrity on Marxist principles.

The second area of special value is that Trotsky's views provide possible solutions to theoretical and practical problems faced by left wing cultural workers in the West, the Third World and in the crumbling post-Stalinist states — all areas where authentic Marxism may still be recouped as the theoretical and practical instrument of liberation. Trotsky's appraisals of tradition, experimentation, literary value, diverse critical schools, and the relation between culture and class, along with the examples of his analyses of texts, remain superb starting points for critical exegesis and cultural policy.

However, in both efforts, we must make every effort to scrutinise critically and update Trotsky's legacy. For example, today, while admiring Trotsky's lifelong devotion to human self-liberation and his intransigent opposition to intellectual mystification and despair, there is reason to conclude that his acceptance of the Enlightenment tradition was too complete. His 'faith' in the Enlightenment's reified categories of science, reason and progress was far too one-sided, as well as Eurocentric.[36] This means that there are good reasons to rethink the basis of his assessment of cultural advance and retardation of the early USSR as compared to the West.

Contemporary Marxist critics might not discern the working class and peasantry of the early USSR as being as barren of cultural achievement as Trotsky suggests in *Literature and Revolution*. While Trotsky was hardly an 'elitist', his examination of the cultural activity of these two classes may in some measure be judged to be vitiated by what contemporary Marxists now regard as a patriarchal, Eurocentric literary tradition — a rendering of judgements according to models of high cultural attainment based too one-sidedly upon Dante, Shakespeare and Goethe. Marxists presently studying the cultures of less industrialised countries are far more alert than Trotsky to the genuine complexity of the daily life, activities and art of women and the subaltern classes — especially of those hitherto regarded as 'primitive', 'uncultured' and 'uncivilised'.[37]

Perhaps the most significant caveat in assessing Trotsky's achievement concerns his theory of the transitional era, which was the basis of much of his thinking on cultural policy and possibility. To what extent has history verified his understanding of the post-revolution USSR — either as he saw it in 1922 as simply the dictatorship of the proletariat; or as he saw it after the consolidation of power by Stalin — as fundamentally the same in its economy, yet qualitatively compromised by bureaucratic degeneration? Unless one succumbs to the characterisation of such societies as being in some sense authentically 'socialist', which I certainly am absolutely unwilling to do, then one must call into question Trotsky's belief that the Russian Revolution inaugurated a transitional stage that would rapidly, over several decades, evolve into socialism and then communism. Was the post-1917 stage of the Russian Revolution something other than a transient transition?

---

36. A stimulating comparison of Trotsky with Walter Benjamin, from a slightly different perspective, can be found in Enzo Traverso, 'Walter Benjamin et Léon Trotsky', *Quatrième Internationale*, no 37-38, August-October 1990, pp97-104.
37. For an influential work bridging literary theory and anthropology along these lines, see James Clifford, *The Predicament of Culture: Twentieth Century Ethnography, Literature and Art*, Cambridge, 1988. Of course, one should not exaggerate Trotsky's tendency towards an emphasis on high school to the point of ignoring his important writings contained in *Problems of Life* of 1924, with its chapters on vodka, the church, cinema, etc.

Will societal transitions occur in far more complex and prolonged ways than Trotsky imagined? Was 1917 an aberration caused by historical peculiarities?

Finally, the utopian vision that closes *Literature and Revolution* requires augmentation by what one has been learning over the past few decades about 'cultural difference' from feminists, people of colour in the external and domestic colonies of imperialism, other subjugated minorities, the environmental movement, and such recent radical religious trends as Liberation Theology. Trotsky, like Marx before him, drew too exclusively and uncritically on what he saw as best in the Western tradition and the Enlightenment. The human ideals — Aristotle, Goethe, Marx — that Trotsky admired came from a tiny portion of humanity; they were by no means as 'universal' in their outlook and achievement as Trotsky portrayed them.

These and other problematic features of Trotsky's cultural contributions could be the worthy subject of lengthy future expositions. Whether or not such inquiries will come to pass may well be bound up in the fate of the world socialist movement as it enters the twenty-first century. The collapse of the Soviet regime in 1989 has unexpectedly opened the door wide to the possibility of a new socialist revival in which a reconsideration of Trotsky's cultural as well as his political writings might well be a significant component. At this point, though, it remains unclear as to just who and how many will pass through that door. However, considering the horrors inflicted by today's global capitalism — hi-tech wars, unrelenting racism, murderous inter-ethnic hatred, mass starvation — it is urgent that alternative courses for humanity receive the utmost consideration by this as well as the next generation of scholars and activists.

History

David Law
The Left Opposition in 1923[1]

In the autumn of 1923, the leadership of the Russian Communist Party was confronted by the activity of a new opposition group. The process of its formation is somewhat unclear, but there is no doubt about the issues which led to its intervention. *The Declaration of the Forty-Six*, the only joint statement of any significance made by the Opposition during 1923, raised two main issues: the economic situation and the party regime. As subjects of opposition, these two issues were not new; what was especially significant about *The Declaration of the Forty-Six* was that it connected them. The statement declared that 'the economic and financial crisis... has inexorably revealed the inadequacy of the leadership of the party... especially in the domain of internal party relations'. It discussed the shortcomings of economic policy, and made the assertion that the party was being replaced by 'a recruited bureaucratic apparatus... which inevitably fails in moments of crisis'.[2]

The economic crisis (the complex 'scissors' crisis, the causes and nature of which are of secondary relevance to this article, and are therefore ignored) helped to promote the Opposition in a number of ways. Firstly, the Opposition regarded

1. This article first appeared in *Critique*, no 2, 1973.
2. *The Declaration of the Forty-Six* was dated 15 October 1923. It brought together supporters of Trotsky (for example, Yevgeny Preobrazhensky, Leonid Serebriakov, Yuri Pyatakov, Vladimir Antonov-Ovseyenko and Ivan Smirnov), and members of the former Democratic Centralist opposition (for example, V Osinsky, Timofey Sapronov, Andrei Bubnov, V Kosior, V Maksimovsky and Vladimir Smirnov). Although by no means homogenous, the Opposition of 1923 can justifiably be regarded as the foundation of the Left Opposition. EH Carr, *The Interregnum 1923-24*, Harmondsworth, 1969, pp373-80, gives the full text of the *Declaration*, together with the various signatures and the reservations expressed. Quotations from the *Declaration* are not footnoted separately.

the inability of the official party leadership to deal effectively with economic problems to be a consequence of a bureaucratic party structure.³ Secondly, those who made up the Opposition found themselves, in general, advocating solutions (for example, efficient planning for industrial development) which clashed with the opinions of the official leadership. Thirdly, the harmful effects of the economic crisis on the working class, the fall in the standard of living and rising unemployment, resulted in strikes which were supported by groups (the Workers Group, Workers Truth) involving party members. This gave rise to a general feeling of disquiet about the internal party situation which went beyond the ranks of the nascent Opposition.

The Declaration of the Forty-Six shows that the primary concern of the Opposition was not with bureaucratism as an evil in itself. Of more fundamental concern were the implications of bureaucratism: the effects on the vitality of the party, and its ability to influence events decisively. As *The Declaration of the Forty-Six* illustrates, the Opposition was worried that the party would not deal adequately with the international situation, which was particularly critical in the autumn of 1923. The position was further aggravated by the enforced retirement of Lenin as a result of illness. His presence might well have reduced the tensions that led to the Opposition's struggle. Perhaps, as in the past, Lenin would have led the party onto a changed course as events demanded, and thus avoided a permanent fracture. In any case, Lenin's absence allowed the friction between Trotsky and the official leadership to find political expression.

The Course of the Struggle

The first stage of the struggle of the Left Opposition, from October 1923 to January 1924, can be divided into three periods: firstly an attempt by the Opposition to raise issues in secret at the highest levels of the party as a prelude to broader discussion — this was met by condemnation; secondly, a period of concessions by the official leadership during which they allowed relatively open discussion of the issues, and agreed to a resolution on party democracy which made considerable concessions to the Opposition; thirdly, repression of the Opposition culminating in a condemnation by the Thirteenth Party Conference in January 1924.⁴

3. The term official leadership is here used as a convenience to denote those party leaders who were against the Opposition, principally Zinoviev, Kamenev and Stalin. The term 'leadership' by itself is insufficient since many prominent Oppositionists could be considered to be party leaders. The use of the term is a convention, and is not meant to imply that there was an unofficial leadership.
4. Since this article cannot deal with the details of the struggle, readers are referred to I Deutscher, *The Prophet Unarmed*, London, 1959, chapter 2; EH Carr, *The Interregnum*, op cit,

The first period opened with a letter from Trotsky dated 8 October to the Central Committee. This letter, prompted in part by an attempt to restrict Trotsky's power on the Military Revolutionary Committee, raised issues of economic policy, and roundly criticised the 'bureaucratisation of the party apparatus' which had developed to 'unheard of proportions by means of the method of secretarial selection'. It concluded by threatening 'to make known the true state of affairs to every member of the party... those whom Trotsky considered to be sufficiently prepared, matured and self-restrained...'.[5] This letter was quickly followed by *The Declaration of the Forty-Six*, which it may well have prompted. At the very least, several signatories of the *Declaration* must have been aware of Trotsky's move, just as Trotsky would surely have been aware of the intention to make such a *Declaration*.[6]

The response of the official leadership was to hold a plenum of the Central Committee, together with the Central Control Commission and delegates of 10 leading party organisations. This meeting, in the absence of Trotsky through illness, but in the presence of 12 invited signatories from the Forty-Six, considered a resolution put by Preobrazhensky (included as an appendix to this article), but rejected it in favour of the resolution *On the Internal Party Situation*. The resolution, accepted by 102 votes to two with 10 abstentions, gave no record of the points raised by the Opposition, but 'resolutely condemned' the action of the Forty-Six 'as a step of factional splitting politics', and characterised Trotsky's action as 'a grave political error', and one which 'has objectively assumed the character of a factional move'.[7]

The causes of the transition from the first to the second period of the discussion are not entirely clear. Certainly, news of the Opposition's statement circu-

---

chapters 12 and 13; RV Daniels, *The Conscience of the Revolution*, New York, 1969, chapter 9. Source references relating to the views of the Opposition and the official leadership are kept to a minimum.

5. Trotsky's letter, the reply by the Politbureau, and Trotsky's response have never been published in full. Lengthy extracts were published in *Sotsialisticheskii Vestnik* (*Socialist Herald*), a Menshevik organ published in Berlin, no 11 (81), 28 May 1924, pp9-12. Partial translations are to be found in M Eastman, *Since Lenin Died*, New York, 1925, pp36, 142-5.

6. Several of Trotsky's closest political associates were among the Forty-Six (see note 2). Trotsky was later accused of playing a leading part in organising the Forty-Six, but it is unlikely that he did so. Throughout the struggle of the 1923 Opposition, Trotsky refused to associate himself directly with the Opposition (although this article considers Trotsky as a part of the Opposition); also the *Declaration* went further than Trotsky by questioning the ruling on factions. EH Carr considers that Trotsky was invited to associate himself with the group (*The Interregnum*, op cit, p305).

7. *KPSS v Resolyutsiyakh, 1898-1924* (*CPSU in Resolutions*), Moscow, 1954, pp767-8. The resolution is translated in *Against Trotskyism*, Moscow, 1972, pp235-6.

lated, possibly creating rumours unfavourable to the official leadership.[8] Perhaps there was pressure from inside leadership circles to go further than simple condemnation; perhaps also the official leadership hoped to keep Trotsky isolated from the rest of the Opposition by allowing various concessions. Whatever the reasons, on 7 November, the anniversary of the Revolution, an article by Zinoviev appeared in *Pravda* proclaiming the indispensability of giving 'practical application to workers' democracy within the party', and admitting that 'almost all very important questions go pre-decided from above downwards'. An editorial footnote announced that *Pravda* would sponsor a debate on questions of party democracy.

The second stage of the struggle began quietly and without the participation of prominent figures. Only near the end of November did the debate sharpen. Preobrazhensky declared in *Pravda* that since the introduction of New Economic Policy, the party had been following 'an essentially incorrect line in its internal party policy'. Zinoviev and Stalin made speeches which, although of course declaring in favour of workers' democracy, carried real warnings to the Opposition.[9] By the beginning of December the struggle had begun in earnest. Particularly in Moscow, Opposition speakers at party meetings were finding considerable support, and the official leadership had become concerned enough to send its major figures to speak.

During December a committee of Kamenev, Stalin and Trotsky, apparently established to find a compromise, produced a resolution which was passed by the Politbureau and the Presidium of the Central Control Commission on 5 December.[10] The resolution, which was long and detailed, bore evident signs of the influence of the Left. Indeed, it was later referred to as 'a mistaken concession to Trotsky'.[11] It began by outlining a series of negative tendencies, which stemmed from

8. A resolution of the Thirteenth Party Conference of January 1924 declared that Trotsky's letter of 8 October and *The Declaration of the Forty-Six* immediately became 'the common property of wide circles of party members'. The resolution is in *KPSS v Resolyutsiyakh*, op cit, pp778-85. Translations are in *International Press Correspondence (Inprecor)*, Volume 4, no 20; and *Against Trotskyism*, op cit, pp236-45.
9. Preobrazhensky's article is in *Pravda*, 28 November 1923. Zinoviev's speech of 1 December at the fourteenth Petrograd provincial party conference warned against relaxing the ruling on factions (*Pravda*, 7 December 1923); Stalin's speech of 2 December to an enlarged meeting of the Krasnaya Presnya district party committee called for the rejection of 'two extremes'; that of wanting 'elections throughout', and that of 'demanding unlimited discussion' (*Pravda*, 6 December 1923).
10. *Pravda*, 7 December 1923. The resolution titled *On the Party Structure* was later accepted by the Thirteenth Party Conference, and is in *KPSS v Resolyutsiyakh*, op cit, pp771-8. A translation is in *Inprecor*, Volume 4, no 7, 29 January 1924.
11. SI Gusev, at a session of the Central Control Commission in 1926, quoted by Trotsky in a declaration to the Politbureau, 13 August 1926. Source: Trotsky archives, document T2998.

the contradictions of the NEP. These tendencies included 'the danger of a loss of perspective of socialist construction as a whole and of the world revolution, and... the process of bureaucratisation which is to be noted in the party apparatus'. It was asserted that workers' democracy was necessary to counter these negative tendencies, and measures were outlined for achieving it. Above all, these included 'liberty of party life', and election of 'all leading party functionaries and commissions... by those bodies immediately under them'. The resolution also urged better provision of information and education for the rank and file, more attention by the Central Control Commission to fighting 'bureaucratic perversion', and greater participation by all in party administration. Factions were condemned, but the party leadership was instructed not to regard every kind of criticism as an indication of the formation of factions. A practical recommendation made was that the next party congress should consider passing a rule that provincial and all-Russian party conferences be held twice a year instead of annually. However, the main proposals of the resolution concerned recommendations about attitudes and practices which depended for their success on the way that they were interpreted and acted upon.

As if to underline his success in having the resolution adopted, short-lived though this success was to be, Trotsky published his own interpretation of the resolution. He did this in the form of a letter to his party branch, expressing regrets for his absence from a meeting owing to illness.[12] The letter ascribed 'exceptional significance' to the resolution, proclaiming that the 'new course' which it opened was to transfer 'the centre of gravity which was mistakenly placed in the apparatus by the old course... to the activity, the initiative and critical spirit of all the party members as the organised vanguard of the proletariat'. Bureaucratism was doing considerable harm to the political education of the 'young communist generation'. It was they, 'the most reliable barometer of the party', who had reacted most sharply against bureaucratic practices. A democratic relationship between the old and young communist generations (later defined as the pre- and post-October party members),[13] was required to preserve the party from bureaucratism. Trotsky offered the example of German social democracy to illustrate the historical possibility of degeneration of a 'revolutionary old guard'. Above all else, the essential change required to guard against such degeneration was a change in 'the spirit that reigns in our organisation'.

The second period of the struggle was concluded by a meeting of the local

Information: Daniels, op cit, p223.

12. The letter was dated 8 December 1923; it was published in *Pravda*, 11 December, and is to be found in LD Trotsky, *The New Course*, Ann Arbor, 1972, pp89-98.

13. Ibid, p17.

party in Moscow on 11 December, attended by over 1000 people.[14] At this meeting, assessed by Carr as 'the last occasion of frank and fully reported debate capable of swaying opinion within the party', Kamenev made the opening speech.[15] He admitted the need to renew party life and the apparatus, and to abolish appointments in favour of elections; however, no groupings must be permitted, whether factional or not. Unlike Kamenev, Sapronov, the principal speaker for the Opposition, freely referred to Trotsky, quoting him in support of his arguments. A general debate followed the two main speeches. Amongst others, Preobrazhensky, Radek and Zinoviev spoke. Stalin, although apparently present, remained silent.[16] Yaroslavsky was the only speaker to make a direct attack on Trotsky, an attack which was not well received; but Kamenev, in his concluding speech, regretted certain aspects of Trotsky's letter, and called upon him to explain his attitude further.

Within days of this meeting, the relative freedom of discussion allowed there had given way to repression. Again, the reasons for the timing of the change are not entirely clear. Perhaps it is best explained by the hypothesis that the official leadership had hoped that the resolution of 5 December would satisfy both Trotsky and the Opposition, and that they would relax their critical posture, but ensuing events proved this to be a false hope.[17] Trotsky himself suggests that the change in attitude may have been due to Zinoviev forcing an attack of sufficient momentum to compel Stalin to join in, and thus preventing a compromise between Stalin and Trotsky being made at Zinoviev's expense.[18] Whatever the reason for the timing of the change, the change itself is not surprising, given the split between the official leadership and the Opposition, which had only been papered over by the resolution of 5 December.

The third period of the struggle, prefaced by growing criticism in *Pravda*, was launched by Stalin in an article in *Pravda* on 15 December, and in a speech made by Zinoviev on the same day.[19] A particular feature of this period was the attack on Trotsky. Previously, Trotsky had not been selected for special criticism; now,

14. JV Stalin, *Works*, Volume 5, Moscow, 1953, p383.
15. EH Carr, op cit, p322. Kamenev's speech is reported in *Pravda*, 13 December 1923. The debate is fully reported in successive issues of *Pravda*.
16. JV Stalin, *Works*, Volume 6, Moscow, 1953, p12.
17. Trotsky's letter was later referred to as 'a platform advanced in opposition to the CC resolution' immediately after that resolution had been unanimously accepted (JV Stalin, *Works*, Volume 6, op cit, p13). Trotsky's relative inactivity made this a propitious time for the official leadership to strike.
18. LD Trotsky, *Stalin*, London, 1947, p387.
19. Zinoviev's speech to a Petrograd party conference attended by over 3000 people is in *Pravda*, 20-21 December 1923. In contrast to the Moscow meeting, only the speech of the major official figure, Zinoviev, was reported in *Pravda*.

however, the official leadership mounted an attack unfettered by political principle. Typical of such an approach was Bukharin's serialised *Pravda* article, 'Down with Factionalism', which accompanied Trotsky's articles 'Groups and Factional Formations' and 'The Question of Party Generations'.[20] Bukharin accused 'the faction of Trotsky, Sapronov and Preobrazhensky' of departing from Leninism on questions of internal party policy. Hinting at Trotsky's former Menshevik associations, he asserted: 'Bolshevism has always distinguished itself from the formal democratism of the Mensheviks... It does not conceal from the party and the working class the fact that the party is led by leaders... The more conscious lead the less conscious... The less conscious and less active become more and more conscious and active. These internal mechanics constitute real democracy.' Besides not understanding 'real democratism', Trotsky failed to understand the 'mass psychology' of the peasants, and in the three major debates since October — the Brest-Litovsk crisis, the trade union debate, and the present controversy — Trotsky had advocated a solution out of touch with reality.[21]

The decisive condemnation of Trotsky and the Opposition, which ended the first stage of the struggle of the Left Opposition, was made at the Thirteenth Party Conference in January 1924. Again Trotsky was not present, due to continued illness, and Preobrazhensky made the major speeches for the Opposition. The official leadership condemned the Opposition in the same terms as previously, and produced a resolution declaring that the Opposition represented 'not only an attempt at a revision of Bolshevism, not only a direct aberration from Leninism, but also a blatant petit-bourgeois deviation'.[22] The resolution, among other things, called for measures to preserve 'an iron Bolshevik discipline', identified the conference with the resolution of the Tenth Party Congress banning factions, and publicised the previously secret point seven of that resolution, which provided for the expulsion of both ordinary members and members of the Central Committee for 'any breach of discipline or revival or toleration of factionalism'. The resolution concluded by declaring the discussion closed, and called on all party organisations to proceed to active work.

20. Trotsky's articles were published in *Pravda* on 28 and 29 December. They were later included in *The New Course*. Bukharin's article was published in *Pravda* on 28, 29 and 30 December 1923, and 1 and 4 January 1924. It appeared as an unsigned article; Stalin stated that the author was Bukharin (JV Stalin, *Works*, Volume 6, op cit, p38).
21. Irony is added to the coarseness of Bukharin's attack if one remembers Bukharin's position on the first two of these issues.
22. See note 8 for the reference to this resolution.

The Issues

In 1923 questions of economic policy and international revolution helped give rise to the debate, and deepened it in various ways. These were, however, of secondary importance compared to questions of party democracy, which were given very considerable attention in their own right.[23] This contrasts with the later situation of 1926-27 when the Left Opposition virtually always raised the issues of decision-making in connection with the actual decisions made, concentrating in particular on the 'hardening' of the NEP, and the subordination of Comintern policy to the demands of socialism in one country. No doubt this was due in part to a changed analysis. In 1923 the Opposition was discussing bureaucratism and the growth of bureaucracy as a system of administration; by 1926 it was beginning to assert the existence of a bureaucracy as an ossifying party leadership, maintaining itself by the exercise of power. The progression from bureaucratisation to bureaucracy in the analysis of the Left Opposition assisted the transition to a more comprehensive and interlinked analysis by pointing to bureaucracy as the central political factor which conditioned policy in all spheres.

Another contrast between the Left Opposition at different stages is that, unlike the Opposition of 1926-27, the Opposition of 1923 never published a programme. This reflected the fact that the Opposition was in its formative stages; apparently, in 1923, it existed without any form of internal discipline. In many ways the Opposition in that year was a much more informal body than it later became; at this stage, far from the organised and subversive force as it was later characterised, the Opposition was a relatively loose collection of individuals grouping together on the specific question of internal party democracy.[24] The nearest it came to a programme was *The Declaration of the Forty-Six*. This statement contented itself with a call for the abolition of the regime existing in the party 'in the first instance by those who have created it', and for its replacement by 'a regime of comradely unity and internal party democracy'. It offered no suggestions as to how this was

---

23. Divisions on issues relating to party democracy were mirrored by those relating to economic policy, with the Opposition in general calling for more widespread and efficient planning as a way out of the 'scissors impasse'. Divisions over the issue of the attempted German revolution were distorted in various ways to exploit the situation in favour of the official leadership, in particular Zinoviev. Unlike the economic situation, where there were real and defined differences, the 'German question' was of importance because it raised doubts about the political capabilities of the official leadership, and because it raised the general level of tension. It also underlined the dangers to the troika of Trotsky's support in the Comintern, and it provided an exploitable situation.
24. The relative looseness of this group is shown by the fact that 43 of the signatories of *The Declaration of the Forty-Six* signed it with reservations. Eleven different reservations are expressed.

to be attained, merely proposing, 'as a first and urgent step', the calling of a conference of the Central Committee with 'the most prominent and active party workers', and including 'comrades holding views on the situation different from the views of the majority of the Central Committee'.

Since the Opposition lacked a definitive programme, in order to assess its ideas, one must look to the speeches, articles and resolutions put by various individuals. Prominent among these individuals was Preobrazhensky, who often took the role of spokesman for the Opposition. In the course of leading the defence of the action of the Forty-Six at the enlarged plenum of the Central Committee in October, he presented a resolution, later repeated in his speech to the Thirteenth Party Conference. This resolution, described by Carr as 'the most concise statement of what the Opposition meant at this time by workers' democracy',[25] is reproduced in full as an appendix to this article. The pleas it made for freedom of discussion and criticism, without reprisal, and for freedom of elections, were typical of Opposition statements at this time.

During the period of concessions, the official leadership met the Opposition's demand for internal party democracy with agreement that change was necessary. This created a problem for the Opposition; on the issue of what to do about bureaucratism, they found themselves apparently in alliance with the official leadership. This situation might well have confused some members of the party's rank and file. Indeed, one railway worker at the Moscow party meeting of 11 December declared: 'The workers will ask me what your fundamental differences are; to speak frankly, I do not know how to answer.'[26] However, there were real differences in the positions of Opposition and official leadership, even if these were somewhat obscure to the party's rank and file.

The Opposition considered bureaucratism as the antithesis of workers' democracy, and viewed it as a fundamental problem, the overcoming of which was of paramount importance. The official leadership, in general, asserted that the Opposition's criticisms were heavily exaggerated, but rather grudgingly admitted that perhaps there was too much red tape, too much appointment, and not enough election, and *perhaps* discussion did not take place as freely as it ought to. The Opposition tended to consider that bureaucratism had become a serious problem since the introduction of the NEP, and that, in many ways, it was strengthened by the contradictions of the NEP. The official leadership preferred to view bureaucratism as a hangover from war communism, although admitting that the NEP could exert negative influences on the party.

At the root of the differences between the Opposition and the official leader-

25. EH Carr, op cit, p308.
26. *Pravda*, 18 December 1923.

ship, there were different conceptions of the respective roles of leaders and rank and file in the party. The Opposition stressed the need for freedom of criticism and interaction both between leaders and led, and between experienced and youthful members, within a framework of democracy. A major task of leadership was the coordination and distillation of the experiences of different sections of the party. However, in the view of the official leadership, the primary task of leaders was to issue directives. The role of the party's rank and file was to be an obedient transmission belt.

The Opposition was seriously concerned that careerism, subservience and a reliance on tradition would threaten the flexibility that the party required if it was to be able to adopt new policies when necessary. Without freedom of discussion and criticism, the party's rank and file would be inhibited. The result would be a reluctance to criticise policies that they were called upon to implement, and a distortion of information reaching the leaders from below. The official leadership countered its critics by referring to the past exploits and the traditions of the party, suggesting that these guaranteed the correct formulation of policy in the future.[27]

On one issue in particular, the Opposition and the official leadership were split, and remained so. This was the issue of factions. The Opposition called for a precise definition of the ruling on factions, asserting that not all groups constituted factions, and that group expression of opinion in certain forms was both desirable and inevitable. It also took the view that a repressive regime in the party was itself a cause of factionalism, since discussion would allow the airing and resolution of grievances and dissent; suppression only resulted in clandestine manoeuvres. Furthermore, the Opposition asserted that the present leadership was, in fact, a faction which employed the power of transfer and disciplinary procedures in its own factional interest. The official leadership denied these claims, admitting only that treating every criticism as factional would lead to factions. It asserted that any relaxation of the ruling on factions would tend towards a splitting up of the party and the opening of the party to diverse social interests which would be very dangerous in the situation of the NEP. The Opposition accepted that factions might become spokesmen for non-proletarian class interests, but asserted that this applied equally to the leadership faction, since bureaucratism threatened to detach the party from the masses. In its turn the official leadership characterised the Opposition as a petit-bourgeois faction, thereby referring implicitly to the influence of the NEP.

The question of factions, described by Trotsky as 'the pivot of the discus-

---

27. For example, Kamenev's speech reported by *Pravda*, 13 December 1923; and Stalin's article in *Pravda*, 15 December 1923.

sion',[28] became critical because on this point the differences between the two sides crystallised. According to a strict reading, the Tenth Party Congress resolution *On Party Unity* differentiated between factions and groupings. Nevertheless, all forms of group criticism were effectively illegal, partly because the official leadership held the power to define and punish factions. Recommendations on free discussion and elections remained formal, and could only acquire meaning at the discretion of the leadership. Although by itself a resolution redefining factions according to the wishes of the Opposition in no way guaranteed freedom of group criticism, it was a first step in this direction. Even during the period of concessions, the official leadership would not concede this point.

The refusal of the official leadership to permit any revision or redefinition of the statute on factions indicated its views on the limits of party democracy. The rank and file was free to have all the elections and discussion that it liked, provided the elections resulted in the selection of the leadership's candidate (the increasing practice of effectively restricting the field to one candidate ensured this), and provided the leadership controlled the form and limits of the discussion. Against this attitude the Opposition vainly repeated its warnings of the dangers of bureaucratism.

Strengths and Weaknesses

There can be no doubt that the challenge of the Opposition carried behind it some force. This is shown by the fact that the leadership was prepared to make concessions. Although, without doubt, sections of the leadership were sensitive to, and seriously concerned about, the charges of bureaucratism, these concessions cannot be regarded as freely given, because they followed and preceded periods of repression. It is not possible to be precise about the strength of the Opposition. However, some indications of the numerical level and the occupational and geographical areas of strength may be given.

The resolution of the Thirteenth Party Conference condemning the Opposition was accepted with only three votes against, out of 128 voting delegates.[29] However, not even spokesmen of the official leadership asserted that this accurately reflected the strength of the Opposition. In the course of the conference debate, Rykov declared that the struggle 'brought the Moscow organisation to the verge of a split'.[30] Opposition representation at the conference was undoubtedly

28. LD Trotsky, *The New Course*, op cit, p27. On this question, see in particular Trotsky's chapter on the subject in *The New Course*, and Preobrazhensky's speech of 11 December in *Pravda*, 16 December 1923.
29. *KPSS v Resolyutsiyakh*, op cit, pp771, 785.
30. *Trinadtsataya Konferentsiya RKP(B)*, Moscow, 1924, pp91, 108.

reduced by the pressure of the apparatus during elections. Sapronov, in a speech to the conference, gave an illustration of how the strength of the Opposition was limited during the process of indirect election. The Opposition had won 36 per cent of the representation at district conferences in Moscow province; from these district conferences they received only 18 per cent of the vote for delegates to the provincial conference which then elected delegates to the all-Russian conference. Sapronov suggested that the Opposition had a majority at cell level throughout the province.[31]

Besides considerable strength in Moscow, perhaps even an actual majority, the Opposition had managed to capture party organisations in Ryazan, Penza, Kaluga, Simbirsk and Chelyabinsk. The Opposition's strength in these provincial towns was plausibly attributed to there being in those centres a predominance of party officials transferred as a reprisal for their dissident opinions.[32] In Moscow the strength of the Opposition lay in the state administration (particularly in economic bodies), and student cells. The Opposition was comparatively weak amongst the working class. No doubt this was partly a result of the past record of various members of the Opposition on questions of industrial management, and also partly because questions of immediate working class interest, such as wages, were not given any prominence. Whatever the reasons, in Moscow, at a time when it was gaining majorities among the students, the Opposition could only win 67 out of 346 cells of industrial workers.[33]

A simple comparison of voting figures does not give an adequate picture of the Opposition's strengths and weaknesses. Even as early as 1923, members of the Opposition were subject to various forms of reprisal and discrimination — workers could lose their jobs, students be expelled from the universities, and party and state functionaries be removed by transfer from positions of influence and responsibility. This tended to mean that there were no passive members of the Opposition, whereas the vast bulk of support for the official leadership was passive: the leadership was supported simply because it was the leadership. Thus a comparison of support by voting figures is misleading. At the level of active and prominent members of the Opposition as against active and prominent members of the official leadership, the comparison in terms of numbers would have been much more even. However, it was power rather than numbers that counted.

The official leadership controlled the party apparatus and means of communication. The Opposition had no independent paper or access to any means of communication. The rank and file of the party outside Moscow depended on the

31. Ibid, pp130-1.
32. Ibid, pp124, 133.
33. Ibid, p134.

party press and the local secretaries for their sources of information. With these firmly in the control of the official leadership, it is most unlikely that the bulk of party members even understood the issues at stake. The Opposition could be — and was — freely portrayed as wanting to do away with the apparatus and allow all sorts of competing factions and groups, if only as a cover for its own ambitions. *Pravda*, although for a comparatively short period giving space to the Opposition, was firmly under the control of the official leadership, and served its interests. After 15 December this was increasingly apparent from the content of the articles and reports published.[34] Besides controlling *Pravda*, the official leadership was able to prevent the publication of *The Declaration of the Forty-Six*, as well as hinder and delay publication of Trotsky's *New Course*.[35]

It must be remembered that the bulk of party members were newly recruited, with no pre-revolutionary experience, and very little political education. Although elements of the rank and file might have been concerned about bureaucratic practices on the basis of their own experience, the statements of the official leadership in favour of democracy would have reduced this concern. On the one issue where there was very clear differentiation, the question of factions, the official leadership could appeal rather emotively for unity on the basis of Lenin's resolution on party discipline at a critical stage of the revolution, and call for action rather than interminable factional wranglings. It is not surprising that the Opposition enjoyed comparatively little support outside Moscow. In the capital they could, to some extent, short-circuit the official leadership's control of communications by personal intervention. However, even in Moscow, the official leadership was able to bring pressure through the apparatus and especially through secretaries of party committees to ensure the defeat of the Opposition.

---

34. During December two sub-editors of *Pravda* who had been responsible for the 'party life' section in which many articles critical of the Central Committee had appeared, were dropped after the intervention of Zinoviev. The change of attitude in *Pravda* brought an unsuccessful protest from Trotsky, Radek and Pyatakov. Cf EH Carr, op cit, pp326-7, 330.

35. Publication of *The Declaration of the Forty-Six* was prohibited on the grounds that it was the platform of an illegal faction. The obstacles put in the way of Trotsky's *New Course* are indicated by M Eastman, *Since Lenin Died*, op cit, p81; and B Souvarine, *Stalin*, London, nd, p374. Trotsky's *New Course* was his major contribution to the party debate. Besides his letter of 8 December and the few articles he published in *Pravda* during December 1923, it contains additional chapters which provide an incisive analysis of bureaucratism. In particular, bureaucratism is treated as a social phenomenon, not as an accidental feature of party administration, nor as consisting only of 'the bad habits of office holders'. The NEP promoted bureaucratism in a number of ways; for example, by forcing the attention of the party to matters of administration (state and party links, and the tempo of development, were important in this respect), and by its tolerance of non-proletarian social groups and classes.

The Question of Tactics and the Dilemma of the Opposition

Various writers have asserted that Trotsky and the Opposition compounded their problems by tactical errors. Trotsky, for instance, should have taken a more aggressive attitude and brought his differences into the open at the Twelfth Party Congress in April 1923, and the Opposition should have organised itself as a faction, which, in any case, it was accused of doing.[36] It is beyond the scope of this article to examine in detail these criticisms, although it must be admitted that they may contribute to an explanation of the defeat of the 1923 Opposition. However, the dilemma of the Opposition should not be ignored.

The Opposition accepted, apparently unanimously, that the party was capable of reform, and it therefore addressed its appeals to the party.[37] It acted in what it obviously regarded as a principled manner, denying the accusation that it constituted a faction, and refraining from publishing a platform illicitly. However, a basic premise of the arguments of the Opposition was that the official leadership was manipulating party administration and discipline in its own interests. Even though the Opposition made it clear that it was not attempting to oust the present leadership,[38] those in power were hardly likely to take criticism in the same fraternal spirit in which it was offered. Thus the Opposition was confronted by a dilemma which it was never able to resolve.

Various reasons can be advanced for the decision of the Opposition to press for reform and to remain within the confines of party discipline (although it must have realised that it would be confronted by the power of the apparatus). To some extent, the decision was probably based on a fear of the consequences of splitting the party. Indeed, the Opposition of 1926 divided on this issue, with the Trotskyist element continuing to maintain that the main danger was a bourgeois restoration promoted by forces outside the party, and thus refusing to act as an alternative party. Also, the Opposition lacked an organisational base from which to launch an effective attack. Nevertheless, whatever the significance of these two factors, the Opposition had no special reason to regard its situation as hopeless. Only with hindsight can the question of tactics be given special significance.

Even after the German defeat, the international situation could not be viewed as totally unfavourable. Much of Europe was still in a state of political and eco-

36. Eastman, Souvarine, Carr, Daniels and Deutscher all make tactical criticisms.
37. Agreement on reform provides a contrast with at least one section of the Opposition in 1927, the Democratic Centralists, led by Sapronov and V Smirnov, both one-time members of the Forty-Six, who called for the formation of a second party.
38. 'However much we differ from them... we assume that the present leaders could not in any conditions fail to be appointed by the party to the outstanding posts in the workers' dictatorship.' (*The Declaration of the Forty-Six*)

nomic instability, and in China there were already portents of the coming revolutionary situation. Internally, the party, by virtue of its political consciousness and inherited traditions, its base in the working class, and its control of the economy, remained the only revolutionary body. Although these factors had their negative sides, the Opposition could realistically hope for some support from sections of the party previously uncommitted to its policies.[39] However, as the struggle developed, the apparatus showed the extent to which its power could control the effectiveness of the Opposition, especially its ability to put its programme to the party's rank and file, a factor which could not have been obvious before the struggle began. It also became apparent that the incumbent leadership would not tolerate any threat to its position. Zinoviev and Kamenev, and later Bukharin, in time were to plead for democracy, but only after they had been ousted from positions of effective influence.[40] At this juncture they felt unable to give real meaning to party democracy. Whether this was through distrust of the political consciousness of the newly recruited members (the vast majority of the party), and a preference for the political experience of the old guard, or whether through antipathy and distrust of Trotsky (a factor not without consequence), their reluctance to concede any ground on this question led to the defeat of the 1923 Opposition, as well as to their own subsequent demotion.

Without concessions from above, the Opposition was faced with very considerable problems. The activity and power of the apparatus was based on the passivity of the rank and file, which, as the Opposition was well aware, arose from the objective situation (the general decline of working class consciousness and self-activity related to various factors — historical, international, economic, and the development of the party, post-1917), but was also promoted and definitely maintained by the apparatus itself. This passivity could be broken only by a changed objective situation, over which the Opposition had no direct power, or an internal regeneration which encouraged political education and activity. The objective situation could not be left to itself to develop in a direction favourable to the pro-

---

39. There were some indications that concern about party democracy went beyond the ranks of the Opposition. Dzerzhinsky, president of the GPU, declared in September: 'The dying out of our party, the dying out of its internal life, the prevalence of nomination instead of election, is becoming a political danger and is paralysing our party in its political leadership of the working class.' (Quoted by Kamenev, speech of 11 December, *Pravda*, 13 December 1923) At about the same time Bukharin made a speech in which he complained in strong terms about the restrictions on discussion and elections (cited by Trotsky at the Thirteenth Party Congress, May 1924, *Trinadtsatyi S'ezd RKP(B)*, Moscow, 1963, pp147-8).

40. Not without some justification, Trotsky was also accused of becoming interested in democratisation only when his position was threatened. See Shliapnikov's article in *Pravda*, 19 January 1924; JV Stalin, *Works*, Volume 6, op cit, p29.

letariat. However, in the view of the Opposition, the adoption of appropriate policy depended on curbing the effects of bureaucratism. Thus, in the short term at least, a changed objective situation *necessarily required* internal regeneration. But this, in its turn, required certain concessions from above. If all information filtered to the rank and file through the apparatus, if all sympathisers and support of the Opposition were rooted out from positions of influence on the rank and file, and if the apparatus prevented the active participation of the rank and file in party political life, then such a regeneration on a broad scale became unlikely.

The argument leads back to the question of tactics. The Opposition was faced with the choice of persistently raising questions of party policy and hoping for concessions from above, or presenting itself as an alternative party leadership, disregarding the limits of party discipline as set by its opponents, and, if necessary, attempting to seize power. For various reasons, among which one might include the hypothesis that not even the Opposition was fully aware of the dangers of bureaucratism, the former tactics were pursued. Perhaps the defeat of the Opposition, in retrospect, damns these tactics. Nevertheless, it should be remembered that, although it was a necessary first step, political regeneration of the party without a changed objective situation would tend to be partial, existing in something of a vacuum, and always threatened by contradictions deriving from the force of circumstances, isolation in particular. Trotsky and the Opposition, with few exceptions, refused to take steps of which the consequences were unforeseeable, the implications of which in 1923 were largely unthinkable, in a situation which did not appear hopeless, and which, in any case, might only lead to the Opposition being forced to manage the isolated Soviet state.

Appendix: Preobrazhensky's Resolution on Party Democracy[41]

In order to carry into effect the resolution of the Tenth Party Congress on party work, and to realise the principles of workers' democracy in party life, it is necessary to put into practice the following measures:

1. It is necessary to implement in reality a number of resolutions on drawing into active work the party periphery, which must be not only a transmission belt from the highest party organs to the working masses, but also the very sphere where party and social opinion is formed on the basis of the link with the masses. It is necessary that broad discussion of all important questions of party, political and economic life takes place in all party organisations with permission to raise in discussion party questions, not only on the rec-

---

41. *Trinadtsataya Konferentsiya RKP (B)*, Moscow, 1924, pp110-1.

ommendation of party committees, but also on the initiative of the cells themselves, and also of individual comrades.

2. It is necessary to remove in fact the ban on discussion, which is the basic form of party criticism, and in particular to revive discussion in the party clubs and the party press.

3. It is necessary to secure effective, permanent control by the public opinion of the party over the work of leading organs, by means of systematic accounts of party committees before local cells and general party assemblies.

4. It is necessary to stop the practice of appointment from above of the leaders of the party organs, and to re-establish the principle of election of executive party organs and officeholders which always existed in the party.

5. It is necessary to cease the existing system of selection of party workers, which is based not only on the degree of their fitness in this or that job, but on the degree of their submissiveness to directives. This system gives rise in the party to negative phenomena in the form of subservience and careerism. In order to combat these undesirable phenomena, it is necessary to change in essence the work of the credentials commission.

6. It is necessary to review transfers of personnel which took place according to the requirements of struggle with dissenting comrades, to reverse those transfers which were, and still are, especially harmful for our party work.

Resolution put to the enlarged plenary session of the Central Committee and the Central Control Commission, 25-27 October 1923.

Natalia Sedova at a picnic, December 1939

Richard Day

The Myth of the 'Super-Industrialiser'

Trotsky's Economic Policies in the 1920s[1]

During the debates of the 1920s, the Left Opposition within the Bolshevik party never seriously considered the possibility of forced collectivisation. In January 1934 Yevgeny Preobrazhensky confessed to the Seventeenth Party Congress that this had been his greatest error. 'In this question', he declared, 'what was needed was the greater far-sightedness of Comrade Stalin, his great courage in the formulation of new tasks, the greatest hardness in carrying them out, the deepest understanding of the epoch and of the relationship of class forces.'[2]

When the preliminary attack on the kulak began in the winter of 1927-28, Leon Trotsky dismissed it as having no lasting significance; the 'centrists', he was certain, were merely undertaking a factional manoeuvre in the form of a 'left zig-zag'. One year later 'sploshnaya kollektivizatsiya' was underway. Even now Trotsky believed that no lasting change of policy was in the offing. The 'elimination of the kulak as a class' was an absurd slogan, for Soviet Russia did not possess the agricultural machinery required to consolidate land holdings and work them collec-

---

1. This article first appeared under the title of 'Leon Trotsky and the Problems of the Smychka and Forced Collectivisation' in *Critique*, no 13, 1981.
2. Cited in A Nove, *An Economic History of the USSR*, London, 1969, p220.

tively. The most he expected from the ultra-left course was a proliferation of 'bogus kolkhozy', which would continue to be dominated by kulaks.

In Trotsky's judgement, the organisational transformation of Soviet agriculture logically presupposed a vast expansion of socialist industry. In the meantime, the party's responsibility was to preserve the smychka, or the alliance between worker and peasant, by increasing the availability of manufactured consumer goods within the context of the New Economic Policy (NEP). As early as 1923 Trotsky had expressed the desire to overcome the NEP and replace it with consistent economic planning. The transcendence of the NEP, however, presupposed that the town would create the industrial preconditions. A study of Trotsky's views on Soviet agriculture must therefore begin with a clear statement to the effect that the Opposition's principal concern was not to reorganise agriculture, but to avoid the impending collapse of the smychka.

The manner in which different party leaders reacted to the growing crisis in grain procurement was determined by their understanding of the smychka and its problems. Bukharin believed that the marketed surplus of grain had declined chiefly due to the breaking up of the large estates and their replacement by scattered small-scale holdings. Before the First World War, the landed estates had been responsible for more than 20 per cent of grain marketings, the kulaks for 50 percent, and medium and small peasants for the remainder. There was no doubt that an increase by about 50 per cent in the number of individual households made an important contribution to the displacement of market-oriented agriculture by subsistence agriculture. To Bukharin it seemed that the way to restore the prewar pattern of grain sales was to give the kulak greater opportunities to lease land, hire labour and expand the scale of production.

Stalin agreed with Bukharin that the pattern of land holdings was the basic problem. The sale of grain was, in his view, restricted because the peasants were eating more than before the revolution. Having emancipated themselves from the landlords, the small and middle peasants had 'obtained the opportunity of considerably improving their material conditions'.[3] It was this agreement on the source of the problem which led both Stalin and Bukharin to seek a solution in the reorganisation of tenure. In Bukharin's case the proposed solution envisaged an expansion of output; in Stalin's case it relied upon both a larger output and the suppression of rural living standards.

In his own assessment of agriculture, Trotsky shared Stalin's opinion that the change of tenure had effected a redistribution of income, freeing the peasants of many of the taxes and rent payments which before the war had squeezed the grain onto the market.[4] Like Bukharin, he pointed to the 'liquidation of landlordism' as

3.   JV Stalin, *Problems of Leninism*, Moscow, 1954, p251.
4   LD Trotsky, *Towards Socialism or Capitalism?*, London, 1926, p33.

one of the factors accounting for the decline in the marketed surplus. But unlike both Stalin and Bukharin, Trotsky considered this to be a 'secondary' problem in contrast with the 'goods famine', or the shortage of manufactured consumer goods required to provide the peasant with an incentive for commercial agriculture.

The goods famine resulted from the change in the pattern of land holdings and the disappearance of fiscal pressures previously exerted upon the peasant. By 1925-26 gross agricultural production regained the prewar level, and total industrial output (including both census and small-scale industry) had reached 90 per cent. This joint approximation to prewar conditions did not ensure adequate incentives to agriculture because the peasant, now exercising greater control over his produce, was less willing to part with it. Although these circumstances appeared to be conducive to a change in the terms of trade favouring agriculture, in fact the 'price scissors', or the relation between the industrial and agricultural price indices, turned against the peasant.

This development was due initially to the slower recovery of industry, and later to an acceleration of inflationary investments in new construction and heavy industry. In the cities, direct government intervention held the prices of manufactured goods in check, thus stimulating purchases by a growing urban population. The result in the countryside was accentuated scarcity and dramatic increases in the market prices of industrial goods, the difference between the officially suppressed wholesale prices and market prices constituting the profit of the private merchant. A greater ability on the part of the peasant to withhold his produce from the market, together with a diminished encouragement to sell — these two factors culminated in the 'grain strike' of 1927-28.

There is no doubt that Bukharin was aware of the implications of the price scissors, and was largely responsible for official efforts to suppress industrial prices by lowering costs of production and accelerating the turnover of industrial capital. He hoped that the spread of cooperative retail merchandising would curtail the activities of private traders so that the benefits of lower retail prices would reach the peasants. What he did not anticipate was the growing momentum of heavy industrial investments after 1925, which contributed to shortages in the villages, and ruptured the smychka.

In principle Bukharin opposed such investments, preferring instead to use existing industrial capital more intensively. For that reason he was viewed by Trotsky and the Left Opposition as an opponent of socialist industry. In turn Bukharin looked upon the proposal of some members of the Opposition to finance industrial expansion by raising wholesale prices as a recipe for plundering the peasant. My intention in this chapter will be to show that Trotsky and Bukharin in reality pursued a common objective — the preservation of the smychka. Bukharin misunderstood Trotsky's position, considering it to be 'super-industrialist' and a threat

The Myth of the 'Super-Industrialiser'

to the peasant. Trotsky was no less critical of Bukharin's views. On the one hand, Bukharin endorsed the theory of 'socialism in one country', implying industrial self-sufficiency; on the other hand he resisted new industrial investment. Bukharin's failure to overcome this inconsistency, together with his 'cooperative plan' for agriculture, caused Trotsky to regard his position as that of a neo-Narodnik littérateur who understood neither Marxism nor elementary economics.

Trotsky's understanding of the smychka was rooted in Marxist dialectics. Socialist industry and private agriculture were viewed as a dialectical unity of opposites. Within this relationship there was unity between the proletariat and the poor and middle peasants, and opposition between these two groups and the kulak. The transcendence of the contradiction between industry and agriculture would require the industrialisation of agriculture. As Trotsky wrote in 1927:

'The industrialisation of agriculture means the elimination of the present fundamental contradiction between town and country and so between peasant and worker. As regards their role in the country's economy, their living conditions, their cultural level, they must come closer together as the frontier between them disappears. A society in which mechanised cultivation forms an equal part of the planned economy, in which the town has absorbed into itself the advantages of the country (spaciousness, greenery), while the country has been enriched with the advantage of the town (paved roads, electric light, piped water supply, drains), that is to say, where the antithesis of town and country has itself disappeared, where the peasant and the worker have been transformed into participants of equal worth and equal rights in a single production process, such a society will be a genuine socialist society.'[5]

Trotsky consistently stressed that the material basis of production was the chief determinant of class relations. Until the material basis of rural production was transformed, he believed that class differentiation was inevitable. Bukharin, in contrast, tended to think of overcoming the rural urban contradiction by restoring the flow of goods between the two sectors of the economy, and by encouraging small-scale rural industry (for example, food processing). When he urged the peasants to 'enrich' themselves in 1925, he did so in the hope that further differentiation might be avoided. Cooperative organisations, he believed, would permit the peasantry as a whole to 'grow into' socialism through the mechanisms of trade and finance. Organising the production and marketing of agricultural products, the cooperatives were to become the 'mediating link' between town and country.

According to the cooperative plan, not even kulak cooperation would repre-

5. LD Trotsky, *Sochineniya*, Volume 21, p436.

sent a threat to socialism. If the kulaks accumulated capital they would invest their savings in Soviet financial institutions or in new equipment. In the first instance such resources might be transferred in order to finance cooperation among bednyaks and serednyaks (poor and middle peasants); in the second they would serve to extend the market for industry and accelerate the turnover of capital. In either case the institutional context of agriculture would guarantee that the kulak's ambition would be harnessed in the interests of socialism.

From Trotsky's standpoint, Bukharin appeared to be fetishising an organisational form and ignoring its content. Socialist agriculture would not be created by 'organisational, credit and state-administrative methods', but by mechanisation, tractorisation and electrification.[6] The mere organisation of primitive agriculture within a cooperative framework would alter neither the reality of class divisions nor their objective cause; that is, the inability of state industry to provide more advanced equipment. By ascribing an implicitly socialist character to cooperatives in general, Bukharin seemed to be restoring the Narodnik vision of a pre-capitalist rural community yet to be disintegrated by capitalist relations of ownership and production. On these grounds Trotsky concluded that Bukharin was the author of both a 'kulak' deviation and 'Soviet Narodnichestvo'.[7]

For the same reasons Trotsky was sceptical of the 'ultra-left' position taken by Yuri Larin and others, who went to the opposite extreme and proposed collectivisation of the bednyak together with a general offensive against private capital. Past experience indicated that communes were prone to ignore the division of labour, to strive for self-sufficiency, and to end by consuming their own capital.[8] Poor peasant collectives were fated by an extreme contradiction between advanced social forms and the most backward methods of farming. At best they were an organisational 'laboratory' and a model for the future. But according to Trotsky, 'the main work in preparing for the future is of a more fundamental nature: it involves the development of industry which will give to the countryside the technical basis for the industrialisation of agriculture'.[9]

In the belief that agricultural reorganisation was a distant prospect, Trotsky concentrated his attention on the more immediate dilemma posed by the price scissors and the goods famine. In the autumn of 1925 retail prices of industrial commodities were more than 50 per cent above agricultural procurement prices (calculating the two indices in terms of 1913 prices). Naum Jasny recounts that 'in the Ukraine and Crimea in October 1926, textiles retailed at 172 per cent above

6. *Izvestiya*, 2 June 1925.
7. Trotsky Archives, T-2975.
8. *Izvestiya*, 28 November 1925; cf *Pravda*, 5 December 1925.
9. *Pravda*, 17 December 1925: cf LD Trotsky, *Towards Socialism or Capitalism*, op cit, p46.

the 1913 price (... in private trade they were 225 per cent above prewar), while producers of farm products were getting a scant 20 per cent in excess of prewar prices for their produce. Hence the "scissors" with reference to textiles was equivalent to more than 200 against the Ukrainian peasant.'[10]

In consequence of these disproportionate prices, grain acreage recovered more slowly than gross agricultural production. By 1926-27 agricultural output exceeded the prewar level by six per cent, but per capita consumption of food grains, even in the rural areas, was below 1913 standards. Part of the problem was the shortage of draft animals. However, the major disincentive with respect to grain production was to be found in the scissors. As Jasny observed: 'The critical impediment to recovery in its later stages... was the unfavourable price relationship between farm and non-farm products. Production for the market... rarely repaid the costs.'[11]

Throughout 1925 Trotsky repeatedly warned that unless the requirements of the villages were satisfied, the peasant would create his own smychka with foreign capital in the form of contraband. To determine the pressure of foreign goods, he proposed to develop a system of comparative coefficients which would compare the efficiency of Soviet production in terms of price and quality with that of other countries. These coefficients would then serve as a guide both to the import plan and new investments. Domestic production would be rationalised and standardised in order to lengthen runs and reduce costs. In the meantime he urged that 'commodity intervention' be undertaken in those cases where the coefficient was least satisfactory. Inexpensive foreign goods were to be sold in the Soviet market, the profits being used to subsidise retail prices of the corresponding domestic commodity.[12]

The proposal for commodity intervention was designed to provide a short-run solution to the scissors. Trotsky's longer-run intention was to use the grain thus brought to market in order to finance the import of new industrial equipment. In contrast with Stalin's vision of Soviet self-sufficiency, Trotsky proposed to stabilise the smychka by drawing upon the 'reserves' of the world market. He summarised the relationship between closing the scissors, the renewal and expansion of fixed capital, and the growth of international trade, in the following comment:

'Our economic system has become a part of the world system. This has made new links in the chain of exchange. Peasant grain is exchanged for foreign gold. Gold is exchanged for machinery, implements and other requisite articles of consumption for town and village. Textile machinery acquired for gold and paid for by the ex-

10. N Jasny, *The Socialised Agriculture of the USSR*, Stanford, 1949, p209.
11. Ibid, p203.
12. See my *Leon Trotsky and the Politics of Economic Isolation*, Cambridge, 1973, pp138-9.

port of grain provides new equipment for the textile industry, and thus lowers the price of fabrics sent to the rural districts. The circle becomes very complicated, but the basis remains the same — a certain economic relation between town and village.'[13]

Trotsky's overriding concern to provide the peasant with adequate incentives set him apart from both Bukharin and Preobrazhensky. Preoccupied with the 'cooperative plan', Bukharin suspected that the 'super-industrialisers' were bent upon accumulating industrial capital by exacting 'tribute' from agrarian 'colonies'. Preobrazhensky confirmed this suspicion by urging that 'primitive socialist accumulation' take place behind the protective barrier of the trade monopoly by means of deliberately manipulating the terms of domestic trade to the disadvantage of agriculture. Although Trotsky shared Preobrazhensky's commitment to industrial expansion, he did not agree with his arbitrary notion of pricing, or with his understanding of the relation between light and heavy industry.[14]

Trotsky was convinced that the world division of labour and international trade were expressions of technological progress and the steady rise in the organic composition of capital. The replacement of living labour power by a constantly growing volume of fixed capital meant that large-scale industry could only remain competitive by increasing the volume of sales in the service of the world market. The fixed capital requirements of modern industry were so great that no country could afford to become self-sufficient or to deny itself the advantages of trade.

Preobrazhensky looked at the problem of industrialisation in a more restrictive context. 'As we know', he wrote in *The New Economics*, '... the development of the productive forces... and the development of technology lead, as a general rule, to an increase in the organic composition of capital, which... means an ever-increasing importance of production of means of production. The possibility of extending the production of consumer goods, and cheapening them, is achieved by a relatively still greater extension of production of means of production...'[15] Given the assumption of a more or less self-contained economy, Preobrazhensky's reasoning could not be refuted. Stalin acknowledged this fact in 1928 when he likened the price scissors to 'tribute'. Trotsky sought to avoid the dilemma posed by Preobrazhensky by husbanding scarce capital, and drawing instead on the capital equipment available in the world market.

This concern to restrain the demands of heavy industry upon the country's

13. LD Trotsky, *Towards Socialism or Capitalism*, op cit, pp44-5.
14. See my 'Trotsky and Preobrazhensky: The Troubled Unity of the Left Opposition', *Studies in Comparative Communism*, Volume 10, nos 1/2, Spring-Summer 1977, pp81-4 et passim.
15. E Preobrazhensky, *The New Economics*, London, 1965, pp186-7.

limited resources was apparent in Trotsky's writings from the early months of 1925. In January of that year Felix Dzerzhinsky, in his capacity as Vesenkha chairman, received a major commitment from the Central Committee to expand metallurgical output in anticipation of new capital construction. This was the first programme for heavy industrial expansion to receive the explicit sanction of the party leaders. Pyatakov, another of Trotsky's associates and deputy chairman of Vesenkha, enthusiastically welcomed Dzerzhinsky's proposals. Trotsky was quick to communicate his personal misgivings. His account of the incident follows:

'Returning from the Caucasus in May [1925], I found a typical picture of speculation. All the trusts were following a course of capital investments. The operations of the Prombank were ceaselessly expanding. In June I wrote to Dzerzhinsky and Pyatakov with a warning that this fever was fatally leading to a financial and industrial crisis. Neither Dzerzhinsky nor Pyatakov understood this, and they accused me instead (especially Pyatakov) of an intervention against industrialisation. I showed them that the overall material base, with a proper policy, could be considerably expanded, but that with the given material base it was impossible to push industrialisation forward with the aid of unreal credits. Probably everyone recalls that in September 1925 a serious crisis occurred, accompanied by the dismissal of workers, etc.'[16]

In all Trotsky wrote three letters to Dzerzhinsky, each time stressing the same theme as appeared in his criticism of Bukharin's 'cooperative plan': socialist construction could not be guaranteed by 'organisational, credit and state-administrative methods'.[17] Three years later Bukharin's *Notes of an Economist*, with their reference to the problem of the gestation period and 'bricks of the future', would prove reminiscent of Trotsky's 'unreal credits'.

Repudiating the autarkic implications of 'socialism in one country', Trotsky insisted that Soviet Russia's dependence upon foreign suppliers of industrial equipment was materially embodied in her existing plant.[18] In order to acquire access to inexpensive foreign equipment, he was even prepared, for a time at least, to contemplate the expansion of kulak agriculture. In June 1925 he declared that it would be a 'reactionary policy' to interfere prematurely with the development of rural productive forces which were currently growing in capitalist or semi-capitalist forms.[19] On another occasion he claimed that concessions to the kulak,

16. LD Trotsky, *Écrits 1928-1940*, Tome 1, Paris, 1955, p186.
17. Ibid, p6.
18. *Pravda*, 14 December 1926.
19. *Pravda*, 29 July 1925.

assuming the growth of state industry continued without interruption, would not pose the threat of 'economic surprises' or of a 'sharp turn to capitalism'.[20] 'There may be periods', he added, 'when the state, sure of its economic power and desirous of increasing the rate of development, purposely allows a temporary increase in the weight of private enterprise in agriculture in the shape of capitalist farms...'[21] In November 1925 he compared the initiative of the kulak with the complacency of bednyak communes, and approved the Central Committee's decision to ease restrictions on land leases and the hiring of agricultural labour.[22] The wager on the kulak, he suggested, should be treated as 'purely a matter of expediency'.[23] At a time when Zinoviev was attacking Bukharin for 'degeneration', 'retreat' and the promotion of 'state capitalism', Trotsky avoided identification with the Leningraders, and awaited the harvest.

By January 1926, in EH Carr's words, 'the kulak had shown himself master of the situation'.[24] During the previous year agricultural taxes had been lowered. The inflation caused by the 'unreal credits' rekindled distrust of the ruble, and the peasant, whenever possible, paid his taxes in cash rather than bringing the grain to market. Shortages and rising prices followed an excellent harvest. The export plan had to be suspended. Trotsky judged the time to be appropriate for an appeal to the party leaders for a reconsideration of priorities.

In a speech on 19 January 1926, he described the smychka as an 'endless ribbon of cloth which is stretched out between town and country. A cloth conveyor — that is what the smychka is.'[25] At precisely the time when the textile smychka needed to be supplemented gradually by a tractor smychka, the conveyor between town and country had broken down. The volume of textiles sent to the villages during the harvest had proven to be inadequate.[26] When the Central Committee met in plenary session in April 1926, he suggested a five-year plan aimed at overcoming the goods famine by 1931: more progressive agricultural taxes; selective increases in wholesale prices, combined with an effort to lower retail prices; commodity intervention for 1926-27; and expanded capital commitments to industry.[27] At the same meeting Kamenev took the view that industry was now lagging behind agriculture. This congruence of opinion prepared the way for the formation of the Joint Opposition.

20. LD Trotsky, *Towards Socialism or Capitalism*, op cit, pp26-7.
21. Ibid, p41; cf *Pravda*, 7 November 1925.
22. *Izvestiya*, 28 November 1925.
23. LD Trotsky, *Towards Socialism or Capitalism*, op cit, p26.
24. EH Carr, *Socialism in One Country 1924-1926*, Volume 1, London, 1964, p295.
25. *Pravda*, 29 January 1926.
26. Ibid.
27. Trotsky Archives, T-2983.

The Myth of the 'Super-Industrialiser'

From the beginning Trotsky's alliance with Kamenev and Zinoviev was fraught with tensions, the most serious of which concerned the issue of industrial pricing policy. Preobrazhensky, Pyatakov, Smirnov and several other of Trotsky's associates were of the opinion that wholesale prices should be raised in order to capture a portion of the profit going to the Nepmen. The proposal was sensible: higher wholesale prices in the cities might have diverted a larger portion of output to the countryside, where retail prices were already as high as the market would bear, and a wholesale price increase would have been difficult to pass on to consumers. Trotsky sympathised with the proposal, but was wary of its possible implications. He feared that any increase at the retail level would intensify pressures on the trade monopoly and worsen the crisis. Ultimately he believed that industrial prices could only be lowered by renovating fixed capital and expanding production. According to Smirnov, Zinoviev exerted pressure on Trotsky to abandon the proposal for higher wholesale prices.[28] Early in 1927 Trotsky complied, provoking the frustration of Smirnov and the Democratic Centralists and the first breach in the Joint Opposition.

The policies of the party leadership helped to exacerbate these tensions. The 'regime of economy', a rigorous campaign to suppress wages and lower the costs of production, had the effect — or appeared to have the effect — of reducing retail prices. In fact, the situation was much more complex. The main reason for the modest decline in retail prices in the autumn of 1926 was a reduction in peasant demand. A portion of the redundant purchasing power had been absorbed by tax increases, and grain prices (or rural incomes) were curtailed by a more orderly procurement campaign. Thus poor peasants were obliged to postpone purchases, while the higher income groups became more selective. The trusts had deliberately avoided producing those commodities whose prices were most strictly controlled. Because these were the commodities which normally met with the heaviest demand in the villages, the production profile adjusted to the 'regime of economy' in a perverse manner — the goods most in demand became relatively more scarce, while inventories of other actually began to grow.[29] Appearances were so deceptive that some observers concluded the goods famine was about to be replaced by a new 'sales crisis'.

The misleading signals coming from the marketplace boded ill for the political prospects of the Opposition. In 1927 the party leaders renewed the campaign to lower retail prices by means of intensified administrative pressure. In the meantime increasing resources were channelled into heavy industry, where they made no immediate contribution to resolving the goods famine. In the year 1926-27

28.   Trotsky Archives, T-931.
29.   Trotsky Archives, T-939.

heavy industry (department I) received 71 per cent of industrial investments, and increased its output by 26.8 per cent. The output of light industry (department II) increased by 14.9 per cent.[30] Because urban incomes continued to grow, the effect of the retail price controls was actually to increase effective demand in the cities and further impede the flow of goods to the peasants. Alec Nove quotes one Soviet writer who described the situation this way:

'Towns are closer to the sources of industrial goods, the villages are further away. Therefore the towns appear to obtain a larger share of industrial goods than they would have obtained at prices which balance supply and demand. The policy of low prices not only failed to lower prices for the village, but on the contrary it lowered prices for the towns at the cost of raising them for the village, and by a large percentage too.'[31]

Throughout this period the Opposition leaders argued that the peasants, and especially the poor peasants, were the main victims of party policy. Apart from the need to deal with the goods famine, they concentrated their attention on the promotion of 'class cooperatives' with the aid of a 'class credit system'. They insisted that a preponderant share of the modest resources being committed to agriculture should go to the bednyak and the serednyak, not to the kulak, who was frequently availing himself of state credits to form fake machine societies and bogus cooperatives.[32] Criticising the 'cooperative plan', they maintained that Bukharin's policies had merely contributed to the furtherance of class differentiation.[33]

When the harvest of 1927 brought with it the 'grain strike', it was none other than Bukharin who found himself obliged to announce a reinforced offensive against the kulak. Trotsky, now about to be expelled from the party, treated the announcement as empty posturing: 'Today it is "enrich yourself", and tomorrow it is "dekulakise yourself" — to Bukharin such things are simple. Pick up the pen — and it is done. From him one can expect nothing better. But the kulak is not given to such about-turns. He will yet have his say.'[34] Convinced that the balance of class forces had shifted decisively, Trotsky was taken completely unawares when Stalin responded to the crisis with the introduction of the 'Siberian method'.

Although the return to civil war conditions did bring in the grain, it is worth considering the question of whether and how the grain strike might have been

30. EH Carr and RW Davies, *Foundations of a Planned Economy*, Volume I, London, 1969, pp291-2.
31. A Nove, op cit, p140.
32. N Jasny, op cit, p269.
33. *Pravda*, 5 November 1927; cf *The Platform of the Left Opposition*, London, 1963, pp29-30.
34. Trotsky Archives, T-3100.

avoided. The evidence leads one to suspect that if Trotsky's proposals had been implemented as early at 1925-26, the final collapse of the smychka and forced collectivisation might not have occurred. There can be little doubt that the principal error of the party leadership was to commit excessive resources to heavy industry during the period of goods famine. This obsessive preoccupation with industrial self-sufficiency, involving the production of equipment never before manufactured in the country at prices which, on average, were up to twice as high as foreign imports, was Stalin's contribution to Soviet policy. EH Carr and RW Davies have described its consequences:

'The individual peasant, having little inducement to spend, developed the traditional peasant propensity to hoard. Grain, whether as a reserve for future contingencies or as a speculation on higher prices, was the most stable and convenient form of wealth. The existence of large holdings in individual hands meant that the holders would surrender the grain only on terms — involving an adequate supply of consumer goods at acceptable prices — which were incompatible with the ever increasing investment in heavy industry...'[35]

Trotsky's proposals would have enabled at least a portion of the resources expended on capital-intensive projects to be used instead to purchase foreign equipment for both departments of Soviet industry. Construction costs in the Soviet Union were even higher in the 1920s, relative to prewar prices, than manufacturing costs. Nevertheless, the Soviet government pressed ahead with prestigious projects such as the Dnieper power station, the Stalingrad tractor factory, the metallurgical works of Kryvi Rih and Kuznetsk, and the Sverdlovsk engineering works, in every case holding the import of capital goods to a minimum. Up to one third of all industrial investments by 1928-29 were allocated to the construction of new factories rather than to the renovation of existing ones, even though new investments in department I tended to result in new production only after a gestation period of between three to five years.

The greater the resources immobilised in this way, the more difficult it became after 1925-26 to regain any degree of flexibility. When the crisis reached the proportions of a disaster in 1927-28, a handful of Soviet officials finally awakened to the need to divert resources into department II. By this time it was already too late. With the campaign against Bukharin and the 'Right Danger' about to begin, the inescapable reality of the situation was quietly recognised late in 1928. The share of investment allocated to department II was once again lowered. At the same time food rationing was introduced in Leningrad.

35.   EH Carr and RW Davies, op cit, p244.

It is true that the implementation of Trotsky's approach would have brought difficulties with the onset of the Great Depression in 1929-30. To continue a high degree of import-dependency would have been costly when the terms of world trade turned sharply against primary producers. All the same, it is difficult to imagine that the resulting dislocations of the Soviet economy would have been remotely comparable to those which issued from forced collectivisation. Moreover, by the time these difficulties materialised, light industry might well have developed to the point where a dynamic internal balance could have been maintained, involving a gradual transition towards the expansion of domestic heavy industry. Textile factories commissioned in 1925-26 would have been built and producing by 1928-29, when Trotsky began his years of exile.

It was in the exile period that Trotsky undertook his final assessment of Soviet agricultural policy, beginning with a paper written in November 1928 entitled 'What is the Smychka?'. Here he wrote:

'Even a genuinely established smychka between industry and peasant agriculture represents not a basis for a future national-socialist economy, but only for a proper stable relationship between the proletariat and the peasantry of a separate country during the time of the "breathing space"; that is, until a war or until a revolution in other countries. A victory of the proletariat in the leading countries would signify for us a radical reconstruction of the economic base in accordance with a more productive international division of labour which alone can create a real foundation for a socialist society.'[36]

The theory of 'socialism in one country', he reasoned, had grown out of a false understanding of the smychka. Bukharin had initiated the confusion with his vision of diminishing class struggle: 'Even a theoretical analysis should have indicated that the coexistence of two systems, the capitalist and the socialist, struggling with each other and at the same time providing each other with sustenance, must from time to time cause unusually acute crises.' Misled by an ideal of social harmony, by 'theoretical scholasticism' and 'practical short-sightedness', Bukharin had pressed for the administrative lowering of prices in 1926-27 which brought on the 'grain strike'. Before the crisis could be mitigated it would be necessary to close the price scissors, and restore first the prewar terms of trade and eventually those prevailing in the world market.

The perpetuation of the price scissors, Trotsky continued, served as a constant reminder to the peasants that socialist industry had failed to demonstrate its superiority over capitalism. It was understandable therefore why the peasant should

---

36. Trotsky Archives, T-3148.

differentiate between the democratic Bolshevik, who had given him land, and the communist, who wished to take it away. Until this dichotomy was erased from the peasant's mind, the danger of counter-revolution would fester and grow.

By the time Trotsky recorded these thoughts, Stalin had already condoned the preservation of the scissors as an object of policy. In the spring of 1930 the Sixteenth Party Congress dismissed concern over the scissors as a 'bourgeois prejudice'. Trotsky responded in the *Bulletin of the Opposition*, forecasting that Stalin's ultra-left bureaucratic adventure would end in panic and retreat. On the assumption that income within the kolkhozy would be distributed in a truly cooperative manner — that is, in accordance with the share of the productive forces contributed by each peasant — he concluded that the kulak would necessarily re-emerge within the collective farm. An entire social class would only be 'eliminated' by a change in technology and in the mode of production, not by administrative methods. It was no more possible to create large-scale mechanised agriculture out of wooden ploughs and kulak horses than it was to create a ship by adding up fishing boats.[37] All-round collectivisation would destroy incentives and lead to 'all-round weeds in the fields'.[38] Paraphrasing Bukharin, Trotsky wrote that 'it is impossible to build kolkhozy today without tractors of the future'.[39] The reactionary utopia of a socialist Atlantis had given rise to 'sploshnaya kollektivizatsiya'; now it was necessary to 'repudiate the "ideals" of a shut-in economy', and work out a new variant of the plan involving 'the broadest possible interaction with the world market'.[40]

As Trotsky groped for a way out of the impasse, Stalin promised a meeting of collective farm shock-workers in February 1933 that the goal of Soviet policy was 'to make all the collective farmers prosperous'. In reality, the contradiction between the form and content of the kolkhozy was about to take its dreadful toll. Khrushchev described this period in his memoirs. He tells of a train which pulled into Kiev loaded with corpses: 'It had picked up corpses all the way from Poltava to Kiev.' An estimated five to 10 million people died in the famine, but no mention of the disaster appeared in the Soviet press. How terrible it was, commented Nikita Khrushchev, that no-one told Stalin. Stalin could not possibly have known what was happening, for he had recently assured the shock-workers that 'no less than 20 million of the peasant population, no less than 20 million poor peasants have been rescued from destitution and ruin, have been rescued from kulak bondage, and have attained material security thanks to the collective farms'.[41]

37. *Byulleten' Oppozitsii*, 9 (1930), p3.
38. *Byulleten' Oppozitsii*, 31 (1932), p6.
39. *Byulleten' Oppozitsii*, 11 (1930), p7.
40. *Byulleten' Oppozitsii*, 10 (1930), p6.
41. JV Stalin, op cit, p568.

This brief survey indicates that a clear theme prevailed in all of Trotsky's writings on Soviet agriculture, a theme which distinguished his views from those of most contemporaries. Economic development, he argued, was invariably constrained by objectivity, and could not be subjectively manipulated. The purpose of economic planning was to exercise foresight in the presence of — and not apart from — objective economic laws. To achieve their ends, the planners must seek to transform the material forces of production. Marx had shown that each mode of production embraces a unique combination of productive forces and productive relations. More consistently than either Stalin or Bukharin, his principal adversaries, Trotsky believed that the one could not change in isolation from the other.

Trotsky's residence at 19 Avenida Viena, Coyoacan, December 1939

Susan Weissman

The Left Opposition Divided: The Trotsky-Serge Disputes[1]

The International Left Opposition in Europe was composed of expelled communists and young recruits. For the most part, they were dedicated but inexperienced militants who were committed to the programme of Trotsky's Left Opposition. In exile in Europe, Lev Davidovich Trotsky alone represented the experience of the first decade of the Russian Revolution. Along with his son Lev Sedov, Trotsky led the struggle against Stalin from Western Europe in the first half of the 1930s. The pressure of organising resistance, educating European comrades, writing, and building the International Left Opposition was enormous. How fortunate for Trotsky and the European Left Opposition that another comrade from the Soviet Union, Victor Serge, was to join them in the West in April 1936. Though Trotsky and Serge were now free to correspond, political circumstances prevented them from meeting, and a combination of political differences, miscommunication and NKVD subterfuge destroyed their relationship.

Surely one of the greatest tragedies of the years 1936-40, from the time Serge was expelled to the West until the time Trotsky died, was that their relationship was so filled with acrimony. The role of the NKVD was large, though real political differences emerged, clouded over by slander, misunderstandings and sectarian debates.

Stalin had erred in expelling Trotsky. Outside the USSR, Trotsky mounted a

---

1.   This is a revised and extended version of the introduction to part four of D Cotterill (ed), *The Serge-Trotsky Papers*, London, 1994.

The Left Opposition Divided

sustained fight against Stalin, exposing his crimes in front of the world. Now Stalin had let another Oppositionist slip through to join Trotsky, another member of the revolutionary generation of Bolsheviks, whose voice was equally eloquent. That these two anti-Stalinist Bolsheviks had survived at all was serendipitous, that they now had the chance to work together in the West was astonishing. Serge had stood with Trotsky's Left Opposition since 1923 in the open, in clandestinity, and through prison and deportation. As Trotsky noted in a letter to Serge in March 1937: 'Victor Serge, you remained in the ranks of the Opposition without wavering, in the midst of an unprecedented repression, when less steadfast persons were capitulating one after the other. In prison and in exile, you belonged to the band of those whom the thermidorian hangmen could not break.'[2]

How then did their relationship unravel? Serge had last seen Trotsky in 1927, and although they corresponded while they were both in exile in Europe, their paths never crossed again. Despite the terribly difficult relationship between these two Left Oppositionists, Serge lived most of his adult political life 'in the tail of Trotsky's comet'.[3] He was perhaps the best known 'Trotskyist' in the West, although he was treated shabbily by Trotsky and the Trotskyists. When Victor Serge first arrived in Mexico in September 1941 — a small miracle in itself — he gravitated to Avenida Viena where the Old Man had lived and been killed. Walking along Rio Churubusco toward Trotsky's compound on Avenida Viena, Vlady recalled, 'my father saw the wall around Trotsky's house, where the Old Man was killed. He began to weep, and then broke into sobs.'[4]

Political differences developed between Trotsky and Serge over their assessment of the then current situation. Their correspondence and articles pursue these differences, in a wide-ranging debate which had an engaging and educational character. The discussion covered the character of the POUM[5] in Spain, the Popular Front in France, the renewed debate over the suppression of the Kronstadt revolt of 1921, and the Fourth International. Unfortunately, the level of discourse had deteriorated by the time Trotsky wrote 'The Moralists and Sycophants Against Marxism' in June 1939, his response to the debate provoked by his earlier *Their Morals and Ours* of February 1938. It is in Trotsky's response that we see how successful the NKVD was in dividing the surviving oppositionists. The publication of Trotsky's splendidly scurrilous essay marks a sad moment for the anti-Stalinist left.

2. LD Trotsky to V Serge, 'On the Subject of Jacques Sadoul', 5 March 1937, first published in *Le Mouvement Communiste en France (1919-1939)*, edited by Pierre Broué, Paris, 1967.
3. The phrase is Vlady's (Serge's son).
4. Private conversation with Vlady in Coyoacan, 20 August 1990. Vlady and I took the same walk that he and his father took in 1941. It was the fiftieth anniversary of the death of Trotsky.
5. Partido Obrero de Unificación Marxista, the Workers Party of Marxist Unification.

The Left Opposition in exile was in constant, real danger of physical liquidation, and they worked in a milieu of suspicion, demoralisation and despair. The role of the NKVD cannot be overlooked in this regard, although it would be equally incorrect to overstate its influence, since real political differences emerged in an atmosphere that was not always conducive to the free expression of critical thought, especially unorthodox thought.

This was particularly discouraging to Serge, who was wrestling with the contradictions he had begun to consider inherent in 'guided organisations'. He often quoted Rosa Luxemburg's dictum that 'liberty is the liberty of the man who thinks otherwise', a principle more easily expressed than practised on the far left, with 'the best-disposed men, professing in principle respect for free thought, ... [who] in reality do not know how to tolerate thought which is different from their own'.[6] From Paris to Mexico, Serge continually associated with refugee revolutionaries who embodied intolerance, with all the concomitant consequences of inquisitions and expulsions. More than simply discouraged, Serge sought to understand the problem which surely undermined their effectiveness. He also noted that back in the USSR, the bureaucracy knew how to mobilise these feelings against the Opposition, and yet the Opposition itself exhibited the same qualities.

The problem, according to Serge, lay in the inability to reconcile intransigence, a necessary quality, with respect for others. In Russia, Serge wrote, politics failed because socialists treated Marxism as a 'faith, then a regime, a double intolerance in consequence'.[7] Serge thought the dilemma could be solved by 'fighting intransigence', and 'by an absolute rule of respect for others... for the enemy even'.[8] These are noble sentiments, but they challenged even Serge in practice. In the final year of his life, he remarked to Hryhory Kostiuk that he remained 'intransigently socialist'.[9] Earlier Serge had observed: 'Respect for the enemy; the totalitarians make it difficult, if not impossible.'[10]

Though Serge himself fell victim to the dirty divisive work done by NKVD agents, he was conscious that political differences and organisational practices were also responsible for straining his relations with Trotsky from 1937 onwards. Serge and Trotsky began to disagree with each other in late 1936, and this grew to a practical rupture by 1939. While Kronstadt and Serge's support of the POUM were the public issues of contention, what angered Trotsky most was Serge's attitude to the Fourth International.

6.   V Serge, 'Intransigence, Intolerance, Conflicts', 2 October 1944, *Carnets*, Arles, 1985, p145.
7.   Ibid, p146.
8.   Ibid.
9.   V Serge to H Kostiuk, 22 June 1947. Kostiuk was a Ukrainian survivor of Vorkuta, who corresponded with Serge from his exile in New York. I interviewed him in October 1985.
10. V Serge, 'Intransigence, Intolerance, Conflicts', *Carnets*, op cit, p146.

Trotsky very much wanted to have Serge as a close political ally. Trotsky saw his mission, once the Great Purge was underway and the Stalinists were strangling the revolution in Spain, as the creation of a new International, a revolutionary pole of attraction for workers the world over who rejected both Stalinism and social democracy. He devoted most of his energy to the Fourth International. Victor Serge, another exiled Russian Left Oppositionist with intellectual standing in Europe, would be an asset to Trotsky's effort.

Trotsky sent Serge a draft adopted by the Conference for the Fourth International that was held in July 1936, entitled 'The New Revolutionary Upsurge and the Tasks of the Fourth International'.[11] Serge responded to Trotsky in 'A New Revolutionary Upturn?'. Serge disagreed with Trotsky's assessment of the readiness of the workers in Europe for revolutionary struggle. Serge said the workers were just 'emerging, awakening out of a long period of depression', which was a product of 10 years of exhaustion brought on by the First World War and the postwar defeats. This was no minor difference.

The different perception of the nature of the conjuncture led to different attitudes toward the Popular Front. Serge saw the Popular Front as a 'useful transitional form', and his slogan was to 'transform the Popular Front from an instrument of class collaboration into an instrument of class struggle which obviously implied a split with... bourgeois-dominated elements, and the regrouping of the working class forces around a revolutionary programme which can assure them of the support of the middle classes'.[12]

Trotsky sent AJ Muste, a minister whose American Workers Party fused with the Communist League to form the American section of the Fourth International (the Socialist Workers Party),[13] to Brussels in late July 1936 to coopt Serge. Serge accepted.[14] After discussing with Muste, Serge wrote a letter to Trotsky on 27 July 1936 in which he put forward his ideas on how the organisation could reach and recruit as many people as possible. Serge envisioned a broad revolutionary party with a truly professional and quality press that encouraged open debate in a fraternal style. Serge emphasised that the organisation be non-sectarian, though ideologically firm, and that the question of the 'nature of the Soviet state and of the defence of the USSR — matters on which enormous confusion reigns among the rank and file', be left open, since it was an important educational concern, but not

11. LD Trotsky, 'The New Revolutionary Upsurge and the Tasks of the Fourth International', *Writings of Leon Trotsky 1935-36*, New York, 1970, pp32-5.
12. V Serge, 'Observations on the Theses of the July Conference of the Fourth International, Sections 1 ,5, and 9', 19 July 1936, Serge archives.
13. For an insider's account of this process, see JP Cannon, *The History of American Trotskyism*, New York, 1972.
14 V Serge, 'My Break With Trotsky', *Carnets*, op cit, p44.

one of principle. Trotsky replied to Serge on 30 July 1936, stating that he couldn't agree. Moreover, he criticised Serge for his 'artistic and psychological' approach, which was insufficiently political.[15]

By mid-1937, Serge and Trotsky began to have serious disagreements. In 1938 Serge entered into a polemic over Kronstadt which was splashed across the pages of *The New International*, *Lutte Ouvrière*, *La Révolution proletarienne* and the *Byulleten Oppozitsii*. The Kronstadt debate came in the wake of the Spanish Civil War, and had everything to do with the role of the anarchists and the POUM. Despite assurances from Trotsky that the Fourth International would pledge themselves to struggle in sympathy with the POUM,[16] they never did, and in fact 'the Trotskyists were directing all their fire at the POUM',[17] which Trotsky's son, Lev Sedov, dismissed as 'destined to stab the revolution in the heart'.[18] Serge nonetheless took part in the Fourth International, including its founding conference, and worked with its members in what he felt was a stifling internal atmosphere, where it was difficult to 'detect the hope of the Left Opposition in Russia for a renewal of the ideology, morals and institutions of socialism'. In the Fourth International Serge found a crude caricature of Trotsky's intransigence, here translated into simple inflexibility. Their shallow dogmatic and sectarian thinking was all very discouraging to Serge: 'In the countries I knew at first hand... the tiny parties of the "Fourth International", ravaged by frequent splits and, in Paris, by deplorable feuding, amounted only to a feeble and sectarian movement out of which, I judged, no fresh thinking could emerge. The life of these groups was maintained by nothing but the prestige of the Old Man and his great, unceasing efforts; and both his prestige and the quality of his efforts deteriorated in the process.'[19]

Furthermore, Serge came to believe that the timing was all wrong: the creation of a party of world revolution during a period of defeat (fascism, war, Soviet totalitarianism) was futile, if not pretentious. Their correspondence reveals conflicting objectives: Trotsky wanted Serge to play a leading role in the Fourth International, but Serge was dubious of the project from the start.

Serge was certain that a non-Stalinist federation would have better suited the new world situation. Serge was less specific than Trotsky about the actual character of the non-Stalinist organisations he hoped would come together in this federation. While Trotsky's misgivings about the non-Stalinist but non-Trotskyist left were important, Serge thought the Trotskyist left 'spent most of their strength

---

15. LD Trotsky to V Serge, 30 July 1936.
16. See V Serge, 'My Break With Trotsky', *Carnets*, op cit, pp44-7.
17. Ibid.
18. Ibid.
19. V Serge, *Memoirs of a Revolutionary*, Oxford, 1978, p 348.

and... their time in intriguing against each other and in running each other down in whole books. I reproached them bitterly for squandering their resources like this...'[20]

Serge cut himself off from the Fourth International in 1937, tried to avoid controversy, and 'made every effort to do the militants and LD all the good turns I could'.[21] Serge did not refrain in 1938 from his polemic with Trotsky over Kronstadt and other vital issues. After all, there was an entire generation of political militants who would benefit from an airing of the issues surrounding the suppression of the Kronstadt rebels. He was subjected to a torrent of abuse from Trotsky's pen in this same period. Yet even as Trotsky attacked Serge publicly, he privately wrote to him: 'I am still ready to do everything to create conditions for collaboration... but only on one condition: if you yourself decide that you belong to the camp of the Fourth International and not to the camp of its adversaries.'[22]

In a letter to Trotsky in Russian, datelined Paris, 18 March 1939, Serge defended his activities, and once again laid bare his differences with the Old Man on the question of the International:

'I can assure you personally that I took no part in any groupings "opposed to the Fourth". Of course I feel closer to comrades-heretics, because I believe they are right: it's time to follow a new road, not to stick to the well-trodden paths of the late Comintern. Nevertheless, not only did I not participate in any "factional activities", but tried whenever I could to soften the inevitable split. You will hardly find another person in existing groups as alien to any kind of "intrigue" as myself... The same thing all over again: one cannot say honestly, calmly and with dignity, "Yes, we have serious disagreements" — one must always discredit or even slightly slander the other side.

'Our disagreements are very great indeed... I am convinced that one cannot build an international while there are no *parties*... One should not play with the words "party" and "International". But there are no parties here... Only small groups manage to hold out somehow in this deadlock, but they have no dynamism, no influence, nor even a common language with the working class movement. One cannot build an international organisation on intolerance and the Bolshevik-Leninist doctrine, for in the whole world there are no more than 200 people (except the surviving inmates of Stalin, perhaps) who are in a position to understand what Bolshevism-Leninism is... For the time being, no one in the Fourth International groups thinks except through your head.

20. V Serge, 'My Break With Trotsky', *Carnets*, op cit, p48.
21. Ibid.
22. LD Trotsky to V Serge, 15 April 1938.

'What should be done? The solution, I believe, lies in an alliance with all the left wing currents of the workers' movement (its platform: the class struggle and internationalism)... one must abandon the idea of Bolshevist-Leninist hegemony in the left wing workers' movement, and create an international alliance, which would reflect the real ideological tendencies of the most advanced sections of the working class (I am convinced that in such an alliance the Bolshevik-Leninists would have a greater influence than in their own high and mighty International).'[23]

Serge's attitude to the POUM, the French Popular Front and the Fourth International were based on his concern that revolutionary Marxists should not be cut off from the political arena that held the attention of the working class. Though Serge was perhaps overly enthusiastic about what could be achieved with the Popular Front[24] and the POUM, he also understood that the Trotskyists would be seen as sectarian, resulting in their isolation, depriving an important struggle of their revolutionary influence. Furthermore, the behaviour of the Fourth International in relation to the Spanish events was disturbing: Serge wrote to Sedov that they 'consider themselves called from above... to lead the revolution in another country, and they see their one path in the creation of factions à la the Comintern and in a schismatic perspective. This path will obviously lead nowhere, if not to the discredit of the Fourth [International].'[25]

Serge's disdain for the Fourth International's tactics in Spain and his insistence on solidarity with the POUM were seen by the Trotskyists as a capitulation to reformism, and Serge was indelibly labelled a centrist.

The stamp 'moralist' came from Serge's renewal of the debate on Kronstadt. This debate took place in late 1937 and throughout 1938 in journals in Europe and America. In 'dredging up' this ignominious chapter in Bolshevik history, Serge had not changed his position of siding with the party, but wanted the party to understand how they came to be in the position of executing workers. The libertarians and anarchists in Europe were quick to point to the similarities between the Mos-

23. V Serge to LD Trotsky, 18 March 1939.
24. But Serge's enthusiasm was less than Trotsky's in 1936 when Trotsky wrote to Serge in envy that Serge would be off to Paris where the 'birth-pangs of the French Revolution' had begun with a massive strike (LD Trotsky to V Serge, 9 June 1936). Serge replied with a cautionary note: 'The wonderful strikes in France and here show clearly that the working class is recovering after its phase of depression and extreme fatigue, and is entering a new period of struggle. In such a situation one may hope for anything, so long as one does not expect an immediate all-round upsurge.' (V Serge to LD Trotsky, 16 June 1936) These letters are now published in English in D Cotterill (ed), *The Serge-Trotsky Papers*, London, pp69-74.
25. V Serge to LL Sedov, 21 January 1937.

cow Trials and the suppression of the Kronstadt rebellion. While the anarchists and 'Poumistas' were being betrayed by the Stalinists in Spain, the Kronstadt debate served as a foil for the larger argument that Stalinism was the natural outgrowth of Leninism. Serge did not share this view, nor was it his purpose in intervening in the debate about Kronstadt.

Serge insisted that it was not only healthy to look back at what happened, and how it could have been avoided, but that this was essential to draw the lessons. Trotsky agreed that it was 'necessary to learn and think', but that advice was very easy to give after the event.[26]

Trotsky aimed his fire at the 'moralists', like Boris Souvarine and Ante Ciliga, who were interested in the question of Trotsky's personal responsibility. Serge entered the fray, in order to defend the ideals of October from those, like Ciliga, who 'judged [the revolution] in the light of Stalinism alone', and who directed personal attacks 'against Trotsky out of bad faith, ignorance and sectarian spirit'.[27] Serge took on Ciliga's ahistorical critique, stating:

'A little direct contact with the people was enough to get an idea of the drama which, in the revolution, separated the Communist Party (and with it the dust of the other revolutionary groups) from the masses. At no time did the revolutionary workers form more than a trifling percentage of the masses themselves. In 1920-21, all that was energetic, militant, ever-so-little socialistic in the labour population and among the advanced elements of the countryside had already been drained by the Communist Party, which did not, for four years of civil war, stop its constant mobilisation of the willing — down to the most vacillating... Eloquence of chronology: it is the non-party workers of this epoch, joining the party to the number of two million in 1924, upon the death of Lenin, who assure the victory of its bureaucracy. I assure you, Ciliga, that these people never thought of the Third International. Many of the insurgents of Kronstadt did think of it; but they constituted an undeniable elite, and, duped by their own passion, they opened in spite of themselves the doors to a frightful counter-revolution. The firmness of the Bolshevik party, on the other hand, sick as it was, delayed Thermidor by five to 10 years.'[28]

Clearly, Serge and Trotsky had much in common in these thoughts. Furthermore, it was Trotsky, not Serge, who dredged up the Kronstadt debate, in the course of

26. LD Trotsky, 'Hue and Cry Over Kronstadt', 15 January 1938, *The New International*, April 1938.
27. V Serge, 'A Letter and Some Notes', *The New International*, February 1939, p 53.
28. V Serge, 'Reply to Ciliga', *The New International*, February 1939.

defending his record against the calumny of the Moscow Trials. In light of the Spanish Civil War, and a need by those like Ciliga to link the Stalinist weeds with the Leninist germs, Serge took the opportunity to raise some issues he thought worthy of reflection because they had an educational value for the left in the West.

Trotsky's tone, in all of his replies, was one of exasperation. He seemed most angry by the debates Serge raised. On 2 December 1938 Trotsky wrote a short piece that was published in January 1939 in the *Byulleten Oppozitsii*, no 73, entitled 'Viktor Serzh i IV Internatsional', which stated that Serge, now a member of the centrist POUM, was an opponent of the Fourth International.[29] When Serge published in *Partisan Review* an article entitled 'Marxism in Our Time',[30] Trotsky replied without any evidence of having read Serge's piece. Trotsky's disagreements with Serge here turn into simple ad hominem attack:

'... the ranks of the disillusioned include not only Stalinists but also the temporary fellow travellers of Bolshevism. Victor Serge — to cite an instance — has recently announced that Bolshevism is passing through a crisis which presages in turn the "crisis of Marxism". In his theoretical innocence, Serge imagines himself the first to have made this discovery. Yet, in every epoch of reaction, scores and hundreds of unstable revolutionists have risen to announce the "crisis of Marxism" — the final, the crucial, the mortal crisis. That the old Bolshevik Party has spent itself, has degenerated and perished — that much is beyond controversy... this does not at all invalidate Marxism, which is the algebra of revolution. That Victor Serge himself is passing through a "crisis", that is to say, has become hopelessly confused like thousands of other intellectuals — is clear enough. But Victor Serge in crisis is not the crisis of Marxism.'[31]

Serge wrote to Trotsky on 18 March 1939:

'I've decided not to react at all to the article in the *Bulletin*. You are too inaccurate, too unjust and unnecessarily offensive. I don't know who keeps you informed and how, but, sadly believe me, there exists a whole nest of intrigues here (which has played its part in the death of Lev Lvovich, and before that, in the death of Reiss, as well as in the failure of the whole Fourth International movement in France).'[32]

29. *Byulleten' Oppozitsii*, no 73, January 1939, p16.
30. V Serge, 'Marxism in Our Time', *Partisan Review*, Volume 5, no 3, August-September 1939, pp26-32.
31. LD Trotsky, 'Intellectual Ex-Radicals and World Reaction', 17 February 1939, *Writings of Leon Trotsky 1938-39*, New York, 1974, pp194-6.
32. V Serge to LD Trotsky, 18 March 1939.

The Left Opposition Divided

In a postscript to this letter, Serge told Trotsky that his rupture with the French Bolshevik-Leninists occurred because he had been told by a 'comrade' that there were serious suspicions about Lola Ya Ginsburg.[33] Serge thought this should be investigated and confided to Rosmer, Wullens and Elsa Reiss. Elsa told the group, who 'refused to look into *the substance* of the affair, or so I was informed through comrade Étienne. Instead — it "brought an action" against me.' While it appears that Lilia Ginsburg, known personally as Lola and politically as Paulsen or Yakovlev, was not the NKVD agent, she protected and vouched for the reliability of Étienne/Zborowski — the real agent. Zborowski was apparently successful in turning Serge into a political pariah for the group. Trotsky fell right in, and subjected Serge to an horrendous offensive of vitriolic prose.

In a fragment found among Trotsky's papers in Mexico, written sometime in 1939, he reached, perhaps, the peak of his animosity:

'Victor Serge claims that his enunciations, statements and corrections always revolving around his own personality, must without exception be printed by the workers' publications. Why? On what basis? What does Victor Serge represent today in the workers' movement? An ulcer of his own doubts, of his own confusion and nothing more...What do people of the Victor Serge type represent? Our conclusion is simple: these verbose, coquettish moralists, capable of bringing only trouble and decay, must be kept out of the revolutionary organisation, even by cannon fire if necessary.'[34]

Clearly with this fragment Trotsky reached beyond viciousness to deadliness. It was as if all his frustrations at being physically prevented from playing a leading role in the struggle in the USSR and Europe were vented in his literary tantrums against comrades like Serge. His own son, Lev Lvovich Sedov, a frequent subject of Trotsky's anger, recognised the deleterious effects of this kind of outburst:

'I think that all Dad's deficiencies have not diminished as he grew older, but under the influence of his isolation, very difficult, unprecedentedly difficult, have got worse. His lack of tolerance, hot temper, inconsistency, even rudeness, his desire to humiliate, offend and even destroy have increased. It is not "personal", it is a method, and hardly good in organisation of work.'[35]

33. For more on the suspicions planted within the Left Opposition as to who was the NKVD agent, see Susan Weissman, *Victor Serge: Political, Social and Literary Critic of the USSR, 1919-1947*, UMI Dissertation Information Service, Ann Arbor, Michigan, 1991, pp76-9.
34. LD Trotsky, 'Petit-Bourgeois Democrats and Moralisers', *Writings of Leon Trotsky: Supplement 1934-40*, New York, 1979, p872.
35. LL Sedov to his mother, Natalia Sedova, 16 April 1936. Having vented his own frustration at

Serge's translation of Trotsky's polemic on means and ends, *Their Morals and Ours*, of February 1938, brought more unwarranted controversy to their relationship. Unfortunately, the controversy was not over the content of the book, which Serge thought contained 'many fine pages at the end'.

The book was subtitled 'Marxist Versus Liberal Views on Morality', and it provoked a debate between Trotsky and John Dewey, among others. Trotsky was at his polemical best in this book, utilising colourful and truculent language to describe his opponents. He set out to distinguish revolutionary morality, which is rooted in concrete historical circumstances, from the abstract and timeless morality argued by the liberals, social democrats and others who Trotsky labelled in vintage descriptive terms. The 'fine pages at the end' contain a discussion entitled the 'Dialectic Interdependence of End and Means'. Here Trotsky insisted that base means lead to base ends, that 'organically the means are subordinated to the end',[36] or in other words, the product could only be as pure as the process.

The dispute with Trotsky was not over Serge's translation, or any unspoken disagreements about the ideas Trotsky expressed, but over the promotional prospectus in the French edition, which crudely attacked Trotsky. Without checking with the publisher, Trotsky assumed Serge wrote this invective:

'For Trotsky, there is no such thing as morality per se, no ideal or eternal morality. Morals are relative to each society, to each epoch, relative especially to the interests of social classes... True morality must defend the interests of humanity itself, represented by the proletariat. Trotsky thinks that his party, once in power, today in the opposition, always represented the real proletariat; and he himself, the real morality. From this he concludes that shooting hostages takes on different meanings depending on whether the order is given by Stalin or by Trotsky or by the bourgeoisie... Trotsky, basing himself on Lenin, declares that *the end justifies the means* (on condition that the means are effective: for example, individual terrorism is generally ineffective). There is no cynicism in this attitude, declares the author, merely a statement of the facts. And it is to these facts that Trotsky says he owes his acute conscience, which constitutes his *moral sense*.'[37]

> his father's inconsistent meddling with the French Trotskyists, Sedov never sent this letter, and he remained publicly his father's most ardent supporter. The letter was found in the Boris Nicolaevsky Collection at Stanford's Hoover Institution, series 231. It was also cited by Dale Reed and Michael Jakobson in 'Trotsky Papers at the Hoover Institution: One Chapter of an Archival Mystery Story', *The American Historical Review*, Volume 92, no 2, April 1987, p366.

36. LD Trotsky, *Their Morals and Ours*, New York, 1969, p37.
37. Prière d'insérer, 1939 edition of *Their Morals and Ours*, Éditions du Sagittaire, Appendix C of 1969 (English) Merit edition.

It is inconceivable that Serge could have penned or inspired these thoughts, so out of character with the body of his published work. Instead of verifying the facts with Serge or Les Éditions du Sagittaire, Trotsky lifted his pen and wrote a furious addendum to *Their Morals and Ours* on 9 June 1939, the essay called 'The Moralists and Sycophants Against Marxism: Peddlers of Indulgences and their Socialist Allies, or the Cuckoo in a Strange Nest'. He wrote:

'... some "friend"... contrived to slip into a strange nest and deposit there his little egg — oh! it is of course a very tiny egg, an almost virginal egg. Who is the author of this prospectus? Victor Serge, who is at the same time its severest critic, can easily supply the information. I should not be surprised if it turned out that the prospectus was written... naturally not by Victor Serge but by one of his disciples who imitates both his master's ideas and his style. But, maybe after all, it is the master himself, that is, Victor Serge in his capacity of "friend" of the author?'[38]

The piece exudes Trotsky's vexation with the 'independents' loosely associated with the Left Opposition. One can detect his obvious frustration at being an ocean away from the discussion, an ocean away from reining in the dissidents. The essay is devoted to a scathing attack against Victor Serge (the moralist) and Boris Souvarine (the sycophant) in language memorable for its viciousness. Trotsky sustained some seven pages of tirade, accusing Serge of 'Hottentot morality', of publicly becoming a member of the POUM, of being a 'petit-bourgeois moralist' who 'thinks episodically, in fragments, in clumps', of wanting 'to purge human history of civil war'. Furthermore, Trotsky berated Serge for dating the degeneration of the revolution from the moment the Cheka began secret trials. Trotsky wrote: 'Serge plays with the concept of revolution, writes poems about it, but is incapable of understanding it as it is.' Apparently one of Serge's worst attributes was that he wrote lyrically, even poetically about revolution; Trotsky returned to this in several articles.[39] More to the point, Trotsky got to the heart of his animosity to Serge: '... when we evaluate from the Marxian standpoint the vacillations of a disillusioned petit-bourgeois intellectual, that seems to him an assault upon his indi-

---

38. LD Trotsky, 'The Moralists and Sycophants Against Marxism', in *Their Morals and Ours*, p41.
39. In a particularly vicious attack on Serge, Trotsky replied to Serge's letter criticising the creation of the Fourth International: 'When the Fourth International becomes "worthy of the name" in the eyes of Messrs littérateurs, dilettantes and sceptics, then it will not be difficult to adhere to it. A Victor Serge (this one, or another) will then write a book in which he will prove (with lyricism and with tears!) that the best, the most heroic period of the Fourth International was the time, when bereft of forces, it waged a struggle against innumerable enemies, including petit-bourgeois sceptics.' (LD Trotsky, '"Trotskyism" and the PSOP', *Writings of Leon Trotsky 1938-39*, New York, 1969, p134)

viduality. He then enters into an alliance with all the confusionists for a crusade against our despotism and our sectarianism... On the other hand, Victor Serge has systematically helped centrist organisations drive from their ranks the partisans of the Fourth International.'[40] He ended his diatribe by saying that 'the moralism of V Serge and his compeers is a bridge from revolution to reaction'.[41] The essay seeks to lump Serge with other anti-Bolsheviks and anti-Leninists, those who see Stalin as the heir to Lenin. It is remarkable for its obvious ignorance of Serge's writings, from his *Year One of the Russian Revolution* to his *Lenin*, his civil war writings, his *From Lenin to Stalin*, his novels, not to mention his articles.

Serge was heartbroken by what this vicious onslaught of ad hominem attack represented. In the *Memoirs* Serge lamented:

'Deplorably misinformed by his acolytes, he wrote a long polemical essay against me — imputing to me an article of which I was not the author and which was totally at variance with my frequently expressed opinions. The Trotskyist journals refused to publish my corrections. In the hearts of the persecuted I encountered the same attitudes as in their persecutors... Trotskyism was displaying symptoms of an outlook in harmony with that of the very Stalinism against which it had taken its stand, and by which it was being ground into powder... I was heartbroken by it all, because it is my firm belief that the tenacity and willpower of some men can, despite all odds, break with the traditions that suffocate, and withstand the contagions that bring death. It is painful, it is difficult, but it *must* be possible. I abstained from any counter-polemic.'[42]

Serge was denied access to Trotskyist journals, but nonetheless attempted internally to refute the charges, to clear the air and his name. Publicly Serge refused to break solidarity with Trotsky. Serge wrote to Dwight MacDonald:

'In his recent attacks on me, Leon Davidovich has so abused me that I'm almost glad I no longer have the means to answer him. He began by criticising me without having read what I wrote, and continues to attribute to me an article that I did not write in a journal with which I have no association. His entire article entitled "Moralists and Sycophants" is thus entirely falsely based, since he ascribes ideas and arguments to me that were never mine. However, I have written a great deal in the last 20 years on these subjects, and he should know this! He would also do well to find out who wrote the article he attributes to me without so much as a

---

40. Ibid, p45.
41. Ibid, p50.
42. V Serge, *Memoirs of a Revolutionary*, op cit, p349.

care. All this is terribly sad. I sent *New International* and LD himself some corrections, the fate of which are unknown. In Europe the publications that attacked me in this way never published my replies. So I stopped replying. I am adamant.'[43]

Serge then penned a reply to Trotsky which he did not publish. It was discovered among Serge's papers by Peter Sedgwick, who translated and published the essay in *Peace News* in 1963 under the title 'Secrecy and Revolution: A Reply to Trotsky'.[44] In a letter he wrote to Angelica Balabanova on 23 October 1941, Serge explained why he refrained from a public debate with the Old Man, who was engaged in a resolute fight against Stalinism, and whose ideas Serge still deeply respected:

'... in all this painful argument with the Old Man, I kept such esteem and affection for him that, even though he wrote a long polemical attack accusing me of writing an article which was never mine and of advocating ideas which were never mine, I first sent a powerful rebuttal to the printers of *La Révolution Proletarienne* (Paris) and then took it back from them, preferring to suffer this unjust attack in silence. And I still think I was quite right: truth can work its way out in different ways than by offensive polemics.'[45]

Serge also wrote to Trotsky on 9 August 1939 denying any connection to the odious prospectus. Trotsky replied on 7 September 1939 in the *Byulleten Oppozitsii*, saying that he 'willingly accepted his declaration', and then proceeded to attack Serge for having 'a confused mood of uncertainty, disillusionment, dissatisfaction and repulsion from Marxism and proletarian revolution'. As to the authorship of the prospectus, Trotsky wrote 'if not he personally, then [it was] one of his disciples or co-thinkers. The supposition that the prospectus was written by Victor Serge occurred to various comrades, independently of one another. And not by chance: the blurb constitutes a simple resumé of Victor Serge's latest sermonisings.'[46]

43. V Serge to D MacDonald, 22 October 1939, MacDonald Papers, Yale University archive. Dwight MacDonald was an American radical journalist and critic, formerly close to Trotsky, but later a pacifist, then an independent liberal. In his role as editor of *Partisan Review*, and together with his wife Nancy, he supported Serge with material help. The MacDonalds were instrumental in obtaining Serge's visa for Mexico in 1941.
44. V Serge 'Secrecy and Revolution: A Reply to Trotsky', *Peace News*, 27 December 1963.
45. V Serge to A Balabanova, 23 October 1941, Serge Archive, Mexico. Angelica Balabanova (Balabanoff) was the first Secretary of the Executive Committee of the Communist International, based in Moscow. After her expulsion from the Comintern, she lived in various European countries. When Serge wrote to her, she was living in the USA, where she lived until her death in 1965.
46 LD Trotsky, 'Ocherednoe Oproverzhenie Viktora Serzha', *Byulleten' Oppozitsii*, no 79-80,

Which comrades? Étienne? Pierre Frank?[47] Whether or not Étienne directly raised the issue with Trotsky, or incited others to do so, he could be justly proud of accomplishing his objective of dividing the two surviving Left Oppositionists, and occupying them with incessant internal intrigue. Yet Trotsky seemed to dismiss the possibility of the hand of the NKVD. In a letter dated 6 May 1939 to Serge published in the *Writings* as 'Victor Serge's Crisis', Trotsky wrote:

'... you are passing through a protracted ideological crisis and... you are turning your dissatisfaction with yourself into dissatisfaction with others. You write about intrigues, false information, etc. I don't know about any of that... I do not lose the hope of seeing you return to the road of the Fourth International. But at present you are an adversary, and a hostile one at that, who demands nonetheless to be treated as a political friend.'[48]

Serge was categorical that he 'never published a single line concerning that work [*Their Morals and Ours*] of his, in any publication or in any shape or form'.[49] Serge continued: 'I am not the author of this prospectus: I have had no part, direct or indirect, in composing it: I have no idea who its author is — and I do not care either. Is that clear enough?'[50] The real author of the prospectus is still unknown. Vlady believes Zborowski wrote it,[51] and I put that question to him several times, without ever being graced with a reply. Pierre Broué believes an editor wrote it,[52] which could have been done under Zborowski's guidance.

The rupture over the prospectus was really the culmination of disagreements over larger issues: Serge's support of the POUM, and his attitude to the Fourth International. Trotsky was offended by this 'defection', and the excessive tone of his polemic reflected his anger. Defection notwithstanding, Serge still functioned in the orbit of Trotskyism, and held the Old Man in great esteem; and he was considered a 'Trotskyist' by the larger political public. He later wrote in his diary:

'I went on translating the Old Man's books, *La Révolution trahie*, *Les Crimes de Staline*, *Leur Morale et la Nôtre*, and to defend him. I remained in the eyes of the

August-September 1939, p31. The English translation, 'Another Refutation by Victor Serge', is published as Appendix B in the Merit edition of *Their Morals and Ours*.

47. Pierre Frank (1906-1984) was a Trotskyist and founder of the French section of the Fourth International, and a member of its International Secretariat.
48. LD Trotsky, 'Victor Serge's Crisis', *Writings of Leon Trotsky: Supplement 1934-40*, op cit, p836.
49. V Serge, 'Secrecy and Revolution: A Reply to Trotsky', *Peace News*, 27 December 1963.
50. Ibid.
51. Private conversation, Mexico City, January 1986.
52. Private conversation, Los Angeles, October 1989.

general public the best-known "Trotskyist" writer — while the "B-L" [53] disparaged me as far as they could. I had become for them a "petit-bourgeois intellectual" of whom they had to "make use of the influence" and the "questionable sympathy". The sense of possession of the truth, the intolerance and the aggressiveness devoid of critical sense of *Leur Morale* made me furious, although there are fine, worthwhile pages at the end of this essay. I said so to some Trotskyists who wrote and told the Old Man, and that at once brought fresh attacks upon me. The saddest thing was that they were always insulting, and always based on inaccurate data. It would have been so simple to state: We're at considerable variance on such and such a point — but the Old Man and his followers had become completely incapable of holding such a straightforward dialogue. The frightening atmosphere of persecution in which they lived — like me — made them inclined to a persecution complex and to the practice of persecution.'[54]

The rupture between Serge and Trotsky was never really completed, and had the character of a quarrel with room for conciliation. Even as Trotsky spewed out the worst venom, some of which is quoted above, he always left open the door for cooperation, provided, of course, that Serge work within the Fourth International. For Serge's part, the pain of Trotsky's vitriol was great, but it did not deflect from Serge's essential appreciation of Trotsky's 'greatness' whose 'traits were those of several generations, developed to a very high degree of individual perfection'.[55]

With this appreciation of Trotsky in mind, Serge replied to Trotsky's invective against him:

'Whether Trotsky wills it or not, no limit has been set to the analysis of the Russian Revolution, which he has served so outstandingly, so tremendously — despite the measure of responsibility that must be laid to his name for certain tragic errors. And no amount of ponderous irony, no broadsides of discredit, directed against men who dare to think and sometimes to pronounce according to their conscience, will render him free to substitute mischievous polemic for the necessary debate to which, with a little less pretension to infallibility, he could bring the most precious contributions of all.'[56]

All the more tragic, then, that Serge and Trotsky were not able to work together

53. Bolshevik-Leninists, that is, Trotskyists.
54. V Serge, 'My rupture with Trotsky', *Carnets*, op cit, pp 44-7.
55. V Serge, 'The Old Man', 1 August 1942, written in Mexico 'to the memory of Leon Davidovich Trotsky', in V Serge and N Sedova Trotsky, *The Life and Death of Leon Trotsky*, New York, 1975, p4.
56. V Serge, 'Secrecy and Revolution: A Reply to Trotsky', *Peace News*, 27 December 1963.

in those dark years, that Serge's generous, comradely and dignified attitude to Trotsky was not reciprocated.

Worse, for Serge, was the destructive behaviour of the Trotskyists. It is clear that Serge did not think Trotsky a Trotskyist in this sense. Trotsky's inflexibility could be understood, wrote Serge, because he was 'the last survivor of a generation of giants'. For the present generation and the future, however, Serge was convinced that:

'Socialism too had to renew itself in the world of today, and that this must take place through the jettisoning of the authoritarian, intolerant tradition of turn-of-the-century Russian Marxism. I recalled, for use against Trotsky himself, a sentence of astounding vision which he had written in 1914, I think: "Bolshevism may very well be an excellent instrument for the conquest of power, but after that it will reveal its counter-revolutionary aspects."'[57]

In an essay Serge wrote to the memory of Trotsky, he described him as:

'... a doer, but one who brought to everything he did a lyrical touch... His absolute conviction that he knew the truth made him impervious to argument towards the end, and detracted from his scientific spirit. He was authoritarian, because in our time of barbaric struggles thought turned into action must of necessity become authoritarian. When power was within his reach in 1924 and 1925, he refused to seize it because he felt that a socialist regime could not be run by decree.'[58]

Furthermore, Serge attested:

'Our Oppositional movement in Russia had not been Trotskyist, since we had no intention of attaching it to a personality, rebels as we ourselves were against the cult of the Leader. We regarded the Old Man only as one of our greatest comrades, an elder member of the family over whose ideas we argued freely... I came to the conclusion that our Opposition had simultaneously contained two opposing lines of significance. For the great majority... it meant resistance to totalitarianism in the name of the democratic ideals expressed at the beginning of the Revolution; for a number of our Old Bolshevik leaders it meant, on the contrary, the defence of doctrinal orthodoxy which, while not excluding a certain tendency towards democracy, was authoritarian through and through. These two mingled strains had between 1923 and 1928 surrounded Trotsky's vigorous personality with a

---

57. Ibid.
58. V Serge, 'The Old Man', V Serge and N Sedova, op cit, pp2-5.

tremendous aura. If, in his exile from the USSR, he had made himself the ideologist of a renewed socialism, critical in outlook and fearing diversity less than dogmatism, perhaps he would have attained a new greatness. But he was the prisoner of his own orthodoxy, the more so since his lapses into unorthodoxy were being denounced as treason. He saw his role as that of one carrying into the world at large a movement which was not only Russian but extinct in Russia itself, killed twice over, both by the bullets of its executioners and by changes in human mentality.'[59]

59.   V Serge, *Memoirs of a Revolutionary*, op cit, pp348-50. These thoughts were echoed in a letter Serge wrote to Trotsky on 27 May 1936. In discussing the strands of thought in the Left Opposition, Serge quoted the Left Oppositionist Yeltsin, who admitted that the 'GPU created any unity we have'.

Debating Trotsky

Michael Cox

The Revolutionary Betrayed

The *New Left Review* and Leon Trotsky[1]

The *New Left Review* under Perry Anderson's theoretical leadership played a critical role on the international left from the 1960s onwards. Accused of elitism by some, and of theoretical eclecticism by others, nonetheless it was without doubt the main standard-bearer of Marxist discussion on the non-Stalinist left. Unfortunately, after the revolutionary flush of 1968 gave way to the quietism of the 1970s, the *New Left Review* gradually shifted its ground, becoming in the process less critical of the USSR and its international role. Part of the explanation for this lay with the influence of Deutscherism upon a number of its board members. However the 'second' Cold War launched by Reagan also made the journal more defensive of the Soviet Union, as the following critique of Anderson reveals.

Anderson on Trotsky

In his provocative discussion of Trotsky's analysis of the USSR, Perry Anderson quite correctly finds much that is praiseworthy and good.[2] Indeed, he insists that Trotsky's contribution was quite unique. 'Trotsky's interpretation of the histori-

1. This article first appeared in *Critique*, nos 20/21, 1987.
2. P Anderson, 'Trotsky's Interpretation of Stalinism', *New Left Review*, no 139, May-June 1983, pp49-58.

cal meaning of Stalinism', he asserts boldly at the beginning of his article, was, and presumably remains, 'the most developed theorisation of the phenomenon within the Marxist tradition.' According to Anderson, Trotsky's analysis of Stalinism had three qualities: historical perspective, sociological richness, and political balance. The first made it possible for Trotsky to situate Stalinism historically. The second is shown by the fact that modern scholarship has been unable to refute his findings. The third enabled him to avoid becoming either a straightforward apologist for or utterly dismissive of Soviet achievements, for he recognised that in spite of its negative degenerate features, the Soviet Union remained a progressive historical formation. The USSR, to use a phrase, was a 'contradictory phenomenon', and Trotsky incorporated this reality into his analysis and characterisation of the Soviet system.

Yet Anderson perceives a basic problem in Trotsky. Having correctly understood the dual character of the USSR, he then failed to apply this insight to his discussion of the USSR on an international level. If the Soviet Union was a contradictory system that was both anti-capitalist and anti-working class, did it not follow that this contradiction would be reflected in its relationship with world capitalism? Here Anderson believes he has spotted a major problem in Trotsky's thought. For while Trotsky was willing to recognise the dual nature of the USSR, he was unwilling (or unable) to apply this idea to the Soviet Union's external role. Hence, Trotsky's argument concerning the absolutely counter-revolutionary role played by the USSR abroad, not only contradicted his basic theory of the Stalinist system, but fails — according to Anderson — to explain important historical developments since 1917 and the part played by the USSR in bringing them about.

Anderson points to several examples of the USSR's objectively progressive role, and the contribution it has made directly and indirectly to the struggle for socialism in the twentieth century. Perhaps most important, he insists, was the part played by the Soviet Union in the defeat of first Nazism and later colonialism. He puts the case forcefully and without ambiguity: 'The two major forms of historical progress registered within world capitalism in the past 50 years — the defeat of fascism, the end of colonialism' were, he maintains, directly 'dependent on the presence and performance of the USSR'.[3] However, that is not all. The USSR has also weakened capitalism by overthrowing bourgeois rule in one part of the world

3. The Soviet contribution to the defeat of Germany after 1941 is obvious. However, Anderson might have mentioned the fact that Soviet policies — in Germany before 1933, in Spain in 1937, and in the shape of the Nazi-Soviet Pact in 1939 — actually contributed to the consolidation and spread of Nazism in Europe. He should have also specified what indispensable role the USSR played in the overthrow of European colonial rule during and after the Second World War — especially as Stalin was utterly indifferent to and even opposed to anti-colonial nationalism!

— Eastern Europe — and by giving support to regimes and movements which negate it in others, especially in the Third World. In short, the USSR has not proved to be purely counter-revolutionary. It has, in its inevitably contradictory fashion, weakened capitalism as an international system, and by definition therefore has advanced the cause of the working class. However, Trotsky — Anderson insists — refused to admit that the USSR could further the struggle, and that Stalinism could spread as a result. Yet, if he had remained true to his original view about the dual contradictory character of the USSR, he could have explained why Stalinism has proved able to advance the fight against the capitalist world system, and how the USSR, in spite of its 'colossal distortions', has proved to be 'persistently anti-capitalist beyond its own frontiers'.

In formal terms there are certain points made by Anderson with which it is impossible to disagree, particularly about the seminal nature of Trotsky's work on Stalinism, and why it has proved to be so influential since his death. In his characteristically elegant manner, he shows why Trotsky retains his fascination for Marxists. Moreover, unlike orthodox Trotskyists, he is prepared to engage with what he sees as the inconsistencies in Trotsky's thought. For this at least, Anderson ought to be applauded. Yet while Anderson has posed a number of problems for those in the orthodox Trotskyist tradition, I would argue that his own analysis is basically flawed.[4]

Firstly, he is far too uncritical of Trotsky's discussion of the USSR. Instead of exposing the underlying ambiguities in Trotsky's theory of the Soviet Union, he seeks to preserve and even celebrate their existence. More seriously, he not only ignores that which is ambiguous in Trotsky, but more obviously that which is important and analytically useful. For this reason Anderson fails to use Trotsky in order to develop a theory of Soviet external relations. Secondly, while he is correct to point to the obvious problems confronting Trotskyists who have argued that the USSR is a status quo power in the world, he is himself unable to provide a theory of Soviet foreign policy, or an explanation of why Stalinism has spread. Finally, although Anderson admits that the USSR has often held back the struggle against world capitalism, in the end the main thrust of his argument is to show the active, sometimes unconscious, role it has played in weakening the market on a

---

4. In his critique of Anderson, Phil Hearse is correct politically, but makes two mistakes. Firstly, unlike Anderson, he doesn't even try to explain why the USSR comes into opposition with the world market. Secondly, like Anderson he treats Trotsky uncritically. See his 'Perry Anderson on Stalinism', *International*, November-December 1983, pp31-4. In his contribution, Chris Arthur makes the somewhat understated criticism that Anderson is 'overgenerous to the Soviet bureaucracy'. However, he seems to agree with Anderson that there is something worth defending in the USSR, and like Hearse, fails to examine Trotsky's thought critically. See his remarks in *International*, January-February 1984.

world scale. Hidden behind his nuances and qualifications there is a clear message struggling to be heard. It reads thus: the USSR is on the side of socialism, and in spite of its internal degeneration and often dubious international politics, it is still a revolutionary force in the world which the left ought to defend. It is this which is perhaps the least acceptable and most questionable part of Anderson's attempt to correct Trotsky. Let us deal briefly with each of these points.

Orthodox Trotskyism

Anderson, it is obvious, is far too uncritical of Trotsky. It is all very well saying that Trotsky's analysis of Stalinism had historic perspective, sociological richness and political balance (whatever that means), but that hardly helps us come to terms with Trotsky's highly ambiguous legacy.[5] To praise Trotsky for what many have seen as his flawed, albeit powerful, analysis of the USSR, evades this real problem. Anderson ignores the simple fact that in spite of its many strengths, Trotsky's discussion of the USSR in the 1930s leaves many questions unanswered. Perhaps we shouldn't blame Trotsky. After all, he was working in isolation, and was separated by thousands of miles from events in the Soviet Union.[6] Moreover, what he was analysing was itself unique and in flux. His work should therefore be regarded as unfinished, as he himself admitted.[7] There were thus good objective reasons why Trotsky's half-developed (albeit frequently brilliant) ideas were bound to be limited. We should treat them, as he did, as only first approximations. Unfortunately, this has not been the case, as the subsequent history of the Trotskyist movement and Anderson's short piece show. Far from engaging with Trotsky, many, including Anderson, have been content simply to repeat his formulae. This is why the 'Russian question' has always been the Achilles' heel of Trotskyism.

Basically, what Trotskyism has taken from Trotsky has been the following propositions about the USSR. Firstly, that in spite of its degeneration, the Soviet

---

5. All serious Marxist discussion about the USSR, however, inevitably has to begin with Trotsky and deal with his contribution. This point is demonstrated forcibly by Antonio Carlo in his useful survey 'The Socio-Economic Nature of the USSR', *Telos*, no 21, Fall 1974, pp2-86.
6. Writing of Trotsky in the mid-1930s, Victor Serge later observed: 'Although he was still at the height of his intellectual powers, what he wrote towards the end did not approach his earlier work in quality. People often forget that intelligence does not exist in a vacuum.' (V Serge and NS Trotsky, *The Life and Death of Leon Trotsky*, London, 1975, p4)
7. Trotsky wrote: 'In our analysis, we have above all avoided doing violence to dynamic social formations which have had no precedent and have no analogies. The scientific task, as well as the political, is not to give a finished definition to an unfinished process.' (LD Trotsky, *The Revolution Betrayed*, New York, 1970, pp255-6)

Union still remains a workers' state. Secondly, that although there is no democracy in the USSR, planning exists. Thirdly, that this new economic system, whatever its shortcomings, is basically superior to capitalism because it is able to grow more quickly and develop technology more rapidly than under the market. Fourthly, that the bureaucracy, almost in spite of itself, is bound to defend state property in the Soviet Union. Finally, that for all these reasons, the left has a duty to defend the USSR. There would be little point here in the space of a short article to restate all the obvious objections to these propositions, but the following questions need to be answered by those like Anderson who would defend Trotsky's theory of Stalinism.

Obviously, how can one use the term 'workers' state' to characterise the USSR, where real workers are exploited by an elite which controls the state apparatus in a society which grants the same workers even less rights than in a bourgeois democracy? Further, how can we talk of planning in the Marxist as opposed to the Stalinist and bourgeois sense, when there is no democracy and thus no possibility of the associated producers exercising conscious control over the society?[8] Moreover, if the USSR were superior to the market (and 'growth' can hardly be used as a measurement of Soviet economic superiority, especially now when there is no real growth), then why is the USSR unable to compete economically with the West, or to come out from behind the administrative shield provided by the monopoly on foreign trade? Equally, if the bureaucracy was 'bound to defend the property gains of October', why has it been attempting to move the USSR and Eastern Europe gradually back to the market over the past two decades? Indeed, what exactly are these gains, and who actually benefits from the system? Finally, while we could make a case for defending the USSR in the 1930s when Nazism posed a threat and the system may conceivably have been regenerated, the case for 'defending' the USSR today seems specious and dangerous; specious because it is never defined exactly what it is we are supposed to be defending and against whom; dangerous because it makes those who would defend the USSR into its effective apologists.

As Anderson is well aware of these obvious objections to Trotsky's analysis of the USSR, we can only assume that he finds them trivial, so trivial in fact that he fails to mention them in his assessment of Trotsky's ideas. However, it seems odd, to say the least, that Anderson simply by-passes 40 years of debate about Trotsky's analysis of Soviet society without mentioning these points. All that is needed, he

8. The crucial distinction between the bureaucratic organisation of the Soviet economy and planning proper is made in an easily understandable form by Hillel Ticktin in his debate with Wlodimierz Brus. See 'Is Market Socialism Possible or Necessary?', *Critique*, no 14, 1981, especially pp13-21, 35-9.

implies, is to study what the great man said before 1940, absorb his theoretical insights, maintain his political balance, and celebrate in the knowledge that Trotsky's account has been 'developed rather than contradicted' by 'professional scholars' such as Alec Nove (who thought Stalin was — and the market is — necessary),[9] David Lane (who has little sympathy for Trotsky's theory of the Soviet Union),[10] RW Davies and EH Carr (whose ambivalence about Stalin is well known),[11] and Jerry Hough (who was once regarded as a modern American apologist).[12] Apart from the fact that these scholars, whom he cites, are not quite so neutral as he pretends, and that he ignores the work of contemporary Marxists critical of the USSR, this approach is a recipe for intellectual stagnation. It simply is not enough to take an unfinished theory developed over 40 years ago, and add,

9. A Nove, *Was Stalin Really Necessary?*, London, 1964. It was in his most recent book that Nove mounted a spirited and lucid attack on socialism under the rather humorous title *The Economics of Feasible Socialism*, London, 1983.
10. D Lane, *Politics and Society in the USSR*, London, 1972, pp182-3. Lane's functionalism of necessity gives his work an uncritical character.
11. Davies has revealed that Carr chose him to be his collaborator in 1958 because there was 'fairly close agreement on basic issues'. Carr, in a private letter, noted that Davies was 'not a Menshevik or (like Nove, apparently) a Bukharinite'. However, nor was he a 'Trotskyite' either, 'in the sense of wanting to spend all his time throwing stones at Stalin'. According to Davies, he and Carr 'shared a common approach to history', loosely defined by the former as being anti-Cold War. This meant that with others — like Baykov, Deutscher, Dobb, Schlesinger and Jacob Millar — they accepted the 'legitimacy' of 1917, and 'regarded the Soviet industrialisation drive and the forced collectivisation of agriculture as in broad outline inevitable and in some sense progressive'. Davies does admit that unlike Carr, he came to believe that 'industrialisation at a modest pace' was compatible with the maintenance of market relations under the NEP. However, nowhere does he repudiate his original belief in the broadly progressive character of Stalinist economic policies. See RW Davies, 'Drop the Glass Industry: Collaborating with EH Carr', *New Left Review*, no 145, May-June 1984, pp56-70. In this fascinating piece, Davies is concerned, amongst other things, to show that there was no great difference between himself and Carr. But he does admit that unlike Carr, he took Stalin seriously as a theorist. It is also very difficult to believe that Davies could have shown the same degree of sympathy towards the Left Opposition in the 1920s as Carr did in the middle volumes of his *History*.
12. Jerry Hough took Merle Fainsod's *How Russia is Ruled*, Harvard, 1953, and turned it into a jointly-authored study, although it was basically Hough's book. While Hough is more sympathetic to the Bolsheviks than Fainsod, his discussion of Soviet history and the Soviet system is not only inferior, it is also uncritical. Amongst other things, Hough manages to tone down Lenin's attack on Stalin, and reduces the great debates of the 1920s to a power struggle. Later he makes the comment that free speech 'in any country is an extremely difficult matter to discuss' (p276), and that it is impossible 'to measure power reliably in a political system' (p550). Finally, Hough underplays the KGB's repressive role, and he also says next to nothing about social privilege. See *How the Soviet Union is Governed*, Harvard, 1979. In other works, Hough has argued that there is a large degree of popular participation in Soviet political life!

or fit, the facts to it. Unfortunately, this is what has passed for Marxist debate on the USSR for nearly a generation, which is one of the reasons why it has been so barren intellectually.

Of course, it might be objected that in a short piece Anderson could not deal with these questions. However, to discuss Trotsky's theory of the USSR without even mentioning the obvious objections to it is strange to say the least, particularly in an article purporting to be a critical assessment of Trotsky's work.

Indeed, Anderson only makes the situation worse by praising what is in fact most problematic about Trotsky's discussion of the USSR, namely its supposedly dialectical character. Trotsky was able — or so it is inferred — to distinguish between the different features of the system, praising that which was good (presumably the economic base), and attacking that which was not (its political superstructure). In fact it was precisely this sort of method which led Trotsky, and has led Trotskyists ever since, up the historical garden path. If one reflects on the problem, if only for a moment, it becomes obvious that with this approach one could say or justify anything. Apart from the fact that it is based upon a ridiculously optimistic view of Soviet economic achievements, this dualistic — rather than dialectical — approach is absurd theoretically. How could the base and superstructure be so out of synchrony, one wonders? Surely, if as Trotsky argued, the superstructure was degenerate, then logically there must have been an equally degenerate set of social and economic relations? One couldn't exist without the other, unless of course one wants to use the absurd Althusserian notion about the autonomy of the superstructure. Yet Trotsky somehow managed to hold on to the view that there was a progressive economic base in the USSR, even though it managed to produce a horribly repressive political system.

Moreover, to assert that the USSR had or has a progressive side tells us nothing, for all systems in history have had a progressive dimension, and have achieved things. After all, the Greeks produced a major culture, the Egyptians built pyramids, and the Romans unified and advanced European civilisation — yet all of these societies were slave-based. Even feudalism constructed magnificent churches, and later colonialism brought backward societies into contact with more advanced ones. Historically, in fact, it could be argued that the market has played, and in many ways still plays, a progressive historic role. Indeed, a stronger case could be made in Marxist terms for defending capitalism rather than Russia. After all, the former has a higher level of productivity, has been able (unlike Stalinism) to develop an international division of labour, and has created an economic foundation upon which some type of democracy has been able to flourish — something which clearly has not happened in the USSR or in any of the 'workers' states'.

Trotsky's Main Theses

However, perhaps the greatest problem with Anderson is not just that he treats Trotsky uncritically, but that he makes no reference at all to Trotsky's main argument, which was not that the USSR was a workers' state that Marxists must defend for eternity, but that in the particular form it had assumed in the 1930s, it would not be able to persist. This is why he maintained that the USSR was at a far higher level of contradiction than capitalism, and should only be regarded as a transitory regime.[13] As he insisted repeatedly throughout the 1930s, the system would have to change if it was to last. It would either have to move forward to socialism — which assumed revolution in the West — or back to capitalism.[14] The USSR could thus only be seen as a temporary phenomenon, for not only was it surrounded on all sides by a more advanced capitalism, but it had a far lower level of labour productivity than its Western adversary. Therefore, unless the USSR broke out of its isolation, and at the same time underwent fundamental internal change, it would either break down, or degenerate to the point where Marxists would have to rethink their whole conception of the era in general, and of what they thought about the Soviet Union in particular.[15] Trotsky considered that it

13. In *The Revolution Betrayed*, Trotsky argued that the USSR was a 'contradictory halfway society between capitalism and socialism' whose character had not yet been decided by history (pp252-6).
14. This argument flowed logically from Trotsky's theory of permanent revolution, to which Anderson does not even refer. In the 1920s, in a veiled polemic against the concept of socialism in one country, Trotsky insisted that if capitalism were to restore its equilibrium, 'socialism in a backward country would be confronted with great dangers'. These were not simply military, but also economic, in particular 'the influx of capitalist goods, incomparably better and cheaper than ours, goods which would break our foreign trade monopoly and afterwards the other foundations of our socialist economy'. See his comments in *Whither Russia? Towards Socialism or Capitalism?*, Colombo, 1973, pp78-80.
15. Anderson — and orthodox Trotskyists — would be well advised to study what Trotsky said towards the end of his life in the polemic with Max Shachtman and Bruno Rizzi. Trotsky rejected their pessimistic thesis, but was honest enough to admit that if the Second World War did not destroy Stalinism and capitalist rule in the West, Marxists would have to draw some radical conclusions: firstly, about the capacity of the working class to become a ruling class, and, secondly, about the character of the USSR. If there were no change, Trotsky wrote that 'it would be necessary in retrospect to establish that in its fundamental traits the present USSR was the precursor of a new exploiting regime on an international scale'. Trotsky, of course, hoped that Stalinist Russia — which he called a 'totalitarian bureaucratic society' — was an 'abhorrent relapse'. However, he admitted that if it remained in being the Stalin regime would inevitably become a 'new' type of 'exploiting society' with the 'bureaucracy' as 'a new exploiting class'. Trotsky was quite unambiguous. If nothing fundamentally changed as a result of war, he would rethink his whole position, which obviously was not final or

was not only socialism in one country which was impossible — so too was Stalinism.

Events did not turn out the way Trotsky had hoped. The USSR emerged triumphant and in some ways stronger from the Second World War. Revolution did not break out in the West. Nor did Stalinism change fundamentally, even with the death of Stalin. Many therefore assumed that Trotsky had been proved wrong, and they forgot (or rejected) his underlying argument about the unviable character of the system. To many his thesis seemed absurd. After all, hadn't the war and the Soviet Union's postwar recovery proved that the USSR was fundamentally strong? Indeed, didn't even bourgeois economists admit that in terms of growth there had never been anything like the USSR? In this way, Trotsky's essential argument was deposited into the dustbin of intellectual history to be ignored by both his critics and supporters.[16]

Of course if the left had looked a little deeper and penetrated behind the cover of crude growth rates, they would have seen that things were not quite as they appeared. The Soviet system may have produced quantitative development, but it also produced immense waste. The growth rates simply obscured the fact that the economy was highly inefficient. Those who eulogised Soviet economic growth in the 1930s (the 'grandeur of industrialisation' as Anderson prefers to call it) also invariably forgot to mention that it was only made possible by the super-exploitation of the masses,[17] and later of Eastern Europe. Furthermore, this primitive accumulation not only presupposed the Soviet Union's huge natural and human resources, but also the creation of a totalitarian police state to keep the system stable.[18] Finally, the Soviet elite had to isolate its own population totally from the West, and manipulate a series of war scares in order to make sure that domestic

       fixed. See his 'The USSR in War', which can be found in *In Defence of Marxism*, New York, 1942. Even the pretentious and dull Baruch Knei-Paz has pointed out that Trotsky had always assumed that Stalinism was a temporary phenomenon, something which was obvious in his last writings on Russia: 'It was almost as if Trotsky were suspending final theoretical judgement on these issues until events themselves decided one way or another.' (B Knei-Paz, *The Social and Political Thought of Leon Trotsky*, Oxford, 1978, p423)

16. In his magnum opus on Marxist economic theory, Mandel speaks of bureaucratic mismanagement of the economy, etc, but completely fails to integrate Trotsky's thesis about the transitional nature of the USSR into his discussion on the Soviet economy. See his *Marxist Economic Theory*, London, 1974, pp548-604.
17. Trotsky often gave the impression that what was being achieved in the USSR was not the result of exploitation, but of planning. See the unfortunate first chapter entitled 'What Has Been Achieved' in his *The Revolution Betrayed*, London, 1973, pp5-20.
18. Not surprisingly, once the Soviet elite could no longer use force as an economic motor, exploit Eastern Europe to its advantage, and call upon huge reserves of labour, Soviet economic growth began to falter dramatically.

discipline was guaranteed. The system was able to persist and grow, but only by taking what amounted to a series of emergency measures — measures which were very much an index of the high level of contradiction assumed by Trotsky. Unfortunately, this problem was never explored by his followers, who managed to turn his work into a dull static parody of the original, while ignoring those ideas which had real potential for development.

However, the failure to develop what was intellectually fruitful in Trotsky not only meant that his followers were unable to explain certain key features of the Soviet system — most notably its repressive unstable character — but also its relationship with world capitalism. For if the USSR was weak, as Trotsky's theory obviously implied, then this was bound to be reflected in its external relations. Concretely, if we accept Trotsky's argument that the USSR was a transitory (and by implication insecure) system, then I would suggest that we might not only explain many of its internal features, but also why it has not been a status quo power. By building upon the arguments implicit in Trotsky's theory of the transition — rather than making a number of apparently clever but basically absurd statements about the dual character of the USSR, which manages to be revolutionary yet counter-revolutionary, progressive but also reactionary, and, according to Anderson, all at the same time — then we might begin to solve the genuine problem which Anderson has at least recognised.

The USSR and World Capitalism

Anderson, it should be recalled, argues that the USSR has been consistent in its opposition to capitalism, and because it remains a non-market system, it must oppose and be opposed by capitalism on a global scale.[19] Let us first examine this argument, and then go on to explain, in the light of our earlier discussion, why the USSR comes into conflict with the West.

There are at least three obvious objections that can be raised against Anderson's argument. Firstly, we can simply point to the various struggles and revolutions the USSR has betrayed. The argument may seem terribly jejune in certain sophisticated circles. Many have even argued that this approach is far too subjective, or is simply a substitute for serious objective analysis. Perhaps so, but the fact remains — as even Anderson admits — that the USSR has opposed all independent revolutionary initiatives since the 1920s. If we accept this then it seems absurd and

---

19. The argument that there must of necessity be a fundamental antagonism between social systems forms the basis of Fred Halliday's theory of the Cold War. Halliday admits that his 'book drew heavily on the ideas and advice of *New Left Review* editorial members' (F Halliday, *The Making of the Second Cold War*, London, 1983, p i).

inconsistent to suggest that the USSR has been persistent in its opposition to capitalism as a world system. Secondly, we could ask him, quite genuinely and seriously, to look at the standard Soviet textbooks on their own foreign policy, which have a lot to say about peace, coexistence, mutually beneficial economic relations, national sovereignty, anti-monopoly alliances and nationalist struggles in the Third World, but hardly anything about overthrowing capitalism. Thirdly, we could point out that if the USSR was a major threat to world capitalism, this would be reflected in American foreign policy. Yet, if we look beyond official statements about the 'threat' (which has a specific role to play in the organisation and legitimisation of postwar capitalism), we discover something which Anderson's argument simply cannot explain — America prefers to keep the USSR 'in play', rather than eliminate it. Better, the State Department argues, to have a bipolar world order with a weak unattractive USSR as the main competitor.[20] Why eliminate Russia? It is the best argument for the market, the most important source of intercapitalist unity, and the reason for Germany — and Europe's — continuing division. That is the official US line, although it is often obscured by their political rhetoric. This doesn't mean, of course, that the USSR is not a problem for the West, or that occasionally arguments about rollback are not voiced in America. It simply suggests that the postwar capitalist order, with America at its head, has come to accept and even depend upon the maintenance of Soviet power — something which would be unthinkable if the USSR were a serious anti-capitalist force in the world, as Anderson seems to believe.[21]

However, as Anderson correctly points out, the situation is contradictory. The USSR has facilitated the overthrow of capital in some parts of the world, and Stalinism has proved capable of taking power under certain conditions. There is little point denying this; the problem, however, is to explain it. Anderson suggests somewhat vaguely that it is the dual nature of Stalinism which is the main reason. I would suggest a very different basis of the USSR's opposition to the West. It is not the USSR's essentially anti-capitalist nature, but its basically unviable character which forces it to pursue a strategy which brings it into conflict with the Western bourgeoisie. It is, in short, the historic failure of the Soviet elite to establish a mode of production which can compete or even coexist with capitalism in any genuine

---

20. As even the unmentionable Sir John Hackett has argued: 'We have to make do with the Soviet regime, barbarian, brutal and based on butchery as it is, because a world in which there are two superpower blocs in abrasive but more or less stable equilibrium is likely to be a safer world than if one of them collapses.' (J Hackett, 'The Soldier's Cautionary Tale', *Observer Supplement*, 4 July 1982)
21. On the importance of the USSR in helping to maintain capitalist equilibrium since 1947, see my 'Western Capitalism and the Cold War System' in M Shaw (ed), *War, State and Society*, London, 1984, pp136-94.

sense that creates the antagonism with the West. This is what we could and should derive from a reading of Trotsky's theory of Stalinism, not a series of ambiguous assertions about its dual nature which explains nothing or — in Anderson's hands — everything.

Understanding the failure of Stalinism as a system is therefore the point of departure for any serious discussion of Soviet relations with world capitalism. Because the Soviet experiment has not been able to achieve any of its stated objectives, it is in a peculiarly vulnerable position at home and abroad. As long as it continues with its flawed economic system, which has not caught up with and cannot overtake the West, the Soviet elite will always have to take what amounts to extraordinary external (as well as internal) measures to remain in existence. It is not just the bureaucracy which is insecure, but the whole system. This has produced an ambivalent relationship with world capitalism. On the one hand, Soviet weakness has forced it to seek an accommodation with the West. This is the real meaning of peaceful coexistence. On the other hand, the same weakness has pushed it into opposition to the world capitalist system in order to reduce the attraction and the pressure which the latter can exert against the Soviet social order. This is why Soviet foreign policy is complex, and often seems inconsistent to its left wing supporters and plainly duplicitous to its right wing enemies. However, there is no real inconsistency involved as long as we recall the underlying dilemma facing the weak Soviet system. It is this which produces both its search for a long term deal with the world bourgeoisie, but at the same time forces it to exploit contradictions within the world system.[22] This is why the USSR cannot be characterised simply as a status quo power, and why it supports some but by no means all forces opposed to the status quo. Given its insecurity, it must relate to the West in ways which appear to the naive as being progressive, and to the right as being a threat.[23]

Historically, Soviet weakness has thus forced it to seek external support in its struggle to survive in a sea of world capitalism. Straightforward survival, rather

---

22. These contradictions were clear throughout the 1970s when the USSR sought the advantages of détente with the West, but then tried to exploit the West's problems in the Third World. In that respect the USSR was as much to 'blame' for the breakdown of détente as the United States in spite of Jonathan Steele's argument to the contrary. See his *World Power: Soviet Foreign Policy Under Brezhnev and Andropov*, London, 1983.
23. When the right argues that there is a Soviet threat, the left responds either by pointing to US military superiority, or by showing how that 'threat' has been manipulated to secure US hegemony, legitimise rearmament, or justify interventions in the Third World. This is all perfectly true; standing outside of and in its own limited and qualified way in opposition to the world market, it does pose a problem — a fact which goes unrecognised by many revisionists including Noam Chomsky in his *Towards A New Cold War*, Sinclair Brown, 1982.

than persistent anti-capitalism, brings it into opposition with the West. In this way we can then explain its links with the communist parties, its need to maintain a stable cordon sanitaire in Eastern Europe, and why it supports anti-imperialist struggles. They are all forms of forward defence utilised by the Soviet elite to help secure its continued reproduction and that of the nonviable system over which it rules. The first places direct pressure upon the Western bourgeoisie — without seeking to overthrow it.[24] The second weakens the pressure which the West can place upon the USSR.[25] The third gives the USSR allies and bargaining counters in its struggle against the West.[26] Finally, while it should be remembered that the main Soviet goal is to weaken world capitalism rather than destroy it, under certain conditions the USSR will give support to movements and regimes actually opposed to the market — but only so long as they remain under Soviet control, or are essentially similar in structure to the USSR. If they challenge Soviet hegemony in any way, the USSR will oppose them. No doubt if Cuba and Vietnam were genuinely independent, or examples of socialist democracy, the USSR would withdraw support. However, as long as they remain dependent, and do not seriously oppose the USSR, the latter will back them for the same reason that it supports all those forces which weaken the West without challenging the Soviet Union and its many allies.[27]

24. This position is reflected in Soviet propaganda advice to the communist parties, which are constantly warned of the twin dangers of ultra-leftism, that is, being revolutionary, and social democratic opportunism, that is, becoming incorporated. As comrade Suslov pointed out, Lenin remorselessly and heroically 'waged an uncompromising struggle against right and "left" opportunism' (M Suslov, *Leninism And The World Revolutionary Working Class Movement*, Moscow, 1971, p19).

25. Significantly, Stalin only finally decided to Sovietise and isolate Eastern Europe in 1947-48; the years which marked the beginning of the reconstruction of Western Europe capitalist democracy. His great fear was not the military prowess of the West, but the attractive power of a successful market upon his own sphere of influence. In fact, we could argue that whereas the Marshall Plan posed a real threat to Soviet hegemony, the formation of a military pact in the shape of NATO helped legitimise it. This why George Kennan supported Marshall Aid, but was sceptical about NATO. Because he wanted to see a Soviet withdrawal from Eastern Europe and a long term change in the Soviet system, he opposed all tough-line military policies. Not surprisingly, he criticised Truman, and today attacks Reagan — and for the same reason. See his recent *The Nuclear Delusion*, London, 1983.

26. The USSR has always made it clear that the struggles in the Third World are anti-imperialist, and not anti-capitalist — and that their main goal is to ensure the unity of the forces of socialism, that is, the USSR, and those of the national liberation movements against the West. See RA Ulyanovsky's unusually interesting *The Comintern and the East*, Moscow, 1979.

27. Milovan Djilas made the point that Stalin did not necessarily oppose communists taking power as long as the USSR was able to control the regimes which emerged. See his *Conversations with Stalin*, Harmondsworth, 1963, pp68-103.

However, the left should not forget that even when the USSR fights the West, its opposition is in no way related to the primary socialist purpose of the emancipation of the working class. The very regimes it has chosen to establish or support are not surprisingly similar if not identical to itself, or are forced to become like it. I have little doubt that if a genuine and independent revolutionary movement emerged outside the USSR — and in Western Europe rather than in some backward distant Third World country — the USSR and its supporters would move to undermine it as rapidly as possible. What happened in Spain in 1936-39 and France in 1968 is perhaps the best argument against those who suggest that the USSR is seriously opposed to capitalism. Supporting nationalist movements in Africa, subsidising dependent non-democratic systems like Cuba or Vietnam, or maintaining fraternal links with mildly critical communist parties is one thing: giving support to genuine socialist movements of self-emancipation is quite another.

Of course, it might be argued that even if Anderson does not provide us with a genuine theory of Soviet foreign policy, he at least recognises that it has played a broadly progressive role. The main enemies of capitalism and imperialism — for whatever reason — have been weakened as a result of the Soviet Union's presence, and we mustn't lose sight of the fact. Moreover — and how often have we heard this argument — it is all we've got, and we must therefore be balanced in our criticism of it. Frankly, I think these arguments are misconceived, and are misleading and short-sighted: misleading, because they ignore the fact that the so-called 'socialist' regimes which have been established in the world are so repressive and inefficient that their main historic function has been to serve as warnings to the rest of humanity not to go down the same dangerous path;[28] and short-sighted, because they must lead those who put forward such arguments grossly to underestimate the negative role which Stalinism has had upon the general struggle for socialism in the twentieth century — not just because it has betrayed, but because it has provided the bourgeoisie with the key argument against socialism on a worldwide scale.[29] This is the main reason why the left is in decline today, when, given

28. Even Zbigniew Brzezinski was prepared to concede that Stalinism had played the historic role of vitiating the appeal of communism, especially in the West, 'the area originally seen by Marx as ripest for historical transformation'. See his *Between Two Ages: America's Role in The Technocratic Era*, Harmondsworth, 1970, p138.

29. We hardly have to admire Jimmy Reid or endorse his back-stabbing approach to the miners' dispute to appreciate that there is a lot of truth in his basic argument: 'The Tories and the right wing parties in Western Europe have managed to equate socialism with the Soviet system of government. I'm concerned that fear and dread of an East European regime is the major obstacle to the advance of socialist ideas in Britain. The labour movement must therefore define its policies and concept of socialism in terms which unmistakably safeguard and expand individual and collective freedom. This is meaningless unless we demonstrate an absolute commitment to democratic rights... It is this which the British labour movement has

the nature of the world crisis, it should be on the rise. It is this tragic impasse which Anderson's discussion of the USSR simply cannot explain. For this, if for no other reason, his analysis of the international role of Stalinism must be rejected.

Conclusion

The left has responded in several ways to the overthrow of the market in different parts of the world in the twentieth century. Some have insisted that nothing new has happened, and that there has only been a series of state capitalist occurrences. At the other end of the scale, we find those who believe that in spite of it all 'we' are winning and 'they' are losing. From Petrograd to Peking, from East Berlin to Pyongyang, socialism, it is argued, is on the move. There is yet a third group, amongst whom I would include Anderson, Mandel and the Trotskyist movement as a whole, who seem to reject both these positions, but somehow still believe the world is nearer to socialism today than it was in 1917. They occupy the ambiguous high ground from which they survey history with more objectivity, or so they think.[30] In fact, they are much closer to the second group than they would care to admit. Herein lies the great tragedy of the Trotskyist heritage, and the great problem with Trotsky, who provided the left with a basic critical foundation for understanding the utopian and reactionary nature of socialism in one country, but then did not break completely and totally from Stalinism. This is why he remained ambiguous in everything which he wrote in the 1930s, and why so many apparent anti-Stalinists like Anderson (and before him Isaac Deutscher) have ended up writing critical apologetics for the system.[31]

The left, in effect, has to come to terms with the enormity of the defeat it has suffered, not just in the past five years, or even since the Second World War, but

---

      failed to do in the case of the miners in the current dispute.' ('The Damage Scargill has Done to the Left', *Observer*, 16 September 1984)

30. See Hillel Ticktin's exposure of this ambiguity in his 'The Ambiguities of Ernest Mandel', *Critique*, no 12, Autumn-Winter 1979-80, pp127-38.

31. Isaac Deutscher, who did so much to educate a political generation with his biography of Trotsky, has been justly accused of providing a Marxist apologia for Stalinism. His influence on the *New Left Review* and Anderson has been self-evident from the early days. In many ways Anderson's tortured logic about the USSR abroad and why it still represents a force for progress is simply a form of Deutscherism writ large onto a world canvas. For two devastating and brilliant critiques of Deutscher see Julius Jacobson, 'Isaac Deutscher: The Anatomy of an Apologist' in J Jacobson (ed), *Soviet Communism and Socialist Vision*, New Brunswick, 1972, pp86-162; and Max Shachtman 'Isaac Deutscher's *Stalin*', *The Bureaucratic Revolution: The Rise of The Stalinist State*, New York, 1962, pp225-44. Significantly, Anderson refers to Deutscher's writings as 'the greatest historical work on the fate of the [Russian] Revolution' (op cit, p55).

since the 1920s and 1930s. One of the consequences of that defeat was fascism. Another was the Cold War, which provided the basis for renewed capital accumulation in the postwar period. A third has been the failure of the left to respond in any serious way to the present world crisis. It is not surprising, therefore, that many socialists faced with this reality have looked for some form of political compensation to mask the defeats they have suffered and the marginalisation they have experienced for nearly two generations. Before the 1960s most of them looked to the USSR. The crisis of Stalinism and events in the former colonies then made some look for comfort in the Third World. For a short period a few even looked to China. Now many, it would appear, are drifting back toward the Soviet fold, after having left it in the revolutionary heat of the late 1960s. This may be understandable given the present situation, but it is something which the left must guard against. The new toughness of US foreign policy in the Third World and towards the USSR should not mislead them into defending the USSR, and becoming yet again its critical supporters from afar.[32] Major changes are taking place in the Soviet bloc as a result of its continuing economic decline, and this will open up new political situations. It would be theoretically illogical and politically disastrous if the left ended up once again in the situation of defending so-called 'workers' states', especially now when these systems are in terminal decline. In the end, the left must choose and not prevaricate while legitimising its ambivalence with talk — like Anderson's — of the dual nature of the USSR.[33]

32. It is clear that because America is the active leader in the arms race, many within the peace movement for instance are less critical and even uncritical of the Soviet Union. If the antinuclear movement attacks NATO alone this is quite acceptable to the Soviet elite. However, those who criticise the Cold War system as a whole are not regarded favourably. For this reason EP Thompson is seen as a bête noir in the East and by communists active in the peace movement in the West. Unfortunately, Thompson has not worked out his ideas on what a new Europe 'without the superpowers' would look like.
33. Nor should they argue, like Anderson, that if one fails to defend the USSR as a workers' state one invariably ends up on the 'other side'. This approach is not only dishonest, it constitutes a form of blackmail which makes it impossible for the left to discuss the USSR in a way not already defined and determined by the Soviet elite or the Western bourgeoisie. See Anderson's comments, op cit, p55.

Michael Cox
Trotsky's Misinterpreters and the Collapse of Stalinism[1]

This short piece on Trotsky has few pretensions. Its basic aim is to provide a simple categorisation of the way in which his ideas have been interpreted and misinterpreted in the West. If it makes any intellectual claims at all, it is in its attempt to rehabilitate what has been consistently overlooked in Trotsky's thought: the argument, repeated by him on several occasions (indeed it lies at the heart of his critique of socialism in one country) that in the form it had assumed by the end of the 1930s, the USSR was ultimately doomed. Consigned into the proverbial dustbin of history for over 40 years, this apparently absurd thesis — absurd even to the Trotskyists who droned on about 'the achievements of the workers' states' — now seems worth dusting down and looking at afresh. As I shall argue, although the way in which Trotsky presented his argument left much to be desired, the absolute failure of Stalinism as a system would indicate that his prognosis about the Soviet future — that in effect it had no future — was less a mental lapse and more a brilliant insight into the contradictions of the USSR.

Interpreting Trotsky

In schematic terms, works in the West on Trotsky can basically be placed into one of five categories: Stalinist, orthodox Trotskyist, the critical but sympathetic, the

1. This article first appeared in *Critique*, no 26, 1994.

sceptical, and finally the anti-utopian which accuses Trotsky of the fatal disease of being unrealistic. Let us deal with each in turn.

Stalinist

Historically, the USSR exerted an enormous influence on the left in the capitalist world. The result was that the vast majority of western Marxists were traditionally 'educated' both to distrust Trotsky and to oppose his ideas. Of course the situation did not remain static. Before the 1950s, for instance, it was quite normal for communists to identify Trotsky and his followers with counter-revolution, and to treat them accordingly. With de-Stalinisation this particular view became politically indefensible; consequently the attack had to assume a more subtle form. However, the basic intention remained the same — to discredit Trotsky's views, and in this way guarantee that the Marxist left remained tied to the USSR. In this respect, anti-Trotskyism played an important political function for the Soviet Union in its struggle to maintain control over the Western left.

A whole generation of Marxists in the West were thus fed a political line whose main purpose was not so much to encourage debate than to demonstrate the obvious errors of Russian Trotskyism. Hence Trotsky, it was pointed out in one typical Soviet publication, was fundamentally at odds with Lenin on all the main questions, proving — if proof were needed — that he wasn't really a Marxist at all.[2] According to a more sophisticated western communist, whose speciality was combating Trotskyism, while Trotsky was to 'play a positive role' in the early years of the revolution, he suffered from one fundamental flaw — 'fatalistic optimism', a deviation that led him to overestimate the possibility of revolution in the capitalist world.[3] Loizos Michail attacked an even more fundamental flaw in Trotsky's intellectual armoury — his theory of permanent revolution. This so-called theory, Michail insisted, provided neither a serious analysis of Russian social conditions nor a guide to revolutionary practice in 1917 itself.[4] Indeed, according to Kostas Mavrakis, whose Maoism led him to write one of the most vitriolic attacks on Trotsky and Trotskyism, the theory was both wrong and dangerous: wrong because it confused the 'democratic' and 'socialist' stages of the Russian Revolution; and dangerous because it was based upon an underestimation of the role of the peasantry.[5]

In the last analysis, however, the principle objection of the communist move-

2. See *Lenin Versus Trotsky and His Followers*, Moscow, 1981.
3. M Johnstone, *Trotsky and World Revolution*, Young Communist League, London, nd.
4. L Michail, *The Theory of Permanent Revolution: A Critique*, Trotskyism Study Group, Communist Party of Great Britain, 1977.
5. K Mavrakis, *On Trotskyism: Problems of Theory and History*, London, 1976.

ment to Trotsky was less theoretical than practical, and ultimately revolved around the issue of socialism in one country. From this all else logically followed, including the antagonism between Trotsky and his various pro-Soviet critics about what was achieved — or achievable — in backward Russia, about the historic role of Stalin, and finally, of course, about the contribution made by the USSR to the struggle against capitalism on a world scale. His political enemies claimed that Trotsky was in error on each of these issues. Socialism, they maintained, was successfully constructed in Russia under Stalin's leadership. And in spite of its flaws, what was established inspired the oppressed and exploited in the rest of the world. Thus far from betraying the revolution as Trotsky claimed, the so-called bureaucracy against which he directed so much bile actually advanced it, and did so moreover under hideously difficult conditions.[6]

Ironically, this critique of Trotsky was complicated by one simple problem — the fact that orthodox Trotskyists, in spite of their antagonism to Stalinism, believed it was necessary for revolutionaries to defend the workers' state. In this sense, the opposition between the communist movement and those inspired by Trotsky was not absolute. Both defended the USSR against its capitalist opponents. Moreover, they agreed that the Soviet economic system was superior in many ways to what was on offer in the West. Indeed, by the 1960s, the real point of dispute between Trotskyists (such as Ernest Mandel) and some of the less Stalinist elements within the communist movement appeared to revolve less around the Soviet Union's socio-economic achievements than what the Trotskyists perceived as Moscow's pusillanimous foreign policy.[7] In fact, by the time the Eurocommunists entered the fray in the 1970s, the gap between the communist parties and their various critics on the Trotskyist left focused almost entirely on the issue of the failure of the USSR to be sufficiently left wing internationally.

Orthodox Trotskyism

Trotsky never succeeded in gaining a substantial popular base in the advanced capitalist countries. Yet amongst intellectuals he did manage to exert some degree of influence. In the late 1930s and again in the 1960s, his ideas (not to mention his romantic and tragic image) proved attractive to a large number of individuals alienated from capitalism, but repelled by the reality of Stalinism in the USSR.[8] Life

6. See Lawrence Ellenstein, *The Stalin Phenomenon*, London, 1975.
7. In his study *The Second Slump*, London, 1980, especially pp147-56, Ernest Mandel draws a sharp contrast between the recession experienced in the capitalist world economy in the mid-1970s and the continued economic dynamism of the 'so-called socialist countries'.
8. For a sensitive portrayal of the appeal of Trotskyism in America in the 1930s, see Alan Wald, *The New York Intellectuals*, Chapel Hill, 1987.

in the Trotskyist movement, however, was definitely not for the faint-hearted. The never ending round of meetings, the disruption to personal life, and the inevitable marginalisation from 'normal' society usually took its toll with the result that the political life-span of an average Trotskyist was never very long. Those few who survived usually then found some 'principled' reason for forming this faction, or that tendency, or of even creating their own separate organisation. The history of Trotskyism, in effect, was the history of greater and greater dissension between fewer and fewer people, all claiming that their group — and their group alone — was the one and only true heir to the Fourth International of 1938.[9]

Basically, the principle objective of orthodox Trotskyism was not to develop Trotsky's ideas so much as to preserve them. Historically, the theoreticians of Trotskyism thus assumed an essentially priestly role; their main function was to restate the basic truths established by Trotsky, rather than to discuss and apply them. Innovation was not encouraged on the assumption that it might lead to an attack upon the very core of ideas that held the movement together. Most orthodox Trotskyists, moreover, really did believe that Trotsky's analysis of Stalinism could not be improved upon. Even a fairly unorthodox and influential Marxist like Perry Anderson agreed that 'Trotsky's interpretation of... Stalinism to this day' remained 'the most coherent and developed theorisation of the phenomenon within the Marxist tradition' — a view undoubtedly endorsed by his more orthodox peers within the Trotskyist movement.[10]

And so, for 50 years, Trotskyists restated the same line about the USSR as put forward by Trotsky in *The Revolution Betrayed* in 1937: namely, that as a result of the isolation and backwardness of the Soviet Union, a new bureaucratic stratum had emerged that first appropriated the Bolshevik party, and then the revolution itself. However, even though this stratum was parasitic upon the working class, it was not a 'new class' in the Marxist sense for the simple reason that it did not own the means of production. Indeed, because of its position, it was impelled to defend the 'gains of October' — specifically the nationalised property forms that had grown up in the USSR after 1917. This placed the bureaucracy in a highly contradictory position. On the one hand, it had to defend itself from the working class from whom it had usurped power. On the other hand, it was forced to preserve the new, historically progressive property relations that had emerged in the Soviet Union. Consequently, its role was not completely without historic merit. Reac-

9. In Britain alone by 1977 there was, according to Paul Thompson and Guy Lewis, 14 groups claiming to be Trotskyist. In 1955 there had been three, and in 1945, one. See their *The Revolution Finished? A Critique of Trotskyism*, Big Flame pamphlet, London, 1977.
10. P Anderson, 'Trotsky's Interpretation of Stalinism', *New Left Review*, no 139, May-June 1983, p49.

tionary and repressive though it undoubtedly was, the new bureaucracy had no option but to defend the economic foundations of the new state; a state that in spite of its Stalinist superstructure still possessed a social and economic base theoretically superior to that of capitalism.

Trotsky's theory of Stalinism was, as Antonio Carlo has pointed out, the starting point for nearly all critical Marxist discussion of the Soviet Union.[11] Yet his analysis left him and his followers open to several charges, one of the most obvious perhaps being ambiguity. At home the bureaucracy, according to Trotsky, played a dual role; abroad, however, it was deemed to be totally reactionary.[12] More seriously, his discussion of the Soviet system came very close to providing an apologia for it. After all, if the Soviet Union was a workers' rather than a bourgeois state, and, according to Trotsky, striding forward economically, did this not imply that there was something progressive about Stalinism?[13] Indeed, if there was not, then why did Trotskyists continue to defend the USSR? Some got around this dilemma by the age old technique of simply ignoring the problem. Others (and here one would include Isaac Deutscher) accepted that there was indeed something 'historically' progressive about Stalinism.[14] Now while Deutscher's argument was officially rejected by Trotsky's followers, the fact remains that the latter seemed to share a position similar to that of Deutscher.[15] Nor was this so surprising given that the original author of the idea that the USSR was progressive (at least at home) was Trotsky himself. Herein perhaps was the great irony of Trotskyism. Established by a revolutionary obviously opposed to Stalinism, it could easily be deployed to provide the basis for a critical defence of the Soviet system.

11. A Carlo, 'The Socio-Economic Nature of the USSR', *Telos*, no 21, Fall 1974, pp2-86. See also my 'Western Marxism and Soviet Society', *Bulletin of the Sociological Association of Ireland*, no 40, January 1985, pp12-17.
12. See Anderson, op cit, pp56-7.
13. In the first chapter of *The Revolution Betrayed*, Trotsky spoke in glowing terms of what had been 'achieved' economically in the USSR under Stalin, in contrast to the 'stagnation and decline' experienced in the capitalist world (LD Trotsky, *The Revolution Betrayed*, New York, 1970, pp5-20). In an article published in November 1937, Trotsky could write that 'the main difference between the USSR and the contemporary bourgeois state finds its expression in the powerful development of the productive forces as a result of a change in the form of ownership' (LD Trotsky, 'Not a Workers' and Not a Bourgeois State?', *Writings of Leon Trotsky 1937-38*, New York, 1970, p90).
14. Critical though he was of Stalin, Deutscher could still write in 1953 that the 'core of Stalin's genuine historic achievement lies in the fact that he found Russia working with the wooden plough and left her equipped with atomic piles' (*Russia After Stalin*, London, 1965, p55).
15. For an uncompromising attack on Deutscher from the left, see Julius Jacobson, 'Isaac Deutscher: The Anatomy of an Apologist', in J Jacobson (ed), *Soviet Communism and the Socialist Vision*, New Jersey, 1972, pp85-162.

Sympathetic Critics

Perhaps the most interesting group of Western commentators on Trotsky have been those who, while sympathetic to his life's work, questioned his interpretation of Stalinism. A number of issues were raised by this fairly heterogeneous group; the first concerned Trotsky's understanding of Bolshevism and the relationship between Bolshevism and Stalinism.

Trotsky, as we know, became an uncritical admirer of 'Leninism' in the 1920s and 1930s, stressing firstly that he had been wrong to oppose Lenin on the question of organisation prior to 1917, and secondly that far from being the logical result of Leninism, Stalinism was its antithesis. Trotsky's relationship to and analysis of Leninism has been criticised on a number of grounds. Firstly, according to Robert Wistrich, Trotsky, having correctly identified the dictatorial strain in Bolshevism before 1917, made a crucial error when he was converted to the Leninist cause after the revolution. As a result he not only forgot his earlier attacks on the Bolsheviks' authoritarian practices, but seemed to adopt some of them himself.[16] Moreover, his adoption of Leninism meant that he was unable to identify one of the main causes of the revolution's subsequent degeneration. As Michael Lustig has argued,[17] Trotsky's analysis of and struggle against the Soviet bureaucracy was always compromised by his failure to recognise that the seeds of Stalinism were sown by the Bolshevik party between 1917 and 1921 — a point also raised in a more subtle way by one of Trotsky's greatest admirers, the libertarian Marxist Victor Serge.[18]

A second criticism directed against Trotsky focused less on his relationship to Leninism, and more on his political judgement. Concretely, he is said to have made two fatal mistakes in his struggle against Stalin — both of which contributed to Stalin's final triumph. The first was his failure in 1923 to unseat Stalin. This, according to many commentators, sealed the revolution's fate. Armed with Lenin's Testament, Trotsky, it is maintained, should have acted decisively and prevented Stalin consolidating his control over the party apparatus.[19] His more important error, however, was that he identified the wrong 'main' enemy in the 1920s. By insisting that the principle danger after 1923 was 'capitalist restoration', Trotsky not only overstated the danger coming from the right, but underestimated the very real and more important threat posed by Stalin. In addition, his fear of the right made it impossible for him to forge a bloc with Bukharin in the late

16. R Wistrich, *Trotsky: Fate of a Revolutionary*, London, 1979.
17. MM Lustig, *Trotsky And Djilas: Critics of Communist Bureaucracy*, New York, 1989.
18. V Serge, *Memoirs of a Revolutionary, 1901-1941*, Oxford, 1963.
19. See I Deutscher, *The Prophet Armed*, Oxford, 1979, pp103-6.

1920s to prevent Stalin's final victory.[20] Indeed, because Trotsky and many of his associates had what one commentator has called a 'thermidorian bee' in their bonnets, they were prepared to give critical support to Stalin when he turned against the right and propelled the party's economic policy to the left.[21] Some former Left Oppositionists (although not Trotsky himself) even rejoined the party in 1930 and 1931 because they assumed Stalin was now carrying through the correct economic policies.[22]

The third question raised by Trotsky's critics related to his mature characterisation of Stalinism as a workers' state. This was a definition that many could not support. Their most obvious objection was political. How, they asked, could one call the USSR a workers' state when the workers themselves were exploited by their new bureaucratic masters? Moreover, if the workers were oppressed in the Soviet Union, then why should socialists defend such a system, an argument which took on even more force in 1939 when the USSR invaded Finland and carved up Poland. This in turn led Trotsky's critics to wonder whether the bureaucracy was not just a parasitic stratum but a class in its own right. Trotsky, we will recall, refused to characterise the bureaucracy as a class on the grounds that it had no legal ownership of the means of production. His opponents viewed this distinction as being purely semantic. Although the Soviet bureaucracy did not own the means of production, they did at least 'control' them. Trotsky's refusal to use the term 'class' was mere formalism.

Behind these internecine disputes there lay a much bigger question: to wit, how far had the Russian Revolution degenerated, and what, if anything, did the USSR have to do with the socialist cause? Trotsky obviously assumed that in spite of Stalinism there was still something 'proletarian' about the Soviet system. His critics, on the contrary, denied this, insisting that Stalinism had destroyed any connection the USSR might have once had with the workers' cause. As Max Shachtman put it in his celebrated article of 1943: 'The Stalinist reaction, the causes and course of which have been traced so brilliantly by Trotsky above all others, meant the systematic hacking away of every finger of control the working class had over its state.'[23]

20. Moshe Lewin argues that by 1929 the differences between the Left Opposition and Bukharin were not that great anyway, thus there was no reason for the groups not to unite. See his *Political Undercurrents In Soviet Economic Debates*, New Jersey, 1974.
21. See Tibor Szamuely, 'The Elimination of Opposition between the Sixteenth and Seventeenth Congresses of the CPSU', *Soviet Studies*, Volume 17, no 3, January 1966, pp318-38.
22. Szamuely argues that while Trotsky and the Left Opposition may not have approved of Stalin's 'methods', it was they 'who had propounded the [economic] programme now taken over by Stalin'. As a result they felt bound to defend Stalin's broad economic strategy (ibid, p323).
23. See M Shachtman, 'Is Russia a Workers' State?', in his *The Bureaucratic Revolution: The Rise of*

Naturally, having rejected Trotsky's argument that the USSR was a workers' state, his critics began to search for other ways of characterising Stalinism. Some, like Raya Dunayevskaya and later Tony Cliff, concluded that in Russia a new form of 'state' capitalism had emerged in which the workers were alienated by a system driven by the logic of accumulation.[24] This position was in turn rejected by Shachtman, who argued that the USSR was neither a workers' nor a capitalist state, but a form of bureaucratic collectivism — a term whose main strength seemed to lie in the fact that Shachtman never precisely defined what it meant.[25] Burnham then went one step further, and drew the most revisionist conclusion of all — that the failure of socialism in Russia proved its impossibility everywhere else. Capitalism may have been doomed as Trotsky suggested. This did not mean that socialism would follow. Burnham concluded that it was not just Trotsky's characterisation of the USSR which was at fault, but his continuing faith in the feasibility of a classless society.[26]

Trotsky had few problems in fending off critics such as Shachtman and Dunayevskaya because both individually and collectively they really didn't provide much of a theoretical alternative. This highly charged discussion, however, did have a number of unfortunate consequences. Most obviously, it tended to push Trotsky and his followers into an ideologically rigid mould from which they never escaped. It also made the whole debate on Stalinism highly sectarian. Thus what began life as a potentially fruitful dialogue on the left about the nature of socialism was soon transformed into a sterile fight between ideological militants who neither cared nor listened to what their opponent had to say.

The Sceptics

In spite of their reservations about Trotsky's theory of Stalinism, his many critics clearly regarded him as a serious, albeit confused, opponent of Stalin who had made a major intellectual contribution to the left's understanding of the USSR. Even a social democrat like Irving Howe admitted that Trotsky was a 'figure of heroic magnitude' who constituted the real pole of opposition to Stalin.[27] There were others, however, who had their doubts.

the Stalinist State, New York, 1962, p45.
24. See R Dunayevskaya, *Marxism And Freedom*, New York, 1958; and T Cliff, *State Capitalism In Russia*, London, 1974.
25. Shachtman's definition of the USSR as 'bureaucratic collectivism' was in fact entirely negative. Having demonstrated to his own satisfaction that Russia was not a bourgeois state and not a workers' state, it followed that it just had to be bureaucratic collectivist. See *The Bureaucratic Revolution*, op cit, especially pp37-106.
26. J Burnham, *The Managerial Revolution*, London, 1945.
27. I Howe, *Trotsky*, London, 1978, p8.

Firstly, there were many — from the anarchist left to the conservative right — who questioned the authenticity of Trotsky's differences with Stalin. After all, they argued, Trotsky believed in and supported the dictatorship of the proletariat, which after 1917 meant the dictatorship of the single party.[28] When he was in power, they say, Trotsky was also as authoritarian as Stalin; witness his opposition to workers' control, his treatment of the Kronstadt rebels, and his support for the militarisation of labour.[29] During the 1920s he made no real effort to go outside of the party to challenge Stalin, thus proving that he shared the same world view as his rival.

Secondly, it was argued that Trotsky and the Left Opposition actually provided Stalin with the economic arguments that he used to justify collectivisation and the Five Year Plans after 1929. Of course, the Left Opposition might not have advocated terror as a means of achieving the economic transformation of Russia, but that is exactly where their policies would have led. As Alec Nove has pointed out, the Left Opposition, like Stalin, believed in 'rapid industrialisation... and urged on the peasants a price structure which would permit the state to accumulate. Yet they did not face up to the measures of coercion that would be required if this policy were to be put into effect.'[30]

This leads to the third and probably the most important weapon in the sceptic's intellectual armoury — Nikolai Ivanovich Bukharin. According to Stephen Cohen, it was not Trotsky but Bukharin who advanced the most consistent programmatic alternative to Stalinism. Thus the view that Trotsky was the main rival to Stalin, or (citing Deutscher) 'the representative figure of pre-Stalinist communism and the precursor of post-Stalinist communism', is a 'serious misconception'.[31] It was Bukharin rather than Trotsky who was the true interpreter of Lenin's last mature thoughts. It was Bukharin who advanced the real economic alternative to Stalinism. And it was Bukharin, not Trotsky, who mapped out a more reasonable evolutionary path for Russia. Moreover, according to Cohen, it was 'Bukharin's outlook and the NEP-style order he has defended' that would remain the 'real alternative to Stalinism after Stalin'.[32]

28. This 'substitutionism' was exactly what Trotsky had warned against in his famous attack on Bolshevism before the 1905 Revolution. For a discussion of this point, see Baruch Knei-Paz, *The Social and Political Thought of Leon Trotsky*, Oxford, 1978, pp175-236.
29. For a libertarian critique of Trotsky on these points, see the pamphlets produced by Solidarity, in particular Maurice Brinton, *The Bolsheviks and Workers' Control, 1917-1921*, London, 1970; Alexandra Kollontai, *The Workers Opposition*, London, nd; and Ida Mett, *The Kronstadt Commune*, London, 1967.
30. A Nove, 'Introduction' to E Preobrazhensky, *The New Economics*, Oxford, 1965, p xiii.
31. S Cohen, *Bukharin and The Bolshevik Revolution*, New York, 1975, p xvi.
32. Ibid, p386.

The Realists

The sceptics doubted whether Trotsky was the real alternative to Stalin. The realists, on the other hand, accused him of a failure to face up to the basic facts of life. As a result he was condemned to that same dustbin of history into which he had verbally consigned the Mensheviks in 1917.

Trotsky's apparent lack of realism assumed a number of forms. Most obviously he, and by implication the Bolshevik party, had a hopelessly optimistic belief in the prospects for world revolution after 1917. Fernando Claudín, one of the theoreticians of Eurocommunism in the 1970s, argued this point with particular force in his highly acclaimed study of the international communist movement. Far from being 'moribund', western capitalism, according to Claudín, still had major reserves to draw upon after the First World War. The Bolsheviks in 1917, and later Trotsky as well, underestimated 'the penetration of reformism into the Western proletariat'. Stalin, on the contrary, did at least have a basic appreciation of the difficulties confronting Russia, and in his own crude, pragmatic way recognised what the more talented Trotsky could not — the 'relative autonomy of the Soviet revolution in relation to the world revolution'. Thus, although the doctrine of socialism in one country may have represented a nationalist deviation, it was at least premised upon a realistic rather than a romantic assessment of the revolutionary potential inherent in the international system in the interwar years.[33]

According to many commentators, Marxism simply could not work in backward Russia, if indeed it could work anywhere. Equality was all very well in theory, but in practice it would not motivate people to work hard. Soviet democracy may have been desirable politically; it was not, however, functional economically. And while internationalism was a fine thing, patriotism was more likely to unite and mobilise the people.[34]

Finally, according to the 'realists', Stalin rather than Trotsky had a clearer answer to the most important question of all — namely, how could the USSR escape from its backwardness and create for itself the foundations of a powerful state that could survive under conditions of capitalist encirclement? Stalin may indeed have betrayed the revolution in the process of modernising the USSR. But this was both inevitable and essential; inevitable, because no revolution can live up to its utopian aspirations;[35] and essential, because the industrialisation of Russia demanded sacri-

---

33. F Claudín, *The Communist Movement: From Comintern to Cominform*, Harmondsworth, 1975, pp56-102.
34. See NS Timasheff, *The Great Retreat: The Growth And Decline of Communism In Russia*, New York, 1946.
35. Even Trotsky himself admitted that 'every revolution up to this time has been followed by a reaction, or even a counter-revolution' (LD Trotsky, *The Revolution Betrayed*, op cit, p88).

fice on the one hand and a strong state on the other. Moreover, didn't the defeat of Nazi Germany and the recovery of the USSR after the war provide retrospective justification for Stalin's policies? In the light of recent historical evidence such rationalisations seem questionable to say the least. However, for a large part of the postwar period, it was more or less the accepted wisdom. Indeed, it is still worth recalling that when Nove responded in the affirmative to his own rhetorical question, 'Was Stalin really necessary?', few Western analysts seemed prepared to disagree with him.[36]

Trotsky Revisited

The extensive discussion around Trotsky is obvious testimony to his historical and theoretical importance. Probably no other twentieth century Marxist has generated such a wide-ranging and heated debate. Yet as we have seen, this discussion has often generated more heat than light. Admittedly, some important problems have been raised by Trotsky's critics — for instance his ambiguous attitude towards Bolshevism, his bizarre view that Bukharin was more of a danger than Stalin, and, of course, his characterisation of the USSR as a 'workers' state'. But at the end of the day, one senses that even Trotsky's more intelligent interpreters have not done him justice, and have failed to understand either the intricacies or the limits of his thought.

That Trotsky has suffered at the hands of friends and enemies alike is incontestable. Even more strange perhaps is the almost total silence of nearly all interpreters about his most interesting and controversial insight — that there was little possibility of the Soviet system surviving over time in a sea of world capitalism. Possessing neither the advantages of the market, nor the benefits of socialism, the USSR, in Trotsky's view, could only be regarded as a transitional regime; a halfway house literally stranded on the beach of history between a bourgeois society that had no future and a classless society that had not yet been born. Whether the Soviet Union would move forward to socialism, or regress to capitalism, would only be decided by the uncertain outcome of the class struggle in the advanced capitalist countries. What was certain, however, was that if such a revolution did not occur, then the attractive pull of the world market would ultimately expose the contradictions of Stalinism, and lead to the dissolution of the system and its reintegration into the international economy.

Unfortunately, Trotsky's argument found little favour amongst his many interpreters, even those sympathetic to his work. Firstly, his gloomy prognosis smacked of a certain catastrophism, implying as it did that the regime could not survive under any circumstances. It also seemed to be refuted by events. After all,

---

36. See A Nove, *Was Stalin Really Necessary?*, London, 1964.

far from disappearing or breaking down after the war, as Trotsky had predicted, Soviet power actually grew and expanded. Finally, his argument about the non-viability of Stalinism stood in opposition to his frequently reiterated statement about the USSR being a workers' state, superior in character to capitalism. If this was the case, then it was obviously absurd to suggest the USSR was a transitional regime that might move back to the market.

Of course, this in turn raises the intriguing empirical question as to why the USSR survived as long as it did. Here, I would suggest that the Soviet Union, firstly, was able to draw upon a unique set of resources that ensured its reproduction. These included, amongst other things, a vast pool of easily controlled labour, an apparently limitless resource base, and, after the Second World War, Eastern Europe too. Moreover, the Soviet elite was highly successful in isolating the USSR and its people from dangerous contact with the more advanced capitalist world. Finally, the very bureaucracy and repressive state apparatus against which Trotsky railed, provided the regime with extraordinary instruments of control and organisation without which the system could not have continued. Now while none of these measures could resolve the dilemma facing the USSR, together they did buy the system time. The problem for the regime was that while it might have been able to contain its difficulties by drawing upon its different resources and constructing a particular type of state, it could not escape from them. Indeed, the very measures adopted by the Soviet elite to guarantee the system's continuation in the end accelerated its collapse. Hence, by isolating the USSR from contact with the more advanced capitalist world, the elite effectively contributed to the country's underdevelopment. In turn, by basing itself on a massive bureaucratic and police apparatus, it only managed to stifle debate and discussion, thereby contributing in a very direct way to the system's technological stagnation. In addition, the very assets upon which the elite was able to draw could not last indefinitely. It was hardly a coincidence, of course, that when the Soviet Union began to run out of labour in the late 1970s, the system began to wind down. The examples could be multiplied, but would only prove the same point: that the USSR managed to endure for over half a century, but after 1985 was no longer able to do so. As Trotsky had insisted, there were really only two choices available in the modern world — socialism or capitalism. The mutation represented by the USSR was theoretically inconceivable, and was thus doomed.

David Law

How Not To Interpret Trotsky[1]

In life and in death Trotsky appears as a hero of Russia's revolutionary tragedy. Isaac Deutscher saw him as a prophet. To his Russian adversaries he became a Satan. Possibly because he was so extraordinary, Trotsky has suffered at the pen of some very ordinary accounts of his life and work. Politicians have refracted his thought to produce some unconvincing, even bizarre accounts. At their head stands Kostas Mavrakis with his resolutely hostile *On Trotskyism*, a shrill denunciation from a Stalinist-Maoist perspective.[2] Neither have academics done Trotsky justice. Between them, Joel Carmichael, Baruch Knei-Paz, Robert Warth and Robert Wistrich have not matched quantity with quality.[3] The only general work to rise above the crowd is Isaac Deutscher's trilogy.[4] Even this is rarely so satisfactory on Trotsky as a theorist as on Trotsky the revolutionary hero.

The latest addition to the literature on Trotsky is John Molyneux's *Leon Trotsky's Theory of Revolution*.[5] It joins the 'centenary studies' by Ernest Mandel and Duncan Hallas to form a trio of somewhat predictable interpretations produced

---

1. This review first appeared in *Critique* nos 20/21, 1987, and was written before the publication of Pierre Broué's *Trotsky*.
2. K Mavrakis, *On Trotskyism: Problems of Theory and History*, London, 1976.
3. J Carmichael, *Trotsky: An Appreciation of his Life*, London, 1975; B Knei-Paz, *The Social and Political Thought of Leon Trotsky*, Oxford, 1978; RD Warth, *Leon Trotsky*, Boston, 1977; R Wistrich, *Trotsky*, London, 1979.
4. I Deutscher, *The Prophet Armed*, *The Prophet Unarmed*, *The Prophet Outcast*, Oxford, 1954, 1959, 1963.
5. J Molyneux, *Leon Trotsky's Theory of Revolution*, Brighton, 1981.

from within the Trotskyist tradition.[6] Unfortunately, it shares with them a restriction of the political debate to familiar lines. Trotsky without politics can only produce shallow interpretations, but the ritual recitation of polemics for and against the workers' state thesis is no more profound.

Like Mandel and Hallas, Molyneux offers an introduction. He wishes to be accessible despite his publisher's decision to set a price beyond the means of most private purchasers. Unfortunately, the book cannot be recommended even for rich novices. Throughout the book the engagement with Trotsky is superficial. Access and depth need not be mutually exclusive. Indeed, an author's depth of understanding should be the basis on which to present a satisfactory introduction.

Scholarship may not by itself provide understanding, as many have shown, but without it what is left? It is clear from Molyneux's text and reference notes that his views do not depend upon an extensive reading of Trotsky. For instance, the assessments of Trotsky before 1905, particularly concerning the early disputes on the nature of a revolutionary party, are based on a very sketchy knowledge of Trotsky's writings of the period. As he states, he has used only a partial and tendentiously edited copy of *Our Political Tasks*.[7] The post-revolutionary Trotsky emerges largely through his major books. Even constrained by dependence on English translations, Molyneux could have done much more to consider Trotsky comprehensively. He makes only slight use of the immensely valuable 14 volume series, *Writings of Leon Trotsky*, which reproduces in English all the published work of the last exile that is not otherwise readily available.[8]

More serious still is the detachment of Trotsky from the political and historical context in which he worked. Admitting its necessity, the author nevertheless does nothing to establish it. We are presented with a work of 'political analysis', as if this were possible without history. Two major consequences flow from this. Firstly, a two-dimensional Trotsky stands before us. The grand themes are there, but the subtleties are absent. Secondly, the historical judgements, which Molyneux cannot in fact avoid, frequently carry no substance. Trotsky on fascism is supported by the historical research of Colin Sparks in *International Socialism*. Tony Cliff is summoned for *empirical* validation of the state capitalist view of Soviet history. Too often the echo calls to its source in circular self-justification.

The alternative is more difficult, but more satisfactory. Trotsky's politics need

6. E Mandel, *Trotsky: A Study in the Dynamic of his Thought*, London, 1979; D Hallas, *Trotsky's Marxism*, London, 1979.
7. J Molyneux, p219. The edition used was produced by Connolly Books for the Irish Communist Organisation in 1969. Presumably Molyneux wrote his book before the New Park translation of *Our Political Tasks* had been published.
8. *Writings of Leon Trotsky*, 12 volumes and two supplements, New York, 1972-80.

to be dealt with in conjunction with the milieu from which they developed. This milieu encompassed alternative positions from both comrades and antagonists, and was textured by Trotsky's orientation to a hundred and one political matters. Appreciating this, would Molyneux then have so confidently told his readers that Trotsky emerged clearly as the head of the Left Opposition in 1923? Had he understood better Trotsky's situation during his last exile, would he still have insisted on such a close relation between perspectives then and the supposed philosophical basis of Trotsky's Marxism? Molyneux's major thesis is that Trotsky only made a partial break with the Marxism of the Second International, a political but not a methodological break. On a series of tactical and strategic questions he rejected the orientation of the Second International, but he did not break with its 'mechanical materialist philosophy'. The main characteristics of this, according to Molyneux, are *determinism*, a view of human activity as being entirely law-governed (ultimately by natural laws), and which, if taken to its logical conclusion, eliminated the role of human agency, consciousness and subjectivity; and *objectivism*, a view of Marxism as a science which had discovered these laws and made it possible to observe them 'objectively'[9] from the 'outside', and thus predict the course of future human activity.

To defend his thesis Molyneux assembles 'evidence' throughout his book. He notes that Trotsky did not recognise methodological questions as problematic. He quotes passages from Trotsky to illustrate his claim that unreasonable predictions were made. He asserts that Trotsky's method led him to consider the relations of production in terms of property relations without due regard for the process of production.

This critique of Trotsky is mounted consciously through Gramsci, and, despite critical reference to Althusser, has surely been influenced by an intellectual fashion to dismiss almost all Marxist thought of the period of the Second and Third Internationals as economistic. At worst this is effectively a repudiation of materialism, at best it is a thoroughly ahistorical amalgamation of theorists as different as, for example, Kautsky, Trotsky, Stalin and Dimitrov. Molyneux's position is inconsistent. He would like to find a basic explanation in Trotsky's methodology for the parts of Trotsky's thought and action which he opposes. Yet he is in general solidarity with Trotsky. He is driven to the conclusion that there must have been a radical separation between politics and theory. But this leaves the origin of the 'good' politics totally unexplained. Furthermore, despite Trotsky's supposed inability to escape the original sin of Second International Marxism, he possessed, in Molyneux's judgement, 'a grasp of historical materialism... in many ways superb'. At another point in the book we hear that Trotsky 'consistently avoided both

---

9.   J Molyneux, p4.

crude economic materialism and idealism', and that 'his ability to synthesise the personal, the psychological (individual and mass), with the political, social and economic in a coherent, integrated analysis on firm materialist foundations, matched that of Marx and was otherwise unequalled'.[10] Who is the intellectual schizophrenic, Trotsky or Molyneux?

No doubt there are some statements in Trotsky on method and general orientation which *appear* capable of bearing inevitabilist viewpoints. There are in Marx, too. But determinism is not at all the same thing as inevitabilism, and where would Marxism be without the notion of historical law? Furthermore, Trotsky's claims were usually conditional. Consider, for instance, this passage from *My Life* in which Trotsky relates something of his intellectual activity between 1905 and 1914:

'During the years of the reaction I studied the questions of trade and industry both on a world scale and a national scale. I was prompted by a revolutionary interest. I wanted to find out the relationship between the fluctuations of trade and industry on the one hand, and the progressive stages of the labour movement and revolutionary struggle on the other. *In this, as in all other questions like it, I was especially on my guard to avoid establishing an automatic dependence of politics on economics. The interaction must necessarily be the result of the whole process considered in its entirety.*'[11]

Trotsky's Marxism was practical and active. He never forgot his early claim that Marxism was above all a method of analysis, not of texts, but of social relations (cf *Results and Prospects*).[12] He always registered his commitment to concrete investigation. An article from 1923, for example, warned that speculative juggling with the concepts and terms of the materialist method leads to 'formalism' and the reduction of analysis to 'rendering definitions and classifications more precise and to splitting empty abstractions into four equally empty parts'.[13] Why sharpen and resharpen a tool, Trotsky asked, instead of using it? The skill of the craftsman is embodied in the product, and this is how Trotsky should be judged.

The theory of permanent revolution, the analysis of bureaucracy, and the investigations of German fascism provide three powerful examples of how far Trotsky was from the mechanical materialism of which he stands accused. In none of

10. Ibid, p195.
11. LD Trotsky, *My Life*, New York, 1970, p223, my emphasis.
12. LD Trotsky, *The Permanent Revolution*, New York, 1970, p63.
13. LD Trotsky, 'The Curve of Capitalist Development', *Problems of Everyday Life*, New York, 1973, p280.

these three cases is the interpretation of the subject ever reduced to economic inevitability. These major parts of Trotsky's work indicate a recognition of the complexity of history. Nowhere is it suggested that an automatic link may be observed between the level of the forces of production and the phenomenon being investigated. Indeed, Trotsky's theory of permanent revolution encountered great opposition precisely because it denied the conventional perception of the economic base of the Russian revolution.

At the very least Molyneux has greatly overstated his case. The evidence on which it rests is far from strong. It is one thing to read detached passages referring to methodological issues through the terms and concerns of recent Marxist debate. It is quite another to see how Trotsky understood his own method in the course of his work. True, Trotsky makes exaggerated predictions, particularly in the second half of the 1930s, and he habitually invokes history as an almost personified force. But there are other ways of explaining this without recourse to the supposed essential features of Trotsky's Marxism. Partly it was a matter of style, and partly, during the last exile, a reflection of circumstances.

As Molyneux observes, Trotsky did not engage in serious and sustained methodological work, and it is a fair inference that this indicated a belief that such matters were not problematic. In fact Trotsky in the last years of his life expounded a rather jubilant orthodoxy, not only on method but on Marx's prognoses, including immiserisation.[14] What should we make of this? Rather less than Molyneux would wish. The implicit equation of orthodoxy and dogmatism is false. In the practice of Marxist analysis Trotsky's approach was far from rigid. Furthermore, there is the danger of emphasising the work of Trotsky's last five years at the expense of the previous 35, and consequently reading Trotsky backwards.

As a highly dedicated and principled revolutionary, Trotsky's main concern was always political. But ideals do not pay the rent. At various times in his life Trotsky needed to earn an income through writing. Trotsky was not a political 'full-timer' supported from party funds. Trotsky's 'party', before 1917 and after 1927, was small and consequently poor. Trotsky, the independent, found a living through journalism, and, in the later period, through advances and royalties on his books. A significant part of his literary output was thereby influenced, and leisure for 'purely theoretical' work was inevitably limited. Five major projects of Trotsky's last exile were undertaken partly for financial reasons — the autobiography *My Life*, the *History of the Russian Revolution*, the biographies of Lenin and Stalin,

14. LD Trotsky, 'Ninety Years of the Communist Manifesto', *Writings of Leon Trotsky 1937-38*; 'Once Again on the "Crisis of Marxism"', *Writings of Leon Trotsky 1938-39*; *The Living Thoughts of Karl Marx presented by Leon Trotsky*, London, 1940; *In Defence of Marxism*, London, 1971.

both uncompleted, and *The Revolution Betrayed*. The first two of these projects were particularly important sources of finance. They produced the resources not only to sustain Trotsky's household in Turkey, but also to support the early development of the International Left Opposition in the years 1929 to 1933.

At times, particularly in Mexico after the break with Diego Rivera, the Trotsky household was extremely poor. On occasion there was not even enough for the grocery bills.[15] The study of Lenin, regarded by Trotsky as a work of primary importance, remained unfinished partly as a result of financial pressure. Attention was diverted towards other projects, in particular the biography of Stalin, possibly to secure financial advantages.[16] Shorter articles, fashioned for what Trotsky supposed to be the tastes of the American general reading public, were composed mainly to produce fees.[17]

Of course, income was only a means to an end. Trotsky was a supremely political person. The few relaxations he permitted himself — fishing in Turkey, collecting cacti and tending rabbits in Mexico — served mainly to regenerate the hub of what was a highly political household. In his last exile, Trotsky was forced to conduct political activity at least one stage removed from the actual arena. He aimed to build a Fourth International as the political instrument for a revolution which, he believed, was held back largely by the betrayals of social democracy and Stalinism. For this it was necessary both to work for the destruction of Stalinism, particularly by exposing the lies of its regime, and for the construction of a new organisation. These twin tasks resulted in an enormous correspondence and body of shorter statements and polemics. In particular, the counter-trial of the Dewey commission in 1937 virtually paralysed other work. Given the volume of writing, published and unpublished, devoted to building the Fourth International and to

---

15. Correspondence of Trotsky's secretaries, in particular T2:11732 (Curtis to Karsner), T2:11756 (Hansen to Karsner), T2:11763 (Hansen to Karsner). T2 indicates the second section of the Trotsky archive, located at Harvard, and open since 1980.
16. Although the evidence is ambiguous, various documents in T2 point to these conclusions. In particular T2:8344 (Trotsky to Gollancz), T2:8366 (Trotsky to Grasset), letters to and from Curtis Brown, in particular T2:635 and T2:669, and T2:10755 (Trotsky to Walker).
17. 'As I see from experience, it is very difficult to place my articles. Possibly they are written in a too Fourth International manner, not sufficiently explanatory, not sufficiently "human", not sufficiently objective, not sufficiently adapted to the average man on the New York street.' (T2:10763, Trotsky to Walker) 'I could write a series of portraits of the most important Soviet personalities... I would give psychological portraits and the ambient milieu with manifold little stories and anecdotes; in one word, a very "human" and very "American" kind of article without any kind of political tendency.' (T2:10765, Trotsky to Walker) 'I am sending you three copies of my article on Yenukidze... If this kind of writing (for the man of the street) proves "marketable", I am ready to write analogous articles...' (T2:10766, Trotsky to Walker).

political self-defence against the calumnies which were broadcast from Moscow, it is easy to see how little time remained for other activity.

Trotsky's major claim to status as a theorist is based upon his formulation of the concept of permanent revolution. This was Marxist theory in the best sense. It was grounded in experience, deepened by historical analysis, and found its utility and confirmation in practice. *Results and Prospects* succeeds because of its intimate connection with activity. In exile after 1929, Trotsky is progressively distanced from direct political action, and after leaving France in 1935 he never experienced again the stimulus of a lively political organisation. The years 1929 to 1935 are a watershed. Despite his being in exile, there is a relative vitality to Trotsky's political activity and contacts during this period. It is a time of reorientation and readjustment in the context of Stalinist economic revolution and the rise of German fascism. An organisation had to be launched, positions had to be defined in relation to the communist parties and to the left wing movements that had split from social democracy. Also, at least until 1932, some contacts with the USSR remained, and there was still a possibility of meaningful action. It is not surprising, therefore, that several of the more significant of the exile writings were produced at this time; for example the *History of the Russian Revolution*, the unfinished biography of Lenin, and various essays on the USSR from the early period, including 'The Soviet Economy in Danger' and 'Alarm Signal!'.[18] It is true that a part of this work had no direct relationship with current political activity, but its subject, even so, was still political. Trotsky's historical work always had both an immediate relationship with Trotsky's experience as a revolutionary, and a political message to convey.

After 1935 Trotsky's work failed to maintain its previous quality. The isolation of residence in Norway and Mexico was partly responsible. There were also major technical obstacles to successful literary work. In particular, the absence of library facilities hampered Trotsky. Much of the basic research had to be done by others, most notably John G Wright in New York. Sections of books were copied laboriously and sent to Mexico. Work was delayed by secretarial problems; there were difficulties in the employment of a skilled and reliable Russian language typist. The most fundamental resources ware lacking. Even *Pravda* failed to arrive regularly. Such problems had beset Trotsky before, and still good work had been produced. Now the technical difficulties were overlaid by intensified political and personal adversity. The fortunes of revolution took a further turn for the worse in

---

18. LD Trotsky, *The Struggle Against Fascism in Germany*, Harmondsworth, 1975; *My Life*, New York, 1975; *History of the Russian Revolution*, London, 1967; *The Young Lenin*, Harmondsworth, 1974; 'The Soviet Economy in Danger', *Writings of Leon Trotsky 1932*; 'Alarm Signal!', *Writings of Leon Trotsky 1932-33*.

1936 and 1937 with the trials in Moscow and the dashing of hopes in France and Spain. Although still in his mid-fifties, Trotsky had become depressed by a sense of impending old age. He was also prone to hypochondria. He and his family were savagely persecuted. In such circumstances it is not surprising that Trotsky's work suffered.[19]

If the quality of Trotsky's work deteriorated during the last five years of his life, and surely it did, the reason need not be sought in a general reference to methodology and orientation. This cannot easily explain the contrast. The catastrophism and triumphalism which becomes evident in the later 1930s had not been so obvious in early years, even during the great upheavals of the period 1917-21. At this time, Trotsky's predictions were rather more conditional. In later years Trotsky needed to be optimistic amidst all the wreckage of earlier hopes in order to continue. Trotsky was a man of action. His statements were intended not only to be diagnostic but mobilising. About him he saw the decline of capitalism and the sharpening of class contradictions. The era of capitalist expansion appeared to be behind him, and much of the evidence, at least until 1937, did support his view. Now things look different; such are the tricks of history, and they can fool us all.

In any attempt to draw even a conditional distinction between Trotsky before and after 1935, or thereabouts, the difficulty arises of assessing *The Revolution Betrayed*. This book, first published in English in 1937, is understandably considered by the Trotskyist movement to be a fundamental work. In the first place, although the book was not published in New York until 1937, it was largely written during the first half of 1936, and was completed by the summer. More importantly, much of it was not new but a direct development from earlier pieces. Certainly the crucial period for the formation of Trotsky's views on the current phase of Stalinism in the USSR was 1930-33. Thus, in a sense, *The Revolution Betrayed* marks a transition between the earlier and the later period of Trotsky in exile.

Perhaps significantly it was not Trotsky who proposed the idea of a major study of the USSR. Although he had somewhat earlier announced an intention to produce a book on the Soviet economy, like many of his other projects, it was never realised.[20] Between 1929 and 1935 Trotsky was extremely prolific, but his ambitions inevitably outran his capacities. In addition to the published work, dur-

---

19. Inter alia T2:6036 to 6072 (Wright to Trotsky), T2:8342 (Trotsky to Gollancz), T2:9036 (Trotsky to Maule), T2:9426 (Trotsky to Novack), T2:10761 (Trotsky to Walker), T2:11741 (Curtiss to Karsner), T2:12488 (Curtiss to Weber). Trotsky's letters to Natalia Sedova, T2:10598-10631, give personal details. See also his diary from 1935, published as *Trotsky's Diary in Exile*, Harvard University Press, 1958.
20. LD Trotsky, footnote in 'Alarm Signal!', *Writings of Leon Trotsky 1932-33*, p101.

ing the first half of the 1930s he hoped to write a full biography of Lenin, and a study of the relationship between Marx and Engels. There were also other more tentative projects — a book on the Red Army, something on philosophy, possibly a study of the American Civil War (probably to justify a stay in the United States). Even amongst the half projects, the possibility of a sustained theoretical work on the USSR does not appear.[21] Evidently, Trotsky was far more at ease when producing works of contemporary history, particularly focused on individuals.

The Revolution Betrayed originated from an idea first put to Trotsky by the American publisher of the *History of the Russian Revolution,* Simon and Schuster. Trotsky was asked to provide a new preface to a one volume edition of the *History.* Taking the opportunity for a serious analytical investigation, he enlarged the preface into a book. It was rejected by Simon and Schuster. Too long they said, but Trotsky saw political motives behind this. Doubleday took it on. It sold poorly at the time, and failed to make much money for either publisher or author, although subsequently it made a major contribution to Trotsky's posthumous reputation.[22]

The Revolution Betrayed is both a defence of the USSR and a critique of Stalinism. It seeks to establish the authenticity of the workers' state by reference to the successes of planning and the supersession of capitalism, but it robustly repudiates the idea that the USSR is socialist. The ambiguities of the workers' state thesis (the counter-revolutionary workers' state) vitiate the whole book. But one is still left with an enormously impressive attempt to come to terms with the development of the USSR in a perspective of historical materialism. Without accepting Trotsky's conclusions, it is still possible to recognise the fertility of the book. Molyneux fails to do this adequately. His discussion is limited by a restricted interest in the internal tensions of Trotsky's work and its development over time.

As an example of the complexities of the analysis in *The Revolution Betrayed,* I shall briefly discuss how the contradictory relationship between production and distribution is presented. This is a problem of central significance for the Trotskyist definition of the character of the USSR. In its standard formulation it appears as an opposition between the 'law of the plan' in production and the 'law of value' in distribution. This underpins the conception of the USSR as more progressive than capitalism, and in need only of a political and not a social revolution; planning, it is held, is an essential expression of the working class nature of the social forma-

---

21. Inter alia, T2:922 (Fadiman to Trotsky), T2:8893 (Trotsky to Lieber), T2:10089 (Trotsky to Scribners). Also Max Eastman, 'Introduction', *The Young Lenin,* p8.
22. Inter alia, T2:702 (Curtis Brown to Trotsky), T2:919 (Fadiman to Trotsky), T2:2771 (Lieber to Trotsky), T2:8437 (Trotsky to Hansen), T2:10573 (Trotsky to Walker), T2:15814 (royalty statements).

tion. This viewpoint is undeniably based in Trotsky, but there we find it in a far less rigid form than it has acquired since 1940.

The premise of *The Revolution Betrayed*, in continuity with all of Trotsky's post-revolutionary writing, is that the USSR has through revolution overthrown capitalism, but it cannot escape from it except by establishing a higher productivity of labour than the capitalist world, and ultimately securing the international consolidation of the revolution. Anticipations of socialism there may be, through the system of planned production, but socialism there cannot be in conditions of generalised want. The USSR is to be understood in terms of the collision between past and future, capitalism and socialism, but in Soviet society the penetration of opposites has mutated the pure form. This is the conclusion that may be drawn from Trotsky, although he himself tended to advance it implicitly through a series of phenomenal observations.

Trotsky pays tribute to the power of planning. The first chapter speaks, without irony, of 'gigantic achievements in industry' and 'enormously promising beginnings in agriculture'.[23] In the body of the book, however, a somewhat more qualified view of planning appears. Trotsky draws particular attention to failures of quality, especially in the consumer goods sector, and to the disproportions which result from economic maladministration. It is possible to derive from Trotsky the view that planning is such only in the formalistic sense of administrative organisation of the means of production, and not in the sense of *conscious, social regulation and control by the associated producers*. Indeed, Trotsky does use the term 'administrative planning', as in the following statement:

'Administrative planning has sufficiently revealed its power but therewith also the limits of its power. An a priori economic plan— above all in a backward country with 170 million population, and a profound contradiction between city and country — is not a fixed gospel, but a rough working hypothesis which must be verified and reconstructed in the process of its fulfilment... For the regulation and application of plans two levers are needed: the political lever in the form of a real participation in leadership of the interested masses themselves, a thing which is unthinkable without Soviet democracy; and a financial lever in the form of a real testing out of a priori calculations with the help of a universal equivalent, a thing that is unthinkable without a stable money system.'[24]

Since throughout his book Trotsky indicates that the first of these 'levers' is completely absent and the second largely so, the conclusion can only be that successful planning (that is, in a strict sense, planning itself) does not occur.

23. LD Trotsky, *The Revolution Betrayed*, New York, 1970, p8.
24. Ibid, p66.

Trotsky sees distribution as operating according to 'bourgeois norms' and, therefore, in contradiction with production. However, throughout *The Revolution Betrayed* Trotsky is constantly referring to the fact that distribution is itself bureaucratically managed. He devotes several pages to money and inflation, and presents in these passages a good example of the necessity of going beyond his general presentation of the contradictions of Soviet society to reach his specific, if brief, evaluations of particular problems. In these pages we can find the following statements, far more penetrating than his general conclusion on the norms of distribution:

'Soviet money has ceased to be money; it serves no longer as a measure of value... The fact seems almost unbelievable now that in opening a struggle against "impersonality" and "equalisation"... the bureaucracy was at the same time sending "to the devil" the NEP, which means the money calculation of all goods, including labour power. Restoring "bourgeois norms" with one hand, they were destroying with the other the sole implement of any use under them. With the substitution of closed distributors for commerce, and with complete chaos in prices, all correspondence between individual labour and individual wages necessarily disappeared... Only the abolition of the card system (that is, rationing), the beginning of stabilisation and the unification of prices, created the condition for the application of piecework payment.'[25]

Thus Trotsky indicates the fiction of the idea that distribution during the first Five Year Plans was in any real sense based upon the law of value. Only in the loosest of senses was this so; distribution took place unequally.

In explaining the growth of inequality Trotsky uses the famous analogy of the near-empty shop.[26] Shortage in the USSR is 'the basis of bureaucratic rule'. Queues for goods, real or implicit, necessitate 'a policeman to keep order'. This is the Soviet bureaucracy. Trotsky's image is powerful and instructive, but it does not support his idea of bourgeois norms of distribution. The state (the 'policeman') intervenes directly in distribution, sponsoring and developing inequalities. Only in the first instance, shortage as the basis for inequality, can distribution be seen as impersonally determined. The low level of the forces of production has parallel consequences in production and distribution. In production the bureaucracy manages and through the use of inequality (bourgeois norms) creates incentives. In distribution the bureaucracy regulates the supply of scarce products, but above all does not forget itself.

25. Ibid, pp70, 72, 80.
26. Ibid, p112.

Much of the intricacies and internal tensions of *The Revolution Betrayed*, a central part of the richness of the book, passes unrecognised in *Trotsky's Theory of Revolution*. Notice is taken only when support for the basic thesis can be derived, or to try to show how close Trotsky came — without realising it — to the positions of state capitalism (despite the fact that he openly opposed the theory)! Molyneux has offered us an impoverished Trotsky. The basic thesis is argued superficially; the contradiction between the mechanical determinism of which Trotsky is accused, and the admitted profundity of many of the major writings, is never explored. There is a useful introduction in the first chapter to 'permanent revolution', but this is counterbalanced by a routine concluding defence of state capitalism, and a polemical assessment of Trotsky's legacy. We are forced to conclude that Molyneux knows something of Trotsky's major writings, but little of Trotsky and his times. Trotsky is too complex, too large and too important to be treated in this way.

John Molyneux

How Not To Interpret Trotsky — Again[1]

Leon Trotsky has been reasonably well served by biographers, but there has long been a need for a clear, concise and comprehensive presentation of his main political ideas. Unfortunately, this book does not meet this need.[2] In the first place, it is extremely long-winded and repetitive, which makes it rather tedious reading. Knei-Paz has little talent for the succinct summary. If one is prepared to read 230-odd pages to find out about the theory of permanent revolution, one would do much better to read *Permanent Revolution* and *Results and Prospects* themselves. Apart from anything else, Trotsky is a much better writer than Knei-Paz. Secondly, although Knei-Paz is extremely scholarly when it comes to Trotsky himself (he seems to have read a considerable amount of Trotsky's truly vast output), his knowledge of the rest of Marxist thought and the Marxist movement is based very much on second-hand sources, and poor sources at that. Thus for 'the relationship between Lenin the thinker and Lenin the doer' we are told on page 437 to see Leonid Schapiro and Peter Reddaway's *Lenin: The Man, the Theorist, the Leader*, a truly abysmal collection of essays. For a survey of theories of the Soviet Union we are recommended on page 439, of all things, Daniel Bell's *The End of Ideology*. The effect, therefore, is rather like a portrait from life set against a background of a cheap reproduction landscape.

But the book has a much more serious defect; namely that Knei-Paz approaches Trotsky as a bourgeois academic with a bourgeois academic's priorities

---

1. This article first appeared in *Critique*, nos 10/11, 1978.
2. Baruch Knei-Paz, *The Social and Political Thought of Leon Trotsky*, Oxford University Press, Oxford, 1978, pp629, £15.

How Not to Interpret Trotsky — Again

and values. He sees Trotsky principally as a theorist of 'backwardness' and of revolution in the 'backward' countries, and he wants to situate Trotsky in the context of debates on industrialisation and modernisation. The focus of the study is thus almost entirely on the theory of permanent revolution and its consequences in Russia. In a work that claims to be reasonably comprehensive (p xi), this leads to a serious distortion of Trotsky's thought. For the world proletarian revolution, as an essentially international phenomenon which for Trotsky was absolutely central throughout his life, is, as far as Knei-Paz is concerned, something peripheral to be added on as an afterthought to the writing on Russia. Thus 'Trotsky's innumerable writings of the 1920s and 1930s on political events in Britain, France, Spain, etc, have been largely ignored... they are... of little theoretical interest' (p x), and: 'It would be merely tedious and, today, hardly illuminating to follow Trotsky's writings during the 1914-24 period on revolutionary developments in the various individual European countries.' (p320)

The same criterion is applied to Trotsky's work in exile and to his struggle to build the Fourth International. Now Trotsky himself considered this to be the most important work of his career, and one does not have to be an uncritical Trotskyist or a partisan of the Fourth International to see his point. For Trotsky at that time was struggling, virtually alone, to defend and develop genuine Marxism, crushed by the dead weight of Stalinism, and to prepare the future world revolution. However much one might disagree with Trotsky here, the fact remains that the work of this period is a major component of Trotsky's political thought, and it should find a place in a 'comprehensive' study of that thought. But it doesn't... 'Trotsky's writings of 1929-40 are on the whole of purely historical interest today, and only peripherally valuable as sources of Trotsky's social and political thought.' (p439) It is worthwhile listing some of the things that are either left out completely or mentioned only in passing as a result of Knei-Paz's approach: the analysis of the crisis of capitalism, the theory of the united front, the critique of popular frontism (surely of great relevance today after Chile and Eurocommunism), the notion of the counter-revolutionary role of Stalinism internationally, the theory of transitional demands, the role of trade unions under capitalism, the attitude to the Second World War, and much more. In other words, those aspects of Trotsky's thought that pertain to the strategy and tactics of revolution which could possibly serve as a guide to action in the here and now are entirely omitted.

Even on its own chosen ground of the theory of permanent revolution there is much to quarrel with in this account. Knei-Paz's central argument runs as follows: Trotsky failed to distinguish sufficiently between industrialisation and modernisation (p100), and on the basis of limited economic development exaggerated the extent to which Russia had become socially modernised (pp102-5). This, according to Knei-Paz, led Trotsky to predict and to work for a socialist revolution for which Russia was socially unready. In the event, this premature revolution could only be achieved through 'the substitute link' of the Bolshevik party, which imposed the revolution from above (pp172-3), and this, of course, is the basic explanation of Stalinism, which grew out of the attempt to impose upon society a social revolution for which it was unprepared, and which, therefore, could be carried out only through the largely autonomous activity of the state and its institutions of coercion (pp367-8).

Thus Knei-Paz's book is yet another episode in the long-running posthumous defence of Menshevism ('the pessimism or cautious reservations of the more orthodox Russian Marxists... was better grounded in Russian reality than the optimism of Trotsky', p106), and arrives once again at the familiar equation of Leninism with Stalinism. Unfortunately for Menshevism, the argument is unsound at each stage. Firstly, it is nonsense to say that Trotsky exaggerated the social modernisation of Tsarist Russia, since the whole theory of permanent revolution was formed on this being an impossibility. If social modernisation had been possible under Tsarism, then either there would have been no revolution at all, or the revolution would have been led by the bourgeoisie. Equally absurd is Knei-Paz's contention that 'very little' had really changed in Russia, 'only segments of the formal economic framework' (p105). If that were so, then the events, not only of 1917, but also of 1905, would be truly inexplicable. What had changed, of course, was the emergence of a numerically small but, in the context of a weak and timid bourgeoisie, politically decisive urban proletariat, and that is precisely what Knei-Paz misses. Trotsky's conviction that 'the Russian proletariat was an independent, vital revolutionary force', is described as 'either perverse or simply naive' (p171).

It is because he 'does not see' the revolutionary proletariat of 1917 that Knei-Paz is only able to conceive of the relationship between the Bolsheviks and the working class as one of imposition of revolutionary goals. Trotsky in 1917, we are told, became 'aware, that left to their own initiative the masses might compromise with less than now seemed, to him, attainable' (p231). But this was not at all the main problem of 1917, for there was abundant evidence of the proletariat's revolutionary aspirations. What was a real danger, however, was the possibility that the workers and soldiers would go into action, as they did in the July Days, spontaneously and without a clear plan, and consequently be decisively defeated. The role of the Bolshevik party was not at all to impose socialist aims on a reluctant working class, but to provide the existing elemental revolt of that class with organisation and a coherent strategy.

Furthermore, it is because Bolshevism achieved that relationship with the working class that Stalinism was unable to triumph as a straightforward evolution from Bolshevism. Rather, it required firstly the destruction, dispersal and exhaustion of the proletarian vanguard as a result of the civil war and economic disintegration; secondly, the bureaucratic degeneration of the party; thirdly, the revision of the party's theory and programme; and, finally, the complete annihilation of its old guard, all of which involved a long and bitter internal struggle. Knei-Paz claims that there is a contradiction in Trotsky's analysis of Stalinism in that, on the one hand, he showed the social and historical roots of Stalinism, yet he maintained at the same time that it was 'in principle avoidable' (p369). But there is no contradiction here. Trotsky never suggested, as Knei-Paz claims, that Stalinism 'was merely an aberration, an accident almost' (p369); but to reveal the historical roots of a phenomenon in no way involves asserting that history could have taken no other course. That is a ludicrous determinism. In a particular historical situation a number of courses of development may be possible, each of which will have profound social roots. Knei-Paz's argument against the specific alternative advocated by Trotsky (the spreading of the revolution), that material aid from socialist Europe would not have made a decisive difference as shown by 'the persistent problems confronting underdeveloped countries today, no matter what the extent of the material aid they receive' (p167), is based on a truly amazing equating of socialist cooperation with 'aid as imperialism'.

Of course, the ideas on which Knei-Paz bases his critique of Trotsky are neither unusual nor original; in broad outline they have long been dominant in this academic field, and a review is no place for their detailed refutation. The point is, however, that the painstaking application of their ideas to Trotsky's thought has failed to generate any striking insights. The 'contradictions' he purports to discover are largely illusory, and the genuine 'problem areas' in Trotsky's Marxism (the tension between his authoritarianism and his commitment to workers' democracy in the 1920s, his vacillations in the struggle against Stalin, the limitations of his theory and strategy when applied to advanced Western Europe) are sometimes noted but never investigated. There are many other criticisms, both general and particular, that could be made of this work, but enough has been said to show that it cannot be regarded as a satisfactory, not to speak of definitive, account of Trotsky's thought. It is a pity to have to condemn so thoroughly a book that is evidently the product of great labour and considerable, though limited, scholarship, and there is no doubt that it will serve a useful function for further work in this field, but the moral would appear to be that Trotsky and liberal academicism do not mix well.

Loren Goldner
Trotskyism and Trotsky
Pierre Broué as Biographer[1]

Pierre Broué, French historian, Trotskyist militant, and editor of the *Cahiers Léon Trotsky*, published in 1988 an imposing biography of the 'organiser of victory' of the October Revolution.[2] As the Soviet state takes timid steps towards the tacit or full rehabilitation of Trotsky, the appearance of this book seems timely indeed. That rehabilitation will be meaningful only when Trotsky's writings become widely available to the Soviet public, and when the historical truth about his role in the revolution and in the establishment of the young Soviet state (a role second only to Lenin's) can be freely discussed in open debate. When virtually every other 'old Bolshevik' murdered by Stalin has been rehabilitated under Gorbachev, the caution with which the partisans of glasnost proceed in the case of Trotsky is testimony to the explosiveness of the questions linked to his name, questions with real implications for contemporary Soviet and world politics. Today, the prospect of a prompt Russian translation of books like Broué's and of their diffusion in the current ferment in the Soviet Union is merely a heady one. Only a few years ago, it would have been surreal.

One can think of few people more qualified than Broué to write this biography. For 45 years, the author has been active in Trotskyist politics in France, where Trotskyism has arguably been of more real political importance than in any other country outside the Soviet Union itself. He has authored massive tomes on the Bolshevik party, the German revolution and the Spanish revolution, each in the orthodox mould of the master; he has edited and prefaced an authoritative French edition of Trotsky's post-1928 writings; he has been at the centre of much

1. This review first appeared in *Critique*, no 25, 1993.
2. P Broué, *Trotsky*, Fayard, Paris, 1988, pp1105, FF198.

'Trotsky research' of recent decades, and he was at the door of Harvard's Houghton Library on the day in 1980 when Trotsky's archives were first opened to the public.

Broué's biography of Trotsky is necessarily read in the shadow of Isaac Deutscher's even lengthier study, whose final volume appeared in 1963. In the postwar decades, the rise of a 'Sovietology' inspired by the Cold War has made possible serious biographical studies of most of the revolutionaries of the Second and Third Internationals. (To their credit, neither Deutscher nor Broué, as politically-committed leftists, can be called 'Sovietologists', let alone Cold Warriors.) Significantly absent from this scrutiny has been a biography of Lenin that even approaches what both Deutscher and Broué have done for Trotsky. Lenin's life blends all too completely into the history of Bolshevism and of the revolution itself.

Some intangible quality in his personality, the supreme product of the century-long evolution of the Russian revolutionary milieu, has defeated every attempt to evoke the man behind the cascade of statistical studies of Russian agriculture, questionable epistemology, factional polemics and central committee resolutions which constitute the bulk of his writings. By partisan accounts, even some of Lenin's most historically significant speeches were delivered with the cool pedagogy of an accomplished schoolmaster. For many, Lenin's utter lack of the qualities conventionally associated with 'charisma', combined with his steeled pursuit of one life-long goal, was precisely the source of an overwhelming charisma. But the 'wine, women and song' in a life devoted to honing an apparatus and leading it to power have thus far eluded a biographer worthy of the man. One even senses that Lenin, lacking any trace of personal vanity, would take pride in this.

The problems confronting the biographer of Trotsky are of a rather different order. Trotsky lost. He is not first remembered, by the average reader, for his unique application of the theory of permanent revolution to Russia, for his almost unparalleled oratorical skill in the 1905 and 1917 revolutions, for his military organisation of the seizure of the Winter Palace or for building the Red Army (indeed, for decades, in both the Soviet Union and even in supposedly 'progressive' circles in the West it was flatly denied that he had done any of these things). Trotsky is remembered as the man who was defeated by Stalin. Lenin had admirers; Lenin had enemies. But there is (unfortunately) little controversy among his admirers and his enemies over what Lenin stood for and what he accomplished. 'Leninism' — a term invented after his death by Stalin — was part of the official ideology of 20 countries and countless political parties in the world today. Trotsky's name, on the other hand, has until very recently been associated with anathema in those same countries and in many of those parties. Where there is discussion of Trotsky, there is a problem of saving him from many 'Leninists' who are in fact merely Stalinists. There is moreover a problem (pace the 57 contemporary varieties of Trotskyism) of establishing Trotsky's true historical stature, almost on a par with Lenin, in order then to laugh, cry or simply understand.

It is therefore hardly surprising, yet is still noteworthy, that both of Trotsky's major biographers, Deutscher and Broué, have come out of the Trotskyist milieu. Deutscher's three volume study appeared from 1953 to 1963, at a time when such a biography was still, even in the West, very much an act of historical recovery. (He had, in 1949, published a single volume on the life of Stalin.) Prior to 1980, Deutscher was one of the very few individuals allowed to consult the closed section of Trotsky's archives at Harvard.

For all its sweep and novelty in the atmosphere of ignorance and calumny still evoked by Trotsky in the West at the time, Deutscher's biography was also a political tract, an advocacy of 'Deutscherism', or an historical accommodation to Stalinism veiled in Trotskyist language. This accommodation was even more palpable in the earlier study of Stalin, a virtual paean to the Stalinist industrialisation of the 1930s. 'Deutscherism' amounted to a belief in the ability of the Stalinist bureaucracy to reform itself, a belief confirmed for Deutscher in the emergence of Khrushchev, and presumably dashed in the emergence of Brezhnev. But the best heirs of Trotsky retained the Old Man's perspective that only a new working class revolution could put an end to Stalinism.

Broué's book is no less a work of political advocacy, and one senses that he wants to polemicise with Deutscher on every page. He admits as much in the preface. One can readily agree that Broué is more restrained, certainly more the historian, and more correctly 'Trotskyist' than Deutscher. But one would also think that 25 years later, after uncovering new archival material, and most importantly after so much world history and so many polemics in which the relevance of Trotsky's ideas has been debated almost as intensely as 50 years ago, Broué would have written a biography showing the marks of these developments. The reader approaching this book with such hopes, however, will be disappointed. Like his earlier orthodox books on the Bolshevik party, Spain and Germany, this is as close to an official Trotskyist work on Trotsky as we are ever likely to see. And there is, ultimately, something dry about Broué's Trotsky.

One major problem for Trotskyism, and for Deutscher, is that almost all the leading figures of the Left Opposition in the Soviet Union capitulated to Stalin after 1928. Many of them did so because they saw Stalin implementing the left's 'super-industrialisation' programme on his own. All their self-abasement and toadying did not stop Stalin from shooting every one of them over the next decade. But Trotsky, to his great credit, realised that there was a political dimension to Stalin's 'borrowing' of the left's economic programme, and did not capitulate. Since his death, a fondness for Stalinist 'productivism' has led many Trotskyists to blunt this political critique and to become the noisy 'left wing' of the Stalinists, an affection which has generally been little reciprocated.

This is not Broué's problem. He shows repeatedly where Deutscher's chiding of Trotsky concealed a covert (or not so covert) political agreement with Trotsky's adversaries, or at the very least a misunderstanding of Trotsky's views. But if we admit that Broué's book is more 'truly Trotskyist', more truly the work of an historian, it must also be said that the 'literary' merits of Deutscher are superior to those of Broué.

The panorama of an epoch moves in and out of Deutscher's trilogy, in which the arena of Trotsky's life is not merely the historical stage of the socialist movement in Europe and North America, but the whole Zeitgeist associated with Nietzsche, Ibsen, Freud, the post-1917 Russian avant-garde, or finally the avant-garde figures such as Breton and Rivera who rallied to Trotsky during his exile in the 1930s. With Deutscher, one is present as Trotsky breathlessly awakens Lenin and Krupskaya in a London dawn in 1902, to introduce himself upon escape from Siberian exile, or when, in 1907, he escapes a second time across the tundra of the Ostyaks; one is present during his emigré life in Vienna before 1914, or when, after his internment in Canada in 1917, he is carried to the camp gates on the shoulders of the German PoWs whom his speeches, in German, won over to revolution. All this evocation of a real life, in its quotidian as in its world historical dimension, does not excuse Deutscher's attempt to enlist Trotsky in his own variant of Trotskyism, but it gives his book a human quality far more intense that Broué's more documented, prosaic and more 'correct' account.

Perhaps the most striking example of Broué's shortcomings is his portrait of the most critical years of Trotsky's life, when from 1923 to 1927 he was losing his battle with Stalin. In some sense what is unique to 'Trotskyism' — as opposed to 'Leninism' — is the legacy of Trotsky in this period, after Lenin's death in 1924. Trotsky and Trotskyism's claim to constitute the real continuity of Bolshevism against Stalin began in the fight against Stalin's doctrine of 'socialism in one country', the struggle against the Bukharinist right and the Stalinist 'centre' in the industrialisation debate, and the battle over the Comintern's suicidal bungling of the Chinese revolution in 1927. One of the most perplexing questions hanging over Trotsky's life is his failure, on several occasions, to fight Stalin inside the party when the fight between them was still undecided. Trotsky allowed Lenin's testament, calling for Stalin's removal from the position of general secretary, to be suppressed by a decision of the party. He repudiated his American follower Max Eastman when Eastman published the testament in the *New York Times* in 1926. On several occasions when Stalin still remained vulnerable, Trotsky sat silently in party proceedings, to the consternation of his supporters. When the Left Opposition was completely defeated and Trotsky was formally expelled from the Bolshevik party, a friend and colleague, Adolf Yoffe, shot himself in protest in his Kremlin office. He addressed his suicide letter to Trotsky, in which he wrote: 'I have always thought that you have not had enough in yourself of Lenin's unbending and unyielding character, not enough of that ability which Lenin had to stand alone and remain alone on the road which he considered to be the right road... You have often renounced your own correct attitude for the sake of an agreement or a compromise, the value of which you have overrated.'

No one had ever talked to Trotsky in that fashion. It goes to the heart of a 'psychological' dimension of Trotsky's inability to carry on the struggle against Stalin without Lenin. (This is not to suggest a psychological explanation for his defeat, but merely a psychological aspect of it.) Yet it is such a dimension which Broué, writing a purely 'political' and 'historical' book, is at great pains to avoid. He thinks that by showing, against Deutscher, the superior Marxist logic in Trotsky's reasons for shying away from several lost opportunities, he has obviated the need for any 'psychology', and gives further lofty Marxist reasons why such a discussion is not necessary. But, while quoting abundantly from Yoffe's testament, he manages to omit the first half of the above passage! For Broué, as for most orthodox Trotskyists, revolutionary politics are exclusively a question of 'correct positions', as he is at great pains to show against Deutscher. Yet by eschewing any discussion of Trotsky's failure of nerve on several occasions, in the 1923-27 period, he appears less honest than Deutscher's politically-motivated, but partially 'psychological' portrait.

Habent sua fata libelli; books have their fates. Deutscher's book, for all its problems, had the good fortune to appear on the upswing of the post-1956 thaw in the world communist movement. When thousands of militants of the 1960s looked around for alternatives to social democracy and Stalinism, Deutscher's book was one place to start. In France and Britain, for the decade after 1968, Trotskyist groups were the most visible organised expression to the left of the French Communist Party and the Labour Party, even if it is patently false to characterise them as the most authentic heirs of the ferment of the 1960s. In Japan, they were even more dominant. Today, Broué's book appears in a context of unprecedented mass ferment in Eastern Europe and in the Soviet Union itself, and it may in the long run be as influential as Deutscher's. But in the West, since the mid-1970s, the important Trotskyist groups have largely shrivelled up, along with most other carryovers from the New Left. And much of the current, vocal opposition in the East is unfortunately clamouring not so much for Trotsky and soviets as for Milton Friedman and more consumer goods.

More importantly, the prestige of the Russian Revolution and its heirs has been drastically deflated as a model or point of reference, and not merely in the West. Still more importantly, from the 1960s onwards, an international discussion has taken place in which the whole concept of Bolshevik vanguardism, and therefore of Trotskyism, has been radically questioned, from various points of view, some of them to the 'left' of Trotskyism. None of this had happened when Deutscher wrote. But, now, Broué's book reads like the words of a man from another era. He writes as if the 'poetry' that the early phase of the Russian Revolution could yet evoke for many in the 1960s were still in the air. Of course, Broué is writing a biography and is not obliged to make his work 'relevant' to the polemics of the present. But he truly writes as if the history of the past 25 years, and therefore the way in which we think about the more distant past, had never occurred. He is certainly to be commended for not bending to the waves of cretinisation which have swept through the French intelligentsia since the appearance of the 'new philosophers' in 1977. But it seems slightly breathtaking to write, in the midst of a deeper crisis of Marxism of which the 'new philosophers' were only the vulgar pamphleteers, without the slightest sense that something has gone wrong, and without attempting to join these developments polemically.

Broué is a militant, and he has written a militant book for a new generation awakening to politics. But he does not seem to have noticed that in the past 15 years, much of the world appears to have exited the political universe defined by the Russian Revolution, that 'historical turning point where history did not turn', as someone once put it. Even the head of the Soviet state has recently expressed a desire to leave that universe. This may of course turn out to be an illusion, and some future turn of the historical spiral may again find the international left debating the 'Russian enigma', the 'philosopher's stone' of twentieth century history, as intensely as it did 15 or 20 years ago.

But I doubt it. Everything that underwrote the centrality of the 'Russian question' in the international left as late as the 1970s rested on the view of Russia as a generalisable model of the future. A future of a society without classes, for some; a future of a new form of class domination, for others; a still valid model of a future proletarian revolution, for still others. Even as they awaited the new working class revolution to restore the power of the soviets and rid the Soviet Union of bureaucracy, the Trotskyists saw the 'gains of the October Revolution' preserved in the system of central planning and state property that assured a steady, if unspectacular, rate of economic growth. But today, with an internal expansion of the market and an entry into the international division of labour, even that mirage has evaporated for the Eastern bloc.

Again, Trotsky was assassinated in 1940, and his biographer is not obliged to deal explicitly with any of these questions. But to the extent that all history is, to some extent, inevitably 'present' history, one might think that Broué would approach Trotsky with the questions of the present. To the extent that he does not, the reader can only look elsewhere for enlightenment on the ever-fascinating 'Russian enigma'.

Trotsky and the World Economy

Leon Trotsky

Two Speeches on Developments in the World Economy

Editors' Note

The two speeches translated below provide for the first time a crucial supplement to Trotsky's writings on the nature of capitalism. They should be seen in the context of Trotsky's report to the Third Congress of the Communist International in 1921, the article on the curve of capitalist development (referred to in the text), and his later introduction to Marx's *Capital*. His conception of inter-capitalist rivalry and the nature of capitalist development are exceptional examples of classic Marxist political economy. Trotsky's dialectical integration of political economy with history is unsurpassed in the twentieth century. The second article continues Trotsky's stress on the political-economic nature of capitalist development, and repeats his differences with Kondratiev, best known in the present day as the author of the Kondratiev cycle. Avoiding the obvious danger of making specific predictions, he nonetheless manages to analyse the main contradictions of the interwar system. In this he proved remarkably prescient; firstly, in terms of grasping earlier than most the central and growing importance of the United States of America; secondly, in analysing the historic decay of Europe; and finally, of course, in recognising the real possibility of a special relationship emerging between an ascendant America and a declining Britain.

Two Speeches on Developments in the World Economy

Translator's Introduction

It is understandable that biographies of Trotsky's life, when they reach the mid-1920s onwards, concentrate upon the power struggle with Stalin and the reasons for Trotsky's defeat. However, this approach has obscured many of Trotsky's writings of that time. Indeed, in general, we still lack a good exposition of the full range of Trotsky's works. The first translations of the two speeches presented here were in part motivated by a desire to 'restore the balance'.[1]

The speeches are important and interesting in that they contain Trotsky's views on a whole range of subjects — developments in the world's economies and their interaction with political and social factors, what is a revolutionary situation, what makes a revolution, the significance of the Russian Revolution, what is the nature of decline, and what is a Marxist analysis. Although Trotsky's predictions have proved to be false with regard to several specific issues, the speeches are still relevant as impressive examples of applied Marxist analysis of a type rarely encountered today.

The first speech was made as part of a contribution to a discussion held on 25 May 1925, and subsequently published on pages 171-81 of the journal *Planovoe Khozyaistvo* (*The Planned Economy*), 6/1925. The second speech was made at a meeting held on 18 January 1926, and subsequently published on pages 185-200 of *Planovoe Khozyaistvo*, 1/1926.

Ian D Thatcher[2]

---

1. Since first completing this translation several years ago, some articles have appeared which utilise these speeches as sources. See, for example, V Barnett, 'Trotsky, Kondratiev and Long Waves', *Journal of Trotsky Studies*, no 2, 1994, pp1-15; Ian D Thatcher, 'Trotsky, the Soviet Union and the World Economy', *Coexistence*, Volume 30, no 2, 1993, pp111-24; and HH Ticktin, 'Trotsky's Political Economy of Capitalism', in Terry Brotherstone and Paul Dukes (eds), *The Trotsky Reappraisal*, Edinburgh, 1992, pp216-32.
2. Ian D Thatcher lectures in the Institute of Russian and East European Studies at the University of Glasgow. He has edited, with Alec Nove, *Markets and Socialism*, Aldershot, 1994, and is editor of the annual *Journal of Trotsky Studies*. He has taught at the universities of Auckland, New Zealand, and Teesside, England, and is author of numerous articles on various aspects of Trotsky's life and thought, several of which have appeared in *Cahiers Léon Trotsky*.

Towards the Question of the 'Stabilisation' of the World Economy: Comrade Trotsky's Speech on Comrade Varga's Report

Comrades, it is very difficult to talk on such a complex question, confined by the framework of someone else's report, especially a report of such abstract foundations, and of an even more abstract exposition. So, from my side, there will inevitably be several improvisations of this alien schema, not very well mastered by me. All of this really complicates my task.

It seems to me that the main defect of Comrade Varga's[3] report is the abstract nature not only of the exposition, but also of its content. He raised this question: are the capitalist forces of production developing or not, and considered world production for 1900, 1913 and 1924 calculated for America, Europe, Asia and Australia. However, this is not relevant for resolving the question of the stabilisation of capitalism. One cannot measure the revolutionary situation in this way. One can measure world production, but not the revolutionary situation, for the revolutionary situation in Europe, in present historical conditions, is determined to a significant degree by the antagonisms between America and Europe, and within Europe itself — interrelations of German production and British production, competition between France and Britain, and so on. At minimum, the economic foundations of these antagonisms determine the revolutionary situation in an immediate way. That the productive forces in America have grown in the last 10 years is beyond doubt. Nor can one question that productive forces in Japan grew during the war, and are growing now. They also grew and continue to grow in India. And in Europe? In Europe they are growing neither in general nor in total. Therefore, the basic question is resolved not by calculating production, but by an analysis of economic antagonisms. The crux of the matter is this: America and, in part, Japan are driving Europe into a blind alley, not giving an outlet to its productive forces that were only partly rejuvenated at the time of the war. I do not know whether you have looked at the recent speech made by one of America's most prominent exporters, Jules Barnes, who has close ties with the American Ministry of Trade. He outlined, apparently at the Conference of American Trade, and proposed at

3. ES Varga (1879-1964) was a Soviet economist and a member of the CPSU from 1920. He was chief editor of the journal *Mirovoe khozyaistvo i mirovaya politika* (*The World Economy and World Politics*) during 1927-47. His books include *Kapitalizm i sotsializm za 20 let* (*Capitalism and Socialism for 20 Years*), 1938; *Osnovnye voprosy ekonomiki i politiki imperialisma* (*Fundamental Questions of the Economics and Politics of Imperialism*), 1953; and *Kapitalizm 20 veka* (*Twentieth Century Capitalism*), 1961.

the Brussels Conference of American representatives, this programme of development: 'We want to appease Europe, but at the same time we want to allocate certain sections of the world market to some European countries so that they will not collide with American products.' These are almost his exact words. So that Germany does not collide with American products and with American trade, we Americans instruct Germany to trade in Soviet Russia, etc. These are not empty words, for Europe depends upon America to an extraordinary degree. Certainly, America cannot successfully organise the chaos of the world market, and in such a way guarantee the stability of capitalism for a long time, if not forever. On the contrary, driving the European countries onto a more and more narrow sector of the market, America is now preparing a new, more unprecedented worsening of international relations, both between America and Europe and inside Europe itself. But at the present stage of development America is realising a whole number of imperialist aims by 'peaceful', almost 'philanthropic' means. Take the question of the stabilisation of currency, which is the clearest feature of the so-called stabilisation of capitalism. The richest country of Europe — Britain — has currently stabilised its pound sterling. But how was it stabilised? By a 300 million dollar loan from New York, so that if British pound sterling drops in value American capital should save it. The consequence of this is that British pound sterling is now becoming a toy in the hands of the American stock exchange, which, at any moment, could weaken it. That which was officially used in relations with Germany; that which ripened in relations with France — the Dawes system[4] — is now, at minimum, partially contemplated in relations with Britain. Certainly, this in no way signifies that America could successfully carry this policy through to the end and stabilise a 'Dawesised' Europe. One simply cannot talk of this. On the contrary, 'Dawesisation', today giving predominance to 'pacifistic' tendencies, in fact worsens Europe's plight, and is preparing a massive explosion.

Comrade Aizenshtadt is incorrect in a similar way when she argues for the general equal development of the productive forces of America and Europe. Is the Reims Cathedral different from the skyscrapers built in New York? They built skyscrapers there because destruction in Europe occurred with the help of American dynamite. The inflow of gold into America did not entail a corresponding development of the productive forces of Europe. One cannot mechanically sum up these two parallel phenomena, the draining of Europe and the enrichment of

4.   Charles Dawes (1865-1951) was Vice-President of the USA between 1925 and 1929, and was American Ambassador in London between 1929 and 1932. He won the Nobel Peace Prize in 1925. He elaborated what became known as the 'Dawes Plan' that was intended to deal with the problems of German reparations and the strengthening of capitalism in Western Europe. It was approved at the London Conference on 16 August 1924. Germany received a $200 million loan, and its reparation payments were fixed at a lower rate.

America. One cannot add up the lost wealth of Europe with the wealth accumulated in America. Although Comrade Aizenshtadt objected to Comrade Varga, in fact she only amplifies his errors. He also combines the value of Europe and America, whereas they now oppose each other both economically and politically — this is what determines Europe's hopelessness to a large extent.

Again, I repeat: if I cite J Barnes's programme regarding the allocation to Europe of strictly defined sectors of the world market, that is, give enough provision to European countries so that they can pay interest on loans and the loans themselves whilst not breaking the American market, it does not follow from this that Europe itself is secure on a certain level, and is preserved for a long time. Nothing of the kind. Any amount of long-term security either in the international or in the internal relations of imperialist capitalism is impossible. It goes without saying that on this point not one of us has any doubts. The Dawes system, the restoration of currency, trade agreements — all of this 'pacifism' and measures of restoration are completed with American 'support', and are under her control. This is characteristic of the present stage in the development of Europe. But in restoring their elementary economic functions, the European countries restore all of their antagonisms, impinging on each other. Insofar as America squeezes the European restoration process into narrow limits, these antagonisms, which led directly to the imperialist war, may be revived earlier than prewar levels of production and trade turnover are reached. Under the financial 'pacifist' control of America, despite present 'appearances', there is now occurring not a lessening but a heightening of international tensions. This also applies to no lesser degree to internal, that is, class relations. The Second Congress of the Communist International[5] has already emphasised the essential point that the postwar decline in the development of the European productive forces involves not a halting, and not a slowing down, but, on the contrary, a strong intensification and sharpening of the process of social differentiation: the ruin of the petty and middle classes, the concentration of capital (without national accumulation), and the proletarianisation and even greater pauperisation of all new national stratum. All subsequent Congresses emphasised this fact. It is in this sense that Comrade Varga is completely correct when he says that in Europe there is now occurring a further polarisation of class relations which has not attained, and cannot attain, any type of stabilisation. The general volume of wealth in Europe is not increasing, or is almost not increasing, but it is amassing into fewer and fewer hands and at a faster rate than was the case before the war. One of the flanks of the proletariat is turning into a lumpen-proletariat. We witness this in Britain. There we observe the phenomenon of a new order, precisely a standing army of unemployed which, for the whole postwar period,

---

5. The Second Congress of the Communist International was held in July-August 1920.

has not dropped below one and a quarter million, and is now at about one and a half million. But the stabilisation of unemployment is absolutely not the same as the stabilisation of capitalism. In one of his latest articles Kautsky said that the socialist revolution will all the same come in its time (a hundred years hence and then smoothly) because the proletariat is growing, its significance in society is becoming greater and so on; in other words, he repeats the *Erfurt Programme*,[6] but in a vulgarised form. Today, one can see that this is incorrect. If the proletariat is growing, then it is growing in Britain, the richest country in Europe, as a lumpenproletariat. And not only in Britain. Here one can repeat Marx's words that Britain only shows other countries the shape of their future.[7]

France faces the urgent task of stabilising the franc. This means that in the more or less near future there will also be chronic unemployment in France. If the whole French proletariat is currently engaged in industry, this is because French industry lives not within its means, but with the help of false money, with the help of inflation. America demands from France what it has already attained from Britain — stabilisation of currency. This requires an influx of gold into France. But one has to pay a high interest for American gold, and this brings great overhead expenses onto French industry. Overhead expenses on French industry result in a worsening of the market, and this market, which France has at the expense of the ruin of its currency and at the expense of undermining its financial economy, will be suspended, and there will inevitably be a standing reserve army as in Britain. If France rejected this, America would force her to move to a stable currency with all the consequences which flow from this. The clearest expression of the restoration process is in Germany, where the capitalist curve fell to its lowest point. But in Germany the restoration process operates within the framework of a struggle for prewar levels, and on the path to this level Germany will be confronted by many economic and political obstacles. Meanwhile, due to a depleted national wealth, we witness a greater and greater intensification of social contradictions. One part of the report of Comrade Varga's exposition is very abstract, but it is correct. I have in mind that section in which Comrade Varga spoke of a deforma-

6. The *Erfurt Programme* was adopted in October 1891 by the German Social Democratic Party. The programme was divided into two sections — the 'maximum' and the 'minimum'. The 'maximum' programme expressed the final goal of a seizure of power by the German working class, and the necessity to link this with international socialism. The 'minimum' programme was directed towards specific demands to be advanced in the pre-revolutionary epoch — a democratic electoral system, equal rights for women, rights of association, progressive taxation, a free medical service, and so on.
7. Trotsky is here referring to the following sentence from the Preface to the first edition of *Capital*: 'The country that is more developed industrially only shows, to the less developed, the image of its own future.' (K Marx, *Das Kapital*, Hamburg, 1867, p ix)

tion of society that cannot be reversed. In order to abolish unemployment in Britain one would need to capture the market, whereas Britain is not gaining but losing it. In order to stabilise British capitalism one needs — neither more nor less — to push America aside. But this is fantastical and utopian. All of the 'cooperation' between America and Britain consists of America, in the framework of peaceful 'pacifistic' cooperation, increasingly pushing Britain aside, using it as a medium, a means, as a broker in the diplomatic and commercial fields. The world share of the whole of the British and of the whole of the European economies in general is falling — and, in the meantime, the economic structure of Britain and of Central-Western Europe arose from the world hegemony of Europe, and depended upon this hegemony. This contradiction, both inevitable and unavoidable, is progressively deepening, and is the basic economic prerequisite of a revolutionary situation in Europe.

In this way, it seems to me that it is absolutely impossible to characterise the revolutionary situation outside the antagonism of the United States and Europe, and this is Comrade Varga's fundamental error.

But here the question was raised about the origins of the notion of stabilisation itself. Why speak of stabilisation? I think that one cannot answer this question only in the framework of economic categories, one cannot avoid raising political issues. Let's take the European economic situation. How was it immediately after the war, and how is it today? Have any changes taken place? Certainly there have been changes, and very serious ones. In France all the destroyed stations were rebuilt, and the Northern departments were to a large extent restored; in Germany one now travels on rubber tyres and not on straw. Much has been restored, repaired, improved. If one approaches the issue with such a limited point of view, it seems as though much has been done in the postwar period. This is how a person, falling into extreme difficulties and even into poverty, who has two or three hours of free time, hastily sews buttons, covers patches, cleans himself, and so on. Now let's take the whole European situation in the state of the world economy. Has it changed? Has it improved or not in these years? No, it has not improved. Europe's position in the world scale did not improve — this is the essential point. But why do we nevertheless speak of stabilisation? Above all, because although Europe has not escaped from its general position of *decline*, it has managed all the same to introduce certain elements of regulation into its economy. One cannot ignore this. This is not a matter of indifference for the fate and struggle of the European working class, and for the correct tactics of the communist parties. But it does not decide the general fate of European capitalism. The gold stabilisation of the pound sterling is undoubtedly an element of 'regulation', but at the same time stabilisation of the currency only more clearly and more precisely reveals Britain's decline and its colossal dependence upon the United States.

What, nevertheless, does the regulation of European capitalism, the restoration of its elementary functions and so on mean? Is this internal regulation only the necessary preliminary condition and together with this an indicator of a future healthy, long-term stabilisation? No, there are no facts to support such a proposition. In order to understand how and why the European bourgeoisie was able to 'regulate' its economy, one has to consider political issues and their mutual interaction with economics. In 1918-19 in Europe we had, on an economic base still bearing the direct consequences of the war, a mighty spontaneous revolutionary upsurge of the working masses. This rocked the bourgeois state at its foundations, and brought about a strong lack of self-confidence in the bourgeoisie as a ruling class — it did not even possess the decisiveness to darn its European caftan. Its thoughts of the stabilisation of the currency stood somewhere on the third or fourth place, if they stood at all, whilst the direct onslaught of the proletariat threatened its supremacy. Then inflation was a measure of direct class self-defence for the bourgeoisie, just as war communism was a measure of self-defence of proletarian power in our country. Comrade Varga correctly remembers that at the First and Second Congresses we considered a seizure of power by the European proletariat extremely likely.[8] What did our mistake consist of? In which field were we unprepared? Was the economy prepared for a social revolution? Yes, it was. In what sense was it prepared? In a fundamental sense, if you please. Already in the prewar period the state of technology and of the economy made the transition to socialism objectively advantageous. What did the changes occurring during and after the war consist of? They consisted of the fact that, if one takes development as a gradual general process, the productive forces of Europe ceased to develop. Prior to the war they developed quickly and within the capitalist framework. Their development went into a blind alley, and this led to war. After the war they stopped developing in Europe. We have stagnation with sharp, irregular fluctuations from top to bottom which do not permit even a holding of the conjuncture. If, generally speaking, the conjuncture is the pulse of economic development, an amount of conjuncture tremors testify that capitalism lives. At the Third Congress of the Comintern,[9] we showed that changes in the conjuncture would inevitably continue and lead to an amelioration of the conjuncture. But there is a difference in the heartbeat of a healthy and a sick man. In 1921 we said that capitalism has not died, it lives. Therefore, its heart would beat, and the conjuncture would change. But when a living being falls into an insufferable condition, its pulse beats irregularly, and it is difficult to attain the necessary rhythm and so on. This is what we had for all that time in Europe. If the cyclical changes in Europe once

8. The First Congress of the Communist International was held in March 1919.
9. The Third Congress of the Communist International was held in June-July 1921.

again become regular and full-blooded (and I speak very conditionally with all reservations), then this, to a certain extent, would show that the bourgeoisie had taken some sort of principled step forward in the sense of consolidating economic relations. But thus far one cannot talk of this. The irregularity, non-recurrence and unperiodical nature of these conjunctural tremors shows that European and above all British capitalism is insufferably constrained in those limits into which it fell after the war. The productive forces, pushing ahead, are confronted with the limits of the world market, which are too narrow for them. Hence the economic twitchings, spasms, sharp and razor-edged tremors without a regular periodisation of the economic conjuncture.

But to return to the question: what did we not take into account in 1918-19 when it was expected that the European proletariat would seize power in the coming months? What was missing for the realisation of these expectations? The economic prerequisites and class differentiation were not missing — the objective conditions were sufficiently prepared. The revolutionary movement of the proletariat was also present. After the war, the proletariat was in such a mood that one could have led it into decisive battle. But there was nobody to lead and nobody to organise this battle — there was no party. This was the factor that we ignored, and this was the mistake in our prognosis. Insofar as there was no party, victory was impossible. And, on the other hand, one could not maintain the revolutionary fervour of the proletariat while a party was being created.

The communist party began to be built. In the interim, the working class, not finding a militant leadership at the proper time, was forced to accommodate itself to the situation which formed after the war. Hence the old opportunistic parties received a chance once again, to a greater or lesser extent, to strengthen themselves. Capitalism also survived. What did capitalism receive precisely because there was no revolutionary party at the critical moment and the proletariat was not able to take power into its hands? *Breathing space*, that is to say, the possibility to orient more peacefully itself to the forming situation: restore the currency, substitute straw with rubber tyres, reach trade agreements, and so on. In summary, serious changes took place in the state of European capitalism which one cannot underestimate, but they are all packed into the same limits of world economic, financial and military forces which were prepared before the war, finally determined at the time of the war, and which have not changed as far as Europe is concerned in the recent period. It is not because capitalism has successfully created for itself conditions for the further development of the productive forces that there is now no revolutionary situation in Europe. There is no further development of the productive forces, and there are no serious symptoms pointing in this direction. The absence of a revolutionary situation is directly expressed by changes in the mood of the working class, most notably in the German, in the ebb from revolution to social democracy. This ebb is a consequence of the fact that the postwar revolutionary wave, during and after the Ruhr events[10] was unsuccessful. As a result of this ebb, the bourgeoisie was able to repair the most tattered elements of its state and economic apparatus. But its subsequent struggle, if only for the prewar economic level, is inevitably fraught with new and newer contradictions, conflicts, tremors, 'episodes' of the Ruhr type, and so on. The mood of the working class, as was once again illustrated in 1923 in Germany, is a factor incomparably and immeasurably more fluid than a country's economic 'stabilisation', which, on each of its subsequent stages, may place a new revolutionary situation before the European communist parties.

Here Comrade Varga mentioned an important fact: the bourgeoisie cannot fatten up the upper stratum of the working class. Now in Britain, Baldwin's Conservative government very much wants peace with the workers. If one follows Baldwin's recent speeches, one finds them full of great concern. Not long ago that classic phrase was heard in Parliament: 'We, Conservatives, do not want to shoot first.' And when the extreme right of his own party introduced a bill to prevent trade unions from collecting political dues (and the Liberals agreed with it fully because the Labour Party which destroyed them depends on these moneys), Baldwin said: it goes without saying that collecting political dues is force, and this breaks with British traditions, and so on, but — 'We do not want to shoot first.' This was his exact expression, which is not only an oratorical device.

If one follows the British economy, politics, the press, the mood of Britain, one gains the impression that the revolutionary situation is moving forward, albeit slowly, but with striking regularity. The hopelessness of British capitalism found its expression in the fall of liberalism, the growth of the Labour Party, the appearance of a new mood in the mass working class, and so on. Baldwin's policies are built on the hope of 'compromise' with the workers. In the meantime, the British trade unions, which we know as the concluders of conservative arrangements (of what was trade unionism an expression for us — an expression of ultimate workshop opportunism), are gradually becoming a great revolutionary factor of European history.

Communism can fulfil its mission in Britain only by combining its work with those processes which are occurring in the British trade unions. And by what are these processes directly determined? Precisely by the fact that that country, which more than anywhere else fattened a broad stratum of the working class, can do this

---

10. On 9 January 1923 the Entente Reparations Committee announced that Germany was not fulfilling the terms of its reparations payments. Two days later French and Belgium soldiers began to occupy the Ruhr, an area rich in natural resources and containing large industrial production plants. This triggered a political crisis in Germany.

no longer. Hence Baldwin's mood of compromise should reject all those modest bills (for example, minimum wages for coalminers) introduced by Labour MPs.

Yesterday we received news by telegraph that the Conservatives had rejected a modest bill from Labour MPs for 10 million pounds sterling for social programmes. From here it follows that the strengthening of opportunism which is an indisputable fact in Germany and in France, can be neither firm nor long lasting. Neither France nor Germany can create a privileged situation for the upper layer of the proletariat. On the contrary, in all places there will be a period of serious pressure on the working class.

And in Britain? Is it not possible that the opportunism of the present leaders of the Labour Party will be consolidated for many years, even decades? If we devote a couple of words to this issue, it would be better to make a general evaluation of the situation. In Britain we had a Social Democratic Federation and an Independent Labour Party — two organisations which existed in the course of decades as competing organisations. Each had 15 000, 20 000, 25 000 members. During the postwar years we witnessed a striking thing in Britain: yesterday's propaganda section, the Independent Labour Party, came to power. True, it depended upon the Liberals, but at the last election, already after the fall of MacDonald, it gathered four to five million votes!

I speak of the Independent Labour Party since it is the ruling fraction of the Labour Party. The Labour Party does not exist without the Independent Labour Party. What explains the so unusual career of the Independentists, and are they stable? In Britain we have a bourgeoisie which has subordinated the proletariat to itself better, more consistently and more intelligently than any other; it has economically fattened up the top stratum of the working class, and has demoralised it politically. There has not been a school like it in history, nor, in all likelihood, will there be one like it in the future. The American bourgeoisie will hardly be able to corrupt and humiliate its working class for so long. To what did the change in Britain's international and internal economic situation lead? To the pressure of the mass of trade unionists on their leaders, and this pressure led to the creation of a Labour Party. If we take the average British worker today, he would hardly consciously reject those prejudices which he had when he voted for the Liberals. But he is disappointed with the Liberals because Liberal MPs, in the light of Britain's changing position on the world market, were unable to speak for him in Parliament to the extent to which they could previously. Hence there arose the need to create his own party. What is the Labour Party? It is the political department of the trade unions. The Labour Party/trade unions needed a treasury, a cashier, a secretary, and deputies in Parliament. It was the pressure of a sharpening class struggle and the elimination of Liberalism that forced the trade unions into creating their own Labour Party. But the trade union bureaucracy was not able to create it under its own steam in 24 hours. And in Britain the situation had changed in such a way that it was necessary to build a party almost in 24 hours. This is how the startling 'union' between the Independent Labour Party, which had existed in the course of many years as a section, and the trade unions took place. 'You need a political department attached to the trade unions? We are at your service.' The Labour Party was formed in this way. The opportunism of the Independentists received a gigantic political base. But for long? Everything points to the answer: 'No!' The present Labour Party is a consequence of a temporary crossing of the path by the Independent Labour Party and the mighty revolutionary rise of the working class; the Independentists correspond to only a short stage of this rise. We have already had MacDonald's government. This was an episodic experiment, not exhausting itself since the first Independentist government did not have a majority.

What are the future prospects? Are there grounds to think that the present Conservative ministry will be directly overthrown in a revolutionary situation? It is difficult to guess, but even without a fundamental push from history one can expect a revolutionary struggle for power between the working class and the bourgeoisie in the coming period. If there is not a war or other events like an occupation of the Ruhr, the Conservative government in Britain, either a year earlier or later, will be replaced by a Labour government. And what does a Labour government mean in such conditions? An extraordinary working class attack, and pressure on the state. And what does this mean, given Britain's hopeless world situation? That the British working class could demand communism with the same mass energy and speed as when they demanded the leadership of an Independent Labour Party. To present the matter as if the number of communists in Britain will grow gradually over the course of decades is to be radically mistaken. Precisely the fate of the Independent Labour Party better than anything else demonstrates that in Britain events develop along other paths and at another tempo. Britain used to own the world market — hence the conservatism of the trade unions. Now it has been relegated, its situation has worsened, and the situation of the British working class has changed radically; the whole orbit of its movement altered. At a certain stage this orbit (the movement's line) intersected with the path of the Independent Labour Party. This creates an illusion of a strong Labour Party. But not everybody supported MacDonald — this was only one landmark, one incision on the path of the British working class. It is perhaps the processes currently occurring in the British working class which most clearly express the deeply critical, that is, revolutionary, character of the whole of our epoch.

A revolutionary situation, in the special sense of the word, is a very concrete situation. It flows from the intersection of a whole number of factors: a critical economic situation, a sharpening of class relations, a combative mood among the working class, uncertainty among the ruling class, a revolutionary mood among the petit-bourgeoisie, a favourable international situation for the revolution, and so on. In its very essence, such a situation can and should mature, and then be maintained only until a certain moment. It cannot last for long.

If it is not utilised strategically, it will begin to disintegrate. From where? From the top, that is, from the communist party which was not able or could not utilise the revolutionary situation. Internal conflicts will inevitably arise in it. That the party inevitably weakens is well known, and sometimes it loses a very significant part of its influence. In the working class there begins an ebb of revolutionary feelings and attempts at accommodation with the order in existence. At the same time, a certain wave of self-confidence washes over the bourgeoisie, which is also expressed in its economic work. It is the existence of these processes that force us to speak of stabilisation and in no way of some kind of radical change of the capitalist base in Europe, that is to say, above all its situation on the world market.

We have to reject European provincialism in our analyses. Before the war we thought of Europe as the ruler of the world's destiny, and we interpreted the problem of revolution in a national and European-provincial way, along the lines of the *Erfurt Programme*. But the war showed, revealed, disclosed and consolidated the very interconnected ties of all parts of the *world* economy. This is the fundamental fact, and one cannot ponder the fate of Europe outwith the connections and contradictions of the world economy. All that has occurred recently on the world market, every day and every hour, shows the growth of American supremacy and increasing European dependency upon America. The present position of America is, in several respects, similar to that of Germany prior to the war. This was also the master who arrived when the whole world was already divided. But America is distinguished from Germany by the fact that she is incomparably mightier than Germany was. She can attain much without ever directly drawing swords, without the use of arms. America forced Britain to cease Japanese-British agreements. America forced Britain to recognise the equality of its fleet with the American when all of Britain's tradition was constructed on the undisputed supremacy of the British fleet. How did she achieve this? By flexing her economic muscle. America has tied up Germany with the Dawes regime. She has forced Britain to pay her share. She pushed France into paying her share, and forced her to quicken her return to a stable currency to enable this. What does all of this mean? A new colossal tax on Europe to the advantage of America. The transferral of power from Europe to America continues. Although the problem of the market is not the primary question, Britain relies on the market as a matter of life and death. However, Britain cannot resolve the problem of the market. Unemployment is the ulcer which is undermining Britain's physiology. All of Britain's bourgeois-economic and political thinkers are saturated through and through with pessimism.

To sum up. I agree with Comrade Varga's conclusion that there are no grounds for assuming the economic stabilisation of Europe for any kind of lengthy period. Europe's economic situation, for all its changes to the better, remains deeply critical. In the coming years its contradictions will take on a profoundly sharper character. Therefore, in relation to, say, Britain, the problem of revolution consists above all in whether there will be enough time for the communist party to form, prepare itself and develop close ties with the working class before the moment arrives, as it did in Germany in 1923, when the revolutionary situation is so acute that it demands a decisive onslaught. In my opinion, this also refers to the whole of Europe. Any 'danger' does not consist of the establishment of stability in Europe, a rebirth of capitalist economic forces, under which the revolution will be put off to the distant future. No, the danger is that the revolutionary situation may form so quickly and so sharply that the communist parties will not have had enough time to become sufficiently formed. All of our attention should be focused on this issue. This is how the European situation, in general and as a whole, appears to me.

On the Question of the Tendencies in the Development of the World Economy

This published article has several stylistic changes to the stenographic report of Comrade Trotsky's speech made in the Business Club on the reports, organised on 18 January 1926 by the Industrial-Economic Council of the VSNKh USSR, on the tendencies in the development of the world economy for 1919-25 made by Professors Bukshpan, Kondratiev, Spektator and Falkner. Because of lack of time, the author did not examine the stenographic report. (Editor)

The first question which I want to examine is whether we can make an attempt at prognosis. If we have in mind the denial of an exact prognosis of a crisis in the coming three years, I would concur. However, I would do this only with great reservations; for without prognosis and without conjunctures in the field of prognosis, as working hypotheses, there can now be not only no theoretical, but also no practical orientation for us.

We are a trading country, we are buyers, we buy and sell. We have to know where to buy and where to sell, and how to use the state of the market — and since we have wholesale trade one cannot do this in a week; it takes place over months and years, and therefore we have to forecast ahead. We will get nowhere without prognosis. If the prognosis is in error, we have miscalculated, and this shows up in the trade balance.

But pessimism in relation to prognosis would be even more misplaced if one is thinking of the general line of development, since one cannot evaluate the developments of the coming three years, and isolate this from the general development of the economic forces of Europe and of the whole world. If I think of the coming three years I do not do this in a simple way, as a continuation of all previous history — here is this segment or curve extrapolated for three more years — I think of this in terms of the three years, as part of a further curve. It seems to me that it is precisely thus with thoughts of prognosis. When it is proven to be mistaken even in relation to three years, it can prove to be correct in general. This is what happened with many of the previous revolutionary prognoses, which, it appears, were mistaken in relation to the rate of development, but which proved to be correct in general.

If we conclude that capitalist development is moving towards a new vigorous upturn in Europe and in the whole world, this prognosis would have several, and hence not insignificant, practical consequences for our fate. And today it is clear that if a rapid development of capitalism were possible, this could, and in certain conditions would, be fatal for us. This is why the question of prognosis has great significance. It goes without saying that prognosis is possible if one correctly utilises the method of materialist analysis.

I think, insofar as I understood the speakers' basic ideas, that several of them applied an economic analysis very schematically and formally in relation to the present epoch.

Professor Bukshpan insists on the cyclical nature of postwar economic development. Can one establish a more or less regular cycle? I think not. Is this an uprising against Marx and against the Marxist theory of cyclical development? There is no uprising at all. Why? Because Marx's theory is not a supra-economic theory. The cycle is an expression of the internal rhythm of the mother of history herself in all of her movement. But in all circumstances? No, not in all. So, for example, the war started in the second year of the crisis. In 1913 the crisis began, and it is undoubted that this was a serious economic fact with, moreover, a social aspect, for a naked economy clothes nobody. What we are saying here is that 1913 was not simply one example of a recurring market crisis, but, at minimum, was a change in the whole European economic situation, and that Europe increasingly flinched against the limits of the market. The further development of the productive forces at approximately the rate observed in Europe for almost all of the previous two decades was extremely difficult. The growth of militarism occurred not only because militarism and war creates a market, but also because militarism is an historical instrument of the bourgeoisie in its struggle for independence, for its supremacy, and so on. It is not accidental that the war started in the second year of the crisis, revealing the great difficulties of the market. The bourgeoisie felt the market through the agent of commerce, through the economic agent and through the diplomatic agent; it felt it as we, a young state, attempt to feel the world market through our agents. The bourgeoisie saw this. This created class tension, made worse by politics, and this led it to war in August 1914.

In 1914 capital concluded a wonderful deal. What does this mean? Where did the market go to? The fact of the matter is that the market was not according to Marx, but according to the managers. That the managers are against Marx is undisputed, but the state of the market was not against Marx, since for the Marxist the state of the market is not a curve which drives into the economy — take it or leave it. This curve springs from the economy. If economics had to flow from politics at this point, despite Europe's growth in arms, you will not find a normal cycle.

And the first years after the war? The Germans called this time — and, in general, the Germans use precise terminology — an apparent-market because 1919-20 saw to some extent a continuation of war methods in the economic field — inflation, coarse privileges for the workers based on inflation, that is, on the squandering of basic capital, and so on.

In actual fact, this amounted to a weakening of basic capital in Europe, but externally it appeared as an upsurge. The destruction in the beginning of the war took place in the form of an upsurge. This was the apparent-market. And then payments for the war began, which were multiplied by the difficulties beginning in 1913.

From their very beginning payments for the war aggravated the new process of decline which started in 1913. What did capitalism need? Capitalism was floundering, it started to have spasms, and it sought a way out. Is there a regular cycle at work here? Comrades, it is difficult to find a regular cycle in spasms if that is what one is looking for. This, however, does not mean that Marx's theory is not applicable. It is applicable, but one has to apply it correctly.

I'll take the simplest example. There is an instrument called a pedometer. It is a very crude device, and does not calculate steps exactly. If you walk in more or less correct human steps, it will tell you how many miles you have walked. If you start to skip then already it will not be so accurate. But if you slip into a pond or on ice and flounder for two or three minutes, the pedometer will register 20, 30, 50 steps while you are getting nowhere. Something similar occurred with capitalism. For it the war was a terrible economic disaster. What did we see after this? We witnessed its attempt to rise from this deteriorated level of economic development in the conditions of the new Europe — the intersecting of new borders with dozens of new tariffs, and experiencing great difficulties.

If one attempts to trace a curve for separate branches of industry, for individual countries, and for Europe, what will such a curve portray? Only the spasmodic attempts of capitalism to rise again. One will not see the rhythm of the normal steps of capitalism — they are not there. Here one needs a profound analysis, and we have data for many elements of this analysis. Many of us are learning a lot from these tables, or, at minimum, we are reminded of many specific things. This will be very useful, but attempts to place this data under a regular cycle, a cycle portrayed as having begun a cyclical pattern, and then on these foundations produce an *optimistic* prognosis for capitalism, would be misplaced.

It is true that the three esteemed speakers, who bear a small amount of guilt in this, did not speak of it from scientific caution. Scientific caution is an admirable quality; not everybody is obliged to be a politician and make the mistakes which already, so to say, lie in the political profession. Economists can allow themselves to be cautious. But sometimes caution embryonically masks recklessness, and it is precisely in cautious evaluations that the dangers and difficulties standing before capitalism can be recklessly lost in overly optimistic evaluations of the fate of its further development. And I am inclined to reproach the three speakers for such caution.

In actual fact here the problem of cycles is not only a problem of methodology concerning an understanding of Marx and an application of Marxist theory, but is also the problem of evaluating the path of future development. Marx's cycles are explained by hints. Marx did not have enough time to give an exhaustive explanation of the industrial cycle. Something from his allusions, valuable to the highest degree, was subsequently elaborated upon by Hilferding.[11] In any case, cycles are undoubtedly at root connected with the expansion and renewal of heavy industry's basic capital — this is undisputed. Therefore Comrade Spektator's acknowledgement that the oscillations of European industry still occur in the framework of old basic capital as it issued from the imperialist war or from the prewar epoch explains, from the theoretical standpoint, why one cannot speak of regular cycles. For similar reasons it would be incorrect to turn the present rate of growth of industry — 40 or 50 per cent a year — into the normal rate of growth for the whole of future development. This is a rate of growth delivered to us as a heritage of basic capital.[12] It is for the same reason, although in different circumstances, that it is wrong to apply cyclical theory and methodology, extrapolating from it, for an analysis of the postwar economic period in Europe.

I want to add further that if, in so-called normal conditions, politics plays a great role in the European economy, this role is the same as that of air to breathing.

In conditions of upheaval, in conditions when the economy spasmodically seeks equilibrium, both political and military factors play a completely different role. We saw this in the case of the occupation of the Ruhr. A vast seizure of natural resources by foreigners occurred, property was transferred from one country to another. A different type of contribution was extracted, and the military hindered economic operations. And such semi-military measures as the creation of artificial corridors and the present struggle for rubber materials between Britain and the United States are a still further continuation of Ruhr methods which may become a colossal, huge factor in the economy. In other words, we see here not the free or semi-free play of economic forces which we were accustomed to analysing in the prewar period, but concentrated and resolute state forces bursting into the economy, and this threatens to interrupt, or is interrupting, regular or semi-regular cycles, if they are noted at all. Consequently, one cannot move forward without taking political factors into account.

11. Rudolf Hilferding (1877-1941) was editor of *Vorwärts* (*Forward*), the journal of the German Social Democratic Party, during 1907-15, and editor of *Freiheit* (*Liberty*), the journal of the Independent Social Democratic Party, during 1918-22. He was German Minister of Finance in 1923 and between 1928 and 1929. His most famous work is *Das Finanzkapital* (*Finance Capital*) (1910).
12. The high industrial growth rates to which Trotsky refers were mainly due to existing enterprises returning to use under the New Economic Policy, rather than to new plant coming into operation.

It seems to me that Professor Kondratiev is even worse in this respect when he advances the theory of long waves. I do not know the history of this theory. Personally, I only came across this issue in around 1920 when I saw, almost for the first time, a logarithmic curve which appeared in the supplement to the January New Year edition of the British newspaper *The Times*. There Kitchen, an old British economist, produced this logarithmic curve. And looking at this curve, I understood why Marx was mistaken in 1849-50. He for the first time hoped for the imminent development of the revolution. Then, in 1851, Marx said that one could not expect revolution now because of an upturn in the economy, 'but', he said, 'with the coming crisis, which is inevitable, so revolution is also inevitable'. Nonetheless, the crisis happened, and the revolution did not.

So, if we look at Kitchen's curve, portraying the conditions of the development of the basic economic processes of capitalism, we understand of what Marx's mistake consisted. In 1851 there began not a simple upturn in the economic curve, but a new period of great upturn in capitalism. What was the essence of this? Capitalism develops in cycles. Cycles consist of rise, halt, depression, crisis and so on, but the interrelation between rise and crisis is not always the same. Periods of capitalist development occur when rise and crisis move closer together and balance each other out — this is a period of stagnation and depression (although certainly not totally). Periods occur when the rise in each cycle strongly exceeds the crises which preceded it and which follow after it, and then the following rise even more strongly exceeds the crises which came before it and which follow after it. What follows from this? That all of these summits are removed by history when they are characterised by a rising curve in general. The whole line of capitalist development in general rises frantically upwards.

At that time Marx was not able to take into account — he only observed the rise in the market — that he was dealing with a new epoch of upturn when crises would only be temporary and delays weak, and an upturn would quickly overcome them and lead the economy upwards. He did not foresee this. Revolution did not come in 1859-60. Instead, there were wars associated with the unification of Italy, then we had the Crimean War, and then the Franco-Prussian War. Urgent questions, questions of state and national order were resolved through battle. It was in the early 1870s that a new line of depression, stagnation and so on began.

At the Third Comintern Congress I spoke against several left opponents. I illustrated that it does not follow that a crisis, a state at a particular time, will inevitably and uninterruptedly worsen, but that there will be fluctuations of crisis. One can think thus on the basis of a curve of stagnation with a tendency to go lower or with an insignificant tendency to go higher, but, in general, there will be a process of stagnation, of a decaying European capitalism with spasmodic strengthening and attempts at an upturn. However, there will also be oscillations in the market.

Although this is a dying capitalism, it still breaths, and its breathing, its palpitations are expressed in conjunctural, cyclical curves.

Then in Professor Kondratiev's book I came across the attempt to portray great epochs (apparently in 1923 or 1924), which characterise certain sections of the capitalist curve, as a new cycle of approximately 50 years. I remember that I even wrote somewhere, perhaps in *Vestnik Sotsialisticheskoi Akademii* (*Herald of the Socialist Academy*),[13] that this was radically wrong. What does this cycle consist of here? Cyclicality signifies regularity, correctness, rhythm; the fact that it grows from the internal property of the curve itself — this is what a conjuncture cycle consists of. But how can one talk of a cycle in this case? If one is haphazardly chronological in order to lead us into error, then our history would be constructed so that these curves would appear to be of approximately equal length — which, in my opinion, is absolutely not the case — and it would be possible to chart, although roughly, great stretches. But if one attempts to do this for an individual country, everything disintegrates into dust. An individual country is subjected to Marx's cycle as a whole; but these long waves are not subjected to an individual country.

And in actual fact this is wrong. But again, what is the heart of the matter? The upheavals in capitalist development do not grow from the internal dynamics of capitalist processes as such, but from the conditions into which it falls in its own development, that is, from the opening of new continents, colonies and markets for capitalist activity, or from military revolutionary tremors which cut across its road. For example, here is the new powerful country of the United States of North America. Is she able to create stagnation for Europe? Yes, she is able. Does this flow from the internal rhythm of Europe's economic development? No. And can the United States keep the revolution in Europe at a standstill for long? If the revolution does not occur — then for several decades.

I would want, as Professor Kondratiev loves to do, to examine European decay in a long wave, but it does not happen in this way. All the same, if we take the example from walking, which I took in relation to short waves, the oscillations of the cyclical conjuncture express the dynamic of capitalist walking. This is how capitalism moves. But where it is going, rising or declining, or sticking in the quagmire, depends upon the relief. Certainly, here the relief is not an accidental thing, and it is modified by the development of capitalism itself, but it is not an immanent process peculiar to capitalist development as such. There are profound differences in this, and it seems to me that Professor Kondratiev is guilty on this count.

13.   Trotsky is here referring to his article 'O krivoi kapitalisticheskogo razvitiya', *Vestnik sotsialisticheskoi akademii*, 4, 1923. For an English translation, see LD Trotsky, 'The Curve of Capitalist Development', *Problems of Everyday Life*, New York, 1973, pp273-80.

It is not clear to me, insofar as I have formulated this accusation, so to say, of potential optimism for capitalist development, in which way Professor Kondratiev shows that America's productive forces are now being transferred from America to Europe. I am absolutely incapable of understanding this. Here I say directly: damn it, I don't understand. In what scale, in which limits, what is the specific weight of this process, of this transferral? It seems to me that one has to study the basis of this. What do such partial transfers mean? If one takes the generally recognised fact that America is the hegemon of the world economy and then makes a prognosis referring to European development as if this were not the case, not taking the growing world power status of America into account, then one has written an account irresponsibly. I think that this has become a generally acknowledged fact, and one does not have to dispute this.

So, if one examines America and one has in mind the fact that America needs Europe, a Europe sufficiently strong to pay interest and purchase those products which cannot be sold elsewhere, and, at the same time, a Europe sufficiently weak so as not to threaten America either in ousting her from markets or opposing her expansion (and here I am not talking of military danger, naval danger or the danger of a land attack), then it becomes clear that America has a defined policy for Europe of allocating a certain corner to Europe, and keeping Europe in the confines of this corner. This is her policy. This explains her oppressive pacifistic role in relation to Europe. She acts how, say, a mighty calculating banker who finances several mutually competing trusts would act. She wants to receive interest from each of them. It is possible that the competitors may accidentally devour one another. However, the destruction of one means the destruction of the other, and one cannot allow this danger to come true. Hence the policy of such a banker will veer towards above all guaranteeing interest payments, but, certainly, not destroying competition, because this would set the debtors free and threaten the banker's domination. On the other hand, to permit the debtors' mutual destruction is also impermissible since this destroys the banker's personal profits. This rough comparison, but in essence true, is more correct in that America is moving from industrial capital to mixed finance and industrial capital of a higher banking-investment type. Such is the relation of America to Europe.

If in the process of her relations towards Europe when she rules over the European economy as Britain never did, since British supremacy, from today's point of view, was a provincial supremacy in terms of resources, America has still not realised all of her potential, this does not mean that it will not be realised in the future.

If revolution does not get in the way, this potential will be realised by 100 per cent as Americans demand. The situation is already such that when Britain attempted to shake off America by raising the price of rubber, on which it possesses almost a monopoly, America shook her fist at Britain, and this threat carried real clout. America has powerful combined repressive measures — economic and financial. Pound sterling is totally dependent upon the United States' banks; the might of the United States is so great that she does not have to mobilise it in total. Just as in electronics one can direct a huge mass of energy using a minority of its quantity, the United States can direct Britain's policy through some kind of pitiful loan which it slips in at the necessary moment, and which guarantees the pound sterling from conjuncture oscillations.

The German loan from the Dawes Plan of 800 million marks (400 million rubles) bears a similar petty character — from the standpoint of prewar proportions, and even from the vantage point of contemporary estimations of Germany's resources, one can see that this is nothing. And what did they do? Germany was wrapped in a package, and its stamps were stuck on — see what they did! And if a limited transfer of productive forces and resources from the transatlantic banker to the European debtors takes place in the framework of this unprecedented process in history, this will in no way be reflected on the balance of the great account books.

In Britain one should expect a tendency of an upturn — this is undoubted. It has already started. In Britain there are certainly a whole number of temporary private crises laid upon its profound historical crisis which began to appear sharply at the end of the 1880s, and which, in the last analysis, was complicated by the war. Recently she has experienced a deflationary crisis in connection with the renewal of the gold parity of pound sterling. In general this is a painful process, but for Britain, an exporting country, it is yet more painful. But when a harsh period of spasmodic pressure on working capital as a result of a sharp increase in banking interest comes to an end, only the painful process remains. This is what is now occurring in Britain. Hence, it was not difficult to foresee a certain inevitable improvement following a period of terrible decline.

But what does this mean? A technical bend of the curve, but by no means a change in its direction. It seems to me that, on Britain, the speakers expressed too much optimism, including Professor Falkner, who spoke of Britain's new strengthened international role. I admit that there will be several improvements upon that terrible time when Britain went cap-in-hand to the New York Exchange to ask for a 600 million dollar loan. But these improvements will occur against a background of Britain's continuing actual decline. By accident, I have a very interesting document whose author did not intend publication (in any case I did not receive it from the press but through other means), namely Klain's, the director of the Bureau for Internal and External Trade attached to the United States' Ministry of Trade, secret report. He here summarises Europe's situation, and says that one can note several improvements in Europe which, certainly, are thanks to the enlightened intervention of American capital. Here I do not agree with him. I agree with Aizenshtadt that American capital works for robbery, and its negative features are changed a little only in those cases where we receive it as a loan.

So Klain himself in the secret report where he happily and optimistically portrayed Europe's situation — and from this point of view we could have invited him to be our fifth speaker — spoke of Britain thus: 'The single dark spot in the more general sense if we exclude, certainly, France's and Italy's financial situation' — [if we exclude two small fry] — 'then we received' — [also not small] — 'the comparatively slow renewal of Germany.' So, in general everything is going wonderfully: Germany has no money, France has no money, and Italy is in no way improving — 'and Britain is also as if situated in an uncertain commercial state'. As we can see, this is another cautious economist. I do not want to be overly pessimistic since Britain is our best customer and our most hopeful ally in business principles (but this cannot change the evaluation). 'But there are a number of factors developing there which, I think, give food for serious thought.' What are these factors? 'Terrible taxes exist there which, in the opinion of several observers, one can put down to greediness and in particular to moneys expressed politely...'

In general this picture is absolutely correct. Britain is suffocating from a peculiar economic and technical conservatism which grew on the basis of its privileged position, and on the basis of its capitalist primogeniture which Germany had previously tried to capture for itself, and which the United States of America has presently assured for itself. All of these inherited features of technical and economic conservatism weigh it down on each step. For example, in Britain the electrical engineering industry is in a poor state, and has a lower profitability. Recently we received news by telegraph that Baldwin was establishing some kind of commission with the aim of consolidating the electrical engineering industry, and the electric power stations, in order to rectify the desperate situation in which British electro-technology is located in comparison with American. In which direction is Britain discovering the way out from this situation? With the growth of the United States, British conservatism is more and more revealing itself. British unemployment is not normal unemployment in the form of a reserve army; it has turned into a gout clot which, in this flagging organism, is not dispersing. What is the solution being contemplated? Not one of the speakers mentioned it. I do not see it. This is why I think those people who criticised Professor Kondratiev from the point of view of his prognosis were correct. From where did 1849 come from? From the cyclical theory, from the theory of long waves, but we see — and I have attempted to show this — that one should look at short waves with caution, and even more so with long ones. Perhaps this flows out of an economic analysis, from an analysis of the economic situation, from the economic processes? Although I am not a sceptic of parts of the prognosis, if one makes a prognosis on the basis of a materialist analysis one needs to note that the state of our current methods of possibility for analysis in no way permit such accuracy; and, in the meantime, the optimistic prognosis gives capitalism a breathing space of 15 years. One can do much in 15 years, including on the theme of our address. No, I think that we cannot guarantee capitalism a respite of 15 years in this evening's discussion.

Professor Bukshpan said that one possible future prospect is that Europe will produce more and more aristocratic goods in contradiction to America, which is all the more specialising in democratic goods. But one can see that Britain does not know where to sell its aristocratic goods. Where will Europe sell its products? One needs to discover a market. This does follow automatically. Europe will produce aristocratic goods for America? No this won't happen. In spite of all its richness, America conducts a very strict policy in relation to the import of luxury items from Europe and, in particular, in relation to us. In any case, if Europe's role came to being turned into America's jeweller and sending elegant slippers and fans to American ladies, then goodbye Europe! But it is absolutely impossible to squander several million European lives in this way.

Much more guesswork is involved in representing the tendencies of developments in the United States, which placed Europe in such a situation; that prognosis in relation to Europe is undoubtedly clearer: this is a temporary improvement, this is a spasm, this is a minor upturn against the continuing growing pressure of the United States. One can speak of the United States in two ways. I allow both variants. If the economic might of the United States grows in the coming 10 to 20 years or in those 15 years which Professor Kondratiev offers the capitalist world, and if in the course of those 15 years the United States develops at the same rate at which it developed over the last decades, at whose expense will this be? Above all, at Europe's expense. They will not only not give Europe the possibility to reestablish its position in the world market, they will also push her back from those positions on which she stands today, and, given American organisation and American technology, this is certainly not difficult. Read what Europeans have written in recent times on the economic development of the United States; economic observers, both practical and theoretical, talk of the United States in this way — 'the rate of American development is a terrible threat...'. If in the next 15 years America moves upward, then this will be at Europe's expense. And what does this mean for Europe? For Europe there will be revolutionary perspectives. And what does a delay of American development mean? A furious growth of American militarism because delayed economic steam seeks an outlet in this direction. Capital and heavy metallurgy will make the following demands from the President, from the government and from Senate: build ships, widen the programmes. One will not accidentally witness Americans proposing the disarming of France, the disarming of the Soviet Union, but without participating in any conference, and not wanting to disarm themselves. For them the Washington Conference,[14] where they disarmed Germany, is sufficient. I said at one of the Comintern Congresses that at about 1925 the United States and Britain would inevitably collide over the issue of the British and American fleets. The left accused me of putting off the revolution until this war, which should occur only in 1923-24. But I did not delay any revolution, for I was not leading one. I only tried to determine the tendencies of development. Britain accumulated its hegemony on the basis of its position in the world and on the colossal supremacy of its fleet, not only creating a market for its heavy industry, but also acting as a tool for the seizure of markets for heavy and light industry right up to the point that it forced the Chinese to buy opium from India. But the ship building programmes of Britain and the United States were such that in 1923-24 Britain should have been relegated to second place, and I said: will Britain really hand over its position? Here we were talking of war. But Britain handed over without war, through diplomatic means. Then I said to myself that, first, Britain is not henceforth a second-rate power, but a power left a long way behind the current leading power, the United States; and that the basic world antagonism is that between the United States and Britain, and that all other antagonisms are of the second and third order. The United States captured first position without drawing a sword, not firing one shot, and organising only one Washington Conference. The United States continues to build its fleet, inferior to the British in its staff, but one still has to show practically the value of British naval traditions. The German fleet showed its qualitative supremacy over the British, although it was grossly inferior to it in quantitative terms.

In Comrade Feldman's article, consideration of the United States' course of development took an algorithmic form. He concluded that the development of North America was all the more resting on a blind alley, and that the present upturn is nothing in comparison to the upturn of previous decades. If such a situation does exist, one is not justified in constructing perspectives of peaceful world development. America's rise to the top, insofar as it will occur without tremors, will drive Europe into an economic dead end, and Europe will either decay as the

14. The Washington Conference was held in Washington between 12 November 1921 and 6 February 1922. This was called at the initiative of the United States' government to discuss military balances and areas of imperialist activity. A number of agreements were reached at the conference, including the Four Power Agreement (USA, Great Britain, France and Japan) which mutually guaranteed each power's territories in the Pacific. This effectively ended the British-Japanese Alliance, considered by America to be an obstacle to its influence in the Far East. The Five-Power Agreement (USA, Great Britain, France, Japan and Italy) set limitations on the size of each power's fleet. Great Britain accepted America's demand for parity. Finally, the Nine-Power Agreement (USA, Great Britain, France, Japan, Italy, Belgium, Netherlands, Portugal and China) resolved to keep an 'open-door' policy on China.

Roman Empire decayed, or it will experience a revolutionary rebirth. But for the time being one cannot talk of Europe's decay. If American economic development is held up, its huge forces will seek an outlet in war. This will be its only chance to overcome the deformations which result from the circumstances of her economic development. This deformation moved as a nucleus. Such a nucleus, full of colossal force and delayed, could cause a huge amount of destruction inside the country.

Let's now examine the situation of the proletariat. In regard to Britain, nothing remains of the previous aristocratic position of the British proletariat. Our brotherliness with the British trade unions is based upon Britain's economic decline. Now the working class of the United States occupies the privileged position. A delay in economic development for America would mean huge changes in the interrelation of internal forces and, consequently, would also entail a revolutionary movement which will arise with characteristic American speed. In such a way, *with both possible variants for America we foresee great upheavals in the coming decades, and not peaceful developments.* Recently an article in the American *Economist* stated: 'We have attained such a level of development that we need a large-scale war.' Just as one needs fattened calves for the nourishment of a large town, so the *Economist* announces that, as the experience of the last war illustrated, America needs a large-scale war. The American imperialists have a preference, but not for peaceful development.

Now let's turn to France. It is not true that France is painlessly experiencing its deflationary crisis. From what do we see this? Firstly, in France, there existed a national bloc which, in the first and second period, monstrously increased inflation, deceived and robbed the petit-bourgeoisie, and then lost its support because it suffered most from inflation. It was on this soil that a change of government occurred; the national bloc had to abandon their places for the left since it was not able to solve monetary problems. First there was Herriot[15] and then Painlevé[16] from the First and Second Ministries and, finally, Briand.[17] That France is a rich country is more or less true. But this country also has sharpening social contradic-

---

15. Eduard Herriot (1872-1957) was elected leader of the French Radical Party in 1919. He held a number of posts in the French government, including Minister for Social Work, Transport and Supply (1916-17), Prime Minister and Foreign Minister (1924-25), Prime Minister (1926), Education Minister (1926-28) and Prime Minister (1932).
16. Paul Painlevé (1863-1933) was a mathematician whose political career started with his involvement in the Dreyfus affair. He was twice Prime Minister of France, in 1919 and in 1925.
17. Aristide Briand (1862-1932) was excluded from the French Socialist Party in 1906 for joining the then 'bourgeois' government. He was French Prime Minister on many occasions between 1909 and 1929, and was Deputy Prime Minister during 1914-15. He was 17 times French Foreign Minister, most notably during 1915-17, 1921-24 and 1925-31. He was awarded the Nobel Peace Prize in 1926.

tions; a country of much suffering among the petit-bourgeoisie and among the peasantry. I am inclined to believe the statistics, produced by Falkner, calculating the French national income, but one can see that, in general, it is very difficult to calculate the national income of any country, and such calculations involve, without fail, the uncertainty of several coefficients. Not to the least degree do I wish to speak against Falkner's competence or scientific honesty, of which I have no doubts, but one can see that it is possible to refer to facts more critically and more cynically. This depends upon the basic intention on a given matter. In France there is the problem of debt, and, to this day, nothing has been done to resolve this problem. In the meantime, America demands the resolution of this issue, and without America France will go nowhere. But how will France solve this problem? France is a rich country in the sense that some have a lot and others have nothing. But those that have do not want to give, and those who have not are not able to contribute something. If the working class and the bourgeoisie are to be robbed, there will be huge disagreements and criticism. The French petit-bourgeoisie has revolutionary traditions. Do Poincaré,[18] Clemenceau[19] and Millerand[20] really not like power? Nevertheless, they leave one after the other, smelling this burning fat, because they know what is dangerous. Even with a weak proletarian party existing as a revolutionary ghost from the banners of the Paris Commune, and even with weak trade unions, in France it is possible that the massive and dynamic revolutionary forces of the petit-bourgeoisie and the French peasantry, who lost both sons and savings in the war, could immediately develop. It is true that one can attain deflation: take the large bourgeoisie, the banks, large metallurgists by the throat and force them to pay, but since France has a greater debt and currency crisis, this would lead to a huge rise in the bank interest rate, a decline in capital turnover, and an industrial crisis. French politicians look at the question of deflation not so happily as our Soviet professors.

It is claimed that the whole of Europe will find some solution to its serious situation. In actual fact, Europe is already not in the state it was in November 1918, or in January 1923, when Poincaré occupied the Ruhr. In connection with

18. Raymond Poincaré (1860-1934) held a number of posts in the French government, including Prime Minister and Foreign Minister (1912-13), President (1913-20) and Prime Minister (January 1922-June 1924, July 1926-November 1928 and November 1928-July 1929).
19. Georges Clemenceau (1841-1929) held a number of posts in the French government, including Minister of Internal Affairs (March-October 1906), Chairman of the Council of Ministers (October 1906-July 1909) and Prime Minister (November 1917). He left politics after his defeat in the Presidential elections of 1920.
20. Alexandre Millerand (1859-1943) was excluded from the French Socialist Party in 1904 after forming a group of Independent Socialists. He was elected President of France on 24 September 1920, a post he held until the left reformist parties came to power in 1924.

the difficulties of recovery in the present time, such a situation cannot last for long. Europe lives. The methods of recovery — the Washington Conference, moving Europe onto a back seat and a worsening of Britain's position; and then the Dawes plan for Europe as a whole — means tying Europe with the American knot. In the short term this is undoubtedly a way out from a desperate situation and from a war situation; but in the long term Germany is just about to breathe again, and then once again choke. Two years ago German industry worked extraordinarily quickly, and now we are witnessing a terrible crisis in which thousands of bankruptcies are occurring, factories are sold in export, and millions are thrown into unemployment. Can there really be a clearer expression of Germany's and Europe's hopeless situation? Before the war Germany possessed colossal versatility and adaptability, then pressure from Britain and from the war accustomed her to a particular flexibility. All the habits of the German capitalists, who are content with small profits, and of the resilient workers who are satisfied with small wages after terrible years of hunger, all this, however, will not remove this terrible crisis. Does this really not illustrate Europe's doomed position?

Now after Washington, Locarno[21] and the Dawes Plan, there are negotiations towards a United States of Europe, and I, judging by Professor Falkner's words, am some type of apostle in relation to this theory.[22] I thank Professor Falkner for

21. The Locarno Conference was held in Locarno, Switzerland during 5-16 October 1925. Representatives from Belgium, Great Britain, Germany, Italy, Poland, France and Czechoslovakia participated. The conference guaranteed the status quo of Germany's western borders, and discussed Germany's entry into the League of Nations.
22. Comrade Trotsky's note is an answer to the following point from Professor Falkner's speech: 'The current slogan of contemporary capitalist Europe is the slogan of the formation of a United States of Europe. The creation of a United States of Europe has the aim of determining those new trade barriers which formed after the war, and those new political demarcations which changed Europe. The formation of the United States of Europe has the aim of resolving the real questions of international economic policy. I should recall that the slogan "United States of Europe" was first put forward in Soviet Russia by LD Trotsky, and now, several years later, capitalist Europe is itself advancing this slogan. This shows that this slogan was not merely empty words. In recent times much has been said and written of the chances to realise this slogan. I think that its realisation, despite the conferences which arose at Luther's invitation to join the League of Nations, the economic conferences to which our government decided to send its representatives as the newspapers informed two days ago, despite the number of demands for the creation of international, interstate organisations, I think that the chances are small. I think that this problem will not be resolved for the complex of contradictions is too complicated and its various aspects will be a burden to the different economic groups of contemporary Europe. I think that the resolution of important organisational questions of contemporary Europe is not a task of federalisation. Federalised leading capitalist groups with the active participation of the United States, international trusts and cartels of the important branches of industry — here is the outcome which one will be able to

remembering what I wrote, but I said something slightly different on this matter. Here something similar has occurred to what Gretchen attached to Fausts' explanation. When Faust expressed himself in a sufficiently clear Jacobin and atheistic spirit, Gretchen said: 'You are saying exactly what the pastor said in church, but in slightly different words.' The pastor in the church said something different. I spoke of a Socialist United States of Europe and of the dictatorship of the proletariat. I had in mind that Europe, trapped in a dead end, would not survive these internal partitions. The contemporary situation in Europe and the growth of the United States supports our prognosis. We said that under the present partitions and borders, Europe's situation is hopeless, and that this amounts to the Balkanisation of Europe, of which I reminded the Second Comintern Congress. Ludwig Dek, whom I cited, is convinced that a Balkanised Europe will be trampled under the charge of the United States. The same was said by a German bourgeois in a book which was recently published. So, from the one side Briand and from the other side the Germans shed rivers of blood in order to overcome competition and expansion — now they all talk of a United States of Europe. This means total decay, disbelief in the possibility of development and conscious vulnerability before the growing might of the United States. The petit-bourgeoisie timidly dream of unification, not for a repulse, but simply in order to exist; not to become fat, but to stay alive. Such is the psychology of the present European governments. I will not be optimistic on their account.

Now several words evaluating the economic situation in the USSR. Certainly, we have minimum influence on the world market, and we are still active on the world market to only a very modest extent. However, we will be of decisive significance for a socialist Europe. A socialist Europe adjoined to ourselves would be invincible against the United States. If we were the enemy at the rear, the European proletariat would not stand a chance against the capitalist United States. But with such a mighty rear as our country on its side, the European proletariat, which will be a socialist federation or a socialist united states, together with us would constitute a huge magnetic force for Asia. If today there was a bloc composed of ourselves and the socialist United States of Europe, and we sold goods to Asia at a fair price, Asia would fall into line behind us, and the transit road from a socialist Europe to Asia lies across the USSR. Then America would not be able to push Europe aside. A United States of Europe against America — this is a totally realistic perspective, and one can make a prognosis along these lines.

If the capitalist world was now able to generate a new organic upturn, and if it found a new equilibrium as a base for the further development of economic forces,

note for the capitalist character of Europe in the coming epoch.' (Stenograph of the meeting — Ed)

we, as a socialist state, would collapse. One can illustrate this theoretically and practically in two words. Theoretically, because an upturn of capitalism in Europe would create colossal technology for the bourgeoisie, and change the psychology of the proletariat. If the proletariat is shown that capitalism can raise the national economy, this would inevitably reflect on the working class which attempted to make a revolution, was smashed, and experienced a disappointment. If capitalism leads the economy upwards, it will have conquered the proletariat for a second time, dragging the working masses after itself. From the theoretical point of view, one can see that socialism has a right to exist precisely because capitalism is not able to develop the productive forces. Our revolution grew on economic foundations, and before the revolution we were an integral part of the world economy. If capitalism is able to develop the productive forces, we would have to conclude that we were mistaken at the root of our prognosis — capitalism is a progressive force, it develops its forces quicker than we; Bolshevism came to power too early, and history deals very thoroughly with premature births. This would be so if the optimistic prognosis for capitalism had a foundation. But has it a foundation? This is difficult to show. *But for the time being the bourgeoisie has not proven this, and it is not able to prove it*. In Europe there is no development of the productive forces. Crises and a fracturing of the productive forces at hand are occurring — this is the basic fact. Therefore one has to say that *socialism has a right to exist, to development and to full hopes for victory*.

European capitalism — for us the closest and the most dangerous — with each year of its postwar existence illustrates that Europe is not increasing the productive forces, and that America is not increasing the productive forces to the extent to which they would be increased if socialist methods of organising the economy were applied to American technology. If socialist methods were applied to American standards, to Ford's conveyor belt, the productive forces would grow much faster.

In Europe they are not growing at all.

One needs a new approach to the questions examined by us — not an abstract-theoretical, but a clear, rational approach. One has to explain Europe's sorry state and American pressure on it, and ask: what does one have to do with Europe, with us, and also partly with Asia in order to make the world economy better?

These issues arise naturally out of our situation. A year sooner or a year later history will raise them, and today we have to place them before ourselves theoretically.

Leon Trotsky
On Party Education[1]

Editors' Note

What follows is Trotsky's letter to AM Peshkov (Gorky) concerning the school in Capri that was held in August 1909. We have included it because of Trotsky's insistence of the necessity of party members to read Marx's *Capital*, and to study political economy. The manuscript is from the Alexinskii Collection at Columbia University's Bakhmetiev Archive.

Dear Comrade
I very much regret that the comrade editing no 4 of *Pravda* could not find space for Comrade Mikhail's announcement of the school. It will go in no 5, together with the article brought by Comrade Mikhail and the resolution. *Pravda* no 5 will come out as soon as we have distributed no 4 and collected some money. I have thought and discussed lately quite a lot about the party school. Many questions and problems have come to my mind. I consider that it is inappropriate at the moment to expound them in the press, that is, in *Pravda*, because in fact it would mean entering the ranks of the school's enemies and opponents, whereas in essence I want to be included in the list of its friends. I consider it my party duty to inform the school organisers of my doubts. I am writing to you as one of the initiators of the idea.

---

1.   This article first appeared in *Critique*, no 13, 1981.

On Party Education

The Content and Object of the School[2]

Having read the programme of the school, first of all I asked myself these questions. Which are the methodological tasks of the school? What does it intend to give its worker-pupils: a certain amount of factual and theoretical knowledge, or method? This is the basic and central question, which determines the significance and fate of the school. The programme, however, produces a poor impression on me, as if its authors themselves did not have the necessary clarity in answering this question.

It would have been a fatal mistake to set a target of providing the pupils with the maximum amount of socialist knowledge. What kind of special knowledge can be acquired or taught in the course of three to four months? The most dangerous thing in such cases is to take part in the formation of *self-satisfied semi-literates*. A repulsive figure — whether worker or intellectual.

The school must, on the contrary, compel each of its pupils to understand that he knows nothing, and the achievement of this difficult result is possible only by arming them with the method of acquiring knowledge. The intellectuals acquire elementary methodological skills in secondary school. Whatever it may be, it disciplines the mind. And in the framework of the party, this gives the intellectual enormous advantages over the worker. The latter, separated from the masses, feels naked and helpless in a chaos of facts. Why? He feels drowned because *he is lacking a method*.

The school must concentrate all its efforts on this particular problem. Give the worker a method, and with it he will find knowledge on a bookshelf.

Of course, method as method cannot be taught in the abstract. It has to be demonstrated in practice, that is, *in its scientific application*. In what field? The answer is self-evident. In that case where it is already scientifically applied, that is, in political economy. Of course, the workers are interested in the question of literature, art and ethics. What do we have in these fields? Attempts, guesses, hints, comments, satirical pieces, 'discussion', polemical collections. This is all necessary, and many successful ideas and comparisons are spread all over. Where, however, is there Marxist ethics or aesthetics? Which would be developed *for teaching at the school*? I am not aware of them, and no one is, because it does not exist, not *yet*. In this case, in the course of things, we are doomed to dilettantism. The worker can hear essays on philosophical, literary and ethical themes outside the school, in Paris, Geneva and even in Moscow. If he has the Marxist method, these essays will give him something; they will give him a couple of new associations, and will lead

2. Literally 'the scientific-pedagogical tasks of the school'. The translation is free rather than literal because of the Stalinist connotations that the words used by Trotsky have since acquired.

him to read a new book. To transfer the 'essays' to the school would compromise the idea of the school itself. Where we have timid (or daring) *attempts* at application of the method, disjointed and unproven attempts, then the person who still has not acquired the method will learn nothing; to a chaos of facts will be added only a chaos of comments and words — and that is all. So, I would put political economy, or more exactly *Capital*, at the head of the whole programme. I would not popularise it, because it is impossible, while keeping its scientific character, for anyone to express himself more popularly, that is, more precisely or lucidly, than Marx. I would read *Capital* aloud to the workers, and explain it to them. I would omit from Volume I only the historical and narrative chapters which the worker could read independently. In Volumes 2 and 3, I would read aloud only those chapters most essential for the understanding of the whole. *Capital* is not simply 'a course of political economy', but a *philosophy* of the history of capitalist society — that is why it cannot be *one* of the subjects of teaching, equal in rank to the others.

The whole programme is planned for 120 lectures: three to four months. It works out at one lecture per day. But one could give four or five lectures per day. Therefore I do not understand what is meant by 'a lecture' in the programme. I take this word simply as a unit of calculation. Out of 120 lectures there are 12 lectures allocated for political economy, 19 lectures for history of the RSDLP, 20 lectures for the history of Russia, 10 lectures for 'realistic' paintings, and eight lectures for artistic paintings. When it is possible to give several lectures at the end of the course, outside the programme, on philosophy or aesthetics, the political economy has to be allocated not less than 40 lectures out of 120, and even that might not be enough, in my opinion.

History of Russia

My remarks on 'the philosophy subjects' have largely covered it. The materialist history of Russia has not only not yet been written, but even the source material has still to be collected. There is here a wide field for personal decision. It would be sufficient for a lecturer to point out the main turning points, and indicate the sources and texts. I do not know whether it is necessary to have a whole 20 lectures out of a course of 120 for this purpose.

I. The History of the Workers' Movement in the West, and the History of Russian Social Democracy in Particular

This material is specifically for the education of the party activists. Here, every lecture is a direct stimulus to action. At the same time, here lies a great danger. Of course, if we have our own Kautsky, and he undertook to give this course, then we would have no cause for concern. But what if this course were given in the spirit of the *History* of Comrade Lyadov? I have great respect for Comrade Lyadov as an active and tireless party worker. (However, I seldom agreed with the direction of his activity.) But I do not consider his *History* to be a suitable textbook for workers in any respect. In it, the history of the polemics on party organisation did not leave any place at all for the history of political self-determination of the working class. And this latter process is, whichever way you look at it, more important than the first. I have no comment to make about other remaining subjects on the second part of the programme.

II. The Party-Political Physiognomy of the School

The party needs educated workers, and the school wants to provide them for the party. However, this poses the problem in a very abstract way. One cannot create leaders by a laboratory method. By taking individual workers, even by means of elections, and after teaching them Marxism abroad, sending them back to the masses, the idea of the school in this context returns the party to the epoch of abstract small-circle propaganda.

I am sure you don't want this. The school must be linked with the politics of the party, in other words, it must be one of the means for building the party. It is from this point of view that I look at the first section of the programme, 'The Methods of Party Organisation'. What line does the school intend on intra-party politics? But you don't intend to 'exclude politics from the school'. Does the school intend to make the factional split permanent? Maybe to spell out its details? Or, on the other hand, it does intend to put at the disposal of the new party which is now being formed on a purely working class basis, the intellectual stock of our old disintegrating organisation? An entirely factional (I readily concede, an unavoidable) way of setting up the school, that is, from an entire section of Bolsheviks, gives rise to suspicion in the minds of many. It would be a pity if the worker-graduates of the school, after returning, should be confronted immediately with this wall of blind mistrust on the part of Mensheviks and Bolsheviks, and especially if they with their future policy should strengthen this wall. Then the school will turn out to be not an element in the formation of a new party, but only a ferment of disintegration of the old one. One cannot change the way the school has been organised. At the moment, everything depends on those ideas of party politics which will find their clearest expression in the implementation of the first and fourth sections of the programme. On this question, I personally cannot say more than the editorial of *Pravda*, no 4, 'Our Party and Its Tasks'. The first section (propaganda, agitation, writing, etc) must be conducted as concretely and practically as possible. The art of oral and written composition (here one must not neglect even the rules of spelling). Pupils must compose experimental speeches, summaries and proclamations. In view of the importance of training workers as newspaper correspondents and political publicists, it would therefore be extremely useful if the whole school were to compose one or two numbers of a workers' newspaper, which could be immediately printed (for teaching printing techniques), and taken into Russia. It is possible, however, that you have all this in mind, so that these practical suggestions are superfluous.

III. Principles of Everyday Living

Twelve Moscow proletarians will arrive at an Italian island — without the language, and without links with the outside world. This situation is similar in some of its features to the conditions of political exile. In this artificial situation, comrades of different intellectual levels and different ways of life are drawn together. The proletariat is wonderful; an individual proletarian, in everyday conditions, can turn out to be awkward. Sometimes the most difficult situation can develop out of this. Let the school be spared these banal complications.

Esteemed comrade, my objections and reservations may seem incorrect or exaggerated to you, as well as to the other organisers of the school. So much the better for the cause. In my letter, I here deliberately painted a blacker picture, in order to emphasise those aspects of the matter, which might not be so clear to its organisers, as they are to a person standing on the side. On the side — but only partly on the side. Together with my closest friends in *Pravda*, we consider the organisation of the school as our very own business. If the school requires my personal assistance — Comrades Bogdanov and Mikhail spoke to me about it — I will do everything I can and am capable of.

Comrade Basok will give every possible assistance in the transportation of the future pupils across the border. *Pravda* will open its pages for the propaganda of the school's ideas and for the discussions on this subject.
I wish you success, and shake your hand warmly.
Your devoted friend
Trotsky

Thank you very much for your warm words about *Pravda*. I have not lost hope that a small spark from your forge will end up — through good luck — on the pages of *Pravda*.
N Trotsky

Address: Herr Leo Bronstein, XIX Friedlgass 40, Wien

PS: I would be very happy if this letter was made available to your closest friends in the organisation of the school.

Index

Absolute surplus — 78, 85
Absolutism — 6, 34
Abstract labour — 49, 71, 83, 97, 106
Accumulation — 5, 7, 35, 45-47, 50, 52-54, 59, 80, 90-91, 93-95, 205, 217, 259, 297, 304, 312, 345
Aesthetics — 223, 372-373
Agriculture — 31, 35-37, 58-59, 254-260, 263, 265-267, 294, 326, 334
Aizenshtadt — 344, 363
Althusser, Louis — 319
Anarchists — 16, 65, 230, 273, 276
Ancient mode of production — 32
Anderson, Perry — 220, 289-299, 302-304, 308-309
Antonov-Ovseenko, Vladimir — 13, 235
Art — 151, 222, 224-229, 231, 372, 374
Asiatic despotism — 6
Autocracy — 26, 33, 37, 39, 58, 118-119, 121, 129-131, 149, 152
Axelrod, Pavel — 124, 149

Bahro, Rudolph — 55, 60
Baldwin, Stanley — 350-351, 363
Barbarism — 66, 205, 217
Barnes, J — 343, 345
Barracks discipline — 154
Bauer, Otto — 179, 183
Bernal, Martin — 223
Bettelheim, Charles — 52
Blok, Alexander — 225, 227
Bogdanov, Alexander — 49, 106-107, 123, 134, 156, 375
Bogdanov (Menshevik) —187
Bolsheviks, Bolshevism, Bolshevik party — 7-8, 13-15, 27-30, 33-34, 38-39, 41, 44, 46, 67, 95, 111-112, 115, 123, 126-127, 132-139, 141-145, 147, 149, 156-158, 160-161, 163, 166-167, 187-189, 191, 196-199, 207, 220, 241, 253, 266, 274-278, 281, 284-286, 294, 308, 310, 313-315, 331, 333-338, 370, 374
See also Communist Party (Soviet), Russian Social Democratic Labour Party
Bourgeois ideology — 62, 118
Bourgeoisie — 6-7, 10, 12, 17, 25, 27, 29-30, 38-39, 42-43, 51, 61-62, 68-70, 79-80, 84, 90-91, 98, 100, 103-105, 127-132, 134, 140, 152, 157-158, 178, 181, 185, 189-190, 198-199, 205-206, 209, 211-213, 215, 279, 299-302, 331, 348-353, 356, 366, 369-370
Breton, André — 221, 228-229, 336
Briand, Aristide — 366, 369
Britain — 34, 90, 94, 206, 302, 306, 308, 330, 337, 343, 346-347, 349-354, 358-359, 361-366, 368
Broué, Pierre — 20, 123, 148, 156, 270, 283, 317, 333-338
Brzezinski, Zbigniew — 302
Bubnov, Andrei — 235
Bukharin, Nikolai — 8, 16, 28, 32, 45-50, 52, 55, 57, 61, 67, 88-89, 99, 207, 241, 249, 254-257, 259-261, 263-267, 311, 313, 315
Bukshpan — 355-356, 364
Bulletin of the Opposition — 266, 273, 277, 282-283, 309
Bureaucracy — 30, 35, 45, 48, 51, 54, 56, 61-63, 66, 68-77, 81, 84, 160, 214, 242, 271, 276, 291, 293, 296, 300, 307-311, 316, 320, 327, 335, 338
Bureaucratic elite — 67-68, 70
Bureaucratic stratum — 308
Burnham, James — 16, 73, 87, 102, 312

Index

Capitalism — 2, 4, 6-8, 10, 12, 15, 19, 24-29, 31-38, 40-42, 47, 50-52, 55, 57-62, 65-67, 69, 71, 77-79, 81-83, 85, 87-99, 101-105, 107, 129-130, 139, 154, 168-172, 177, 180, 182, 190, 193, 201-202, 204-205, 207-210, 212-215, 217, 232, 254, 261, 290-293, 295-302, 307, 309, 312-316, 324-328, 330, 341-350, 355, 357, 359-360, 364, 370

Capitalist decline — 7, 26, 38, 93, 207-208, 212

Capri school — 371

Carlo, Antonio — 19, 113, 115, 117, 123, 133, 138, 292, 309

Carmichael, Joel — 317

Carr, EH — 52, 197-198, 235-237, 240, 243, 247-248, 261, 263-264, 294

Céline, Louis-Ferdinand — 228

Centralisation — 13, 82, 177-178, 180, 183

Centralism — 118, 120-121, 125, 150-151, 154-155, 177, 180, 183

Centrism, centrist — 16, 18, 46, 57, 66-67, 73, 80, 85, 204, 275, 277, 281

Chiang Kai-Shek — 18, 51

China — 5, 18, 33, 43, 51, 249, 304, 365

Chinese revolution — 160, 336

Ciliga, Ante — 74, 276-277

Civil war — 12, 14-15, 140, 166, 168, 197, 224, 227, 263, 273, 276-277, 280, 325

Class struggle — 7, 91, 113-114, 117-118, 121, 127, 133, 136-137, 168, 175, 198, 202, 205, 216, 265, 272, 275, 315

Claudín, Fernando — 40-41, 314

Clemenceau, Georges — 367

Cliff, Tony — 9, 16, 112, 115, 133, 136, 224, 312, 318

Cohen, Stephen — 46, 313

Cold War — 43, 96, 202, 289, 294, 298-299, 304, 334

Collectivisation — 12, 60, 81, 253, 257, 264-266, 294, 313

Combined development — 6, 100, 130

Communist International — 5, 16, 25, 28-29, 40, 47, 60, 62, 66, 88, 90-93, 96, 101-102, 202, 204-205, 207, 209-215, 222, 242, 274-276, 282, 301, 314, 319, 334, 336, 341, 345, 348, 359, 365, 369

Communism, communist — 8, 16, 25, 29, 40-41, 43, 47-49, 51, 60-61, 65-66, 70, 81, 90-93, 96, 101-103, 143-144, 202, 204-207, 209, 211-212, 226-227, 235, 239, 266, 272, 276, 282, 301-302, 306-307, 310, 314, 318, 321, 323, 337, 341, 345, 347-349, 353-354,

Communist Party (Soviet) — 48, 65, 70, 143-144, 226, 235, 276
   See also Bolshevik party, Russian Social Democratic Labour Party

Competition — 49, 59-60, 84, 229, 343, 361, 369

Concentration of capital — 345

Conciliationism — 112, 133, 137-140, 142, 145, 191

Conservative, conservatism — 27, 350, 352, 363

Contradiction — 36, 45-47, 52, 74, 76, 82-83, 88-89, 106, 154, 167, 169, 173, 196-197, 211, 213, 215, 223, 256-257, 266, 290, 296, 298, 326-328, 332, 347, 364

Crisis — 7, 19, 25, 40, 42, 46, 65, 92, 95-98, 101, 104, 107, 157, 202, 204, 207-208, 211, 213, 218, 304, 330, 350, 355-356, 359, 362, 366, 368

Critique — 9-10, 49-50, 52, 55, 71, 147, 187, 235, 253, 289, 293, 303, 305, 317, 329, 333, 371

Cuba — 100, 301, 302

Cultural revolution — 5, 159

Cultural theory — 219, 225, 230

Curve of capitalist development — 87, 93, 208, 217, 341

Cycle — 90, 92, 207-208, 341, 356-360

Dan, Theodore — 33, 39, 126

Daniels, Robert — 3, 139, 236, 238, 248

Dante, Alighieri — 231

Dawes Plan — 344-345, 353, 362, 368

Day, Richard — 19, 45, 57, 81, 88, 92-93, 207

Degeneration — 15, 46, 51, 70, 88, 104, 120, 160, 231, 239, 261, 280, 292, 310

Democracy, democratic — 4-5, 8, 13-18, 24-25, 28, 33, 38-39, 43-44, 51, 53, 55-56, 61-62, 71, 74, 79, 83-84, 98, 100-101, 103, 106-107, 116, 118-121, 124-126, 129, 133-138, 141-142, 149, 156-157, 159, 165-166, 168-169, 173-174, 176, 178-179, 181-184, 187-191, 195-199, 202, 211-214, 216, 236-239, 242-

245, 247, 249-250, 266, 272, 286, 293, 295, 301-302, 306, 314, 322-323, 326, 332, 337, 346, 350, 364
Democratic centralist, democratic centralism — 16, 47, 235
Democratic Centralists — 15-16, 248, 262
Democratic dictatorship of the proletariat and peasantry — 51, 55, 134, 138, 156-157, 191, 196, 198
Depression — 1, 15, 38, 40, 94, 96-97, 107, 208, 265, 272, 275, 359
Deutscher, Isaac — 2, 17, 33, 45-46, 52-54, 57, 59, 69, 111, 126-127, 132, 136, 140-141, 143, 147, 149, 159, 165-166, 171, 222, 236, 248, 294, 303, 309-310, 313, 317, 334-338
Developed countries — 104
Dialectic, dialectical — 49, 67, 69, 74, 87-89, 97, 99, 107, 189-190, 192-195, 198-200, 202, 223, 227, 256, 295, 341
Djilas, Milovan — 301, 310
Dual power — 56, 63
Duma — 126-128, 133-136, 155
Durnovo — 133
Dunayevskaya, Raya — 312
Dzerzhinsky, Felix — 249, 260

Eastern Europe — 34-35, 214, 291, 293, 297, 301, 316, 337
Eastman, Max — 237, 247-248, 325, 336
Economism — 148, 150-151
Elite — 30, 63, 66-68, 70, 72-73, 77, 81, 152, 276, 293, 297, 299-301, 304, 316
Empiricists — 30
Epoch — 2, 7, 10-12, 17, 19, 46, 55, 61, 63, 66, 68-69, 76, 78-80, 87, 93-94, 97-98, 101-102, 124, 159, 168, 171, 177, 182-183, 201-204, 207-209, 210-211, 213, 215-216, 218, 221, 227, 253, 276-277, 279, 336, 346, 352, 356, 358-359, 374
Equilibrium —8, 19, 89-90, 92, 94-96, 169, 204-209, 217, 296, 299, 358
Ethiopia — 75, 100
Eurocommunism, Eurocommunists — 307, 314, 330
Europe, European — 5-6, 8, 11, 19, 25, 28-29, 34-35, 39, 41, 80, 91, 99, 129-133, 138-140, 160, 163, 165-185, 190, 200, 205, 209-211, 214-215, 219-220, 248, 269-270, 272, 275, 278, 282, 290-291, 293, 295, 297, 299, 301-302, 304, 316, 330, 332, 336-337, 341, 343-350, 353-364, 366-370

Falkner — 355, 362, 367-368
Falling rate of profit — 91, 96
Fascism — 1, 14, 19, 40, 66-67, 76, 78, 96, 103-105, 107, 160, 202, 212, 230, 273, 290, 304, 318, 320, 323
Fetishism — 49, 202
Feudal, feudalism — 10, 32, 37, 72, 188, 193, 196, 222, 295
Finance capital — 41-42, 88, 91, 93, 99-100, 205-206
First World War — 7, 11, 28, 38, 133, 137, 145, 165, 189, 207, 209, 218, 254, 272, 314
Forces of production — 31, 34, 40-41, 81, 99, 130, 267, 321, 327, 343
Form — 2, 11, 14, 24-25, 28-31, 34, 36-37, 54-56, 62-63, 68-69, 71-76, 78, 80, 83-84, 88, 90-91, 100, 102, 105-107, 111, 113, 115-116, 118-120, 123-126, 128-129, 131, 134-136, 142, 144, 150-151, 153, 156, 168-169, 171, 173-175, 177, 181, 183-184, 203, 205, 212, 216-217, 220, 225, 227, 229, 239, 242, 245, 251, 253, 257-258, 263-264, 266, 272, 276, 283, 293, 296, 303-306, 309, 312, 317, 326, 338, 346, 354, 357, 363, 365
Formalism — 115, 227, 311, 320
France — 34, 36, 79, 160, 172, 184, 205, 270, 275, 278, 302, 323-324, 330, 333, 337, 343, 346-347, 351, 353, 363-368
Franchise — 10-11, 14
Free trade — 181
French Revolution — 7, 275
Futurism — 227

Garaudy, Roger — 148, 192
Germany — 12-14, 25-27, 29, 60, 67, 76, 78-79, 103, 105, 118, 129, 166-169, 172-173, 175, 179-180, 184, 191, 193, 204, 212, 214, 239, 242, 248, 290, 299, 315, 320, 323, 333-336, 344, 346-347, 350-354, 358, 362-365, 368-369
Gogol, Nikolai — 220
Goldenberg — 187

Index

Gollancz, Victor — 322, 324
Goethe, Johann — 231-232
Goods famine — 255, 257, 261-264
Gorbachev, Mikhail — 333
Gorky, Maxim — 371
Gorter, Herman — 218
Gosplan — 47
Gramsci, Antonio — 12, 227, 319
Grossman, Henryk — 90
Guchkov, Alexander — 133

Hackett, Sir John — 299
Hallas, Duncan — 317-318
Halliday, Fred — 298
Hansen, Joseph — 322, 325
Hearse, Phil — 291
Heavy industry — 255, 259, 263-265, 358, 365
Hegel, GWF —19, 88, 187, 192-195, 200
Hegemony — 126, 128, 169, 275, 300-301, 347, 365
Herriot, Eduard — 366
Hilferding, Rudolf — 91, 96, 99, 358
Historical materialism — 193, 222-223, 319, 325
Hitler, Adolf — 12, 16, 66, 103, 105
Holland — 34
Hough, Jerry — 294
Hungarian Soviet — 204

Ibsen, Henrik — 220, 336
Immiserisation — 321
Imperialism — 7, 18-19, 42, 75, 88, 91, 94, 96, 98-99, 139, 157, 164, 166, 168, 174, 176-177, 180-183, 202, 206, 232, 302, 332, 343
Imperialist war — 139-140, 157, 166, 174, 176, 179, 182, 203, 205, 209, 217, 345, 358
Independent Social Democratic Party of Germany — 204, 358
India — 17, 42-43, 343, 365
Industry — 31, 37-38, 41-43, 53, 58-59, 79, 99, 102, 105, 107, 149, 169, 210, 254-259, 261-265, 320, 326, 346, 357-358, 363, 365, 368
Inflation — 76, 261, 327, 346, 348, 356, 366
Intellectuals — 91, 98, 119, 133, 160, 277, 307, 372
Internationalism — 27-28, 99, 138-140, 142, 144-145, 173, 181, 275, 314

Iskra — 126, 148-149, 151, 160

Jacobson, Julius — 303, 309
Japan — 15, 42-43, 79, 169, 337, 343, 365
Journal of Trotsky Studies — 3, 124, 136, 219, 342

Kamenev, Lev — 135, 187, 198-199, 236, 238, 240, 244, 249, 261-262
Karatayev — 222
Kautsky, Karl — 4, 25, 116, 189, 190-194, 319, 346, 374
Khrushchev, Nikita — 266, 335
Kitchen — 359
Kondratiev, Nikolai — 90, 92-93, 95, 341-342, 355, 359-364
Korea — 42, 43
Kosior, V — 235
Krasin, Leonid — 127, 156
Kulaks — 60, 62, 253-257, 260-263, 266
Kuzovkov, D — 52

Labour — 10, 15, 25-26, 31, 34-36, 43, 49-50, 57-58, 71-72, 76, 78, 81, 83, 85, 91-92, 97, 100, 104-107, 129, 141, 154, 182, 206, 210, 220, 254, 257, 259, 261, 265, 276, 295-296, 302, 313, 316, 320, 326-327, 332, 338
Labour Party — 39, 111, 135, 149, 337, 350-352
Lane, David — 294
Law of planning — 45, 48, 53-54
Law of value — 40, 45, 48-49, 51, 53, 78-79, 83, 102, 107, 325, 327
Left Communists — 28
Left Opposition — 19, 45-47, 50, 53, 60, 62, 67, 69-70, 77, 87-88, 101, 159, 235-236, 241-242, 253, 255, 259, 263, 269, 270-273, 278, 280, 283, 286, 294, 311, 313, 319, 322, 335-336
Lenin, Vladimir Illich —
  As politician — 12, 29
  Culture — 5
  Differences with Trotsky on other socialists — 133-142
  Differences with Trotsky on the party — 113-128, 147-161
  Differences with Trotsky on permanent revolution — 128-132
  Internationalism — 24, 27-28, 34, 43
  In 1905 — 122-128, 155-157, 189-191

In 1917 — 131, 142-144, 158, 195-200
Party — 14, 111-145
Philosophy — 187-200
Political economy — 88
Revolutionary strategy — 25, 29, 187-200
April Theses, The — 19, 141, 144, 157-158, 188, 195, 197, 199-200
Development of Capitalism in Russia, The — 88
Imperialism: The Highest Stage of Capitalism — 139
Letters From Afar — 140, 196
Right of Nations to Self-Determination, The — 164
State and Revolution — 142, 158, 160
Two Tactics of Social Democracy — 125, 131
What Is To Be Done? — 106, 111, 114, 116-119, 121, 126, 144-145, 148-150, 155, 161, 163
Lieber, Mark — 325
Liebman, Marcel — 123-124, 136, 138, 141, 143-144, 155-156
Literary criticism — 219-223
Literary theory — 1, 231
Long waves — 93, 359-360, 363
Luxemburg, Rosa — 7, 12, 25, 28, 99, 115, 147, 149-151, 154, 156, 160-161, 179, 188, 212, 222, 271

MacDonald, Dwight — 281-282
MacDonald, Ramsay — 351-352
Machinery — 37, 41, 50, 83, 181, 253, 258
Maksimovsky, V — 235
Managers — 48, 50-51, 84, 356
Mandel, Ernest — 9, 52, 92-93, 95-96, 163, 297, 303, 307, 317-318
Maoism — 65, 306
Market — 6-7, 15, 33, 35-36, 41-43, 47-54, 59, 61, 67, 69-70, 74, 76, 78, 80-85, 88, 91, 103, 129, 180-181, 209-210, 254-255, 257-259, 261-262, 265-266, 291, 293-295, 298-303, 315-316, 338, 344-346, 349, 351-353, 355-357, 359, 364, 369
Martov, Yuli — 115, 126-127, 149, 165
Marx, Karl — 4, 8, 15, 18, 20, 26, 30-34, 39-40, 50, 58, 67, 81-82, 89, 91, 95-99, 104, 117, 170, 179, 189, 192-195, 208, 216, 222-223, 232, 267, 302, 320-321, 325, 341, 346, 356-360, 371, 373
Capital — 34, 43, 49, 91, 97, 104, 106, 209, 341, 346, 358, 364, 371, 373
Communist Manifesto — 8, 321
Contribution to the Critique of Political Economy — 208
Critique of the Gotha Programme — 170
Grundrisse — 34
Holy Family, The — 189
Marxism, Marxists — 2-4, 7-9, 12-14, 18-20, 23, 25-26, 30, 34, 38, 41, 49-50, 58-59, 65, 67, 69, 71, 73-74, 77, 81-82, 87-90, 94-95, 97-98, 100, 106, 113, 117, 119, 135, 150, 153, 164, 175, 178, 182-183, 187-195, 197-198, 202, 209, 214-215, 218-225, 227, 229-231, 256, 270-271, 275, 277, 279-280, 283, 285, 289-297, 303, 306, 309-310, 312, 314-315, 318-321, 323, 329-332, 337-338, 341-342, 356, 358, 372, 374
Marxist ethics — 372
Marxist history — 30
Marxist method — 372
Mattick, Paul — 90
Mavrakis, Kostas — 306, 317
Mayakovsky, Vladimir — 225
Mehring, Franz — 222
Mensheviks, Menshevism — 16, 24-25, 33-34, 38-41, 112, 115, 126-128, 133-137, 139-140, 142-143, 145, 149, 187-189, 191, 196, 198, 207, 237, 241, 294, 314, 331, 374
Merchants — 32, 34, 42, 58, 59, 255
Methodology — 319, 324, 357
Mexico — 270-271, 278, 282-284, 322-323
Middle peasants — 254, 256, 257
Millerand, Alexandre — 367
Mode of production — 9-10, 23, 30-32, 36, 41, 59, 60-61, 67-68, 73, 75, 85, 102, 266-267, 299
Molyneux, John — 317-328

Narodniks — 256-257
National socialism — 67, 80, 212, 290, 315
Nationalised property — 17, 66, 71, 73, 79, 308
Nationalism, nationalists — 35, 183, 290, 299, 302, 314
NATO — 301, 304

New Deal — 104, 215-216
New Economic Policy — 29, 32, 51-52, 58-59, 62, 67, 70, 80, 82, 84, 103, 238-239, 242-244, 247, 254, 294, 313, 327, 358
New Left Review — 93, 289, 294, 298, 303, 308
Novack, George — 222, 324
Nove, Alec — 81, 253, 263, 294, 313, 315, 342

October Revolution — 8, 15, 28, 37, 39, 43, 63, 72-73, 76, 78-79, 90, 93, 97, 101, 111, 139, 144, 147, 193, 203, 205, 211, 215, 227, 333, 338
Opportunism — 165, 172, 301, 350-352
Organicism — 103
Orthodox Trotskyism — 308
Overthrow of capitalism — 10, 25-26, 33, 154

Painlevé, Paul — 366
Pannekoek, Anton — 179, 211-212, 218
Partisan Review — 229, 277, 282
Party — 13, 39, 41, 47-48, 51-53, 59, 65, 70, 90, 103, 111-145, 147-162, 164-165, 172, 204, 212, 214, 226, 235, 237-238, 241, 243, 245, 248-250, 253, 266, 270, 272, 276-277, 306, 337, 346, 350-352, 358, 366-367, 371, 374
Party education — 18, 371-375
Party organisation — 116, 119, 123-125, 237, 246, 250, 374
Parvus, Alexander (Helphand) — 4, 39
Pauperisation — 345
Peasants — 27, 29-31, 36-39, 42, 131-132, 141, 156-157, 165, 191, 195, 197, 199, 226, 241, 254-257, 262-263, 266, 313
Permanent revolution — 4, 6, 10-11, 17-18, 26, 39, 51, 55, 88, 100-101, 111-112, 128-132, 136-142, 145, 147, 156-157, 163, 165, 296, 306, 320, 323, 328-334
Philosophy — 19, 187-200, 319, 325, 373
Pilnyak, Boris — 225
Planning — 16-18, 45, 48-58, 61, 67, 69, 74, 76, 79-83, 102-103, 236, 242, 254, 267, 293, 297, 325-326, 338
Plekhanov, Georgi — 4, 30, 58, 187, 189, 191-194
Pokrovsky, M — 23-24, 28, 30, 32, 37, 49, 58
Poincaré, Raymond — 367
Pravda — 135-136, 142, 187-188, 196, 198, 224, 238-241, 243-245, 247, 249, 257, 260-261, 263, 323, 371, 374-375
Preobrazhensky, Evgeny — 18, 28, 45-56, 59, 63, 67, 76, 80, 83, 96, 101, 103, 235-238, 240-241, 243, 245, 250, 253, 259, 262, 313
Prices — 37, 255, 257-258, 261-265, 327
Primitive socialist accumulation — 46-47, 50, 52-54, 59, 80, 259
Privileges — 74, 356
Productive forces — 35, 40-41, 53, 74, 93, 98-99, 130, 175, 203-204, 207-209, 211, 216-218, 259-260, 266-267, 309, 343-345, 348-349, 356, 361-362, 370
Productivity — 31, 42, 53, 57, 60, 72, 78, 81, 175, 180, 182, 295-296, 326
Proletarianisation — 47, 156, 345
Proletariat — 4-7, 10-18, 24, 26, 28-30, 37-39, 42-44, 51, 53, 55, 57-58, 61, 66, 69-70, 72-73, 77-80, 82-83, 89-91, 94, 97-98, 101-106, 113-114, 116-117, 119, 121, 123-125, 128-132, 134, 138-142, 148-150, 152-154, 158-160, 165, 169-172, 174, 178, 181-185, 190-191, 193, 196-197, 199, 203-206, 209-211, 213-218, 231, 236, 239, 241, 246, 249, 256, 265, 272, 274-275, 279, 290-291, 296, 302, 308, 313-314, 331, 335, 338, 345-354, 366, 369-370, 374-375
Pyatakov, Yuri — 235, 247, 260, 262

Radek, Karl — 179, 240, 247
Rakovsky, Christian — 45, 48, 69-70
Reid, Jimmy — 302
Retail prices — 255, 257-258, 261-262
Revisionism — 114, 312
Revolutionary situation — 200, 213, 249, 342-343, 347, 349-350, 352-354
Rivera, Diego — 221, 230, 322, 336
Rizzi, Bruno — 16, 73-74, 160, 296
Roosevelt, Franklin — 216
Rosdolsky, Roman — 91
Rousset, David — 41
Russian Social Democratic Labour Party — 39, 111-112, 114-116, 118, 120, 122-124, 133-135, 139, 149, 151, 155, 161, 165, 373
Second Congress — 111, 114-115, 136, 149, 150
See also Bolshevik party, communist party

Rühle, Otto — 97, 218
Ruhr — 350, 352, 358
Russian Empire — 23-38, 41-42, 44
Russian mode of production — 23-44
Russian Revolution — 3, 6-7, 10-12, 23-24, 26-27, 66, 88, 131, 141, 150, 171, 188, 190, 196, 203, 206, 210, 217, 221, 223, 226, 230-231, 269, 281, 284, 306, 321, 323, 325, 337-338, 342
Rybakov, Anatoli — 30
Rykov, Alexei — 45, 245

Sapronov, Timofey — 235, 240-241, 246, 248
Scissors crisis — 65, 82, 235, 242, 255, 257-259, 265-266
Second enserfment — 31
Sedov, Lev — 269, 273, 275, 278-279
Sedova, Natalia — 279, 284-285, 324
Serebriakov, Leonid — 235
Serfs — 36
Serge, Victor — 19, 47, 102, 269-286, 292, 310
Shachtman, Max — 2, 9, 16, 73-74, 87, 102, 296, 303, 311-312
Shakespeare, William — 231
Shaw, George Bernard — 299
Short waves — 360, 363
Sinclair, Louis — 20
Smirnov, Ivan — 235
Smirnov, Vladimir — 46, 47, 52, 248, 262
Smychka — 253, 265
Social democracy, social democrat, social democratic — 15, 25, 38-39, 49, 68, 79, 82, 98, 101, 107, 114, 116-119, 121, 123-124, 133-134, 138, 141, 148-149, 154-157, 160, 165, 167, 172-173, 177-179, 182-184, 188-189, 191, 202, 207, 211-217, 230, 239, 272, 279, 301, 312, 322-323, 337, 350
Social Democratic Party of Germany — 13, 103, 118, 212, 346
Social patriotism — 138, 140, 143, 173
Socialism — 4-5, 8, 10, 12, 14-15, 17-18, 20, 24, 26, 29, 33-34, 39, 41, 46-47, 49, 50-53, 55, 59, 60-61, 67, 69, 74, 77-84, 97-98, 101-104, 106-107, 114, 119, 131, 141, 165, 168-170, 172-175, 179-180, 182-183, 185, 188, 190-191, 193, 195-199, 202, 204, 210-211, 214, 217, 221, 223, 231, 242, 254, 256-257, 259-261, 265, 273, 285-286, 290, 292-294, 296, 301-303, 305, 307, 312, 314-316, 318, 326, 336, 342-343, 346, 348, 370
Socialism in one country — 8, 14, 17, 24, 26, 33, 39, 41, 46, 51-53, 84, 106, 170-175, 183, 242, 256, 260, 265, 296-297, 303, 305, 307, 314, 336
Socialist construction — 181-182, 239, 260
Socialist knowledge — 372
South Korea — 42, 43
Souvarine, Boris — 247-248, 276, 280
Soviet achievements — 290
Soviet Union — 1, 3, 8-9, 11, 13-14, 16-17, 19-20, 25, 27-30, 32, 36, 41, 45-48, 50, 57, 61, 63, 65-66, 68-80, 82-85, 87, 100-102, 106, 155-160, 188, 197-198, 200, 204, 210, 214, 221, 224, 226-227, 230-231, 250, 253, 258, 264, 269, 271, 273, 278, 286, 289-309, 311-312, 314-316, 323-327, 329, 333-338, 342, 355, 369
Spain — 160, 270, 272, 275-276, 290, 302, 324, 330, 335
Spektator — 355, 358
Spontaneity — 84, 116, 118, 123, 142-143
Stabilisation — 90, 216, 327, 343, 345-350, 353-354
Stagnation — 94, 114, 208, 294, 309, 316, 348, 359-360
Stalin, Joseph Vissarionovich — 1-2, 8-9, 12-19, 27, 34, 43, 45, 47, 50-52, 55, 57, 59, 62, 67, 69-70, 72-73, 77, 80, 103, 112, 158, 161, 167, 221-222, 231, 236, 238, 240-241, 244, 247, 249, 253-254, 258-259, 263-264, 266-267, 269-270, 274, 279, 281, 290, 294, 296-297, 301, 303, 307, 309-315, 319, 322, 332-337, 342
Stalinism, Stalinist — 2, 9, 11-12, 14-18, 24, 27, 30, 34, 41, 47, 55, 66-67, 72-73, 76-80, 82, 84-85, 96, 98, 101, 103, 106-107, 160, 202, 211, 214, 221, 230, 272, 276, 281-282, 289-293, 295-297, 299-300, 302-313, 315-317, 322-325, 330-331, 335-337, 372
Stalinist epoch — 11
Stankevich — 187
State — 1, 5-6, 8-10, 16-17, 25-27, 29, 31, 34-37, 39-40, 43, 47-48, 50-54, 56-57, 59, 61-62, 65, 68-69, 73-74, 76, 79, 81, 84-85, 89-92, 94-95,

Index

98-99, 101, 103-104, 113, 122, 129-130, 133, 144, 158, 168, 169, 172-179, 182-184, 192, 197, 204, 207, 212-214, 216, 218, 220-221, 223, 227, 237, 246-248, 250, 257, 260-261, 263, 284, 293, 295-297, 303-305, 307, 309, 311-318, 325, 327-328, 331, 333, 338, 347-349, 352, 355-356, 358-359, 363, 367, 370

State capitalism, state capitalist — 16, 65, 261, 303, 318, 328
Steele, Jonathan — 300
Stolypin, Peter — 36-37, 133, 135
Stolypin reforms — 36
Substitutionism — 119, 121, 153, 158, 164, 313
Suffrage — 133
Sukhanov, Nikolai — 188
Surplus product — 9, 30-32, 35-38, 40, 42, 72-73, 75-76, 78, 80, 84-85, 93, 254-255
Surplus value — 30, 42, 93
Surrealists — 229
Suslov, Mikhail — 301

Taiwan — 42-43
Taylorism — 19, 105-106
Terms of trade — 255, 265
Third International — see Communist International
Third World — 11, 18, 43, 100, 230, 291, 299-304
Thompson, Edward — 304, 308
Ticktin, Hillel — 201, 216, 293, 303, 342
Tolstoy, Lev — 220, 222-223
Tomsky, Mikhail — 45
Trade unions, trade unionism — 58, 90, 113, 116, 151, 159, 206, 241, 330, 350-352, 366-367
Transition period — 12, 41, 47-48, 50, 52, 54, 63, 67, 85, 102-103, 106, 132, 204
Transitional epoch — 10, 19, 46, 55, 61, 63, 68-69, 87, 94, 97, 101-102, 201-203, 207, 210-211, 218
Trotsky, Leon Davidovich —
    Abilities — 1, 12
    Analysis of the Soviet Union — 1, 3, 9, 15-18, 45-63, 65-85, 160, 253-267, 289-316, 323-328, 335
    As politician — 12-16
    Analysis of Tsarism — 23-44
    Analysis of capitalism — 7, 87-107, 201-218
    Capitalist trends — 343, 351, 353-367
    Character — 1, 336-337
    Communist party tactics — 347-350
    Culture — 5, 219-232
    Differences with Lenin on the national question — 163-185
    Differences with Lenin on other socialists — 133-142
    Differences with Lenin on the party — 113-128, 147-161
    Differences with Lenin on permanent revolution — 128-132, 163-185
    Fascism — 103-105, 320
    In 1905 — 122-128, 155-157
    In 1917 — 142-144
    Influence — 2, 337-338
    Inter-imperialist rivalries — 343-346, 353-354, 358, 360-370
    National question — 163-185
    Party education — 371-374
    Party structure and democracy — 8, 13, 111-145, 147-161, 235-251, 318, 331
    Permanent revolution — 4-6, 10, 18, 39, 55, 128-130, 320, 330, 334
    Planning and market — 45-63, 66-67, 76, 80-84
    Relations with Victor Serge — 269-286
    Rise of the Soviet bureaucracy and Stalinism — 45-63, 66-69, 72-73, 77, 80-81, 84, 228-231, 235-251, 253-267, 321-323, 332, 335
    Second International Marxism — 319-320
    Soviet-Western relations — 355, 369
    Transitional epoch — 10, 63, 66-69, 78-80, 85, 87, 101-103, 201-218
    Working class consciousness — 201-218
    Class and Art — 226
    Diary in Exile — 324
    Europe vs America — 99
    Germany: The Key to the International Situation — 212
    History of the Russian Revolution — 3, 12, 88, 141, 171, 196, 321, 323, 325
    In Defence of Marxism — 71, 74, 77, 81, 87, 100, 214-215, 296
    In Defence of the Party — 136-137
    Literature and Revolution — 219, 221, 224-

225, 227-228, 230-232
Living Thoughts of Karl Marx, The — 89, 91, 97, 99, 104, 321
My Life — 127, 143, 320-321, 323
New Course, The — 62, 239, 241, 247
1905 — 24, 31-32, 37, 58, 91, 122, 128,
On Lenin — 28
Our Political Tasks — 28, 115, 117-118, 147, 150-152, 154-155, 164, 318
Our Revolution — 4, 165, 188
Permanent Revolution — 35, 199, 329
Platform of the Opposition — 70, 101, 159
Problems of Everyday Life — 92, 106-107, 221-222, 320, 360
Report of the Siberian Delegation — 115, 150, 152
Results and Prospects — 4, 35, 128, 130, 191, 320, 323, 329
Revolution Betrayed, The — 65, 68, 72-73, 76-77, 80, 83, 101, 224, 230, 292, 296-297, 308-309, 314
Stalin — 59, 72, 80, 84
Stalin School of Falsification, The — 62
Terrorism and Communism — 159
Their Morals and Ours — 270, 279-281, 283-284
Third International After Lenin, The — 62, 215
To the Social Democrats — 135
Towards a Free Revolutionary Art — 229
Towards Socialism or Capitalism — 60
Transitional Programme, The — 60, 62, 202-203, 218
War and the International — 171
What Next? — 212
What Next? Vital Questions for the German Proletariat — 212, 214
Young Lenin, The — 323, 325
'Alarm Signal' — 43, 53, 323
'Another Refutation by Victor Serge' — 283
'Bonapartism, Fascism and War' — 78
'Bonapartist Philosophy of the State, The' — 78
'C'est la Marche des Événements' — 46
'Curve of Capitalist Development, The' — 92

'Culture and Socialism' — 107
'Defence of the Soviet Republic, The' — 63
'Degeneration of Theory and the Theory of Degeneration, The' — 54, 68, 74, 76
'Dialectics and the Immutability of the Syllogism' — 87
'Does the Soviet Government Still Follow the Principles Adopted 20 Years Ago?' — 55
'En Route: Thoughts on the Progress of the Proletarian Revolution' — 205
'Fragments on the USSR' — 75
'Groupings in the Communist Opposition' — 61
'Hue and Cry Over Kronstadt' — 276
'Intellectual Ex-Radicals and World Reaction' — 277
'Leninism and Workers' Clubs' — 106
'Manifesto of the Communist International to the Workers of the World' — 91-93
'Moralists and Sycophants Against Marxism, The' — 270, 280-281
'New Revolutionary Upsurge and the Tasks of the Fourth International, The' — 272
'Ninety Years of the *Communist Manifesto*' — 321
'Not a Workers' and Not a Bourgeois State?' — 69-70, 309
'Notes on Economic Questions' — 53, 67
'On Tolstoy's Death' — 223
'Once Again on the "Crisis of Marxism"' — 321
'Petit-Bourgeois Democrats and Moralisers' — 278
'Philosophical Tendencies of Bureaucratism, The' — 87
'Planned Economy in the USSR, Success or Failure?' — 74
'Preface to *La Révolution Defigurée*' — 53, 71
'Problems of the Development of the USSR' — 69
'Report on the Fifth Anniversary of the October Revolution and the Fourth World Congress of the Communist In-

ternational' — 90, 93, 101
'Report on the World Economic Crisis and the New Tasks of the Communist International' — 25, 92, 96, 202, 207
'Sixth Congress and the Opposition's Tasks, The' — 70
'Soviet Economy in Danger, The' — 48, 52, 59, 323
'Speech in Honour of the Communist International' — 66, 102
'Theses on the Economic Situation of Russia From the Standpoint of the Socialist Revolution' — 60
'To PB Axelrod' — 124
'Tolstoy: Poet and Rebel' — 222
'"Trotskyism" and the PSOP' — 280
'Victor Serge's Crisis' — 283
'What is the Smychka?' — 265
'Where is the Soviet Republic Going?' — 70
'Where is the Stalin Bureaucracy Leading the USSR?' — 55
'Who is Leading the Comintern Today?' — 88
'World Situation and Perspectives, The' — 73
See also capitalism, collectivisation, imperialism, industry, Left Opposition, nationalisation, scissors crisis, Stalinism
Trotskyism, Trotskyists — 2, 15, 20, 65, 79, 128, 199, 201-203, 215, 218, 230, 237-238, 248, 270, 272, 274, 280-281, 283-285, 291-292, 303, 306-309, 317-318, 324-325, 330, 333, 335-338
Trotskyist movement — 292, 303, 308, 324
Two-stage theory — 18, 51
Tukhachevsky, Mikhail — 27

Underconsumption — 91
Unemployment — 49, 78-79, 83, 94, 102, 216, 218, 236, 346, 363, 368
Uneven and combined development — 6, 130
Uneven development — 6, 42, 99, 130, 205
United States of America — 19, 43, 79, 90, 95, 99, 163-175, 182, 183-184, 209, 219-220, 299-300, 325, 341, 347, 358, 360, 362-369
United States of Europe — 19, 99, 163, 165-175, 182-184, 368-369
Upturn — 89, 93-96, 107, 122, 126, 128, 133-138, 142, 355, 359, 362, 364-365, 369
Uritsky, Moshe — 28

Valentinov, G — 48, 69
Value — 30, 32, 40, 42, 45, 48-49, 51-53, 66, 76, 78-79, 82-83, 88, 93, 97, 102, 107, 180, 230, 277, 325, 327, 337, 344-345, 365
Vanguard — 114, 118, 120, 124-125, 135, 152, 158, 213, 239
Varga, Evgenii — 343, 345-348, 350
Vietnam — 301-302
Von Laue, Theodore — 43

Warth, Robert — 317
Weak link — 27
Western Europe — 8, 25, 29, 35, 39, 41, 130, 166, 219-220, 269, 301-302, 332, 344, 347
White terror — 14
Wistrich, Robert — 310, 317
Workers' state — 1, 5, 8-9, 16-17, 26, 47, 54, 56-57, 74, 85, 293, 295-296, 304-305, 307, 311-312, 315-316, 318, 325
Working class — see proletariat
Working class consciousness — 12, 89, 153, 201-218, 249
World market — 7, 33, 35, 41-42, 129, 210, 258-259, 265-266, 291, 300, 315, 344-345, 349, 351-353, 356, 364, 369
Wright, John G — 172, 323-324

Yessenin, Sergei — 225
Yoffe, Adolf — 337

Zalezhsky — 187, 197
Zasulich, Vera — 126, 149
Zinoviev, Grigori — 158, 236, 238, 240, 242, 247, 249, 261-262